D0464462

BIBLE COMMUNISTS.— PROPHET AND FAMILY.

# The Stammering Century

## Gilbert Seldes

**In *Adam's* Fall**
**We finned all.**

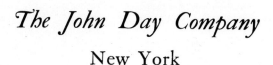

## The John Day Company

New York

COPYRIGHT, 1928, BY GILBERT SELDES
FIRST PUBLISHED, SEPTEMBER, 1928

PRINTED IN THE U. S. A.
FOR THE JOHN DAY COMPANY, INC.
BY THE QUINN & BODEN COMPANY, RAHWAY, N. J.

*To A. H. S.*
*Laetificat Dies Meos*

# About the Author

GILBERT SELDES was born in the ruins of an ideal-istic community in New Jersey and the first twenty years of his life were spent in more or less constant communication with radicals, reformers, faddists, cranks, and colonists of the ideal. He was graduated from Harvard in 1914, did newspaper work in Phila-delphia, Pittsburgh, and London, during the war, and was a sergeant in the American army. He joined the staff of *Collier's* in 1919 and from 1920 to 1923 was managing editor of *The Dial*, since when he has been a free-lance. He is, as far as is known, the only regular contributor to both *The Saturday Evening Post* and *The Dial*. Among the other pub-lications in which his work has appeared are *The New Republic*, of which he is an associate editor, *The New Yorker*, *The North American Review*, *The Encyclopedia Britannica*, *Vanity Fair*, *The New Criterion* (London), *The Nation*, and *l'Echo de Paris*, for which he wrote political despatches from Washington during part of 1918. He has lived a year or so in England and almost as long in France; generally he spends winters in New York and sum-mers elsewhere.

Before the entrance of this country into the war, he wrote an explanation of the American attitude for English readers; it was published in London, under the title of *The United States and the War*, on the day the Senate declared war. In 1924 he pub-lished *The Seven Lively Arts*. In collaboration with his father he translated the plays of the Musical Studio of the Moscow Art Theatre.

# Contents

# Contents

# List of Illustrations

# A Note on Method.

THIS book is not a record of the major events in American history during the nineteenth century. It is concerned with minor movements, with the cults and manias of that period. Its personages are fanatics, and radicals, and mountebanks. Its intention is to connect these secondary movements and figures with the primary forces of the century, and to supply a background in American history for the cults and manias of our own time: the Prohibitionists and Pentecostalists; the diet-faddists, and dealers in mail-order Personality; the play-censors, and Fundamentalists, and Point Loma theosophists; the free-lovers and eugenists; the cranks and, possibly, the saints. Sects, cults, manias, movements, fads, religious excitements, and the relation of each of these to the others and to the orderly progress of America in the past hundred years, are the subject matter. They suggest at once that this is a history of what Mr. Mencken calls the *booboisie*. It is, however, nothing of the kind. In private conversation—and possibly also in print—Mr. Mencken maintains that no quackery has ever been given up by the American people until they have had a worse quackery to take its place. He holds, explicitly and implicitly, that the difference between intelligent and unintelligent people is the gullibility of the boobs, their irremediable tendency to believe anything sufficiently absurd. The distinction is one of the reasons for Mencken's distrust of democracy and the history of manias and crazes in America annihilates that distinction entirely.

The astounding thing about almost all the quackeries, fads, and movements of the past hundred years in America is that they were first accepted by superior people, by men and women of education, intelligence, breeding, wealth, and experience. Only after the upper classes had approved, the masses accepted each new thing. The boob-haters need to correct their theory. They should study the list of endorsers of Perkins Tractors; and note how the faculty of Harvard College felt about phrenology; and read the accounts of

Mesmer's triumphs in Paris; and remember that the two most famous vegetarians in history are Shelley and Bernard Shaw; and
consider the experiments of the Fourierite era in relation to almost all the active intelligence of America at that time; and, keeping in mind the fact that the vast majority of Americans were
far too preoccupied to care about any of these fanaticisms, they
should try to reconcile their easy attack on the stupidity of the mass
of mankind with the appalling sentence that Nathaniel Hawthorne
passed on his ancestors for their part in the execution of Matthew
Maule on the charge of witchcraft:

"He was one of the martyrs to that terrible delusion which
should teach us, among its other morals, *that the influential classes,
and those who take upon themselves to be leaders of the people,
are fully liable to all the passionate error that has ever characterized the maddest mob.* Clergymen, judges, statesmen—the wisest,
calmest, holiest persons of their day—stood in the inner circle round
about the gallows, loudest to applaud the work of blood, latest to
confess themselves miserably deceived."

The history of fads and fanaticisms in America destroys Mr.
Mencken's concept of a boob-class peculiarly given to gusts of
mass-feeling. The religious revivals alone are overrun with stupid
people, and even there, at the very head, stands a profound intelligence, that of Jonathan Edwards. In nearly every other case, the
more gifted, the more intelligent, the more experienced classes
were the first to accept an absurdity and the last to give it up. The
preoccupations of the lower orders may have been ignoble and silly;
that is beside the point. The fact remains that one cannot distin-
guish the herd-majority from the civilized minority by ascribing
to the former any special tendency to be taken in by charlatans. The
minority is as susceptible to mass-suggestion as the majority. It
gives fresh names to its idols, Bergson, or Freud, or Internation-
alism, or Eugenics, but it has no superior power to resist fads or
crazes. It goes to Harlem in a taxi while the rustics go to China-
town in a bus. It spends its days answering crossword puzzles or
questionnaires in the waiting rooms of the more popular psycho-
analysts.

There are, of course, superior human beings, marked by independence. These, however, are not a class, but individuals, capable of resisting both the majority and the minority, untouched by suggestion, resisting or following the current *as they choose*. These are extremely few in number; and the existence of a few human beings who are out of the rut hardly calls for comment. Mr. Mencken is, in fact, not concerned with the few isolated independent individuals. He assumes the existence of an intellectual aristocracy, a class notable for its independence and individuality. If such a class does exist, it is only a smaller herd as much swayed by herd instincts as the majority. It accepts the theories of evolution, or of psychoanalysis, as blindly as the majority rejects them. It accepts anti-Christ as faithfully as the majority accepts Christ. There is no profit in comparing the clarity of vision of two groups which are equally incapable of using, or unwilling to use, their eyes.

§

Almost all of the American cult leaders created grandiose illusions for themselves: illusions of purity or perfection, of economic justice, of physical or spiritual happiness. That was their way of seeking salvation. Most of them rejected the common means of salvation, and having by that rejection persuaded themselves of their own superiority, they infected others with their illusions, to fortify their own faith or to multiply their personality. That was their way of seeking power. These illusions and the cults founded upon them were appropriate to their time. The camp-meeting served a useful purpose in the backwoods of Kentucky in 1800 and New Thought was influenced by the capitalism of 1900. This relation of cults to their environment has virtually dictated my attitude toward the material in this book.* If one believed that cults and crazes were isolated phenomena of a specially stupid class, one could treat them satirically. If one believed that they were all aberrations, separated from the facts of common life, the method of psychoanalysis might be appropriate. But if one takes these cults

---

* I have placed opposite the opening page of many of these chapters a group of notes on the domestic life of the time. The important events are known and the significant movements are alluded to in the text. It seemed to me that some of the commonplaces and some of the oddities of daily life could be rescued from obscurity and made to serve as a background and a contrast to a study of cults and fanaticisms and eccentricities.

and movements as more or less natural phenomena, as abnormalities closely connected with normal life, as part of the continuous existence of the nation, one need only describe them and set them in their true perspective. Thrown against the background of history, they provide their own irony.

For a special reason, I have avoided explaining the messiahs and mountebanks of this book in the terms of modern psychology. I am not a professional psychoanalyst and I consider that the critic and biographer who is only an amateur analyst and attempts to apply the analytic method, is making a pretty bad job of his criticism. For myself, I have too profound a respect for Freud to take his name in vain. I have no quarrel with his analysis of Leonardo which is altogether proper as an essay in psychoanalysis. The impropriety comes when those without technical training apply the literary skimmings of the psychoanalytical method and, if they discover a suppressed desire or an inferiority complex, fancy they have illuminated the work or character of their subject. The claims which Freud, and Jung, and Adler, make for psychoanalysis are not small; but they have the modesty of science in comparison with the assumptions of the amateur. In the early part of the past century, the work of Spurzheim and Gall created a new science of human nature now discredited. While the serious phrenologists were attempting to give their work a scientific basis, charlatans passed up and down the country and read "bumps," precisely as the uninstructed and impudent to-day interpret dreams and discover complexes. Where the 1840's said "amativeness," the 1920's say "libido." The name of the counter is changed, but it is still a counter; it becomes current coin only when it is stamped with authority. It is impossible to read a single page of Freud without observing how scrupulously he employs his weapons and with what solicitude he examines every item that may have bearing on the subject. It is hardly possible to believe that the psychoanalysis which finds its way into common print has employed equal safeguards and merits equal respect. There are significant exceptions but, in most cases, we find that psychoanalytical criticism of artists or men of action is bad psychoanalysis and negligible as criticism.

I have avoided, as far as possible, the use of the terms of psychoanalysis because I consider that, unless they are used by competent analysts, they give a false appearance of scientific authority to what must after all be lay judgments. Where I have used, but not specifically explained them, it has been in their journalistic sense. These words have passed into the common tongue with a meaning roughly approaching the scientific. But they are short cuts and nothing more.*

Another reason for avoiding the method of psychoanalysis is that I suspect it of being inapplicable. In its present state, psychoanalysis, although part of the general body of scientific knowledge, is preëminently a system of therapeutics. Its intention is to analyze and to cure. Its claim is to reveal the sources of disorder. But merely to discover sources will not carry us very far. With Freud's instrument in our hand, however awkwardly we use it, we can not discuss the conversion of John Wesley and omit the story of Sophia Hopkey. But Wesley's love affairs will no more account for all the phenomena of the Methodist revival than the factory system of Great Britain will explain the infidelism, and spiritualism, and millenarianism, which were as important in the founding of New Harmony as Owen's economic ideas. Even in the field of religious excitement, where the connection with sexual instability is most clearly marked, there is room for a little skepticism. The period of conversion roughly corresponds with the period of adolescence, but there have been conversions at twenty and preoccupation with religion is often liveliest as death approaches. The fact that phenomena occur together is not adequate proof that one causes the other. But even when we are assured of a causal relationship and have given a scientific name to it, we have not entirely explained it or exhausted its points of interest.

The instance of the Mormons (too exhaustively treated by Mr. Werner to need reëxamination here) is a case in point. We may

---

* Nor do they improve much in general, on the rough-and-ready system of Horace Greeley. He quotes, in his autobiography, a high-falutin analysis of the character of Margaret Fuller and adds that, if he had been called upon to write it, he should have "blundered out, that noble and great as she was, a good husband and two or three bouncing babies would have emancipated her from a deal of cant and nonsense." In Greeley's opinion, Mrs. Greeley had a good husband. She also knew the glories of motherhood. And she was as given to cant, she was as faddish, as nonsensical, as Margaret Fuller herself. The modern version of Greeley's remark would substitute lover for husband, but it suggests the same satisfactions as cure for the same ills.

discover hallucination, epilepsy, and lust in the character and person of Joseph Smith. He wished to be a Messiah and he became a martyr. Yet the phenomenon of Mormonism has scores of other bearings. It not only satisfied longings for a fresher and more intimate communion with God than was offered by established religions; it offered also a certain adventure. And the principle of polygamy was exceptionally appropriate in an underpopulated domain where men were scarce and fecundity was a prime virtue. The phenomena, in short, are far too complicated for any single system of judgment. In fact, after spending a considerable time in the company of men and women who made simple clothes, or diet, or a single formula of any kind, a panacea for all ills, I begin to doubt whether any one theory, even psychoanalysis—with its masterly trick of accounting for opposites—can cover anything so complex as the impulses or operations of the human spirit.

Most of all, I hesitate to use the literary débris of psychoanalysis because of the complexion which that method gives to criticism. I recall that, when I was at school, I became enchanted with a phrase of Friedrich Nietzsche's. When I incautiously quoted it, I was asked, "Ah, but you know what happened to the poor man, don't you?" As if the sanity of Ella Wheeler Wilcox could add dignity or truth to her utterances or the imputed impotence of Poe could subtract grandeur from his. There is a specific place for the appraisal of works of art in relation to the psychology of the artist, just as there is a place for criticism of the artist in relation to his time and his environment, or judgment of the accomplished work of a man by the standards of social effect. But none of these methods can be entirely adequate and none of them can criticize the object itself. Neither the psychoanalytical nor the social explanation of the motives which underlay the production of the work of art has anything to do with its artistic value. Nowadays, to discover a motive which can be related to sex, or snobbery, is supposed to be the whole function of criticism.

This is bad enough when the critic speaks of literature. When he speaks of such a complex endeavor as founding a religion, or discovering a system of human relations, the business of criticism by motives becomes entirely trivial and beside the point. Heaven knows the Messiahs turned mountebank often enough. They were so ex-

treme that they provided their own burlesques. They were so ridiculous that ridicule failed to touch them. But what makes them important is what they did and the various ways in which, from time
to time, they laid hold on the imagination of a group, or community, or country. The fact that a Christian community could
exist for a score of years in Massachusetts, is far more important
than any speculation as to its motives.

I began this study of reformers and founders of movements
in America with a leading idea much simpler even than that supplied by psychoanalysis. Presently, I had to give it up, not because
it was untrue, but because the strange phenomena I met with refused to be attracted and to cluster round my private magnet. My
original idea was a timid protest against the arrogance of reformers
in general—the arrogance which consists of mortgaging the future
by analogy with the past. The method is familiar. The persecuted
reformer reminds you that Socrates drank the hemlock, that Christ
was crucified, that Bruno was burned at the stake. He implies that
he is persecuted because he is a Christ or a Socrates. The logic is appalling; the attitude, humorless and offensive. It occurred to me
that a study of self-constituted saviors might serve as a check
to this form of spiritual snobbery. In the endless procession of Messiahs accepted by the few and mercilessly persecuted by the many,
there is one Christ, one Buddha, one Garrison, marching like file-
closers to thousands of crack-brained charlatans whose good intentions pave the road not to hell, but to oblivion. The suggestion that
persecution in any way proves greatness is simply absurd. The
world has persecuted enough of its great men to justify a little hesitation and a deal of humility before it persecutes anyone else;
but it has also persecuted so many criminals, and derided so many
fools, that proof by persecution ceases to be admissible. Two thieves
were crucified, and only one Christ.

This, as I say, was my leading idea and required me, without
pre-judging the nature of any experiment in religion or sociology,
only to find a sufficient number who were persecuted in their time
and are remembered, if they are remembered at all, as objects of
derision. I found enough of these. I found others, like Frances
Willard, who were foully slandered in their time and who conquered in the end. I found a surprising number of cult-leaders

upon whom the respect and wealth of their contemporaries were showered, but who now seem to us scoundrels for whom even self-delusion is no excuse. The more my theory was proved, the less important it became. The active presence of these extreme men and women sparkled in so many other lights that my own illumination was not needed.

I came gradually to want to prove nothing What I did want was to compose a sort of anatomy of the reforming temperament and to follow it, by winding roads, to the spiritual settlements it made for itself. What the man thinks who sets himself apart from humanity and expects humanity to follow him, how such people acted, what they did, where they found strength to struggle and consolation in defeat, what victories they won, how they held their faith or lost it, why they ended in an all-embracing disaster—all these things seemed to me exceptionally interesting. The facts became my actual subject—not debunking, not analyzing, not interpreting—only the facts themselves, the strange and incalculable movements of human beings in the stress of life, the mysterious designs of baffled men and women to whom common life was a labyrinth without a clew and without a door.

GILBERT SELDES.

New York City
1926-1928.

# PART I

*"The morbid are our greatest danger."*
NIETZSCHE

# I.

## The Stammering Century.

THE shout of the camp-meeting announced the nineteenth century to the young Republic. Ninety-nine years later the disciples of New Thought met in their first annual Convention, and their delicate, flute-like tones served as a valedictory. In the intervening years, other voices were heard. To hear voices, especially from the Beyond, became a mark of distinction. To be a Voice, was the supreme good. Greeley called it "this stammering century."

The air was full of voices. The sharp hoarse command of the pioneer, guiding his wagons over mountain roads deep in mud; the suave argument of De Witt Clinton, projecting the Erie Canal; the anxious pleading of Robert Fulton, protesting that his steamboat would not ruin navigation; the precise accents of Eli Whitney, explaining to the government his principle of interchangeable parts in the manufacture of guns; the war cry of the Indians on the western plains drowned out by the nasal laconic speech of the Yankee and, later, by the strange, broad tongue of the immigrant; the cries of the Forty-niners; the yelping of Boston mobs, attacking fugitive slaves; the patriotic hymns of William Cullen Bryant; the rounded phrases of Webster; Edward Everett saying, "Our government is in its theory perfect, and in its operation it is perfect also. Thus we have solved the great problem in human affairs."

These were the voices which made America. They spoke of a successful experiment in democratic government; of a western wilderness explored and conquered; of a physical world subdued by unparalleled feats of engineering and invention; of a Federal government slowly establishing itself in superiority over independent states; of immigration and pioneering in an interplay which continued so long as free lands were available; of industry gradually taking dominance over agriculture; of enormous fortunes founded; of the United States as a world power.

These were the fluent speakers. While they were proclaiming

the Gilded Age and the promise of America, other men were vehemently stammering out God's curse on material progress and announcing Christ's Kingdom on earth, or the New Eden in Indiana.

There were the three young men so emancipated that they cursed every time they spoke, causing the fastidious Emerson to remove them from the front porch to the back, out of the hearing of passers-by; and the earnest, incoherent denunciations of Robert Owen, telling Congress what was right and what wrong with the world; and the soft, Swabian accents of the Rappites, who held that sexual intercourse was a sin; and the Scots burr of Fanny Wright, who believed in Free Love. Margaret Fuller held Conversations, trying "to vindicate the right of women to think," confessing "we cannot show high culture and I doubt about vigorous thought," and consoling herself with "manifesting free action as far as it goes, and a high aim." The abolitionists clamored. P. T. Barnum worked his ballyhoo for Temperance. Joe Smith, barely in command of English, dictated the Mormon Revelation. Emerson delivered an inspiring word of Command. Reformed drunkards described the terrors of delirium, and revivalists imitated the Passion in drab meeting houses, and scientists sent people into trances that they might speak the word of Truth. Men and women announced themselves Christ incarnate.

The voices of the century seem at first a clamor of discords but, if we listen carefully, we discover a certain relation between the major voice of progress and the minor voice of radicalism. What the stammerer offered was deliverance, compensation, escape. When crops failed, when the Indians burned a clearing, when waters rose, when women began to grow mad with eternal childbearing in the wilderness, the evangelist came with his promise of streets of gold and heavenly choirs. Likewise, the founders of communities offered salvation for economic ills to the underpaid driven worker in factories, promised the sweetness of Mother Earth to the suffocated dweller in shabby tenements. To the weary the fanatic promised the instant coming of Christ. The Mormon offered to the harassed and hysterical farmers sexual freedom and the adventure of the West. The spiritualists promised release from death. The mesmerists knew a way to escape from one's own personality. The phrenologists could determine and correct the weaknesses of character which hindered success in life. The food faddists pointed the way to health. The Transcendentalists communed with the Soul.

These were the illusions offered to beaten men and women. Their popularity in the nineteenth century is evidence enough that the March of Progress, grandiosely saluted by the orators of the time, left wreckage behind it. At the same time, the ultimate failure of all the eccentric movements suggests that, on the whole, America prospered, that material success was sufficient for the majority of men. Progress, in fact, went in one direction; radicalism, whether religious, or social, or personal, in another. The orators of America's progress—the Websters and Everetts—were fluent enough. The stammerers were those who spoke of its soul.

Yet, as they fumbled for words, the exalted revivalists, and the fanatical food-faddists, and all the other radicals of the time, said something which the world did not forget. In the third decade of the twentieth century, we are living in a spiritual world they helped to form. Our radicals, and reformers, and faddists, and charlatans, are all descendants of the "ultraists"—the radicals—of the 1840's. Our John Roach Stratons, and Tennessee legislators, and Aimee McPhersons, stem from the revivalists who flourished from 1800 to 1860. There is a continuity in our mental habits.

Less obvious than this continuity is the interrelation of all the secondary movements of the past century. Isolated, each leader of a sect is amusing, fantastic, a little incredible: a Miller, giving the exact date of the second coming; a Matthias, declaring himself God; a Joseph Smith, writing the Book of Mormon; a Noyes, combining socialism, religion, and sexual innovations. But their full bearing only begins to be seen when we discover that they were all the children of the 1830 revivals when Charles Grandison Finney, the brigadier-general of Jesus Christ, stamped up and down the state of New York. Nor is Finney's full significance clear, until we discover his relations with abolition and prohibition and see him, near the end of his life, associated with the co-educational college at Oberlin where Frances Willard knew him and where, appropriately, the Anti-Saloon League was founded half a century after his death. The interrelation of spiritualism, medical quackery, Christian Science, and New Thought, with mesmerism and phrenology is equally illuminating. And all of these things bear a specific relation to the decline of the Calvinist theology brought over in the *Mayflower*. The hysteria of the Methodist camp-meeting is connected with the hard doctrine of Jonathan Edwards. The revivalist movement is close to prohibition. Prohibition had a tremendous effect on woman's suffrage. There were other connections even more obscure: between vegetarianism and the doctrine of the sinlessness of man; between the Rappites, who held sexual intercourse in abhorrence, and the Christian Scientists; between the resurgence of censorious Puritanism in our own time and the collapse of American radicalism in all its forms.

To those who still care for liberty, this last point is of exceptional significance. The moral history of America can be traced in the changes which have come over the meaning of the word "reformer." In the middle of the nineteenth century, the word meant one who wanted to give liberty to others; to-day it means, briefly, one who wants to take liberty away. The change in meaning is accompanied by a change in method. There is a dislocation of the center of fear. Laws, lobbies, censors, and spies, have displaced God as the object of awe and veneration, sometimes even as the object of faith. The great social and religious movements of the middle of the century were based on the belief that man could be made perfect. The current belief is that machinery, including the machinery of government, can be made perfect. The former method of arriving at the perfect state was Association. The present one is Prohibition. The change demanded in those days was in the human heart, not in the civil law; it was moral, not legal. Even in religious disputes there has been a marked degradation for, so long as the Bible was not challenged, all men were concerned with the awful tragedy of sin; they were all fundamentalists quarreling about the essence of religion, not about the mistakes of Moses. For a hundred years, there was but one question among men of religion: Are we saved or damned? It was not an academic question. It was present. It was real, urgent, more important than questions of health, or wealth, or social standing. It was the question of life and death. From the moment that the answer was "Saved," all disputes lost dignity and significance.

Whether the goodness or the justice of God eventually determines the course of human life and its destiny hereafter, exercised the imagination and the intellect of the great men of the last century. In the end, the placid assumption that God, if he exists at all, is the All-Good, set minds free to ponder the advantages of a high tariff, or the amount of alcohol one man should permit another to drink. For fifty years, a parallel question in the economic field agitated all men: could not some form of association, or cooperation, or communism, lift the burden of material necessity and set men free for the enjoyment of life? From the moment that question was answered in the negative, practical politics and economics became humanly less interesting. They became problems for technicians and engineers to solve.

The opponents of Prohibition, Censorships, Blue Laws, and other attacks on private rights, are in the habit of referring these disasters to a revival of Puritanism. Actually, the religious connection is more complicated. When the theology of outraged Omnipotence, universal damnation, and natural corruption, began to break down, it split into many divisions. A number of sects, in a natural reaction against the religion of fear, became radically libertarian. The extreme types gave to man every liberty because they seriously believed that the sanctified man—i.e., the man who had accepted Jesus—could do no wrong. Such a sect was Perfectionism. It was defeated by the more orthodox Protestant churches. And even the moderate cults of universal salvation could not overcome the impetus gained by Methodists, Baptists, Presbyterians, and Congregationalists in the early years of the century. Most of the Perfectionist leaders happened to dislike liquor and tobacco. Some of them abhorred all manifestations of sex. Others were violent in their distrust of romantic love. But all of them believed in liberty. The triumph of any form of Perfectionism would have made impossible the existence of the bureaucratic censor, for the Perfectionist was always individualistic. Within the limits of civil existence, he made each man the judge of his own actions. Liberty was part of the Perfectionist way to salvation.

Libertarianism was a religion appropriate to the early days of the Republic when people believed that a perfect government had been discovered for a perfect race; it succumbed to harsh reality, and the stricter code of Protestantism conquered. This was natural in a commercial civilization because that code provides balance sheets of right and wrong, rigid book-keeping of errors and atonements, and prizes for self-improvement. In the early Protestant

way of salvation there was room for liberty of conscience, but in
the application of morals to politics, liberty vanished. Out of the
wreckage of Calvinism, the dominant churches saved the drama
of salvation, casting out the desperate doctrine of the few elect.
Grace was no longer entirely a divine gift. The government of
Heaven, too, was put on a business basis. Eternal happiness had to
be earned.

Presently self-improvement turned into uplift and uplift into
prohibition. It is a complicated process and, in a sense, this whole
book is a sketch, a preliminary study, of the psychological turn which
has affected our customs, manners, habits of mind, and ideals. I
have summarized the process in the last chapter and do not want
to anticipate the evidence here. We know that the typical zealot of
1800 was a man fanatically busy about salvation; in the 1840's, he
was as fanatically busy about improving himself; later he turned
to uplifting his fellowmen and, later still, to interfering with their
pleasures. I suggest the breakdown of Calvinism as a partial explanation of these changes. Another is the revival system.

For a hundred years there had been revivals but, beginning
with the year 1800, revivalism began to be considered as proof of
a living spirit in the churches. As one by one the bars between man
and his salvation were thrown down, it began to be important to
God's ministers that they should be honored by numbers. Truth
was demonstrated in proportion to its popularity, and doctrine
shown to be sound by the number of people on whom it had been
imposed. Revivalists boasted of the number they had "slain" and
openly proclaimed their indifference to the means chosen for salvation and to the permanence of the reformations they effected.
They were selling salvation, at bargain prices; they were "selling"
it also, in the modern use of the word. The institution of the anxious seat—translated in our time as the "sawdust trail"—the giving
of testimony in public, the vast propagandas of the revivalists, all
tended to make a man's religion no longer a thing between himself
and his God, but a matter of public concern. Morals promptly became corporate, not personal. It became the duty of each man to
convert his neighbor. If he could not convert men, the atmosphere
of revivalism encouraged him to pass laws, to establish guardians
for morality, to dictate, and limit, and deny.

The Christian and the infidel have coöperated to create the modern type of reformer. The zealot often believed that before Christ could come again, all men had to receive grace. It was one of the promises of revivalism that every soul brought to Christ hastened the Second Advent. Hence to perfect the world—by force if need be—became a Christian duty. The infidel, too often accused of deserting the church in order to indulge his licentious passions, remained as austere as the Puritan. Hugo Münsterberg has noted the identity of morals in the Puritan and the Unitarian (who in 1830 was considered worse than an infidel). Neither Deists nor disbelievers threw over the strict moral code. On the contrary, dissenters, since they were unorthodox in religion, had to exalt morality, and say, as no Christian said, that morality alone was sufficient for salvation. The Transcendentalists reinforced this worship of ethics and their descendants, the uplifters and New Thoughters of our own time, have given it an almost sinister significance. They conceived the moral law as an emanation from all good men. They clung to the belief that injurious mental action was possible so that it became their duty to fight off the evil thoughts of evil men, lest evil corrupt the Universal Good. The belief that all men could be good was soon changed into the doctrine that those who were not good were dangerous to Goodness itself. Thus it became a moral duty to destroy evil, so that the circle of goodness would not be jeopardized. Our actual censors and prohibitionists have come from the Protestant churches; but the absence of an enlightened opposition is probably due as much to the flabbiness of unorthodox thought as to the psychological identity of the altruist, the uplifter, and the puritanical prohibitionist.

§

Particularly, all are alike in their intense desire for an assured salvation. In the débâcle of Calvinism, theology suffered; the way to achieve salvation was broadened and made pleasant; but the value placed on salvation remained undiminished. The stammering century was made an era of exploration by the work of those who looked for grace in unaccustomed places. There were materialists (they had an odd habit of turning spiritualist in their later days), who believed that Paradise could be found on earth as soon as man was emancipated from the wage system and who founded colonies on the model of Owen, or Fourier. There were monomaniacs who held that all men would be saved if they gave up holding slaves, or smoking cigarettes, or eating meat, and that women would be relieved of all ills if they wore sensible clothing. There were mystics who thought that raising and using cattle was the great sin against the spirit. There were reformers of the sexual relation who went through every variety of doctrine. There were believers in the sacredness of manual labor and disbelievers in sound currency. There were those who made salvation of doubtful value by proving that there is no death and others who hoped that life could be created by spiritual communion. Some of these stammerers proclaimed to Americans that life was all evil and some that success in business was the all-good. A number of them implied that they were divinely appointed and that salvation was only to be had from them.

They were eccentrics, fanatics, fools, faddists, and madmen; but they were all concerned with the same thing: salvation. They looked for some end to earthly sorrows, to some perfection which could atone for our imperfect life on earth. The disaster to Calvinism was already understood when the new Republic was founded; although the revivals kept a modified form of it alive, men turned to political experiment. Religion still assured the somewhat froward American that he was a worm and must abase himself before God. The political experiments suggested to him that he could escape economic misery only by associating himself with others as miserable as himself. And all the time the greatest experiment of all, the experiment of America, was prospering, proving pragmatically that man was the master of all things and that he who labored ruthlessly, tirelessly, and alone, could make a million dollars. The prosperity of America was the one thing which neither orthodox religion nor radical economics could overcome; religion gave ground and radicalism broke entirely. Progress in America went in one direction, reform in another and, at the end of the century, new religions, without shrines, or relics, or authority, or penalties, assured men that, by concentrating on two phrases for ten minutes a day, they could become rich and beatified.

These cults were the more successful because a third form of salvation had supervened when religious and economic grace were both found to be so difficult to achieve. This was salvation by personal effort. Like nearly everything else of importance in the American mind of the nineteenth century, this also has its source in Jonathan Edwards. It received a dignified and modern rendering in the self-reliance of Emerson. To the hermit, Thoreau, it meant independence. The mystic, Alcott, knew that no reform was worth anything unless it began with a reform of the human heart. All of these, and all the other Transcendentalists, knew that there could be no salvation for humanity until man became aware of the moral law of Nature and could identify himself with it. Oneness with this great Law lifted man from the irritations and disappointments of common life. He had compensations. He could live with the over-soul. To each man then came the "revelation of nature . . . that the highest dwells with him." At the very moment when Science was speaking in terms of struggle, when it became certain that Nature was utterly indifferent to the morals and ambitions of men, the Transcendentalists held out this great promise. To Emerson, preoccupation with sin was an adolescent disease. He and his disciples exalted the independent man. And, presently, the religion of success managed to draw from these teachings the cult of Personality and the worship of the Omnipotent Good which turned, oddly enough, into salvation by mail and cures by absent treatment.

The last phase is to be found in Christian Science and in Oriental mysticism. The degree of their relationship is hard to determine; but both are close kin to New Thought, and both are religions of death. Like New Thought, in one of its many phases, they are religions evolved to console those whom the successful materialism of American life no longer attracts and satisfies.

To understand them, it is necessary to follow the long revolt against the theology of the eighteenth century—the revolt of which Christian Science and New Thought and the religion of apathy are the culmination. In order to do that, one must pass behind the stammering century, must go back to Jonathan Edwards, the great figure of Colonial New England, the expressed essence of the Puritan's attitude toward life which was based on his attitude toward God.

† "The effect of Mr. Treat's preaching was that his hearers were several times in the course of his ministry awakened and alarmed. On one occasion a comparatively innocent young man was frightened nearly out of his wits, and Mr. Treat had to exert himself to make hell seem somewhat cooler to him." † In Connecticut no person whose estate was less than two hundred pounds was permitted to wear "gold or silver lace or any lace above two shillings a yard." † In 1748, copies of Bulls and Indulgences of Pope Urban the eighth were sold in the colonies, "by single Bull, Quire or Ream," to be used as writing paper. † In 1752, Franklin was a director of the Philadelphia Contributionship, for insurance against fire. † The preaching of Whitefield caused disunion between liberal and conservative churchmen. † Dutch and German struggled hopelessly against the supremacy of the English language. † "From mansions that were castles, the Johnsons ruled the upper Mohawk Valley with a sway that was half feudal and half barbaric." † At Harvard and Yale, students were listed not alphabetically but in accordance with the social rank of their families. † The Quaker, John Woolman, protested against Negro slavery, and white teachers were "sold" by the indenture system. † The Puritans made liberal divorce laws and insisted on the civil status of marriage. † Franklin invented an improved stove. † The title of mister was reserved for gentlemen—mechanics and farmers being known as goodman. † The gentry wore claret or peach-blossom coats, ruffled shirts, lace cravats, knee-breeches, and shoes with showy buckles; a caricature of the times shows a woman in heavy ruffles, tight long skirts and hoops and a monstrous "craped" head-dress—combed over a "rat" of artificial hair with broad ribbons—feathers three feet long, and imitation fruit and vegetables. A barber stands on a step-ladder and his assistant takes the elevation with a quadrant. The usual time for a perfect coiffure was two hours. † Horse races were frequent in Virginia. † Philadelphia led the colonies in prison reform, Franklin established a circulating library and, in 1789, the American Philosophical Society. † New Jersey and Pennsylvania developed exceptional pottery and glass works. † Benjamin West succeeded Sir Joshua Reynolds as president of the Royal Academy. † In 1765, the first medical school was founded. † The works of Rousseau, Montesquieu, and the French Encyclopedists were promptly translated and published. † The Union Society of Carpenters at Philadelphia struck for a ten-hour day.

# II.

## A Stormer of Heaven.*

ON the eighth of July, 1741, a lecture was delivered in the little town of Enfield, Connecticut. The lecturer was a young, already respected divine; but the Enfieldians had not invited him. His coming, in fact, was an intrusion. For many months the inhabitants of neighboring villages, duly exercised and in great distress about the salvation of their souls, had been dismayed by the backslidden state of Enfield where the villagers remained "secure, loose, and vain"; so much so that the neighbors feared lest God pass them by, and many of them "were prostrate before Him . . . supplicating the mercy of Heaven" in behalf of the irreligious. It was at the instance of these neighbors that a lecturer had been appointed by the clergy, a man of proved power. Ten years earlier, he had descended upon the liberal clergy of Boston and warned them against preaching the soft doctrine that the grace of God extended to all men. A few years later, in his own parish of some two hundred families, he had savingly brought three hundred souls home to Christ. His name was Jonathan Edwards. As he stood in the pulpit, a tall, slender man, with a gentle, slightly feminine cast of features, he was not exceptionally impressive. He was not a great orator. But his logic was like a dagger of cold steel and his imagination was on fire. He was thirty-eight years old.

"And when the time appointed for the lecture came, a number of the surrounding ministers were present, as well as some from a distance—a proof of the prayerful interest felt on behalf of the town. When they went into the meeting-house, the appearance of the assembly was thoughtless and vain; the people scarcely conducted themselves with common decency. But as the sermon proceeded, the audience became so overwhelmed with distress and weeping, that the preacher was obliged to speak to the people and

---

* The reader is warned that the following chapter is not in any sense a complete account of the work of Jonathan Edwards; it is only a sketch of those elements in his work which appear in action in the following chapters. I have simplified, perhaps too much, the subjects which interested Edwards and have almost entirely omitted the more abstruse problems of the freedom of the will.

desire silence, that he might be heard. The excitement soon became intense. Many of the hearers were seen unconsciously clinging by their hands to the posts, and the sides of the pews, as though they already felt themselves sliding into the pit."

The words he uttered were not to be forgotten for a century. Whenever men spoke of the anger or the power of God, or of the cruelty of Calvinism, they cited this sermon of Jonathan Edwards. He had heard that the men of Enfield were assured of their safety, considered themselves among the elect, fancied themselves free from temptation, and destined to Paradise in the hereafter. The text he chose was a threat: "Their feet shall slide in due time." The title of his discourse was *Sinners in the Hands of an Angry God:*

"So that thus it is that natural men are held in the hand of God over the pit of hell; they have deserved the fiery pit, and are already sentenced to it; and God is dreadfully provoked: his anger is as great towards them as to those that are actually suffering the execution of the fierceness of his wrath in hell; and they have done nothing in the least to appease or abate that anger, neither is God in the least bound by any promise to hold them up one moment. The devil is waiting for them, hell is gaping for them, the flames gather and flash about them, and would fain lay hold on them, and swallow them up; the fire pent up in their own hearts is struggling to break out; and they have no interest in any Mediator, there are no means within reach that can be any security to them. In short they have no refuge, nothing to take hold of; all that preserves them every moment is the mere arbitrary will, and uncovenanted unobliged forbearance of an incensed God."

As a child he had observed the field-spider and written a remarkably accurate and vivid description of its habits. The memory of it supplied him now with his most terrible image:

"The God that holds you over the pit of hell, much in the same way as one holds a spider, or some loathsome insect, over the fire, abhors you, and is dreadfully provoked; his wrath towards you burns like fire; he looks upon you as worthy of nothing else but to be cast into the fire; he is of purer eyes than to bear to have you in his sight; you are ten thousand times more abominable in his

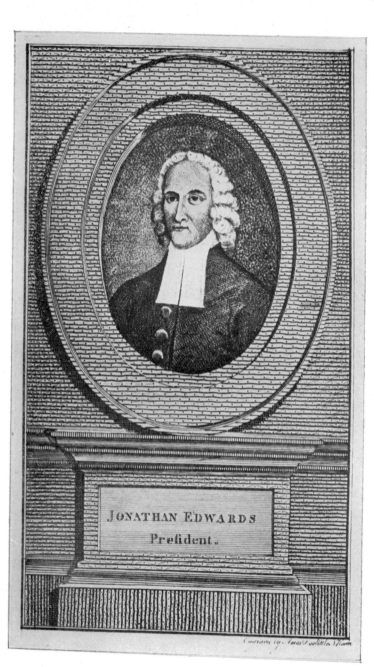

JONATHAN EDWARDS
President.

eyes than the most hateful venomous serpent is in ours. You have offended him infinitely more than ever a stubborn rebel did his prince: and yet, it is nothing but his hand that holds you from falling into the fire every moment. It is to be ascribed to nothing else, that you did not go to hell the last night; that you were suffered to awake again in this world, after you closed your eyes to sleep; and there is no other reason to be given, why you have not dropped into hell since you arose in the morning, but that God's hand held you up. There is no reason to be given . . . but his mercy; yea, no other reason can be given why you do not this very moment drop down into hell."

A fellow minister, sitting beside the preacher, was so overcome that he caught him by the skirt of his dress and cried out, "Mr. Edwards! Mr. Edwards! is not God a God of Mercy?" Mr. Edwards knew how to answer such appeals. Under ten heads, he could prove that nothing but the mere pleasure of God keeps the wicked for one moment out of hell; since they are worms and deserve the universal, extreme, intolerable punishment, which only an infinite God, infinitely enraged, can devise. Divine Justice only encourages the exercise of Divine Power, and God has made no promise, contracted no obligation, to keep any natural man out of hell. Does God ever save a soul? Then it is to his own glory for "the work of God in the conversion of one soul, considered with the source, foundation, and purchase of it, and also the benefit, end, and issue of it, is a more glorious work of God than the creation of the whole material universe."

Damned to eternal torture, the congregation at Enfield could only ask how to achieve salvation; was there a chance for every man to escape? The remorseless voice of the preacher answered coldly that the greater chance was for every man to be damned, since nothing he could do could alter his destiny. Even as he exhorted them to be violent in storming the gates of Heaven, to press into the Kingdom, the cold honesty of his logic made him add that for ninety-nine out of a hundred the effort was foredoomed. What free will could they have, since only God was free, since their freedom could only diminish the Divine Power and belittle the Divine Indulgence which might spare them? Only the possibility remained that, if they were diligent in the fulfillment of every duty, God, out of his goodness and power, but by no compulsion, might give them grace. If grace were given, they might lean on the bar of Heaven and "lost in adoring wonder at the mystery of love which elected and redeemed them" look down upon fathers, husbands, wives, and children in the torments of hell, and rejoice in the operations of Divine Justice!

§

The members of the Enfield congregation were not aware of it but, as they dispersed to their homes, they carried with them the promise of libertarian religion in New England, of religions without Hell and cults without God. The rest of this book is concerned with the results of Edwards' work. Its intention is to show how the religious exercises begun by Edwards affected the life of the American people. The Enfieldians joined the men and women of Northampton, hopefully saved seven years earlier, in the revival which specifically prepared the way for the Great Awakening in the early days of the Republic, and so, in a direct line, for Moody and Sunday, for every exaltation of the individual's sense of communion with God, for every attack on the theocracy by which Edwards lived. The theology of Jonathan Edwards suffered the most spectacular defeat in the history of American religious life, his methods gained the greatest victory. Between them they are responsible not only for the normal development of religious theory, but for nearly every deluded Messiah, every strange cult and, indirectly, for a hundred political experiments, fads, pseudo-scientific social crazes, and movements. Whoever wishes to know the workings of the New England mind of the eighteenth century and the throbbing of its heart, wrote Bancroft, must spend his days and nights in the study of Jonathan Edwards. It is equally true that, if we want to understand the peculiar complex of activities which made the next hundred years so notably and so absurdly a century of reforms, we must begin with the solitary eminence of Edwards' spirit.

§

In any number of ways Jonathan Edwards justifies our interest. Even when he called children "little vipers" there was something magnificent and awful in his utterance. He was the greatest of the New England theocrats, of the Puritans who had the exalted idea that the legitimate ruler over mankind was not a king, not a congress, nor a press, nor a lobby; but God. In the practice of Massachusetts or Connecticut, theocracy came to mean that only churchmen could vote. Inversely, and more liberally, as late as 1834, every citizen of Massachusetts had to contribute to the support of some religious sect. Theocracy meant Establishment, the collaboration of Church and State. But it is impossible to dismiss in these terms, which are modern political interpretations, what was to Edwards, as to every Puritan, a natural and (as it is to any religious mind) a sublime conception, and a fixed reality. The God they worshiped was the undiminished God of the Bible. He was the only possible ruler, governing through the church, which Edwards, to the end of his life, considered superior to the State. Without God, there was no meaning in life; no authority in government. And God was God, an awful Presence, an Immanence, in whose mind alone the puny material universe had existence. He was not the Power which makes for Righteousness. He was not the Good. He was certainly not Nature or Providence. He was sublimely and awfully God, as real to Jonathan Edwards as his wife or children. God's laws were as easy to comprehend as the edicts of the Privy Council. It was this feeling of the immediacy of God's existence that gave point to the whole life of the Puritan; without it, his story becomes insignificant and the Puritan is dwarfed to the puny and irritating figure of a cartoon. Passing behind modern controversy and criticism, recapturing as far as we can the spirit of the time, we find Edwards, the highest expression of Puritanism, a giant.

Even in the firmly established Church of his day, he had a giant's work to do. There had been unlisted cargo in the hold of the *Mayflower:* a cargo of heresy. For, within a generation of their landing, the Puritan fathers found obtaining "nine unwholesome opinions" and no less than eighty-two other doctrines, some blasphemous, some erroneous, and all unsafe, which they consigned "to the devil of hell from whence they came." But heresy refused to be banished. It flourished and New England, ill at ease in its clearings in the forest, hemmed in by cold, threatened with starvation, attacked by Indians, lacking every amenity, and forced to search everywhere for the evil which filled it with misgivings, concentrated all its apprehensions in the dreadful fury of the witch-hunt at the end of the century. This was the last convulsion of intolerance. Spasmodically thereafter, New England broke into violence, but the systematic oppression of the heretic began definitely to decline. To the embittered Puritan, aware in his heart that the grace of God was still withheld, toleration was compacting with the Devil. In 1702, Increase Mather, father of Edwards' only rival in divinity, saw "the glory departing from New England." The tone of reproach can still be heard in his jeremiad:

"We are the posterity of the good old Puritan Non-conformists in England, who were a strict and holy people. Such were our fathers who followed the Lord into this wilderness. Oh, New England, New England, look to it that the glory be not removed from thee, for it begins to go. Oh, degenerate New England, what art thou come to at this day! How are those sins become common in thee that once were not so much as heard of in this land!"

A year later, a fifth child, the only son in eleven children, was born to Timothy Edwards and the granddaughter of the Reverend Solomon Stoddard. He was to be the great glory of colonial New England and to imagine a greater glory still—the Latter-Day Glory—the redemption of the world which, by the application of logic to Biblical texts, Edwards had persuaded himself would radiate from the New World. To the end of his life he embraced hardship. He was the child of pioneers. The wilderness and the clearing marked him for austerity. As a little child, he would go to a hidden place in the forest to pray. The habit remained with him and he has left a record of his experience which still throbs with emotion. In all its harshness, nature rarely frightened him. He studied it, with the curiosity of a boy. But he was not long a child. When he was twelve, his mother joined the church. A year later, he entered Yale College, to which he afterwards gave a line of three Presidents in direct descent.

§

His intellectual curiosity, his range, were rare in his time. The New England mind was preoccupied with God, inquiring how man could prepare for conversion when God was its sole author, asking whether the threatened punishments for sin were out of proportion to its guilt. These were not academic problems, since the conduct of life depended upon the answers. But Jonathan Edwards stepped beyond them and, in his *Notes on the Mind*, he asks boldly "Why is Proportion more excellent than Disproportion?" The voice in which he answers does not tremble with the fear of God; in complete sincerity it carries across the misunderstandings of two centuries: "Life itself is the highest good." That note of vehement affirmation comes again and again into his speech and writing. On the twelfth of January, 1723, he dedicated himself to God, with the whole-heartedness and intensity which mark every movement of his spirit:

"I made a solemn dedication of myself to God and wrote it down; giving up myself and all that I had to God, to be for the future in no respect my own; to act as one that had no right to himself in any respect; and solemnly vowed to take God for my whole portion and felicity, looking on nothing else as any part of my happiness, nor acting as if it were; and his law for the constant rule of my obedience, engaging to fight with all my might against the world, the flesh and the devil, to the end of my life."

And, in the Seventy Resolutions upon which he based his conduct, we find the same intrusion of his adoration of Life. They are the resolves of a Puritan: "Never to lose one moment of time, but to improve it in the most profitable way I possibly can." They are the thoughts of a Calvinist: "Resolved, to act, in all respects, both speaking and doing, as if nobody had been so vile as I, and as if I had committed the same sins, or had the same infirmities or failings as others; and that I will let the knowledge of their failings promote nothing but shame in myself, and prove only an occasion of my confessing my own sins and misery to God." And of an ascetic: "Resolved, if I take delight in it as a gratification of pride, or vanity, or on any such account, immediately to throw it by." But the very first of the vows which he made is that he will do whatsoever he thinks most to the glory of God and "my own good, profit, and pleasure . . . and most for the Good and advantage of mankind in general." And he has barely set down his duty to God when he breaks out: "Resolved, to live with all my might, while I do live."

§

In the year of his dedication to God, he came to know the qualities of Sarah Pierrepont, "a rare and lustrous beauty," then thirteen years old. "They say," he wrote with the modesty of a lover, "there is a young lady in New Haven who is beloved of that great Being who made and rules the world, and that there are certain seasons in which this great Being, in some way or other invisible, comes to her and fills her mind with exceeding sweet delight, and that she hardly cares for anything except to meditate on Him; that she expects after a while to be received up where He is, to be raised up out of the world and caught up into Heaven; being assured that He loves her too well to let her remain at a distance from Him always. There she is to dwell with Him, and to be ravished with His love and delight forever. Therefore, if you present all the world before her, with the richest of its treasures, she disregards and cares not for it, and is unmindful of any pain or affliction. She has a strange sweetness in her mind, and singular purity in her affections; is most just and conscientious in all her conduct; and you could not persuade her to do anything wrong or sinful if you would give her all the world, lest she should offend this great Being. She is of a wonderful calmness, and universal benevolence of mind; especially after this great God has manifested Himself to her mind. She will sometimes go about from place to place singing sweetly; and seems to be always full of joy and pleasure, and no one knows for what. She loves to be alone, walking in the fields and groves, and seems to have someone invisible always conversing with her."

He married her when she was seventeen, and it was said that, throughout her life, she knew a shorter way to Heaven than her husband had found; so that he had always in his sight an example of God's indulgence.

§

His grandfather had preceded him at Northampton and had been five times blessed with harvests of souls; but when Edwards took up the work, "licentiousness greatly prevailed among the youth of the town; there were many of them greatly addicted to night-walking, and frequenting the tavern, and lewd practices. . . . It was their manner very frequently to get together, in conventions of both sexes, for mirth and jollity which they called frolics." In the autumn of 1734, Edwards began a series of sermons which developed into a revival—began, in fact, the Great Awakening.

He descended upon his congregation like a visitation of Nature, "as if he spoke in the Divine name." They must know that they are damned; they must recognize themselves as "inferior worms" (which he called himself, seeking an abasement which made "humbled to the dust" seem prideful, and desiring to "lie infinitely low before God"). They must know the reality of damnation. People spoke of their willingness to be damned, either for the glory of God or in atonement for the pleasures of their sins. Edwards warned them they could not know the actuality of the unimaginable tortures of hell-fire. He placed his imagination in their service with the most appalling power. When he spoke of coming to God, of pressing into the Kingdom, he made of it a great tragedy. The feeling of unworthiness spirals higher and higher, in a sort of ecstasy of fear and abasement, until the great fact of infinite sinfulness touches the great fact of forgiveness; or fails, and brings eternal damnation. He dealt always with infinities. The worm, the viper, that was man held intercourse with the Holy Spirit; the event could not be without magnificence, and its grandeur lay in its tragedy. Damned or blessed hereafter, man is associated with the eternal. If the choice is easy, if all men are or may be blessed, the tragedy sinks to melodrama; if they are damned, it remains noble and full of dignity. Then the saving grace of God becomes also infinitely precious, since it is rare, and His power and Justice are not mechanisms of a tawdry play, but high elements in an immortal tragedy.

Edwards' delivery was not moving; authority and conviction carried the bitter logic of his argument. His audience trembled as under the impact of a blow; it bent under the merciless wind from Heaven. Men and women shrank from the ghastly picture presented to them, shrieked in agony, saw visions, and came to God. Edwards wrote a *Faithful Narrative of the Surprising Work of God* "wherein it pleased God . . . to display his free and sovereign mercy in the conversion of a great multitude of souls—turning them from a formal, cold, and careless profession of Christianity to the lively exercise of every Christian grace and the powerful practice of our holy religion."

"God was then served in our psalmody," he exults; "religion was with all sorts the great concern, and the world was a thing only by the bye." It is this account which John Wesley read one day while walking alone along the high road from London to Oxford. Surely, he exclaimed, "surely this is the Lord's doing and it is marvelous in our eyes."

"There was scarcely a single person in the town, old or young, left unconcerned about the great things of the eternal world," Edwards wrote. "Those who were wont to be the vainest, and loosest; and those who had been most disposed to think and speak slightly of vital and experimental religion, were now generally subject to great awakenings. And the work of conversion was carried on in a most astonishing manner, and increased more and more; souls did as it were come by flocks to Jesus Christ. From day to day, for many months together, might be seen evident instances of sinners brought out of darkness into marvelous light, and delivered out of a horrible pit, and from the miry clay, and set upon a rock with a new song of praise to God in their mouths. "This work of God, as it was carried on, and the number of true saints multiplied, soon made a glorious alteration in the town; so that in the spring and summer following, anno 1735, the town seemed to be full of the presence of God; it never was so full of love, nor of joy, and yet so full of distress, as it was then. There were remarkable tokens of God's presence in almost every house. It was a time of joy in families on account of salvation being brought into them; parents rejoicing over their children as new born, and husbands over their wives and wives over their husbands. The goings of God were then seen in his sanctuary, God's day was a delight, and his tabernacles were amiable. Our public assemblies were then beautiful; the congregation was alive in God's service, everyone earnestly intent on the public worship, every hearer eager to drink in the words of the minister as they came from his mouth; the assembly in general were, from time to time, in tears while the word was preached; some weeping with sorrow and distress, others with joy and love, others with pity and concern for the souls of their neighbors."

So Edwards wrote of the work he had accomplished; but there was a witness he cared for more than for any other. He does not give her name; the decency of the husband is as pleasing as his earlier reticence as a lover, but he quotes Sarah Pierrepont Edwards:

"Part of the night I lay awake, sometimes asleep, and some-times between sleeping and waking. But all night I continued in a constant, clear, and lively sense of the heavenly sweetness of Christ's excellent and transcendent love, of his nearness to me, and of my dearness to him; with an inexpressibly sweet calmness of soul in an entire rest in him. I seemed to myself to perceive a glow of divine love come down from the heart of Christ in heaven into my heart in a constant stream like a stream or pencil of sweet light. At the same time my heart and soul all flowed out in love to Christ, so that there seemed to be a constant flowing and re-flowing of heavenly love, and I appeared to myself to float or swim, in these bright, sweet beams, like the motes swimming in the beams of the sun, or the streams of his light which come in at the window. I think that what I felt each minute was worth more than all the outward comfort and pleasure which I had en-joyed in my whole life put together. It was pleasure, without the least sting, or any interruption. It was a sweetness, which my soul was lost in; it seemed to be all that my feeble frame could sus-tain. . . . The glory of God seemed to overcome me and swallow me up, and every conceivable suffering, and everything that was terrible to my nature, seemed to shrink to nothing before it."

There were some extraordinary manifestations in this descent of the spirit, so that, the account goes on, "some compared what we called conversions, to certain distempers. And (so far as the judgment and word of a person of discretion may be taken, speak-ing upon the most deliberate consideration), what was enjoyed in each single minute of the whole space, which was many hours, was worth more than all the outward comfort and pleasure of the whole life put together; and this without being in any trance, or at all deprived of the exercise of the bodily senses. And this heavenly delight has been enjoyed for years together; though not frequently so long together, to such a height. Extraordinary views of divine things, and the religious affections, were frequently attended with very great effects on the body. Nature often sunk under the weight of divine discoveries, and the strength of the body was taken away. The person was deprived of all ability to stand or speak. Sometimes the hands were clinched, and the flesh cold, but the senses remaining. Animal nature was often in a great emotion and agitation, and the soul so overcome with admiration, and a kind of omnipotent joy, as to cause the person unavoidably to leap with all his might, with joy and mighty exultation. The soul at the same time was so strongly drawn towards God and Christ in heaven, that it seemed to the person as though soul and body would as it were of themselves, of necessity mount up, leave the earth, and ascend thither."

A little jealous of the purity of these signs, the young preacher adds that they were no new thing, and certainly "arose from no distemper catched from Mr. Whitefield," whose labors, indeed, they preceded.

"These effects appeared in a higher degree still, the last winter, upon another resignation to and acceptance of God, as the only portion and happiness of the soul, wherein the whole world, with the dearest enjoyments in it, were renounced as dirt and dung. All that is pleasant and glorious and all that is terrible in this world, seemed perfectly to vanish into nothing, and nothing to be left but God, in whom the soul was perfectly swallowed up, as in an infinite ocean of blessedness. . . ."

Nevertheless, these effects were the "physical jerks" which were to become common phenomena of the camp meeting and the revival. Even then they did not pass without rebuke. The Pentecostalism which, in 1927, stirred the congregation of Dr. John Roach Straton, was denounced by the General Convention of Congregational Ministers in Massachusetts Bay as early as 1743, with testimony against "errors in doctrine and disorders in practice." The staid Episcopalian, Dr. Chauncy, who disagreed with Edwards on essentials of religion, disapproved of these methods. He led the Old Lights, the serene Fundamentalists of his time, in believing that man cannot press into the Kingdom, but can only take care to observe the appointed means of salvation: prayer, reading, and hearing the word of God. He held that emotion, impulses, impressions, were all due to a debased and abnormal condition of the spirit, and that bodily effects were not the proof of divine power, but of human weakness.

Edwards himself admitted that "enthusiasm, superstition, and intemperate zeal" marked the course of revivals, but he did not condemn the outcries and fainting fits. These interruptions were not unwelcome, since they testified to the efficacy of the work, as though a company should meet in the field to pray for rain and should be halted by a plentiful shower. "Would to God that all the public assemblies in the land were broken off from their public exercises with such confusion as this the next Sabbath day! We need not be sorry for breaking the order of means by obtaining the end to which that order is directed. He who is going to fetch a treasure need not be sorry that he is stopped by meeting the treasure in the midst of his journey."

Edwards was too powerful for direct attack. We can best measure his work and the hostility it evoked by noting a related case. Dr. Chauncy brought charges, not against Edwards, but against a less intelligent, and more violent practitioner, the Reverend Mr. Davenport, whose methods are described by an eyewitness:

"At length he turned his discourse to others and with the utmost strength of his lungs addressed himself to the congregation under these and such-like expressions, viz.: 'You poor unconverted creatures in the seats, in the pews, in the galleries, I wonder you don't drop into Hell! It would not surprise me. I should not wonder at it, if I should see you drop down this minute into Hell. You Pharisees, hypocrites; now, now, now you are going right into the bottom of Hell. I wonder you don't drop into Hell by scores and hundreds. . . .' And in this manner he ended the sermon! 'Tis then added: After a short prayer he called for all the distressed persons (which were near twenty) into the foremost seats. Then he came out of the pulpit and stripped off his upper garments and got up into the seats and leapt up and down some times and clapt his hands together and cried out in these words: 'The war goes on, the fight goes on, the Devil goes down, the Devil goes down'; and then betook himself to stamping and screaming most dreadfully. And what is more than might be expected to see people so affrighted as to fall into shrieks and fits under such methods as these?"

So, in Edwards' own time, we find the whole paraphernalia of revivalism in action, the loud denunciation, the pretended secret assurance that the world was soon to come to an end, the personal appeal, the anxious bench, the stamping and leaping to induce frenzy, the frenzy induced and communicated to others. The Great Awakening had begun. Three months after Wesley had read Edwards' account of the work of God in Northampton, physical manifestations first occurred in his own revivals. When Whitefield came he specifically prayed for physical signs, and John Wesley approved, although his brother Charles was aloof and once, seeing signs of approaching convulsions, notified his hearers that the victims would be carried out of the assembly; his assumption that jerks were motivated in part by a desire to exhibit one's grace before others, was right; on that occasion, at least, the audience did not jerk. Edwards had noted that there was a rivalry in "bodily effects," that converts were puffed with pride, and recorded one case in which envy of another's salvation was the cause of conversion. But he believed intensely in the immediate contact between the Holy Spirit and the human heart; and in spite of its abuses, he clung to his doctrine.

§

It is easy to miss the point of Edwards' revivalism by saying that he hated gaiety in others—perhaps because he had none himself—and was determined, by envy, to put down what he could not enjoy. This may be true of the "sour Puritan," of those who lacked vitality, or heartiness, whose lives were meager, whose blood cold. But in Edwards we have a man of a higher type. He lived intensely and to him the Will, determined to evil though it was, remained the essential quality of mankind and the chief glory of

God. He was an energetic man, violent in godliness. It is not what he hated, but what he loved, that determines his character. He loved the power of God and the ecstasy of communion with God. He refused to make light of God's grace by assuming that it was a free gift to all men. What time could there be for night-walking and frolics when the tremendous business of salvation was not yet done?

He had perhaps the most acute mind of his time. His work on the Will is a masterpiece of logic directed to the resolution of a paradox. He is never off his guard. Yet he failed to foresee that his doctrine of direct communication between man and God was certain to break down the whole authority of the church and eventually to make each man the judge of his own salvation. This doctrine was a necessary part of his system but, as he let himself be carried away by violent manifestations of divine grace, he opened the way for others less austere than himself. If conversion was so important, the means could not matter. Presently, the ignorant saw visions, the unscrupulous caused miracles to happen, all to the great end of causing conversions and so hastening the Millennium. Men spoke to God without the intervention of his appointed ministers, and said that God answered. They stormed Heaven or testified that Heaven descended upon them. Edwards had made conversion difficult. He was accused of giving or withholding certificates of regeneration. He insisted upon intelligence as a factor in knowing God. But the weakness of his method overcame its strength. Wesley was to come and preach a softer doctrine, calling for repentance, conviction of sin, and conversion to Christ's holiness. He made conversion easy by weakening the Calvinist's distinction between elect and non-elect, and by letting men believe that it was in the competence of their will, as much as of God's, to be saved.

By setting a high price on salvation, Edwards had deterred thousands from attempting to achieve it. The unregenerate refused to make the effort. But when an easier way was shown them, they took it. In the century after Edwards' death, the most precious thing to him in the world was cheapened and, as a result, the great influence of his church, the Congregationalist, was weakened. Sects, promising anarchy, sprang up. Colleges were denounced as heretical. Famous chapels went over to the doctrine, abominable in Edwards' eyes, of universal salvation. The doctrine that Christ's death had actually saved mankind, not merely given the chance of salvation, was accepted. Saved men, taking an easy way to glory, encouraged Messiahs everywhere. Some believed that man, accepting Christ, was incapable of sin. Others, thinking that all labor for glory showed a lack of trust in the Lord, remained utterly passive, awaiting His pleasure. By making salvation the single end of man, by insisting that it was wholly God's work, and at the same time accepting the physical signs of personal communication with the Holy Spirit, Edwards broke down the wall surrounding the ministry, and cleared the way for cults, which he utterly abominated. He had over-reached himself.

§

This was not the only way in which Edwards defeated his own ends. Everything essential in his work was confuted and destroyed by time and most of it either through inherent weakness in his methods, or because of the austerity and violence of his temper. We say, casually, "If he could have foreseen the end!" But there was something incorruptible at the heart of Edwards' character which would not have been touched by the prophecy of failure. He had more than the assurance of righteousness; he had himself the immediate contact with Divine Grace which he held out as possible for every man. This hard man who condemned humanity to Hell was a poet. The merciless logician was a mystic and experienced the mystic's ecstasy. Thinking of him in the dim dreary churches of colonial New England, engaged in disputation, driving grim men and starved women into frenzies of fear and hysteria, we find it hard to say the word but, in justice it must be said, he knew the essence of rapture. He had what he brought once to a young woman, one of the greatest company-keepers of his town: "a new heart, truly broken and *sanctified*." He rejected the phrase "Godded with God and Christed with Christ," but he could not help believing that the saints came close to union with God. Of his fellow-preacher, David Brainerd, Edwards wrote: "His love of God was primarily and principally for the supreme excellency of His own nature, and not built on a preconceived notion that God loved him, had received him into favor, and had done great things for him, or promised great things to him: so his joy was joy in God, and not in himself."

He could have said the same thing of himself. He did not ask special gifts, feared them rather, preferring one quarter hour of enjoying "the sweet influences of the Spirit" to a whole year of visions and revelations. But when, as a youth, he attained conversion, nothing of vision, nor of the ecstasy of saints, was denied him:

"After this my sense of divine things gradually increased, and became more and more lively, and had more of that inward sweetness. The appearance of everything was altered; there seemed to be, as it were, a calm, sweet cast or appearance of divine glory in almost everything. God's excellency, his wisdom, his purity and love, seemed to appear in everything; in the sun, moon, and stars; in clouds and blue sky; in the grass, flowers, trees; in the water and all nature; which used greatly to fix my mind. I often used to sit and view the moon for continuance; and in the day, spent much time viewing the clouds and sky, to behold the sweet glory of God in these things: in the meantime singing forth, with a low voice, my contemplations of the Creator and Redeemer. . . . It always seemed natural to me to sing, or chant forth my meditations; or, to speak my thoughts in soliloquies with a singing voice. Holiness, as I then wrote down some of my contemplations on it, appeared to me to be of a sweet, pleasant, charming, serene, calm nature; which brought an inexpressible purity, brightness, peacefulness, and ravishment to the soul. In other words, that it made the soul like a field or garden of God, with all manner of pleasant flowers; all pleasant, delightful, and undisturbed; enjoying a sweet calm, and the gently vivifying beams of the sun. The soul of a true Christian, as I then wrote my meditations, appeared like such a little white flower as we see in the spring of the year; low, and humble on the ground, opening its bosom, to receive the pleasant beams of the sun's glory; rejoicing, as it were, in the calm rapture; diffusing around a sweet fragrancy; standing peacefully and lovingly, in the midst of other flowers round about; all in like manner opening their bosoms, to drink in the light of the sun. There was no part of creature-holiness, that I had so great a sense of its loveliness as humility, brokenness of heart, and poverty of spirit; and there was nothing that I so earnestly longed for. My heart panted after this,—to lie low before God, as in the dust; that I might be nothing, and that God might be All."

§

Psychologists have yet to discover from the meager biographical details available, what it was that turned Edwards away from his early interest in philosophy to the dark theology he adopted, but whatever the explanation, they cannot deny the authentic tone of rapture in these words. It is rapture without hysteria, without sham, and it never left him. Whenever he saw Nature he recovered the emotion, because he knew that the world was the work of God, created to communicate "an Image of His own excellence." The golden edges of an evening cloud, the sun in his strength, the apparition of comets, the ragged rocks, all exalted him. His heart was lifted up.

How high it was lifted is not hard to guess. There is no trace of common hallucination in any word he uttered but there is a tone of authority which we meet often in the voice of those who begin by believing themselves divinely appointed and end, this side of lunacy, in believing themselves divinely inspired. The confidence with which Edwards spoke of the ways of God was not uncommon in his time. It was when he began to speak of the Will, that his spirit soared. There are few trivial things in Edwards' life. His belief that America, New England, possibly Northampton, would be the center from which the last Redemption would radiate was one; not because it was humorless (what place has humor in the saving of the world?), but because it is self-aggrandizing. He had a habit, also, of seeing miracles. A balcony in one of the churches fell, and no one was killed; Edwards saw the hand of God directing each single person to sit where no timber would fall. The French Armada was shattered off Cap Breton, "the very night after our day of fasting," proving the Almighty's special interest in New England. But these small things join with great: the sense of God's exceptional concern with all that concerned himself is parallel to the ecstatic abasement before God which Edwards practiced. He lowered himself infinitely, and the infinity of his lowness met, in the infinite, the Infinity of God; met, and became one with it. The two poles of man's life, as Edwards knew them, were to be lower than the dust before God, and to know God: the ecstasy of abasement and the ecstasy of union. As he accomplished both it is possible that somewhere, in the obscure places of his heart, he felt himself God.

§

For when we ask what it is that Edwards chiefly worshiped in God, we find that it was neither Power nor Goodness. It was Will; and not strength of will, but freedom. God alone is infinitely free. The whole mystery of Edwards' denial of free will to man is in this: that he would not diminish, by the slightest degree, the glorious freedom of God. Even in the all-important matter of moving toward Heaven, man was not free; for if man were free, if he could move in this direction or another, what became of God's foreknowledge, what became of His freedom? The action of the Divine will would become subject to mortal power, or mortal whim, and God, too feeble to govern the world he created, would be at the mercy of man. To the jealous lover of God's omnipotence and freedom, this was an unthinkable blasphemy; it is the essence of God's freedom that man should have none. In lesser disciples of Calvin, we feel that the natural corruption of man and his tied will are whips to lash the unworthy; in Edwards, they become banners to honor the incorruptible, illimitable essence of God.

The element of nobility is thus not omitted from Edwards' determinism. The fact of our damnation contributes to the glory of God. The terminology seems archaic, the problem irrelevant. But we may remember that, since his time, science has again and again been interpreted in similar terms. Every fresh discovery of law binds us further. From Evolution to Psychoanalysis each decade has cut in on our freedom. We are continually being persuaded that our heredity, our environment, or the dreams of our immemorial ancestors, condition every move we make. We are all a party in a parlor—if not all silent, at least all damned. Damned to Hell, said Edwards, and to the glory of God; damned anyway, say the moderns, to no Hell but life, and to no glory.

The fires of hell pale in Edwards' discussion of the Will. He is more interested in the fact that our Will is not ours. To enlarge and ennoble the power of God, he endows the human will with every attribute, except freedom. He gave it a prime place in religion, and what he denied in man he worshiped in God. The contemplation of God's free will brought him to a state of exaltation. It was one source of God's satisfaction. Only let God be supremely happy, he cried, as a lover might, or a father. It was to this end that God created the world, not to love it, since God cannot love any other thing but Himself—as Spinoza says, "with an infinite intellectual love." The movements of the Divine Will conform to Divine Wisdom, are identical with Divine Necessity. God alone is free to do only what is right, while man, not free, is bound to evil and wrong. In God, Edwards found the harmonious operation of the spirit, the essential unity. In man, he was aware, there was division between what we want and what we ought, what we intend and what we accomplish. In God there was no break between necessity, will, and action. Edwards, says Allen, his biographer, was "penetrated with the mystic's conviction of some far-reaching, deep-seated alienation which separated man from God" and saw a counterpart of this separation in the divided nature of man himself, impotent, at the end, to do the thing he desires.

Like most philosophies which glorify the Will, Edwards' doctrine is pessimistic. But in comparison with his, modern pessimism is tawdry and modern worship of the will is hysterical and feeble. The Will to Edwards, is the essence of life; lack of it is annihilation, nothingness, "that which the sleeping rocks do dream of." He worshiped the Will and gave it to God and then, in a maze of logic, he set out jealously to defend it. He met his own paradoxes fairly. He reconciled predestination with man's moral responsibility. He said that consciousness was a delusion implanted in man to give him a sense of responsibility. His definition of the will is a little ambiguous, he seems to say that freedom consists not in making a choice, but in pursuing an inclination, and that the acts of the human will are caused otherwise than by mere power of willing. He somehow makes it appear plausible that men, who cannot be converted except by God's will, should attempt to force that will. Despairing perhaps of making clear what was so necessary to his thought, he exclaims that language contradicts itself!

It is left for philosophers and theologians to confute or uphold

Edwards' *Freedom of the Will*. What the layman knows is that it never falters in exalting the Will. He knows that Edwards' worship can be translated, in a moment, from God to Man. He attributed all things to God, but New England Puritanism after having accepted his ideas of the Will, gradually applied them to Man. Here, again in Edwards' own despite, he stands at the beginning of a long series of movements and cults. Remove from his work the idea of God, and there remains a powerful impulse to self-development, to exercise of the Will. The cult of the Will moved exactly away from Edwards, but he is the starting-point none the less. It runs through Emerson and, gradually losing power and dignity, it reappears in our own time in anarchism on one side and, on the other, in the combination of a feeble variety of New Thought with commercialized will-culture.

Just as the Will Edwards exalted had little in common with the Will-power of our current advertisements, the Infinite before which he sank was far removed from the Infinite of New Thought, an Infinite with which the worm man can be "in tune," a friendly, consoling Infinite. For Edwards, the word had not lost its meaning; it had not become a sales-point of popular philosophy.

§

Edwards' life was not easy. He was uncompromising wherever God was concerned and, after a time, he found himself unable to admit unconverted Christians—those who had been baptized, but had never experienced the conviction of sin and regeneration—to full communion in the church. A great principle was involved in the politics of both the church and the state. As only members could vote, the pressure for looser requirements for admission to the church was always great. The Halfway Covenant had gone a little way, but the communion of the Lord's Supper was still refused to those who failed to give proof of Christian experience. Edwards' grandfather regarded the Last Supper as having a magical property, regardless of the fitness of the communicant, and had made concessions. For a time Edwards followed him; then, feeling that this doctrine led to sacramentalism in violation of the Puritan spirit, he rejected it. He proposed a series of sermons to discuss certain improper admissions to the church. The town rebelled.

Allen, Edwards' biographer, notes that the quarrel might have been composed except for another difficulty. "As the story runs, a discovery had been made that certain books of an obscene character were in circulation among the young people of the parish of both sexes, the result of which was licentious conversation and immoral practices. The first act of the pastor was a sermon in which the facts were known to the congregation,—an impressive sermon, which led the officers to unite with him in calling for an examination of the offenders. But when Edwards came to read from the pulpit the names of the guilty persons and of those also who were summoned to give their witness in the case, it appeared that almost every family in the church of any consideration was involved. Those who had hitherto favored an investigation now resisted it. The consequence was that the proposed discipline was dropped, while a certain disaffection towards Edwards began to be felt which put an end to the extraordinary influence he had hitherto exercised."

Edwards resigned. The town, infuriated, voted that he should not enter the pulpit even while another preacher was being sought. He left and, at the age of 47, went with his wife to convert the Indians in the wilderness. He was beset with difficulties there; among other things, a member of a prominent family subverted funds intended for the savage. But finally he made his way out. One of his daughters, Esther, had married Aaron Burr, the president of Nassau Hall and, at his death, the aging Edwards was called to the Presidency of Princeton. He wanted much more to write a history of Redemption, but accepted the call. He was inoculated against smallpox and died, shortly after, in his fifty-fifth year. After his death, rumors persisted that he had written an heretical work. In 1851, Dr. Bushnell refused to make public Edwards' manuscripts owing to the nature of their contents. Thirty years later, on the insistence of Oliver Wendell Holmes, a manuscript was published. Whether it is the only one seems uncertain. It is not shocking. Edwards last published word to humanity is a description of the Trinity: Life, Light, Love.

§

When he decided upon a topic for meditation, he would walk or ride into the woods, making notes on bits of paper, and pinning them to his greatcoat. His manuscripts are described by a descendant: "He used to make rough blank-books out of odds and ends, backs of letters, scraps of notes sent in from the congregation; and there is one long parallelogram of a book made entirely out of strips from the margin of the old *London Daily Gazetteer* of 1743. There is another most curious manuscript, made out of circular scraps of paper, 147 leaves, being in the shape of half moons, intermingled with the patterns of caps and such other like remnants of house-wifery."

From his account books, biographers have culled a few items: "A gold locket and chain, £11." "One dozen long pipes" occurs twice in three months. And, for a "little viper," the devout Dwight, or the mother perhaps of the traitor Burr, or possibly for Pierre-pont who was to disgrace the name, there is "1 child's plaything, 4/6."

§

Nobody can hate God, said Spinoza. Looking ahead to a century of men who sought God with fury and impatience, by devious routes, with strange purposes, one wonders whether many of them loved Him as devoutly as Edwards did.

# III.

## Times of Refreshing.

THE work of Jonathan Edwards was interrupted by the War of the Revolution. It was resumed, with a difference, in 1800. In the half century following his death, a new nation came into existence and, in the judgment of the faithful, the old religion was jeopardized. Deists (generally called atheists), infidels, and Universalists had been as prominent as orthodox Christians in directing the war.

When the time came to frame a constitution, God was considered an alien influence and, in the deliberations of the Assembly, his name was not invoked. "Inexorably," say Charles and Mary Beard in their story of *The Rise of American Civilization*, "the national government was secular from top to bottom. Religious qualifications . . . found no place whatever in the Federal Constitution. Its preamble did not invoke the blessings of Almighty God . . . and the First Amendment . . . declared that 'Congress shall make no law respecting an establishment of religion. . . .' In dealing with Tripoli, President Washington allowed it to be squarely stated that 'the government of the United States is not in any sense founded upon the Christian religion' "— a sad issue, surely, of the theocracy of Edwards.

Among the evangelizing religions, Methodism alone was favored by the break-down and change in authority which came with the creation of the Republic, and Methodism created, in the first years of the century, the characteristic revival form, the camp-meeting. Baptists and Presbyterians were eventually to shriek and fall into fits as their preachers were driven to emulate the enthusiasm of the Methodist itinerant but, at the beginning, religion fell away, was lost in the jumble of new interests and opportunities, or was rejected because it was not spiritually appropriate to the new order. Essentially, the established religion, which had its roots in English soil, taught obedience; America taught freedom. Calvinism looked backward to the glorious past before the Fall: the eyes of new America were toward the future. The great hope offered by

Congregationalism was redemption from sin; America had definitely begun to be interested only in Progress.

Wherever we turn, the irreligion of the early republic is evident. In the churches themselves, the movement away from Calvinism, theocracy, and the trinity, toward religions of universal forgiveness, is marked. "In 1782, King's Chapel in Boston formally and officially declared in favor of unitarianism" and, a generation later, the movement which was to split Congregationalism in two was openly inaugurated by Channing in the same city. The work of Francis Asbury, the Methodist, claimed three hundred thousand converts between the 1770's and the 1820's; and each conversion, although a religious exercise in itself, was a fresh danger to the more austere churches. The association of Church and State, abolished in the Federal Government, grew gradually weaker in the several states. The association of the church with education, art, literature, science, mechanical progress, and international policy was either totally lacking or persistently on the losing side. In the home, romances supplanted volumes of sermons. And even New Englanders learned to go to the theater instead of being satisfied with "meetings." Colleges which had been founded to supply ministers of the Gospel began to be heretical or infidel. The New World, which had been exploring the mysteries of Heaven, began to press across the frontiers of the West, to search out the mysteries of the Mississippi basin or of the Oregon. The American Republic had come into existence at the beginning of the scientific era which was to reach its climax with the trans-continental railway and the publication of the Origin of Species.

If all this shows how irrelevant the Great Awakening was to the problems of the new country, or how disappointing the fruits of that revival had been, it also shows why the revivalists of 1800 felt their call so deeply. The infidelism of "Voltaire, Paine, and Volney" (to adopt the usual grouping of the time) had made headway. The French Revolution had not entirely discredited the Encyclopedia. Infidels were in the Federal Government. They were representing us abroad. They were making fortunes as merchants in Philadelphia. Everywhere they were breaking down the authority of God's word. A thousand new names were spoken daily: names signifying political conflict, westering convoys, ships around the Horn, research into the nature of things, speculation (in both the philosophic and the financial sense), material problems, material ambition, material conquest. Only the name of the Lord was not heard. Infidelism was the spur to the evangelist's spirit; the enemy was the universal, gross, unmitigated materialism of the early Republic. And insofar as the revivals inspired social experiments and led to the foundation of coöperative colonies, they provided the only break in the prevailing system of unscrupulous selfishness, a system of craft, of guile, and of gain.

This does not mean that there was no honest man, no charitable man, in America. There were thousands of noble and generous individuals. And there existed a notable idealism, in intellectual men and women. The dominant interest was, none the less, conquest of nature. The dominant methods were self-seeking and guile. This had been so even before the Revolution; but the removal of foreign discipline, the opening of fresh fields of exploitation, the liberation of hundreds of thousands from imposts and disabilities at the close of the war, made the Yankee of the early days of the Republic a man who not only could, but had to, conquer a world. He had to be hard in the forest and smart with his adversaries, and eternally watchful. He had to be ingenious and inventive. Opportunities crowded round him. Remorseless necessity weighed him down. Many of the Europeans who came early to this country are reliable guides. They came before catchwords were applied to our national habits and their judgments are based on fresh observation. Thus a French engineer, Chevalier, who came in the 1830's, has analyzed for us the character of the Americans upon whom the revivalists were earnestly at work. While others accused us briefly of trying only to get rich, Chevalier (although he remarked our devotion to "*le make-money*") recognized the deeper motives. To exist at all we had to subjugate nature. To exist as a nation we had to develop a system of transportation quicker and cheaper than Europe needed to conceive. "His [the American's] single means [of satisfaction] and his single thought is the domination of the material world,—industry in its divers branches, business, speculation, action, work." Education, politics, art, the laws of family life and of the state, all are made to serve this solitary enterprise. The American cannot imagine himself without a job. And the Yankee does not even suspect the existence of that variety of the human species which is known as "a man of leisure." The American system of government, the independence and individualism which are the essence of Protestantism, are favorable to business enterprise, to inventiveness, to movement and to work: the four great characteristics of the American. "No one assimilates a new method more rapidly; he is always ready to change his tools, his system, or his profession. *He is a mechanic in his soul.* Among us, every college boy has written his skit, or his novel, or his Constitution of an ideal republic or monarchy. In Connecticut or Massachusetts there isn't a farmer who hasn't invented his machine, nor a man of reasonable means who hasn't projected his railway or planned his city or town, or secretly nourished some great speculation. . . . A colonizer par excellence, the type American . . . is not only a laborer, he is a wandering laborer. He has no roots in the soil, is a stranger to the cult of native land and ancestral house; he is always in humor to be off, ready to go by the earliest boat even from the place where he has only just landed. He is eaten by the necessity of locomotion—he must go and come, must always be moving his muscles. If his feet are not in motion, he has to move his fingers and whittle with his ubiquitous knife, his eternal piece of wood."

Chevalier's summary is equally remarkable:

"If movement and the rapid succession of ideas and sensations constitute life, in America you live a hundred-fold. Everything is circulation, mobility, and a terrifying agitation. Experiences crowd on experiences, undertakings on undertakings. Wealth and poverty are on each other's trail and pass each other in turn. While the great men of to-day are busy dethroning those of yesterday, they are themselves already half unseated by the great men of to-morrow. Fortunes last a season, and reputations are as brief as lightning flashes. An irresistible current drags everything along, melts everything down, and recasts all things in new shapes. People change houses, climate, business, conditions, parties, and religion; states change laws, governors, constitutions. The earth itself, or at least the buildings on it, partake of the universal instability." *

* The passage of houses on rollers up Broadway, or through the new streets of Cincinnati, never failed to entertain Europeans.

Another friendly observer, Morris Birkbeck had seen, years earlier, another manifestation of American mobility. In the frontier West (of 1818), he found a hunter who had in twelve months built three cabins, each one deeper in the forest than the other, each one further west and, having sold them, was preparing for his fourth remove. "Not a settlement in this country," he writes, "is of a year's standing—no harvest has yet rewarded their toil, but our approach, as I anticipated, will dislodge many of them, unless they should be tempted by our dollars to try the effect of labor, instead of the precarious supply derived from their beloved rifle. Half-a-dozen of these people, who had placed themselves round a beautiful prairie, have, in fact, come forward to sell us their all,—fat cattle, hogs, and this their first crop of corn, now just maturing; if we purchase they will go to some deeper recess, and build other cabins, and prepare cattle and corn, to be again quitted at the approach of some succeeding adventurers like ourselves. . . ."

To illuminate Chevalier's "*mécanicien dans l'âme*," we have capital testimony of another sort. On January 14, 1789, Eli Whitney made a contract to supply ten thousand stand of arms to the Federal Government. The exceptional merit he claimed for his workmanship was this: that by substituting the scientific accuracy of machinery for the variable workmanship of the human hand, he could make his product uniform. A contemporary, visiting Whitney's factory at East Rock, near New Haven, was impressed by his cotton gin, but much more by his gun-making machinery "so accurate that any article belonging to any one of the muskets will equally well fit any [other] of them." The "uniformity system" as it was called in 1880—the system of interchangeable parts, as we call it, in a Ford factory—was therefore in practical operation before 1800, with all its essential advantages foreseen. The Yankee mind, dealing with machinery, has been uninterruptedly ingenious. It early discovered the essential problem of machine production—and its unique merit—and for a century and a half has been solving the problem in more and more effective ways.

Widely conceived, this was the great American preoccupation. It produced a manufacture suitable to a wide domain. It assumed transportation and the conquest of the wilderness. It involved big business by swift stages. In the half century before the Civil War, the United States was becoming preëminently a manufacturing country. By the time Lincoln took office the dominance of industry was obvious. For such a revolution to take place, the minds of the entire population had to be turned unwaveringly to a single object. Call it conquest of the frontier, or progress of mechanics, or desire for gain; when compared with the earlier absorption of the colonists in the affairs of the next world, it amounts to the same thing.

In the time of Jonathan Edwards and John Wesley, the average man had to be recalled from sloth and indifference to a contemplation of the horrors of hell. In the times of Eli Whitney, Fulton, Howe, Boone, Astor and the glorious companies of nameless pioneers who made the West, the average man was expectant of man-made miracles. He had to be called from wonder at his own achievements to think of the glories of salvation. It was not only a change of color, it was a change of focus.

§

At this time, when the typical activities of post-Revolutionary America were ungodly, the evangelists began their labors in the backwoods and the hinterland. They caught the pioneer in that unhappy middle period when he had already become a settler, but was not yet a villager. The ardor of pushing on had ebbed and the charred clearing, the inundated cornfield, and the solitude pressed down upon him. It is easy to overestimate the dreariness of these secluded lives, if we compare them with the comfort and variety of our own. The frontiersman, who had no such standards, suffered much less than we imagine. His willingness to "get along" without every comfort, his indifference to the society of his fellowmen, his apathy before disaster, his failure of emotional life, are themselves sharp lights on his dim way of living. The face of the first stranger seen in three months excited his instincts of hospitality, but evoked no curiosity and hardly any interest in the richer background from which the visitor came. Mrs. Frances Trollope, mother of the novelist, in her journey from New Orleans to Cincinnati, descended on a farm which, materially, was far above the worst:

"We visited one farm," she says, "which interested us particularly from its wild and lonely situation, and from the entire dependence of the inhabitants upon their resources. It was a partial clearing in the very heart of the forest. The house was built on the side of a hill, so steep that a high ladder was necessary to enter the front door, while the back one opened against the hillside; at the foot of this sudden eminence ran a clear stream, whose bed had been deepened into a little reservoir, just opposite the house. A noble field of Indian corn stretched away into the forest on one side, and a few half-cleared acres, with a shed or two upon them, occupied the other, giving accommodation to cows, horses, pigs, and chickens innumerable. Immediately before the house was a small potato garden, with a few peach and apple trees. The house was built of logs, and consisted of two rooms, besides a little shanty or lean-to, that was used as a kitchen. Both rooms were comfortably furnished with good beds, drawers, etc. The farmer's wife, and a young woman who looked like her sister, were spinning, and three little children were playing about. The woman told me that they spun and wove all the cotton and woollen garments of the family, and knit all the stockings; her husband though not a shoe-maker by trade, made all the shoes. She manufactured all the soap and candles they used, and prepared her sugar from the sugar-trees on their farm. All she wanted with money, she said, was to buy coffee, tea, and whiskey, and she could 'get enough any day by sending a batch of butter and chicken to market.' They used no wheat, nor sold any of their corn, which, though it appeared a very large quantity, was not more than they required to make their bread and cakes of various kinds, and to feed all their live-stock during the winter. She seemed contented, and proud of her independence; though it was in somewhat a mournful accent that she said, ' 'Tis strange to us to see company: I expect the sun will rise and set a hundred times before I shall see another human that does not belong to the family.' "

Travelers remark on the mirthlessness of the lives they observe. Even the school children play seldom at games. In the "triste little town of Cincinnati," the theater is meagerly patronized. Young people preferred Dorfeuille's Hell with its chamber of horrors and electrical shocks; their elders, the same gentleman's "lecture on the Fifth (or Gallinaceous) Order of Birds, after which the Nitrous Oxide will be administered."

In the larger cities, almost every report of social intercourse indicates a feebleness of imagination and a lack of grace. Except for dancing, upon which most of the churches frowned, almost all forms of entertainment were practiced by one sex in complete isolation from the other. Dinner parties were rare and at a small dinner, a family and friends, one ate or, if one talked at all, it was of business. Then the gentlemen gathered together "to spit, talk of elections, and the price of produce, and spit again; the women kept up a fluttering and feeble conversation about food and frivolities."

Most common amusements were forbidden by law, frowned on by religion, or simply passed by. This does not, of course, apply to the very rich nor to artistic and intellectual circles. Such exceptional groups easily provided the quaintness and attractiveness of this period. We have records of crazes for European knickknacks and, in the Thirties, "the exquisite from Philadelphia" finds that even his delicate person can pass along the streets of a middle western town without offense or molestation, and that "an artificial butterfly big enough for Tom Thumb to navigate the heavens with" is considered quite the latest thing for ladies' adornment.

But the very pleasures of society are so dreary, so unhappy and discouraged. A Frenchman, passing through a popular watering place in the 1830's, exclaimed that American women must indeed be bored with home life to prefer the rattle without gayety and the noisy discomforts of Bedford Springs—bad meals, bad beds, noisy rooms, stuffy dances, and the overwhelming dullness. At another equally popular resort, an intelligent Englishwoman who was enchanted with the heartiness of village life in America saw "young ladies tricked out in the most expensive finery, flirting over the backgammon board, tripping affectedly across the room, languishing with a seventy dollar cambric handkerchief, starting up in ecstasy at the entrance of a baby, the mothers as busy with affectations of another kind; and the brothers sidling hither and thither . . . in no way imparting the refreshment of a natural countenance, movement, or tone. . . ." (The fathers, one suspects, were absent on business.)

Such was the society of this period. The tone was given by

women who were always ill and, if not actively unhappy, were generally languid, adoring Byron and taking up collections for the Greeks under Marcos Bozzaris, but keeping themselves isolated from any reality and fleeing from the sinfulness and discomforts of their own nature. The mother of Susan B. Anthony, when she was pregnant, hid herself and never spoke of her condition to anyone, not even her mother. But the pioneering woman was different. As Arthur W. Calhoun has pointed out, fecundity in the early 19th century was the supreme virtue—he might have said the supreme occupation. Even in the plague-stricken swamps and the barren clearings, children had to be raised so that they might soon help in hoeing and planting and shooting game and defending the settlement when their fathers went down the river to the town, or were scalped by the Indians. The government encouraged marriage by giving a whole section of land to a married couple, and only half to a bachelor. In Tennessee, children gave additional claim to land: triplets entitled parents to take up six hundred acres. In North Carolina, there were grandmothers at the age of 27. Even later, when the pressure of an undeveloped country was somewhat slackened, women were considered old at twenty-five. "Sweet sixteen" (the phrase occurs early) was not the winsome age of prettiness and frivolity, but the appropriate period for love and marriage.

A propaganda for romantic love covered the brutal actuality but, as early as 1805, protests against the fictional doctrine that "love is all" were common in the literary magazines. On one side a false glamour was thrown over the forms of love-making: on the other, all the emotions of the sexual relation were beaten down by the mastering necessity of propagating in numbers. The American woman became artificial or cold. The texture of her sexual life was impoverished, or broken down under the burden of children. Stendhal (who never came to this country but obviously based his remarks on reports of other Frenchmen), is almost chagrined at the thought of American boys and girls going sleigh riding together and returning home still boys and girls.

"A little bundling" was customary in many parts of the country—in Pennsylvania, in the Connecticut valley, in Massachusetts and elsewhere. Among the Dutch and German settlers "parties of men and girls spend the night together at inns both sexes sleeping together. Such great control have the females acquired, that several who have bundled for years, it is said, have never permitted any improper liberties. Indeed, it is considered as not in the least indelicate." In a variety of ways this delicacy and restraint were to be erected into an ascetic principle on which religions and communities were founded. It was a natural counterpoise to the unexpressed theories and the constant practice of breeding. Another counterpoise appears with startling frankness in advertisements for contraceptives, "intended for married ladies whose health forbids a too rapid increase of family," and possibly used by women who went out in carloads along the westward routes to join unknown men who needed children beyond woman's capacity to bear.

The hardihood of the pioneers made loneliness a positive pleasure. Many of them felt crowded when their fellowmen appeared and fled from their settlement of a dozen cabins to a further loneliness. Even those who stayed were scattered over vast holdings and their comings together were rare and brief. This was another side of the conquest of nature. It compelled as complete an absorption in material things as speculation in canal bonds or the invention of machinery, but its fruits were neither so full of promise nor so rapid in ripening. Both the commerce and the agriculture of the pioneer shrank and belittled the soul.

§

However tawdry and hysterical was the appeal made by the itinerant evangelist shouting "sin" and "hell," after all, it was to the soul that he addressed himself. From the first, he touched on the very thing which made him successful: he invited more than two or three to gather together. The day of his coming was appointed far in advance, often as long ahead as a year. To make his rounds he had to be as hardy and as patient as the pioneer himself. In desolate regions of forest the word of his coming spread and from single cabins, or clusters of log houses, men and women and children traveled days and nights over trails and log roads, by fords and through swamps, to the wider clearing where the meeting was to be held. To these outlying regions the political rally could not penetrate; in fact it had not yet developed into a second great social phenomenon when the camp-meeting began.

Men and women who had perhaps seen no strange face in half a year, or had been huddled together in a group of twenty or thirty for many months, suddenly found themselves in crowds of thousands. This was in itself an excitement of the happiest kind. The timid and the arrogant both reacted to it. The change of setting, the mill-race of people, the prospect of novelty and adventure, touched nerves which had long been dormant. The unaccustomed contact sent a galvanic spark coursing from one to another and spasmodic shivers of apprehension mingled with a great anticipation of delight.

Before he began to speak, the preacher had already affected the release of his audience. He had set them free from loneliness and the burdensome companionship of their own troubles. He had moved them bodily, had changed for a moment the orbit of their lives. The strange wind that had blown them together swayed the multitude like a field of grain. The preacher had only to put in the sickle and reap.

What the traveling evangelist said was important enough, but the circumstances gave it a nervous intensity far more thrilling than arguments or threats or promises. He was a man violent in the cause of God which, in the forest, in spite of carefully guarded Bibles and prayers and observations, was a lost cause. Here was fervor in a land which required only obstinacy. It was a sort of elated confidence, almost joy, to those who lived, without exaltation of any kind, in continual fear and misgiving. For hours the preacher shouted to men whose speech was crabbed and confined. He gesticulated passionately to indifferent whittlers of sticks. His whole discourse was in the tradition of evangelism. The flood of his images swept over arid souls in which imagination had become a withered stalk. It was, as the evangelist called it, a "time of refreshing," and a "copious out-pouring of grace." Both the words and the tones of revivalism were foreign to the hard-bitten country upon which they fell. It is not remarkable that strange weeds sprouted.

To a world which was always moving, the evangelist brought news of another world where there was peace. He had eternity to offer as a compensation for the uncertainties of life. The theology of the frontier revival was more democratic than that of the colonial had been. A country which had given every man a vote on earth was unlikely to relish a theology according to which only a few of the spiritual nobility, the inheritors of great moral estates, were elected for everlasting mercy. The mechanism of election was becoming familiar. The ancient threat of damnation went further, but it was no longer tyrannical. It gave every man hope, provided he paid his moral taxes. Even the older order of Calvinists were almost as welcome as the Methodist revivalists. For they, too, gave the people a new direction for their thoughts. They also set the stammering and inexpressive and inhibited multitude in direct communion with the gentleness of Jesus and the magnificence of God. For two days, or five, or ten, the merciless inclosure of common unlovely tasks, of meager interests and unsatisfied emotions was broken through. For that brief time, the brutal requirements of physical existence were over-run. In their degree, men and women threw off the burden of living and thought about godliness or sin. They reached upward to the hem of Christ's garment or threw themselves face downward in abasement before the Lord.

The psychology of the itinerant was inspiring. From the moment he spoke the name of God, he released his hearers from the exacting tyranny of Mother Earth. When he spoke of Christ he put an end to the terror of their loneliness and promised them a communion, an intercession, a friend, in their friendless lives.

While from these circumstances we may compile a credit side for the evangelical movement, the discredit is enormous. The revivals from 1800 to the 1830's have been called the source of almost unimaginable evil in the United States. They settled on it the hysteria-system of approaching salvation. They were responsible for a state of nervous uneasiness which was reflected in politics, in domestic life, and in social practice. From the Tree of Life, as conceived by Edwards, they cut off all the noble branches: the intellectual fervor and honesty, the clear sense of logic, the ecstasy arduously gained and reverently cherished. They held fast only to excitement. Where the earlier revivalists demanded proof of conversion, and withheld their approval until they were persuaded that regeneration was genuine and promised to be permanent, most of the later winners of souls had no standard but numbers. How many were saved—not how they were saved, or how lasting their safety—was their great question. Their methods were ignoble, brutalizing. They made sick souls or intensified maladies which might have been cured. The testimony of contemporaries exempts only two or three evangelists from charges of the gravest nature.

To remember the other side, therefore, is all the more necessary; to recall that the very utterance of the name of the Lord by the revivalists smashed for a moment the systematic impoverishment of the American spirit. If we fail to see this, if we do not recognize the unconscious clamoring for release to which the evangelist was the living answer, we cannot understand fully the witches' sabbath of religion which his labors created.

We shall come in a moment to contemporary descriptions of revival meetings so vivid in their delineation of hysteria and abnormality that they send a shiver through us. It is well to pause a moment and consider that in general there are two explanations. The enthusiast for religion says that the mouthings, the ravings, the convulsions, the singing in strange tongues, are the pure work of the Lord and that the slight evils which follow all revivals are amply justified by the grandeur of the souls that are saved. This is a justification which science has long since repudiated. The hater of religion, using the full battery of scientific or pseudo-scientific terms, counts the evangelist as a celebrant of the black mass, his followers the victims of mob psychology, and the marks of conversion as symptoms of libidinous desire. This is the current criticism and there is much truth in it, but we must not forget that, for all its presumable accuracy and the exactness of its scientific terms, this accusation merely implies that revivalism is witchcraft. It is not possible to combine these two interpretations and it is not needful to make a compromise between them. It is only necessary to give each its proper place. In a survey of the field of revivalism, which also includes the physical and emotional complexes out of which it sprang, we may think of it as a necessity and as a godsend no less than as debauchery and pestilence. Something was needed to break down the monotony of an exceptionally materialistic existence. Circumstances favored neither art, nor sport, nor intellectual, nor physical diversion of any kind. No release of the physical pressure was to be found even in immorality or perversion. There was no welcome intrusion into the pioneer's solitude. The camp-meeting originally performed the function of a carnival, or a kermesse, or an orgy—festivals established by the wisdom of ages in three great civilizations to give release to the impassioned body or the tortured mind. In that view, it matters comparatively little that conversions were unsubstantial and fleeting. Possibly even the rapes and seductions and drunkenness, the loosening of tongues and the liberation of every carnality, contributed, in spite of the hysteria which accompanied them, to a healthy life.

† The new republic turned its eyes to the West. † French visitors marveled to see young girls go driving with their sweethearts unchaperoned. † The fictional doctrine that "love is all" was condemned by literary magazines. † At girls' schools the subjects were needlework, music, and moral instruction. Mary Wollstonecraft's *Vindication of the Rights of Women* was published in Philadelphia and Eliza Southgate wrote to Moses Porter that not one woman in a hundred marries for love. Remedies for sexual ills and accidents were advertised in the press. † By the opening of the century, there were 2,000 miles of post roads traveled on horseback, by stage and by sulkies. † The first office for the disposal of public lands was established at Chillicothe, Ohio.
† The piano was manufactured domestically, and Jenner's Vaccine was introduced by Dr. Waterhouse. † Carrots were scarcely used and the tomato was known as the "love apple" and considered poisonous. Salt was available, but had to be powdered. † Eli Terry began to sell wooden clock movements for $25. † Women's skirts grew scantier and they abandoned almost all underwear. "Shepherds, I have lost my love" was parodied:

> "Shepherds, I have lost my waist,
> Have you seen my body?"

† Captain Elias Bunker announced a hundred-ton sloop sailing up the Hudson. Beds, bedding, food, and liquor were procurable on board.
† Foreigners complained that Americans are always in a hurry.

# IV.

## Gasper River.

"IT is a glorious assurance, a whispering of the everlasting covenant, it is the bleating of the lamb, it is the welcome of the shepherd, it is the essence of love, it is the fullness of glory, it is being in Jesus, it is Jesus being in us, it is taking the Holy Ghost into our bosoms, it is setting ourselves down by God, it is being called to the high places, it is eating and drinking and sleeping in the Lord, it is becoming a lion in the faith, it is being lowly and meek, and kissing the hand that smites, it is being mighty and powerful, and scorning reproof. . . ."

§

The setting of the camp-meeting is a clearing in the Kentucky forest, around the bend of the river and away from the village. The underbrush has been fired and fresh grass has come up. Around the blackened stumps of the trees there is no plan, no arrangement of streets but, as the men come from the backwoods, they draw up their wagons as close to one of the platforms as they can get, forming a rough square. New arrivals are pushed deeper into the forest. The day before the camp-meeting, the roads baked by the June sun begin to be crowded. After the sun is set, tallow dips are lit inside the wagons and wood fires upon the ground. New arrivals find their way by the light of pine torches. At the end of 200 miles of travel by day and by night, they are broken, but as they press forward toward the center their spirits revive. The loosening of tongues begins. Voices cross and blend and increase in volume. A straggler coming in hears in the woods first an unwonted sound, then something like a heavy rain, and finally joins himself in a roar of sound. As it dies away, the people crawl into or under their wagons to rest for the ordeal of the preaching on the morrow. But occasionally, through the night, there are hidden sounds of some early revelers or groans and shrieking of those who are prematurely exercised. Within the circumference of the meeting there are perhaps ten or fifteen thousand souls, but each one imagines himself part of a vast crowd of twenty-five or fifty thousand. In the morning, this whole multitude presses into the open space before the preacher's trestle but, even in the dead silence which he demands, his voice cannot carry to the periphery of the crowd. Another preacher sets out for a strategic tree-stump and gathers part of the crowd about him. A third, of another denomination, makes the seat of a wagon his pulpit. The exhorting begins. A fourth and then a fifth evangelist stand above the crowd and add their shouting. The preachers pitch their voices higher and wave their arms in wider gestures, calling for repentance and threatening vengeance. The pictures of hell grow more vivid. The cries of "O, Lord" and "Jesus, save us" and the roared "amens" rise up automatically from the crowd. As one speaker gives up, exhausted, another takes his place. A fresh voice beats down on the people before the speaker in the hot sun. The odors of humanity rise up and overcome the sweet air of the forest. The people crowd and jostle each other, sway forward, and are pushed back, and gasp for breath. A spectator deliberately holding aloof from the excitement stands on the shaft of a wagon and counts seven preachers all speaking at once. He hears the "amens" and "yes Lords" coming more and more quickly with panting breath and great sighs.

Suddenly a little child is lifted to a tree stump and begins to make strange noises, to utter a babble of meaningless sounds. A girl of seven falls senseless and the crowd makes a little room for her to lie on the ground. At the end of two hours she is revived from her stupor and, raised to her father's shoulder, delivers, it is supposed, "the greatest body of divinity ever pronounced by human lips," until she is exhausted and her head drops but, at a word of sympathy, she quickly turns and cries out, "Don't call me poor for Christ is my brother, God my father, and I am rich in the blood of the Lamb." At these ecstatic words, men and women fall to the earth, their faces in the mud and bodies in the path of the restless horses, their hands in dung, and cry out the glories of God. The contagion spreads, the groans grow deeper and more agonized. As a man or woman begins to shout, or sing, or scream, the others turn from the preacher to encourage the sufferer. Slowly the extremities begin to twitch, the fingers clutch in the air, the arms strike out wildly and a convulsive dance begins. The rhythm affects the on-lookers until many are in movement and the leader with a growing wildness and ecstasy in her expression shrieks loudly and falls in a faint to the ground. "She has taken it," the others cry, and the news is reported to the preacher who glorifies the Lord for this visible sign of his grace. The stricken convert is carried to one side and one of the preachers sits by until consciousness returns and then, after a few on-lookers join in an appropriate hymn, the token of conversion is accepted.

Through the noon-day heat the preaching continues and, as the sun goes down, the torches are lit and fires burn in front of every camp and on the tables spread for administering the Lord's Supper, around which the communicants eagerly press. Under the moon the scene becomes unearthly and terrifying. The groans of the spiritually wounded intermingle with the shouts of heaven-born souls. Those who have gotten religion work their way through the crowd seeking relatives and friends, kneeling beside them and praying to them to give in to God. Others try to beat their way out of the encampment, but are paralyzed and some are torn with indecision, fearing the descent of the spirit and powerless to escape it.

"They were struck down and exercised in many different ways, although they generally trembled exceedingly, and were remarkably cold in their bodily extremities. After they recovered, some said they felt a great load about their heart, a little before the severity of the stroke; others said they were rather in a slumbering and inattentive way, not at all affected at that moment, with what they were hearing or had heard when they were struck down in an instant as with a thunderbolt.

"Some were totally insensible of everything that passed for some considerable time, others said they were perfectly sensible of every word spoken in their hearing, and everything done to them although to the spectator they appeared in a state of equal insensibility. Many cried out exceedingly when they were first struck down; their cries were like those of the greatest bodily distress imaginable. But this was generally succeeded, in a little time by a state of apparent insensibility which generally lasted much longer; and which, in some, was succeeded by the strongest appearance of extreme agitation and distress exhibited by incessant cries for mercy, and acknowledgments of unworthiness and ingratitude to a blessed Savior."

All night long the work goes on and, in the early morning, the converts and the unregenerate lie upon the ground in weariness, or are convulsed by movements beyond their control. Again the voice of the preacher, hoarsened but fervent, cries out. In an outlying part of the meeting, a handful of men and women are down on all fours growling and snapping their teeth and barking like dogs, making a sudden rush into another group or roaming around. In other places they mew like cats or snarl like wolves. A preacher leaps down and begins to dance slowly and rhythmically around the stand crying softly, "This is the holy ghost—glory," for an hour, until he falls. In places a convert goes into a trance without any warning and is not aware of his own condition until he sees others crowding around him and, making an effort to move, finds himself powerless. Those who come out of the trances regain their strength and recount their experiences. A rivalry sets in for the wildest movement. As the day goes on the "jerks" begin.

"Nothing in nature could better represent this strange and unaccountable operation than for one to goad another, alternately on every side, with a piece of red-hot iron. The exercise commonly began in the head which would fly backward and forward, and from side to side with a quick jolt which the person would naturally labor to suppress but in vain, and the more anyone labored to stay himself and be sober the more he staggered and the more rapidly his twitches increased. He must necessarily go as he was stimulated, whether with a violent dash on the ground and bounce from place to place like a football, or hop round with head, limbs and trunk, twitching and jolting in every direction, as if they must inevitably fly asunder. . . . By this strange operation the human frame was commonly so transformed and disfigured, as to lose every trace of its natural appearance. Sometimes the head would be twitched right and left to a half round with such velocity that not a feature could be discovered but the face appear as much behind as before, and in the quick progressive jerk, it would seem as if the person was transmuted into some other species of creature. Head-dresses were of little account among the female jerkers. Even hand-kerchiefs bound tight round the head would be flirted off almost with the first twitch, and the hair put into the utmost confusion; this was a very great inconvenience, to redress which the generality were shorn, though directly contrary to their confession of faith. Such as were seized with the jerks wrested at once, not only from under their own government, but that of everyone else so that it was dangerous to attempt confining them, or touching them in any manner, to whatever danger they were exposed."

Toward morning of the third day, a light rain begins to fall. The preachers cry out that it is a signal of God's anger, and no one makes a move to depart. The agitation of those on the ground grows more violent. The jerks and trances become so frequent that the bodies of the convulsed are in danger of being trampled under foot, and friends carry them away and lay them out as though for burial. As they recover, they are drawn magnetically to the scene of their seizure and supernatural eloquence possesses them. Their voices are terribly penetrating and they talk for three or four or five hours without a stop. The preachers beg them to be silent, but it is impossible. They keep on crying out their guilt and danger, their hard heart, their desire to die and be damned, and the infinite justice of God if He sent them to the hell they deserve. A little boy, coming out of a seizure in the middle of the night, cries out, "O, I am lost forever, I am going right down to hell. O, I see hell and the breath of the Lord like a stream of brimstone kindling it." Some remain in a state of torpor from the moment they are seized. Others, when the talking fit has passed, are serene and confident. Some who have been seized before lash themselves in the hope of another visitation. Stories of miracles pass. Deists and infidels have come to sneer at the meeting. One reproaches the preacher and the preacher utters one word in return. The man falls as if dead and rising confesses the Savior. Supercilious young women in silks, jewelry, and prunella come at the beginning of the fourth day and bring with them Northerners visiting the great plantations. They smile with mockery at the scene but, suddenly, their heads and arms jerk so that bonnets and combs fly off, bangles jingle at their wrist, and their hair works loose and cracks like a wagoner's whip. On the outskirts of the meeting there is roistering in the dead of night. Women, half demented, think they give themselves to Christ in the body of a drunken fornicator and, struck suddenly with the awfulness of their sin, return and shriek and pound their way into a fresh ecstasy. Still the meeting goes on. The resisters are broken down one by one.

"Finally a large man cursed the jerks and all religion. Shortly afterward he took the jerks and started to run, but he jerked so powerfully he could not get away. He halted among some saplings, and although he was violently agitated, he took out his bottle of whiskey, and swore he would drink the jerks to death; but he jerked at such a rate that he could not get the bottle to his mouth, though he tried hard. At length he fetched a sudden jerk, and the bottle struck a sapling and was broken to pieces, and spilled his whiskey on the ground. He became very much enraged and cursed and swore very profanely, his jerks still increasing. At length he fetched a very violent jerk, snapped his neck, fell, and soon expired, with his mouth full of cursing and bitterness."

The meeting has come to an appropriate climax.

§

At Gasper River and Cabin Creek in Kentucky, at Spartanburg, South Carolina, at Turtle Creek in North Carolina, in Tennessee, at Holly Springs, Mississippi, in Tuscaloosa and Knoxville, at Muddy River and Red River, the McGreadys, the Cartwrights, the Burkes, the McNemars, the Cummins, the Campbells, and the Stones labored. What is written above is largely drawn from their own accounts and from the reports of their fellow-workers and friendly eye-witnesses in these places. Not all of these phenomena occurred at a single meeting, but at Gasper River, in 1800, the American camp-meeting came into being, and there and in near-by states all of these things took place, and more.

The camp-meeting is the violent form of the revival; the movement they represent has had profound influence on the spiritual history of America giving birth to missions and colleges, to cults and manias, to reform movements of the purest idealism, and to prurient and officious interference with private lives. The actual events are therefore worthy a little more attention. I follow the natural division, noting the physical signs in connection with the camp-meeting, where they were given an intense and almost sinister expression; and leaving for the later revival meetings all questions of doctrine and the meaning of the conversions which they gained.

The camp-meetings of the 1800's were exceptional even to the people who took part in them and that is probably why the evangelists who conducted them left such vivid accounts of their successes and those who took part so frequently wrote letters describing their experiences. These range from the sophisticated correspondence of indifferent spectators to the naïve enthusiasms of the illiterate. The testimony they bear is identical and out of them we get a composite picture of a long series of events and many hints at hidden motives. A physician, who observed the early meetings and the later decline in frequency and fervor, after making every reservation, still maintained that the good results vastly preponderated over the evil. The camp-meetings roused people from indifference to their destiny, but these effects "were of a mixed nature. They were doubtless attended for improper purposes by a few licentious persons and by others with a view of obtaining a handle to ridicule all religion. . . . The free intercourse of all ages and sexes under cover of the night and the woods was not without its temptations. It is also to be feared that they gave rise to false notions of religion by laying too much stress on bodily exercises, and substituting them in place of moral virtues or inward piety. These were too often considered as evidences of a change of heart and affections, though they neither proved nor disproved anything of the kind."

One of the great objections was the unnatural excitement to which children were subjected and the prominence which any evidence of hysteria gave them. The revivalist, McNemar, clearly exulting in these signs of heavenly approval, tells of a sacramental meeting near Flemingsburg, in April 1801, where there was "much weeping, trembling, and convulsion of the soul. Two little girls, nine or ten years old, cried out in great distress during the meeting and continued praying and crying for mercy till one of them re-

ceived hope. She turned to the other and cried, 'O! you little sinner, come to Christ! Take hold of his promises!—trust in him!—
he is above to save to the uttermost—O! The Precious Savior!
Come just as you are, he will take away the stony heart and give
you a heart of flesh! You can't make yourself any better.—Just
give up your heart to Christ now! You are not a greater sinner
than me! You need not wait another moment!' Thus she continued
exhorting until the other child received a ray from heaven that
produced a sudden and sensible change; then rising with her in her
arms, she cried out in the most affecting manner—'O, here is another star of light!' "

A more normal symptom is the amount of eager discussion in
which the people engaged, disputing points of doctrine with each
other, or questioning the preacher for further light. It is also pleasing to discover how sectarian differences were sunk in enthusiasm
for conversions. Presbyterians, Methodists, Baptists, and subdivi-
sions of these, preached simultaneously or in succession to the same
gathering, possibly out of jealous intention to seize every opportunity, but also in the specific belief that the particular pathway
was unimportant if it eventually led to the high road of salvation.

The jerks themselves, around which raged a religious controversy as impassioned as any doctrinal struggle between the Early
Fathers, have been carefully analyzed for us. Here are some accounts, beginning with the first symptoms of those who were "struck
down" and going on to the full development of the fit.

"I suppose I saw as many as 800 that were struck down mostly
in the following manner: they say they feel very weak in their
knees and a want of breath as one in the agony of death and instantly fall and lay insensible from 15 minutes to six, eight, or
ten hours. Some are cramped in the extremities. The first words
generally spoken by them after their recovery is, Lord, have mercy,
increasing from words to sentences, to exhortations to believe in
Christ, to cease to do evil and learn to do well, to depend wholly
in the Righteousness of Christ. Their exhortations are accompanied with instant power to the hearts of their hearers."

"The persons who are struck are generally first observed to pay
close attention to the preaching; then to weep and shed tears plenti-

fully for a while; after this a twitching or jerking seizes them, and they fall to the ground helpless, and convulsed through their whole frame as if in the agonies of death."

"It is impossible to give an account of all the various shades of difference in the appearance of those who are affected. The following may serve as a general outline of the work: when a person begins to be affected, he generally sinks down in the place where he stood and is for a few minutes overwhelmed in tears; he then makes a weeping noise—some person near lays hold on him—he shrieks aloud—and discovers a desire to be on his back—in this he is indulged—and a friend sits down and supports the head of the person in his lap. Every tear now leaves his eye and he shouts aloud for about twenty minutes. Meanwhile the features of his face are calm and regular. His voice becomes more and more feeble for about twenty minutes more. By this time he is speechless and motionless and lies quiet perhaps an hour. During this time his pulse is rather lower than the usual state,—the extremities are cold, the skin fresh and clear, the features of the face full, the eyes closed, but not so close as in sleep. Speech and motion return in the same gradual manner; the features become more full than before. Pleasure paints the countenance as peace comes to the soul, and when faith is obtained the person rises up, and with most heavenly countenance shouts—'Glory to God.' This ecstasy abates in about a quarter of an hour and the person is generally led away by a friend to his tent."

An evangelist writes, "It would be exceedingly difficult to draw an intelligible representation of the effects of this work upon the human body. Some are more easily and gently wrought than others, some appear wholly wrapped in solitude while others cannot refrain from pouring out their whole souls in exhortation to those standing round;—different stages from mild swoons to convulsive spasms, may be seen;—The nerves are not unfrequently severely cramped;—The subjects generally exhibit appearances, as though their very hearts would burst out of their mouths.—The lungs are violently agitated and all accompanied with an helation;—They universally declare, that they feel no bodily pain at the moment of exercise, although some complain of a sore breast and the effects of cramping, after the work is over;—The pulse of all whom I observed beat quick and regular, the extremities of the body are sometimes perceptibly cold.—In short no art or desire could imitate the exercise.—No mimic would be able to do justice to the exhibition."

Two general descriptions both taken from letters and apparently describing the same meeting, follow.

"A more tremendous sight never struck the eyes of mortal man. The very clouds seemed to separate and give way to the praises of the people of God ascending to the heavens; while thousands of tongues with the sound of hallelujah seemed to roll through infinite space; while hundreds of people lay prostrate on the ground crying for mercy. Oh! My dear brother, had you been there to have seen the convulsed limbs, the apparently lifeless bodies, to all of which the distorted features exactly comporting you would have been constrained to cry out as I was obliged to do, the Gods are among the people; nor was this confined to the commonality alone; but people of every description lay prostrate on the ground. There you might see the learned Pastor, the steady patriot and the obedient son crying holy, holy, holy, Lord God Almighty: behold the honorable matron and virtuous maiden crying with all the appearance of heart-felt distress, Jesus thou son of the most high God, have mercy upon us. Cast your eyes a few paces farther, and there you might see the prodigal in the arms of the professed libertine, crying hosannah to God in the highest, there is no other name under heaven whereby the man can be saved; but by the name of Jesus. See the poor oppressed African with his soul liberated longing to be with his God."

* "The camp was exlenonined by candles furneshed by the congration which was in a thick grove of beach timber the apperance of itselfe gave a solem apperance but ad to that preaching exorting singing praying sinors rejoicing publickly testifoying that the ware delivered from the bodage of sin and death others under deep conviction lementing that the wore dredful sinors the whole to gether struck eavery person with a solem aw a few excepted.

"In gaveing my opinion I will describe it as not yet being a

* The spelling is throughout that of the original.

subject of that extrodenery work I have seen of eavery age sects
and description from eight years upwards those that has been subject has been operated on differently some has had symtoms before
the fell the have felt it in the grait arteraye of the thyes and arms
but like a shock closed in emedently to the hart the hart sweels lik-
ing to burst the bodaye occasions shortness and quickness of breath
the become motienless the feet and hands become cold but the pulse
generaly regular the ceace breathing hard and become easaye before the can speake the heart returns to the extremety one of two
subjects the talke on either that the are dredful siner some times
in a state of despere aledging that there is now salvation for them
or the have got a hope of salvation through Christ and recoment
Christ to sinors in the most presint manow caling on their friends
to fly to christ that if the are damned it will be their own blame
that christ dyed for sinours that he is able to save the vilest
sinour . . ."

§

Other observers note symptoms which are more important to
the pathologist: the swaggering pride of those who fall, the envy
of their friends, and the recurrent imitation of the symptoms, mingled with a fury of rivalry to outdo the experience of everyone else.
The extraordinary itinerant, Lorenzo Dow, who covered two hundred thousand miles in the course of his preaching, supplies another
interesting feature. On several occasions he notes that conversions
begin as a dance in definite rhythm, apparently under full control.
Gradually the rhythm breaks and tears itself loose from measure
and discipline until it becomes a series of disconnected leaps and
jumps which end in a fit.

Dow, incidentally, is easily the outstanding figure of the early
revival. He was not the most violent; but his gaunt figure, "his
long hair, his flowing beard, his harsh voice, and his wild gesticulation," make him the most picturesque. He was generally called a
clown. His rude manners, his filthy clothes, were as offensive to
his enemies as the illogical "insults upon the Gospel" which eventually shut the doors of the Methodist Conferences against him.
He was, as a child, subject to musings about God, attacks of remorse and fear, and dreams as vivid as hallucinations. When he

was twenty-two, he sailed, like Asenath Nicholson after him, to investigate the conditions of the Irish, but an attack of smallpox frustrated his intention to save these people from Catholicism and the three thousand handbills warning Dublin of the wrath to come were wasted. He returned home and, for two years, walked or rode through the greater part of the South preaching the gospel, and is credited with being the first to establish camp-meetings in central Virginia. On a trip North, he heard that the sister-in-law of a Methodist tavern keeper had determined never to marry anyone but a preacher who would continue his wanderings. The story of his proposal is told in his own words: "When going away I observed to her that I was going to the warm countries, where I had never spent a warm season, and it was probable I should die, as the warm climate destroys most of those who go there from a cold country; but, said I, if I am preserved, about a year and a half from now I am in hopes of seeing this northern country again, and if during this time you live and remain single, and would be willing to give me up twelve months out of thirteen, or three years out of four, to travel and that in foreign lands, and never say, Do not go to your appointment, etc.—for if you should stand in my way I should pray God to remove you, which I believe he would answer—and if I find no one that I like better than I do you, perhaps something further may be said upon the subject; and finding her character to stand fair, I took my departure."

Two years later he returned. They were speedily married and Peggy Dow endured every hardship with her husband until her death in 1820. Dow's second marriage was also unconventional. His biographer says, "There came a day when in an open-air sermon under the great elm on Bean Hill Green at Norwich, Dow extolled the virtues of his former companion and at the end of his sermon asked, 'Is there anyone in this congregation willing to take the place of my departed Peggy?' Up rose Lucy Dolbeare from Montville, six feet high, and said, 'I will.'" Whether Lorenzo and Lucy had previously arranged this dramatic proceeding we do not know. We do know, however, that she too made a loyal companion. She survived her husband for several years.

Dow's methods were dramatic, but he seems never to have

*Permission of Kennedy & Co.*

An American Camp-meeting

struck down more than a few people at a time. He would preach violently and, when he had "gathered their wandering minds into a train of good thinking," he would draw the penitents and the hesitants closer to him and pray for them with such intensity that soon they sprawled as if lifeless before him. "Here some supposed they were dying, whilst others suggested, 'It is the work of the Devil.' I observed, 'If it be the Devil's work they will use the dialect of hell when they come to.' Some watched my words in great solemnity, and the first and second were soon brought through happy, and so were all of them in the course of the night, except a young woman who had come, under good impressions, much against her father's will, thirty miles. She continued shrieking for mercy eight hours, sometimes on the borders of despair, until near sunrise, when I exhorted her, if she had a view of her Savior to receive Him as appearing for her. Here hope revived, faith sprang up, joy arose: her countenance was an index of her heart to all beholders: she uttered a word, and soon she testified the reality of . . . the peace she had found."

In addition to this work of salvation, Dow was a tireless missionary to convert Roman Catholics and was one of the great evangelists who fought for abolition. Catholicism and slavery he joined together in a sort of mystical combination for which later observers have found a rational excuse. From Dow we get also some sense of the hostility which the camp-meetings roused. He was continually fighting collegians or Conferences, leaping from the pulpit to chase noisy critics from the church or stripping for a fight when the occasion demanded. In a movement which is by no means anonymous, but in which the participants are obscure and without significant personality, he is a singular and arresting figure.

§

What remains to be noted is the opinion of a hostile critic and for this, since we are not looking for justice, no one could be more available than Mrs. Trollope herself. That estimable and angry lady, who managed to write two volumes on her year in the United States, without quite confessing that she was doing anything so vulgar as engaging in trade, was offended by many things and disliked everything. It remained for the camp-meeting to shock her.

"Out of about thirty persons thus placed, perhaps half a dozen were men. One of these, a handsome youth of eighteen or twenty, kneeled just below the opening through which I looked. His arm was encircling the neck of a young girl who knelt beside him, with her hair hanging disheveled upon her shoulders, and her features working with the most violent agitation; soon after they both fell forward on the straw, as if unable to endure in any other attitude the burning eloquence of a tall grim figure in black, who, standing erect in the center, was uttering with incredible vehemence an oration that seemed to hover between praying and preaching; his arms hung stiff and immovable by his side, and he looked like an ill-constructed machine, set in action by a movement so violent, as to threaten its own destruction, so jerkingly, painfully, yet rapidly, did his words tumble out; the kneeling circle ceasing not to call in every variety of tone, on the name of Jesus; accompanied with sobs, groans, and a sort of low howling inexpressibly painful to listen to. . . .

"One of the preachers began in a low nasal tone, and, like all other Methodist preachers, assured us of the enormous depravity of man as he comes from the hands of his Maker, and of his perfect sanctification after he had wrestled sufficiently with the Lord to get hold of him, et cætera. The admiration of the crowd was evinced by almost constant cries of 'Amen! Amen!' 'Jesus! Jesus!' 'Glory! Glory!' and the like. But this comparative tranquillity did not last long: the preacher told them that 'this night was the time fixed upon for anxious sinners to wrestle with the Lord'; that he and his brethren 'were at hand to help them,' and that such as needed their help were to come forward into 'the pen.'

" 'The pen' was the space immediately below the preachers' stand. . . .

"The crowd fell back at the mention of the pen, and for some minutes there was a vacant space before us. The preachers came down from their stand and placed themselves in the midst of it, beginning to sing a hymn, calling upon the penitents to come forth. As they sung they kept turning themselves round to every part of the crowd, and, by degrees, the voices of the whole multitude joined in chorus. This was the only moment at which I perceived anything like the solemn and beautiful effect, which I had heard ascribed to this woodland worship. It is certain that the combined voices of such a multitude, heard at dead of night, from the depths of their eternal forests, the many fair young faces turned upward, and looking paler and lovelier as they met the moonbeams, the dark figures of the officials in the middle of the circle, the lurid glare thrown by the altar-fires on the woods beyond, did altogether produce a fine and solemn effect, that I shall not easily forget; but ere I had well enjoyed it, the scene changed, and sublimity gave place to horror and disgust. . . .

"Above a hundred persons, nearly all females, came forward uttering howlings and groans, so terrible that I shall never cease to shudder when I recall them. They appeared to drag each other forward, and on the word being given, 'let us pray,' they all fell on their knees; but this posture was soon changed for others that permitted greater scope for the convulsive movements of their limbs; and they were soon all lying on the ground in an indescribable confusion of heads and legs. They threw about their limbs with such incessant and violent motion, that I was every instant expecting some serious accident to occur.

"But how am I to describe the sounds that proceeded from this strange mass of human beings? I know no words which can convey an idea of it. Hysterical sobbings, convulsive groans, shrieks and screams the most appalling, burst forth on all sides. I felt sick with horror. As if their hoarse and overstrained voices failed to make noise enough, they soon began to clap their hands violently. . . .

"Many of these wretched creatures were beautiful young females. The preachers moved about among them, at once exciting and soothing their agonies. I heard the murmured confessions of the poor victims, and I watched their tormentors, breathing into their ears consolations that tinged the pale cheek with red. . . .

"After the first wild burst that followed their prostration, the moanings, in many instances, became loudly articulate; and I then experienced a strange vibration between tragic and comic feeling.

"A very pretty girl, who was kneeling in the attitude of Canova's Magdalene immediately before us, amongst an immense quantity of jargon broke out thus: 'Woe! woe to the backsliders! hear it, hear it Jesus! when I was fifteen my mother died, and I backslided, Oh, Jesus, I backslided! take me home to my mother, Jesus! take me home to her, for I am weary! Oh, John Mitchel! John Mitchel!' and after sobbing piteously behind her raised hands, she lifted her sweet face again, which was as pale as death, and said, 'Shall I sit on the sunny bank of salvation with my mother? my own dear mother? Oh, Jesus, take me home, take me home!'

"Who could refuse a tear to this earnest wish for death in one so young and lovely? But I saw her, ere I left the ground, with her hand fast locked, and her head supported by a man who looked very much as Don Juan might, when sent back to earth as too bad for the regions below.

"One woman near us continued to 'call on the Lord,' as it is termed, in the loudest possible tone, and without a moment's interval, for the two hours that we kept our dreadful station. She became frightfully hoarse, and her face so red as to make me expect she would burst a blood-vessel. Among the rest of her rant, she said, 'I will hold fast to Jesus, I never will let him go; if they take me to hell, I will still hold him fast, fast, fast!'

"The stunning noise was sometimes varied by the preachers beginning to sing; but the convulsive movements of the poor maniacs only became more violent. At length the atrocious wickedness of this horrible scene increased to a degree of grossness, that drove us from our station; we returned to the carriage at about three o'clock in the morning, and passed the remainder of the night in listening to the ever increasing tumult at the pen. To sleep was impossible. At daybreak the horn again sounded, to send them to private devotion; and in about an hour afterwards I saw the whole camp as joyously and eagerly employed in preparing and devouring their most substantial breakfast as if the night had been passed in dancing; and I marked many a fair but pale face, that I recognized as a demoniac of the night, simpering beside a swain, to whom she carefully administered hot coffee and eggs. The preaching saint and the howling sinner seemed alike to relish this mode of recruiting their strength.

"We soon after left the ground; but before our departure we learnt that a very satisfactory collection had been made by the preachers, for Bibles, Tracts, and all other religious purposes."

The time of the revival which Mrs. Trollope witnessed was much later than those described above. By that time revivalism had lost a little of its violence and gained new objectives. Before 1800, America had no Bible society and none for foreign missions or the distribution of tracts but, in the next decade, we find the names of Pliny Fisk and Adoniram Judson and Samuel Mills and Knott and Rice, all pioneers in these fields and all influenced by and associated more or less directly with the early revivals. The first violence of the new way of finding God was bound to die out, but it left its mark indelibly on the social and religious character of America.

† The War of 1812 was over, the Spanish dam to Mississippi traffic was broken and the domination of the conservatives had been shattered by the election of infidels and radicals like Jefferson and Madison. † Gentlewomen read Addison and refined selections from Shakespeare, Young's *Night Thoughts* and Thompson's *Seasons*, but not Byron. Men did the marketing and "a considerable part of the slip-slop work." † Peale's Museum was illuminated on certain nights by "gas-lights which will burn without wick or oil." † Women wore long gloves rucked down and, in Tennessee, Leghorn hats costing $50 and gunboat bonnets. Men, who were giving up wigs, still wore the enormous cravats which had been introduced by George the Third to hide the swelling on his neck. The long trouser was coming in and with it the shoestring.

† In the North, there was virtually no hunting or coursing but, in Virginia, there were established races and Eclipse, backed by the North, defeated the Southern favorite Sir Henry. † In Ohio, the Regulators or sheriff's posse kept order. In the East, Ballston Spa and Saratoga Springs were popular. † Arks and flatboats went downstream on the Mississippi and were then sold for lumber. Fulton's steamboat was opposed because it would ruin shipbuilding and the United States Navy. The great boom in canals had an unfavorable effect on farming in New England. By 1817, twelve steamers had penetrated to western waters; and the conestoga wagon which covered the ninety miles between Philadelphia and New York City in three days was called The Flying Machine. † Rags were being imported to manufacture paper. † The first land office fraud was reported. † Indiana, with a population of 100,000, had no cases of insanity. † In 1817, an advertisement in a New York paper informed gentlemen that no smoking was permitted in a certain theater. † The grouse of the Pocono Mountain was a delicacy in Philadelphia, where also the Lombard Poplar had been introduced. † It was remarked that Princeton College was not as respectable as it had been. † Charcoal and plank roads were being abandoned in the older states and macadamized streets given a trial.

† In 1818, there were many protests against deforestation and waste of timber. † Pittsburgh was known as the Birmingham of America and also as its dirtiest city; and Lancaster was the largest inland town. † Government lands remaining after auction were sold at two dollars an acre.

# V.

## The New Eden—.

AFTER each of the great revivals in America, there came a period of social experiment in founding communist colonies. John Humphrey Noyes, himself a convert during a revival and later the founder of the most successful of American communities, noted the alternation of the two movements, but he was too intelligent to claim that the communities were brought into being by the revivals. He noted a coincidence and further remarked that, while the revivals were native products, the social experiments were made under foreign influence. Others were not so cautious. The revivalists of the first half of the century insisted that the American Revolution could not have occurred without the preparatory work of the Great Revival. According to them the moral and religious tone of the country had to be aroused to a high pitch before the sublime idea of democracy could be understood and the sacrifices of war undertaken. To make this point, they had to minimize the significance of men like Paine and Jefferson. They were on much surer ground when they bracketed the camp-meetings of the first decade of the century with the colonies founded under the inspiration of Robert Owen. Had they wished to prove a general argument, they would have been entirely justified in linking the revivals of the 1830's, as conducted by Charles Grandison Finney, with such diverse social movements as Mormonism, Noyes' Oneida Community, the Phalansteries founded under the inspiration of Fourier, the rage of the Millerites expecting the last trump in the 1840's, and a variety of other movements with which this book is in part concerned.

The first of the great American communities, however, the New Eden founded by George Rapp, was entirely beyond the range of the revival system. It illustrates only Noyes' other contention, that communistic experiments in America are imported.

The followers of Rapp came out of Germany and, after they were settled first at Harmony, Indiana, and later at Economy,

Pennsylvania, discouraged the admission of non-Germans to their society. In many ways the print of Teutonic origin is marked in the features of the Rappite colony. In other ways, however, the experiment of Rapp is typical of one group of native American experiments, and its long-continued success had a deep influence on other colonists. It was a theocracy like Mormonism and the Zion City of Dowie. It was millenarial, expecting the quick coming of Christ, like dozens of other communities. It was, like the Shaker colonies, based on the principle of rejecting sexual intercourse. Its economics were a peculiar blend of communism—"from each according to his ability, to each according to his need"—and absolute despotic control. Over the background, the foreground, the middle-ground, lies the shadow of a single man, as at Oneida, or Hopedale, Fruitlands, or Zion. And, as in some of these (and in many other communities) this man held his position by direct order of God, and had received God's promise. All in all, the Rappite colony runs true to the American form. It excels its rivals in a peculiarly American way: it made a great deal of money.

In 1814, George Rapp, a Swabian of considerable advancement, rejoicing in communication with the Almighty and expecting the present return of Christ to Jerusalem, led a band of several hundred men and women, not to the Syrian shore, but to the deep backwoods of America. Like Jonathan Edwards (whom he otherwise does not resemble), he seems to have believed that America was the place to prepare for the second coming. Rapp and some companions went ahead to look over the ground. Presently they discovered an almost ideal situation in the southwestern part of Indiana: a tract of thirty thousand acres of virgin land along the Wabash and the Ohio. The soil promised fertility, and the good Germans were not discouraged by the lack of water power, for they soon bought a steam engine—the first to be used for milling in that part of the country. Later, they made themselves flatboats and projected a steamer to navigate the Wabash when it was at high water.

Here they founded a town, called Harmony, which became the first long home of the Rappites. They set immediately to planting and to building. Rapp and his adopted son Frederick, both men of taste, and both believers in simplicity, saw to it that the buildings were neat and not expressed in fancy. Father Rapp held the economic theory of the protectionist: that the prosperity of the settlement would depend on the degree to which it supplied its own wants. The docile men and women, dressed in buckskin and dark woolen adaptations of their Swabian peasant dress, went to work at an amazing variety of occupations. Within a few years after the foundation, Johann Lenz took a cargo by flatboat down the river to New Orleans and sold for $1,369, kegs of lard and butter, barrels of whiskey, flour, and pork, and various produce, oxen, and hogs. In the same year, Frederick Rapp was offering for sale other products: blue or black broadcloth (first quality at $7 a yard, fourth at $2: the intervening grades may have been used by the communists themselves); fur hats, flannels, and woolen stockings ($12-$18 a dozen). The society in the meantime was providing its members with all the necessities of life, and not neglecting its refinements. They had barely arrived in Indiana when the younger Rapp, who was a stone-cutter and architect, ordered a copy of Klopstock's epic, *The Messiah,* and two paintings, *Christ Healing the Sick,* and *Peter Preaching at Pentecost.* A few years later, two men sent to collect money due in Germany returned with slips of some excellent grapes, a pocket telescope, a camera obscura, and some astronomical charts. From the first year the group subscribed to some ten newspapers and, at the end of a decade, the general store had about two dozen books in its stock, including *Webster's Grammar, Plutarch's Lives, Memoirs of Napoleon, The Vicar of Wakefield, Son of a Genius,* and various practical works on mathematics and navigation.

Everybody worked at Harmony, spinning or weaving, brewing or planting; making shoes, laying bricks, dyeing; making soap, leather, watches, cider, or wine; painting homes; making barrels, boxes, pottery, or silk. Managers were appointed for the separate industries. Money which came in from the outside world was turned over to Father Rapp, who gave no account of it, and never indicated what he intended to do with it. He and the overseers and headmen lived a little more comfortably than the others, using a better grade of flour, and having wine, beer, and "groceries" * of which

* "Groceries" generally signified anything purchased at a store—"boughten goods" as opposed to those raised on the farm.

the others had none, or little. Yet each house was well built, had a vegetable and flower garden, and was supplied, from various depots, with milk, meat, and other necessities. The tailor would come running down the road if he saw a rip in a Sunday coat. The shoemaker took pride in having every man, woman, and child well-shod. Travelers would stop at the inn and find it excellent. After noonday dinner they would go out and look over the field of wheat, two miles square, in which a hundred and fifty men and women were all reaping at once, all advancing regularly under the western sun and not one with the sense of any property in the harvest. Precisely at sunset the laborers came in from the fields and workshops. One night each week they answered the meeting-house bell, filing in gravely, men at one end and women at the other, to listen to a lecture from Father Rapp. On Sundays, they spent nearly all day in religious observances, with music. Music, in fact, was the great diversion. When Bernhard, Grand Duke of Saxe-Weimar, visited the Rappites at Economy, the factory girls asked him to come after work was done to hear them sing "in a naturally symphonious manner" sacred songs from old Württemberg hymnals, and some "of a gay character." The observant Duke also noted that the factory was warmed in winter by means of pipes connected with the steam engine and that "vessels containing fresh sweet-scented flowers" stood on each machine.

The settlement at Harmony was the primitive stage of the Rappite colonization. There is a naïve quality in the spectacle of a dog turning the bellows-wheel at a forge where nails were made. There is charm in the Labyrinth which represented the difficulty of arriving at Harmony (symbolized by a little temple in the center of the maze, "rough in exterior, to show that at distance it had few attractions but smooth and beautiful within"). There were Botanic Gardens and a collection of plants "carefully arranged agreeably to the Linnæn System" and, at gatherings, there was the music of three violins, a double bass, a clarinet, a flute, and two French horns. If the industrious Rappite tossed uneasily in his simple bed, he could hear at the four dead hours of night the watch crying out, "Again a day is past and a step made nearer to our end; our time runs away and the joys of Heaven are our reward." At three in the morning the first part changed to, "Again a night is past and the morning is come." But the reminder of our mortal plight and of our immortal hopes remained the same. It was idyllic, and should have ended plaintively and promptly, like all idylls.

§

What carried the colony through to practical success was the iron hand of Father Rapp, and his followers' deep belief in his doctrine. In church he taught them, and out of it directed every move they made. A traveler might ask the landlord at the tavern why marriage was forbidden and what became of all the monies collected. The only reply would be, "We never answer these questions." Even renegades from the order remained obstinately silent. The money continued to flow in: a single settlement near by paid $60,000 to the Rappites in the course of a few years, and cargoes to New Orleans went at regular intervals. The surrounding country, once grateful for the exceptional variety and quality of supplies afforded at the Harmony store, soon began to fret because there was no mutuality in dealing: Harmony sold everything, and bought nothing. (It imported raw material as needed, but everything the neighboring communities could make was better made in Harmony.) Instead of keeping money in circulation, the ageing Rapp was hoarding it or, it was suspected, sending it for some obscure purpose back to Germany. The only ones who refused to be curious were the Rappites themselves. Rapp may have threatened eternal damnation to seceders (it is very unlikely, as the Society later made handsome arrangements with any member who desired to go), but his great argument was the contrast between the amenity of life led in Harmony and the cold struggle for existence in the surrounding country. In 1822, Rapp began a systematic devolution of authority, appointing his foster son to most of the chief positions, and so gradually accustoming his people to hereditary leadership—an idea peculiarly inappropriate in a society opposed to the propagation of children and eagerly awaiting Christ's return. Two English visitors passed through Harmony at this time, one of whom found the Rappites "a set of well-fed, well-clothed, hardworking vassals. They are very grave and serious . . . they enjoy only a sort of melancholy contentment." The absence of children depressed him as it did most other visitors. The other Englishman came into business relations with the Rappites and his opinion was therefore based on close experience. He was Robert Owen, the ultimate owner of Harmony, and he wrote: "I have not yet met with more kind-hearted, temperate, and industrious citizens, nor found men more sincere, upright, and honest in all their dealings, than the Harmonists."

It would appear, however, from other sources that Owen was not deluded into buying Harmony without some knowledge of why the Rappites wanted to leave. There were a number of reasons, but the "imputation of malaria" was the gravest, and it is on record that the sufferers from this fever shook it off when the colony was transplanted to the higher ground at Economy. The Rappites were so anxious to sell that they offered an Englishman, Richard Flower, five thousand dollars as commission to make the sale. He returned to England, and found Robert Owen, flushed with the success of New Lanark, willing to buy the Harmony lands and buildings, with some of the effects, for $150,000. At five dollars an acre for improved land the Rappites were not being avaricious.

Ninety mechanics and farmers went in advance of the other colonists to their new home, a high bluff on the right bank of the Ohio, seventeen miles below Pittsburgh which was already famous for its industry and smoke. These men cleared the ground, laid out streets, put up a cabin a day, and prepared for the coming, in May, 1825, of the Rappites' own-built steamer, carrying the community and its goods.*

Considered as an economic experiment, the rest of the story of the Rappites is less interesting. The town flourished and the directors invested in manufactures outside their own domain. They inspired the foundation of Beaver Falls. They manufactured the first silk in the United States and imported 500 coolies, whom they treated very well, to work in their cutlery mills, the largest in America. Twice the society faced dissolution—the second time owing to the absence of all account-keeping, the first because of a religious adventure. Stern measures in each case were successful. As finance does not illuminate the inner nature of the society it is only necessary to note that, in the end, when there were only three survivors, a

---

* The steamer, which was toasted in Wabash wine was named *William Penn*, and with the *Bolivar* and other boats, ferried the entire group to their new home.

Pittsburgh syndicate bought the town, with all it contained, and all the Rappites' property in the charming Sewickley Valley, and left two old women and one man possessors of several million dollars.

This was the natural end of Economy, which dwindled in population from 522 members in 1827, to 385 in 1844 (we have the division by sexes in that year, 170 men and 215 women) and to four on the 12th of May, 1903, when John S. Duss, trustee, resigned and withdrew from the Society. He was one of the married members—i.e., one who joined after marriage, and his wife, who succeeded him as trustee, was one of the last survivors. As the children of the original married members grew up, they were allowed a choice of career: to stay in the Society as full members, or as hired laborers (being in either case obliged to conform to all of the regulations of the Society including the unchanging ban on sexual intercourse); or to go outside, in which case a small sum of money was provided for them. Most of them left and, after a time, the Society ceased to encourage recruits, who might be spurred not by a love of celibacy, but by visions of the millions which Rapp and his successors had amassed. It is said that, as they grew old, the Rappites retained a serene complacency and an alertness of mind which made conversation with them a pleasure.

§

The celibacy of the Rappites is their obvious point of supreme interest. I should say at once that I have made no special effort to uncover irregularities in the record. I have found it none the less surprising that of the dozens of investigators of Economy, many of them entirely dispassionate, and of the many hostile critics, not one has suggested that the Rappites were not as they claimed, i.e., opposed inexorably to the practice of intercourse between the sexes; nor is there any suggestion, anywhere, of sexual inversion. The specialist in sexual psychopathology can make surmises, but the material for proof is utterly lacking. Married people were accepted into the Society, but they also foreswore cohabitation, and accepted the religious basis imposed by Father Rapp.

In a variety of ways the doctrine of non-intercourse reappears in other groups, some of which are noted presently, and is hinted at by leaders of religious divisions as far down as Mary Baker Eddy. Like many other cults, Rappism intended a restoration of man to the supposed ambi-sexuality of Adam—an event mystically linked with the second tenet of the Rappite, the general cult-faith in the immediacy of the Second Coming.*

Of the two accounts of Creation, Father Rapp accepted in all literalness the one which says that God made man in his own image: "in the image of God created he him; male and female created he them." From this he judged that Adam, at the moment of Creation was, like God, endowed with the essential qualities of both sexes, and that Adam could have procreated, in that state, had he so desired. Adam's discontent persuaded God to remove from his body the female part or principle, and to give it to him as a companion. This—and not the eating of the fruit—constituted the Fall. Hence God's displeasure with man, and hence the promise that, when the world is regenerated, man will recapture his divine attribute of containing both sexes in one body. This consummation will occur, of course, at the return of Christ who, being divinely born, is a dual being, and who will instantly accept into his company those who have lived in his image—i.e., denying the separation of the sexes—while all others will have to undergo a probationary, lustral period.

For their special explanation of the origin of celibacy the Rappites drew to an extent on the mysticism of Jacob Boehme in which, also, the perfection of Adam before the Fall is centered in his duality of sex. What Rapp saw practically was that the sexual impulse was the mastering cause of human ambition, rivalry, and confusion. So long as these existed, the Kingdom of Christ was delayed. Being convinced that the delay could not be long, he desired men to live

---

* All the authorities on the Rappites agree that celibacy was a fundamental tenet and an observed practice. But there is a curious note to the passage in *Don Juan* quoted below which asserts that the colony (still flourishing when the note was written) "does not entirely exclude matrimony," but imposes restrictions to prevent "more than a quantum of births within a certain number of years" and these births, according to the author of *Hints to Emigrants*, arrive "in a little flock like those of a farmer's lambs, all within the same month perhaps." It is likely that complete abstention from sexual intercourse was not imposed upon the Rappites at the beginning of the experiment; by 1807 it was being warmly supported and gradually became the fixed and, as far as I have found, the universally observed rule of the community. I may note here that to avoid confusion I have omitted mention of the very first stopping place of the Rappites at Harmony, in Butler County, Pennsylvania; everything essential developed in the more substantial colonies at Harmony and at Economy.

in the Adamic state, in preparation for the Return. It had a logic of its own, this doctrine and, in practical affairs, it worked to perfection. Rapp felt that celibates gave themselves more completely to a common cause than those whose sexual lives were woven into the lives of others. He may have counted on the dullness, the placidity, which an ordained celibacy often brings. He had the example of centuries of monastic life to go by and, indeed, his city was only a modern monastery, with a nunnery within its precincts. It remained for a purely American experiment to work from Rapp's basis to precisely opposite ends. In the Oneida Community not only marriage, but love concentrated in one person, was recognized as fatal to the free gift to the Community of all the individual had. But, instead of banishing love, Noyes liberated it and canalized it "for the greatest good of the greatest number." Oneida would have interested Byron at least as much as the Rappites; and would not have puzzled him so much. In *Don Juan*, Byron wrote:

> "When Rapp the Harmonist embargoed Marriage
>     In his religious settlement (which flourishes
> Strangely enough as yet without miscarriage,
>     Because it breeds no more mouths than it nourishes,
> Without those sad expenses which disparage,
>     What Nature naturally most encourages)
> Why called he 'Harmony' a state sans wedlock?
> Now here I've got the preacher at a deadlock.
>
> "Because he either meant to sneer at Harmony,
>     Or Marriage, by divorcing them thus oddly;
> But whether reverend Rapp learned this in Germany
>     Or no, 'tis said his sect is rich and godly,
> Pious and pure, beyond what I can term any
>     Of ours, although they propagate more broadly.
> My objection's to his title, not his ritual,
> Although I wonder how it grew habitual."

The unnatural sexual life of the Rappites had, then, two sources: the very beginning of creation and the end of life. The beginning gave it authority in the story of Adam and the end gave it purpose: it was only the Second Coming that could make celibacy natural and desirable. Father Rapp expected this event from day to day. The stored up money was reserved to be used at the very end when the whole Society would be again uprooted and taken to Palestine to greet the Redeemer. A few rather trivial commands from God are ascribed to Rapp—as for instance the plan of Economy and particularly that he should build a certain house in the shape of a Greek cross—but the divine communications upon which he laid the utmost stress were those which seemed to promise the coming of Christ in Rapp's own lifetime.

It is the intensity of this belief that makes the Society's one great schism, alluded to above, noteworthy. Hospitality was carried to an extraordinary extent by the Rappites: a visitor once counted twenty tramps who were fed, lodged, and given breakfast, without any conditions except that the tramp be not a professional beggar. But on an occasion when the Society opened its doors to one who claimed to have "special illumination in spiritual things," it came close to disaster. Economy was then an important town; it had cheap water-routes and lay on a main stage-line, and its fine inn made it a natural stopping place for travelers. Its integrity in business had given it a great market, and there was still sufficient young blood, as a survivor later told the publicist, Charles E. Nordhoff, to give the required energy to trade and manufacture. Its prosperity was in flood; the members sang songs every day and made music every evening. In short, with its prosperity and its simplicity, it invited the charlatan.

He came, announcing himself as Count Maximilian de Leon, "the Ambassador and anointed of God, of the stem of Judah, of the root of David." These credentials were set forth in a letter written by himself—his real name was Bernhard Müller—and were never questioned. He had already collected some forty disciples, two of whom he had sent ahead, to prepare for his coming, while he rested in Pittsburgh. Rapp, who had been flattered by the Count's preliminary correspondence and had so often preached of the coming of One, planned a magnificent reception. "As soon as the coach approached the town it was greeted with a salute of the finest music from the band stationed on the tower of the church. The Count was met at the hotel and escorted to the church, where the whole Community were assembled awaiting his arrival. He enters in state, attended by his Minister of Justice, in full military garb and sword at his side. He is shown into the pulpit by Mr. Rapp, and all eyes are fixed upon him and all ears are open. He expresses the belief that this meeting is the most important since the creation, and that henceforth all the troubles and sorrows of the Lord's people will cease."

This was late in 1831, the colony having been settled only six years in its new home. The new recruits made a welcome addition, but Rapp soon discovered that Count de Leon, who was continually reading to him from a Golden Book of doctrine, had ideas far removed from the asceticism of his own principles. The Count suggested better food and clothing, livelier gatherings, and, surprisingly, the toleration of marriage. It was obvious that the impostor would have to be expelled, but Rapp hesitated to turn the Leonites out in the midst of winter. By the next spring, the Count had acquired so large a following that they could call for a vote between Rapp and Leon. The Society, then at its maximum of 750, divided two to one in favor of the old believers but, before the dissenters could be dispossessed, the Society had to give them notes amounting to over $100,000. With this money—which was promptly paid, a proof of the Society's financial strength—the Leonites founded a communistic society, with marriage. It failed miserably and, after an attempt to extort more money from Father Rapp, Count de Leon vanished for a time and presently died of cholera.

So ended the Rappites' unique fling in Messianic delusions. It did not discourage them. On his death-bed, still confident, Rapp said, "If I did not so fully believe that the Lord has designed me to place our Society before his Presence in the land of Canaan, I would consider this my last day." It was; but the Society continued to live in his faith; and when a visitor, mournfully looking over the closed factories and unoccupied houses of Economy after the members had almost all died out, asked whether there was no monument anywhere to the founder, an old man, wholly unaware of a more famous use of the words, answered simply, "This, all that you see here, around us."

† William Cobbett, the Englishman, knew the wild strawberry and considered the cranberry "the finest fruit for tarts that ever grew." † The property qualification for voters was gradually dropped. † A family of fourteen lived comfortably on $3,000 a year in a large city and, until 1825, there was no stock market in New York. After that "when the members are assembled the president proceeds to call the list and, as each stock is named in succession, those who have orders to buy and sell make their offers, and the transactions are recorded (and) become binding upon the members."

† The Americans were becoming the best shipbuilders in the world, but the frontier still held its own. It was considered an impropriety to shoot a squirrel or turkey anywhere except in the head. † Noah Webster's Elementary Speller was the accepted standard and Lindley Murray's grammar was displacing *The Ladies' Accidence* as a text-book. † It was proposed to transfer the remains of Washington to Richmond in which city the bust of Lafayette had been mutilated. The capitol at Washington was being repaired after the ravages of the war and nineteen marble capitals had been imported from Italy to crown its columns. † By five o'clock in the morning the markets and stores of Cincinnati were crowded. † The word "elegant" meant eligible or useful. † In Pennsylvania, barns as well as houses were of stone and, throughout the East, even in winter, wagoners drove without gloves. † Broccoli had been introduced and the tomato accepted. † English visitors missed singing birds and honeysuckle, daisies, primroses, bluebells, and daffodils. † Chocolate was cheap enough even to be used by slaves; raisins and currants were imported from the Levant. † Men were addressed by their full names without title. Children of tender years tipped off drams. † On the westward trek it was said that New Englanders walked in front of their wagons, Jersey people sat within, and Pennsylvanians crept reluctantly behind. Twelve thousand wagons passed between Baltimore and Philadelphia in one year. Taverns improved as one went westward but there were still too many "hot rooms and swarming beds"; tips were not expected.

# VI.

## —And the Old Adam.

THE Adamic Rappite had barely quitted the soil of his Eden when it was occupied in force by the Old Adam, lusting for pleasure, experimenting in sexual relations, and convinced that the millennium was coming—not with the second advent of Christ, but with the liberation of man from his unnatural servitudes. New Harmony was bought by Robert Owen who, after addressing the House of Representatives in terms a little offensive to solid citizens, invited all men of good will to participate in his new experiment. The paternalistic Communism of New Lanark, in Yorkshire, had proved a success. No sooner had Owen's call gone out, than the inspired and the shiftless began to crowd their way into New Harmony. Presently they overran the tidy German streets and so overcrowded the inn and the church that immigration had to be checked until some sort of order could be established. A few men of parts—a pioneer among women agitators, an enthusiast for new methods in education—gathered about Owen; but the general run was disappointing. Owen had succeeded with his own people, a homogeneous body whose life was parallel to his own. He hoped to repeat the experiment in conditions totally different, with men strange to him in habit of mind, and only held together by their aversion to the current system of society. The colonists were repellent particles and Owen, with his countless schemes, plans, foibles, interests, and experiments was not powerful enough to hold them together. Owen was, in fact, neither excessively interested in New Harmony, nor extremely radical. He considered private property a curse, but he did not think that man was ready for entire communal ownership. He kept title to New Harmony in his own hands, but allowed the colonists to use the land, and established equality in rank and payment.

Dissensions began almost as soon as work began. Religious differences—Owen ranked organized religion with private property as one of the curses of humankind—separated the settlement into inharmonious groups attempting to exist independently. Yet Owen allowed them to remain on his land. There was, among these ideal-ists and forerunners of Heaven on earth, a strong impulse of snob-bery. Certain foreigners were not considered suitable associates by the more lofty members. There was racial hostility and a measure of spiritual condescension. The people hated a great deal of the necessary work. Although the factory buildings of the Rappites re-mained, the New Harmonists could grow enthusiastic only over the land—not the actuality of farming, but the idyllic picture of a happy (and intellectual) peasantry drawing sustenance from the great breast of Mother Earth, discussing the laws of chemistry or Platonic love while they gently weeded a vegetable patch, and singing behind the cows as they drove the herd in for the milking at sunset. This picture was to recur hundreds of times in the minds of American colonists. Whatever had to do with the land was natu-ral, healthy, beautiful, sacred. Almost all colonists suffered from this form of mother-worship, but the most intelligent of them, we shall see, saw through it and founded his community not on land, but on factories. Owen's was the hungriest of the land hungry colo-nies—in a country where there was too much land, where ma-chinery was destined to become the supreme agent of progress!

New Harmony was only an episode in the life of Owen. It was only a forerunner in the history of American communities. It lasted three years; and that, significantly enough, is far above the average. In Noyes' record of colonies founded on the Owenite model, we find that they lasted "a short time," "three months," "five months," and only Macluria, which was virtually a part of the original Owen-ite colony, lasted as long as two years. The corporate mortality was shocking and, with each bankruptcy, revolution, or dispersal, a share of high human hopes was lost. The break-up of New Harmony is important because it foreshadowed so many other disasters.

§

In part, the failure of New Harmony was due to the violent character of Owen himself; in part, to the stupidity and unfairness of his adversaries. He had issued from the pit of hell—the English factory under the benevolent system of *laissez faire*—and he genu-inely hated property and wage-slavery. As honestly he hated other things, and was determined to abolish them all at one blow. "I now declare to you and to the world, that Man, up to this hour has been in all parts of the earth a slave to a Trinity of the most monstrous evils that could be combined to inflict mental and physical evil upon his whole race. I refer to Private or Individual Property, Absurd and Irrational systems of Religion, and Marriage founded on individual Property, combined with some of these Irrational systems of Religion."

So, in two sentences, he invited the name of demagogue, infidel, and free-lover. He did not have to wait long for rancor. He believed, from his own experience, that man is the creature of circumstance, that if you exchanged the environment of thirty little Hottentots and thirty little aristocratic English children, the aristocrats would become Hottentots, for all practical purposes, and the Hottentots, little conservatives. From this he deduced the principle of abandoning rewards and punishment.*

The acute Protestant, alert for his own dignity and the safety of the state, saw that this theory was doubly dangerous. It not only did away with the principle of the just wage (the *reward* of labor), but with the divine principle of moral responsibility, which holds that the wages of sin is death. Add to this the Spiritualism which became associated with Owen's name, and his belief in an earthly (hence non-Messianic) millennium, and you had a compost of all heresy, all licentiousness, all the excesses of the French Revolution, all the anti-Christian theories of the Illuminati—in short, Satan's Kingdom on earth. In 1826, the Philadelphia *Gazette* published some topical verses on the "Permanent Community." The Devil has

> "heard that a number of people were going
> To live on the Wabash with great Mr. Owen"

(the rhymes are not all as bad as that) and decides that, in the Owenite phraseology "circumstances require" him to be there:

> "Since Adam first fell by my powerful hand,
> I have wandered for victims through every known land,
> But in all my migrations ne'er hit on a plan
> That would give me the rule so completely o'er man.

* Pestalozzi was doing the same thing in his schools, and the whole progress of statutory and prison reform was tending in the same direction.

"I have set sects to fighting and shedding of blood,
I have whispered to bigots they're all doing good,
   Inquisitions I've founded, made kings my lies swallow,
   But this plan of free living beats all my plans hollow.

"I am satisfied now this will make the coast clear,
For men to all preaching will turn a deaf ear:
   Since its plain that religion is changed to opinions
   I must hasten back home to enlarge my dominions.

"The devil then mounted again on the ice,
And dashed through the waves and got home in a trice,
   And told his fell imps whom he kept at the pole
   Circumstances required they should widen the hole!"

The press of the time published sarcastic reports of the progress of New Harmony. Vicious satires in German and English, in prose and verse, appeared everywhere. Although Owen was a lover of children—he was as much responsible as any single man for the first laws controlling child labor and was an actual pioneer in education—he was accused of drilling them by the methods of the hollow square, of taking tots from their mothers' breasts and giving them to girls of twelve and fifteen to educate, of omitting discipline from education, and of treating human beings like machines.* He was unhappy in his phrases. "Circumstances" was turned into "mechanism" and, when Owen was asked how he would account for evil, he invented the notion of the "counteracting principle" which, as indicated in a contemporary satire, had a suggestion of prenatal influence:

"The first born of this new and perfect race in perspective, was a little boy, who, from the moment of his birth, was allowed to hear nothing but the repetition of the great precept, not to harm his play-fellows, but to do all in his power to make them happy. At three years old he was launched into the playground and made his début by biting the finger of one of the matrons who presided over our sports, and who attempted forcibly to keep him from in-

* Owen's ideas, wherever he got them, curiously foreshadowed experiments of our own time. He wanted children to have no books before they were ten; he preferred teaching by objects to verbal exercises, and he dramatized everything, even Grammar in which appear General Noun, Colonel Verb, and so on, down to Corporal Adverb, which isn't, in spite of the names, exactly a barrack-square method of instruction.

dulging the instinct of the Man-Machine for dabbling in mud-puddle. Our master cast about for the 'counteracting principle' that had produced this enormity, that he might give it a sound drubbing, and to his great satisfaction discovered it in a habit which the mother a long time indulged, of biting her nails. This practice was strictly forbidden; but, as one of the fundamental principles of my master was, that no punishments were necessary to keep the Man-Machine in order any more than the steam engine, nobody minded the prohibition, and the women bit their nails, as usual, when vexed or perplexed."

The same pretended history of New Harmony comments on the principle of equality:

"Some of the married women had prettier children than others —and this was a source of inequality. Some were without any children at all, and sorely envied their more happy next door neighbors, whose pretty little curly-pated machines were playing themselves into perfectibility on the lawn before their doors. On the other hand, some of the men had better, younger or prettier wives than others who not being specially instructed in such matters, did frequently break the tenth commandment. My master was, in truth, for a long while, the victim of 'counteracting circumstances,' he at one time as I have heard, had serious thoughts of cutting off all the women's noses, to bring them to a level, and so organizing his men and women machines by the mere force of education, so that they should conform to the law of nature which ordains that every bird shall lay only so many eggs within a certain period. He had no doubt of bringing this about if he could only begin above, and dodge his old enemies, the 'counteracting circumstances.'"

§

While hostility mounted outside, disagreements plagued the New Harmonites internally. Owen, says one of the members, "advised that they should appoint a committee from amongst themselves, every week to inspect the houses in the village and to insert in a book to be given for that purpose, a faithful report of the state of each house as they might happen to find it. They almost unanimously resolved to meet the visitors with closed doors. They bestowed upon them the appellation of 'Bug Hunters,' and Mr. Owen escaped not without his share of the general odium." The Duke of Saxe-Weimar, moving on from the new home of the Rappites to their old one, found that their successors were not so universally happy in democracy. The incident he notes is utterly trivial; it must have occurred a thousand times in democratic communities; but one can still feel the unimportant, but symptomatic heartbreak it records:

"In the evening I . . . saw the philosophy and the love of equality put to a severe test. She is named Virginia and while she was playing and singing very well on the piano she was told that the milking of the cows was her duty. Almost in tears she betook herself to this servile employment, execrating the Social System and its so much prized equality. After the cows were milked, in doing which, the young girl was trod on by one and mired by another, I joined an aquatic party with the young ladies and some young philosophers in a very good boat upon the Wabash. The beautiful Miss Virginia forgot her stable duties and regaled us in a sweet voice."

Owen meanwhile gave his usual lectures and it was unanimously voted that the entire population should meet three times a week for the purpose of being educated together. Five days later, we learn that the sixth successive constitution was adopted. This most important event is chronicled in a diary as follows:

"Aug. 25. The people held a meeting at which they abolished all officers then existing, and appointed three men as dictators."

Owen departed for a time. There were many other things for him to do. There was Hands' Machine for preventing shipwrecks which the inventor wanted Owen to back. A shoemaker, who had been giving lectures in astronomy in pot-houses, would be pleased if Mr. Owen would buy him a van, so that he might extend the radius of his activities. A friend would like a peerage: could Owen help? Frances MacCrone has invented the art of flying "and wants £100 for two months" which does not seem excessive. J. Westbrook has invented a secret voting machine. Not to mention the Universal

FRANCES WRIGHT D'ARUSMONT.

Devastator, of Sweetlove and Cowen, which was so terrifying that the mere threat of its use would bring all nations to universal peace. All the cranks of the world were crowding around Owen and it is remarkable that he kept his head as long as he did. Eventually, he was to issue Weekly Letters to the Human Race, to embrace Spiritualism *à l'outrance*, and to succumb to the temptation to speak a little wildly. On the first of May, 1855, he called a meeting "to prepare the public for the introduction of the knowledge of the Millennial State of human existence and to explain how the people of the world might immediately commence it in peace and with universal good-will," and set the date—the 14th of May of the same year—as the inauguration of the Millennium.

In the midst of all these activities, Owen had returned to America, had met the fantastic Santa Anna in Mexico (who offered him a county or so for a colony under certain conditions), and had faced the disagreeable fact that New Harmony was not a going concern. In its first three years there had been no less than ten secessions. One of these resulted in the foundation of Macluria, named after its founder, presumably the scientific amateur who visited Pestalozzi at Yverdon in 1805 and is credited by Beard with a profound influence in humanizing and making truly democratic the American system of education. MacClure was one of the first Americans whom Mrs. Trollope met. Her reactionary bias and her sarcasm were however ready. Her suggestion of the "intimate acquaintance" and the "nephew-son" are in her best manner:

"In the shop of Miss C—— I was introduced to Mr. M'Clure, a venerable personage of gentlemanlike appearance, who in the course of five minutes propounded as many axioms, as 'Ignorance is the only devil'; 'Man makes his own existence'; and the like. He was of the New Harmony school, or rather the New Harmony school was of him. He was a man of good fortune (a Scotchman, I believe), who after living a tolerably gay life, had 'conceived high thoughts, such as Lycurgus loved, who bade flog the little Spartans,' and determined to benefit the species, and immortalize himself, by founding a philosophical school at New Harmony. There was something in the hollow square legislations of Mr. Owen, that struck him as admirable, and he seems, as far as I can understand, to have intended aiding his views, by a sort of incipient hollow square drilling; teaching the young ideas of all he could catch, to shoot into parallelogramic form and order. This venerable philosopher, like all of his school that I ever heard of, loved better to originate lofty imaginings of faultless systems, than to watch their application to practice. With much liberality he purchased and conveyed to the wilderness a very noble collection of books and scientific instruments; but not finding among men one whose views were liberal and enlarged as his own, he selected a woman to put into action the machine he had organized. As his acquaintance with this lady had been of long standing, and, as it was said, very intimate, he felt sure that no violation of his rules, would have place under her sway; they would act together as one being: he was to perform the functions of the soul, and will every thing; she those of the body, and perform every thing.

"The principal feature of the scheme was, that (the first liberal outfit of the institution having been furnished by Mr. M'Clure), the expense of keeping it up should be defrayed by the profits arising from the labors of the pupils, male and female, which was to be performed at stated intervals of each day, in regular rotation with learned study and scientific research. But unfortunately the soul of the system found the climate of Indiana uncongenial to its peculiar formation, and, therefore, took its flight to Mexico, leaving the body to perform the operations of both. . . . When last I heard of this philosophical establishment, she, and a nephew-son were said to be reaping a golden harvest, as many of the lads had been sent from a distance by indigent parents, for gratuitous education, and possessed no means of leaving it."

Macluria lasted two years. Another secession rejoiced in the name of Feiba Peveli which "calls for explanation." According to the New Harmony *Gazette*, "Stedman Whitwell, its godfather and presumable founder, invented a system of nomenclature under which the name of a place should contain an indication of its latitude and longitude; a or b representing 1, e or d—2, the diphthong ei—8, and so on. Thus Feiba Peveli is 38′ 11″ N., 87′ 53″ W. Under this system New Harmony (38′ 11″ N., 87′ 55″ W.) might be called Ipba Veinul; London and Paris might be known henceforth as Lafa-Tovutu and Oput Tedou respectively. The system is recommended by its author as 'agreeable alike to the man of common sense and to the man of taste'!"

There was also Nashoba, which was not a secession but an off-shoot, founded by Fanny Wright and directed by her with the aid of Owen's son, Robert Dale Owen. Against appalling opposition, Fanny Wright bought slaves, freed them, and started for them a school and community, on approved principles. It did not work and, after a short time, she translated her freedmen to Haiti and settled them there. The Grimké sisters, who merely freed their slaves, escaped the worst persecutions which Fanny Wright incurred. By combining practical abolition with Communism and the taint of free-love, Miss Wright figured as everything hateful and corrupt, and her name became the symbol for vice and disruption.*

While these experiments continued, and a few others, New Harmony was rapidly breaking up. The actual end, which was a signal for the end of all the others, is involved in financial difficulties. Owen lost much, and was presently to lose still more in England and become "an endearing old bore." A scene near the end of New Harmony's life is sad enough for an epitaph:

"A traveler who saw the village at this time describes it as a scene of idleness and revelry. There were, he declares, a thousand persons of every age, sex, and condition gathered in the town, with no visible means of support save the generosity of the visionary Mr. Owen. In the school, which was held in the old brick church of the Rappites, were three hundred and thirty children who were under no control whatever, for the plan of Education was that of Pestalozzi, in which the sole punishment for bad behaviour was a short confinement. The teachers, he was amazed to find, had thrown aside the Christian faith, and taught doctrines not unlike those held by the German Illuminati at the opening of the French Revolution. In and about the Village, no man seemed to be busy. The houses were falling into a state of dilapidation, the gardens were full of weeds, the fences were down, and the curious labyrinth constructed by Rapp had been destroyed by cattle."

* See pages 341, 342.

Presently it ended. Robert Dale Owen remained in America, entered Congress, fought for the rights of men and women. The colony radiated influence in spite of its failure. In spite of its failure, too, it had done an essential work in providing a tangent to the vicious circle of work and profit which then circumscribed the American mind. We think of trusts and strikes, of Russian communism and radical labor, as phenomena of our own day and cannot imagine that they had their counterparts a century ago. It seems unreasonable that there should have been labor troubles in a new country dedicated to freedom and equality, with so much land to be had for the asking, so many roads and canals and machines to be built, so many articles to be made and sold. But the troubles existed none the less. Before 1800, strikes were known. There were strikes for wages and strikes for human rights. The country was plunging headlong into the factory system which was presently to become pestilential almost beyond our power to imagine. Within a few years after Owen's experiment, the wage and property system he attacked was to result in whole cities built to order by manufacturers, in tenements (they were already noted as a civic disgrace in the 1830's), and in a brutalizing poverty. There were men and women who could not face the rigors of the wilderness, its prompt demands and slow returns, without assistance. There were exploiters of labor utterly conscienceless, engrossed in making profit, accepting a moral standard which approved trickery, default, dishonesty of every sort. Between these the first communities stepped, offering a hand to the one, and a warning to the other. They were obviously hopeless, these experiments. Their economic theory was almost purely one of moral ideas. The leaders were more often high-minded than highly intelligent. By principle they refused to reject applicants whom they must have recognized as fools or knaves. And the societies they built were wholly unattractive, lacking luster and heart and beauty. It is, perhaps, the special fatality of communist experiments that they consistently lose the very quality they exalt. The colonies which are meant to exalt beauty, are mean and ugly; the love colonies are peculiarly unhappy as settings for a great passion. Their failure is in that nature of things which they did not understand. But they did say, with the violent emphasis of all the reformers of that time, "there is a greater freedom than man now possesses, there is a freedom from the tyranny of money and of materialism. The system which glorifies only money is not the only system." They failed to prove their point; but at least they announced it.

† "At Cincinnati one came upon vineyards." † Cautionary Verses for Children were widely read; the American Bible Society was founded in 1816; and eternal damnation was preached to the Indians. † From 1801 to 1820, the American publishers had an association which was broken up by competition in pirating the novels of Walter Scott. James Fenimore Cooper had the greatest difficulty in getting an American publisher since it was cheaper to pirate than to pay royalties. † In December, 1802, the United States Navy had a 74-gun ship in the Pacific, the frigate *Constitution* in the Mediterranean, the corvette *Cyane* off the coast of Africa, and the brig *Spark* in the West Indies. † Broadway, in New York, was considered more attractive at night than by day. † Lawyers were as common in that city as paupers in England. "A gentleman walking on Broadway seeing a friend pass, called out to him 'doctor' and immediately sixteen persons turned around." † Banks and public buildings in Philadelphia were an unsightly combination of brick and marble. † Pins cost a dollar a paper. † In New Orleans the theater, circus, and public poolrooms were open on Sunday and gambling houses and coffee houses were occupied from morning to night by gamesters, in spite of the fact that Louisiana was now a part of the United States. † It was the custom of bridegrooms to hold a levee the day after the wedding and on this occasion the bride did not appear. † In the backwoods marriage without legal or religious sanction took place with propriety and awaited the arrival of itinerant judges or preachers.

# VII.

## Winners of Souls.

THE infidel communities inspired by Robert Owen failed; revivalists pointed to them as the work of Anti-Christ and continued to prepare for the Kingdom of the Lord. The work of preparation continued for a century. Between 1800 and 1860, it was the one great religious movement in America, overshadowing the progress of liberal theology. It entered so fully into the lives of ordinary men and women that it became almost equal in importance to the conquest of the West, the struggle over slavery, the progress of mechanics, and the other decisive movements of the time. Like them, revivalism had a share in creating the national character. It became part of the national background and left a mark on the mind and soul of America.

§

The ultimate object of revivalism is to hasten the coming of Christ by effecting the regeneration of mankind. The object of any single revival is to quicken the Christian soul and to convert the sinner. The crisis of a revival is in conversion and the crisis of conversion is when the anxious seeker for salvation undergoes the conviction of sin. The revivalist's object, then, is to persuade his hearers of their sinfulness and to urge them to regeneration by accepting the intercession of Christ. To these ends various means have been used and various effects have followed them. Thus briefly we may conceive the subject.

§

By 1815, the revival system had successfully established itself as the working method of many Protestant churches in America. It was inspired by the theology of Edwards, the fervor of Wesley, and the wild enthusiasm of the camp-meetings—all of them singularly successful in their time. Whether the age so desperately called for refreshing as the revivalist assumed, is, after all, only an abstract question. Men rose by hundreds who were so moved by their vision of saintliness, or damnation, and so constituted psychologically in relation to their fellowmen that they had to go and exhort and threaten and pray. There remained a deal of passive infidelism, and here and there Deists were active. Graver still for the Calvinistic preachers was the progress of Universalism which challenged their first assumptions and particularly the one on which revivals were based. If we put ourselves for a moment in the position of a stern Calvinist or even of a moderate like Finney, we can see how dangerous Universalism appeared. As Calvinists, we ourselves believe that man by nature is depraved, that Christ has atoned for our sins and that, by this atonement, he has given to those of us who accept him, a *chance* to escape the damnation which we deserve, to partake of his substance and become changed men. At our right is the strict Calvinist who makes regeneration unbearably difficult and offers faint hope even to the regenerate since the world is divided inexorably between the elect and the non-elect. Opposite both of us stands the dangerous Universalist who believes that Christ's atonement is all that is necessary and that by it salvation is open to all men, as an almost certain grace from heaven. As good Presbyterians we suspect that this is much too easy a form of salvation. As good Christians we envy it only the appeal it makes to the multitude but, in that very appeal, we see its gravest dangers. For by giving men a false sense of security and a misleading hope of escape, it leads them from the true path. The Universalist thus stood in greater peril of damnation than the utterly unregenerate, greater than the atheist and the blasphemer. The others might still seek the true way, but the believer in Universalism had already rejected it and gone by another path.

The churches, moreover, were appallingly dull. Instead of "the beaten oil of the sanctuary" which the evangelist, Daniel Baker, was to offer his listeners, he himself was brought up on "dry logical sermons, with rounded periods, delivered in a cold, formal, and heartless manner" which he could never relish, "however beautified by the superficial elegances of composition." What he and others wanted was "warm, animating, lively, evangelominous preaching, full of fire, breathing love and compassion." What they got may be judged from Finney's description of one of his first pastors at work: "To give some idea of his preaching, let me say that his manuscript sermons were just large enough to put into a small Bible. I sat in the gallery, and observed that he placed his manuscript in the middle of his Bible, and inserted his fingers at the places where were to be found the passages of Scripture to be quoted in the reading of his sermon. This made it necessary to hold his Bible in both hands, and rendered all gesticulation with his hands impossible. As he proceeded he would read the passages of Scripture where his fingers were inserted, and thus liberate one finger after another until the fingers of both hands were read out of their places. When his fingers were all read out, he was near the close of the sermon."

To the Catholic and the Anglican there can be no such thing as dullness in church, since the service depends on an appointed ritual; and certain sacraments, administered with propriety by priests who hold from God, constitute the major function of worship. To the Catholic, the Mass can never be barren. To the Protestant, a whole year of church-going may be entirely fruitless. The more pedantic and less enthusiastic preachers in the Protestant churches of the 1820's, although they sought to defend themselves against the accusation, were finally convicted of lowering the religious vitality of their flocks. Again and again they protested that the evangelist and the itinerant brought the regular clergy into disrepute and over and over again the revivalists pointed to their own ingatherings and baptisms of the spirit. Gradually the revivalists persuaded the ministers and carried with them another doctrine: that professors of Christianity who had not actively felt the presence of the Holy Spirit were not really saved. These "cold and lazy professors" were held to stand in the way of Christ. Until they had been "seriously exercised," they could not count themselves among the children of God.

To all criticism the revivalist replied that evangelism was God's own plan. Quite apart from the direct inspiration of God, which many evangelists claimed, the whole terminology of revivalism was worked out of the New Testament and, in particular, from the description of the descent of the Holy Ghost at Pentecost. Scoffers on that occasion thought that the receivers of grace had drunk of a heady wine. The opponents of revivalism accused the preacher of hysteria. The very accusation seemed to prove the Pentecostal origin. A defender of revivalism goes further and cites the following passages as an exquisite representation of a revival: "Drop down ye heavens from above, and let the skies pour down righteousness. . . . I will pour water upon him that is thirsty, and floods upon the dry ground: I will pour my spirit upon thy seed, and my blessing upon thine offspring: and they shall spring up as among the grass, as willows by the water-courses. One shall say, I am the Lord's; and another shall call himself by the name of Israel."

"The divine economy of revivals" is proved by the following points: first, that from the beginning God has wrought permanently through revivals; second, that scriptural utterances assume revivals; third, that God's providences are adapted to move people in masses; fourth, that by revivals atheists are rebuked; and so on. It is hardly necessary to examine these defenses of "the Work."

Notably this divine plan functioned five times according to the canon. From the day of Pentecost to the Reformation, revivals are not counted. In the Protestant churches, Luther stands as the first great evangelist. The second work of God is the Puritan revival, in which John Bunyan is the best known figure. Fifty years later came the great awakening in England and America which has already been noted in connection with Jonathan Edwards. After another lapse of fifty years, the fourth revival period began with the camp-meeting and continued until about 1840. The fifth and last important one ran from 1857 to 1860. Whether the tremendously organized revivals of Moody and Torrey and Sunday can be considered as great national awakenings is questionable. Except for an elaboration of publicity and management they added very little to the technique of revivalism.

§

This technique was a long development. We have seen it already at its best and at its worst, and can now observe it in the average. If we return to the early days, we find the "spiritual pickpocket," Whitefield, preëminently an orator. It was of him that Garrick said he could pronounce the syllables of the word "Mesopotamia" and draw tears. He was the great persuader and, as he was collecting funds for the first orphanage to be established in this country, it is said that people would empty their pockets before attending his sermons. The skeptic Benjamin Franklin not only yielded and contributed to the project but wrote that it seemed as if all the world was growing religious, "so that one could not walk through Philadelphia in the evening without hearing psalms in different families of every street." Admirers followed Whitefield from Philadelphia as far as New Brunswick and there, according to the preacher, "God's power was so much amongst us in the afternoon sermon that the cries and groans of the people would have drowned my voice." This was a much more emotional preaching than that of Edwards and it gave rise to those "distempers" of which Edwards was sincerely dubious. In New England, in fact, Whitefield was never cordially received. A critic said that the flagrant enthusiasm and ill-pointed zeal of Whitefield and his adherents cost the people of Boston one thousand pounds every time he spoke. The "testimony" of the Harvard faculty accused him of being an "enthusiast . . . uncharitable, censorious, and slanderous man" and, in regard to the orphanage, a "deluder of the people." His fellow-worker, William Tennent, escaped the worst of these accusations. His preaching rather resembled the close arguments of Edwards. "It was frequently both terrible and searching . . . his laying open their many vain and secret shifts; their refuges, counterfeit resemblances of grace, delusive and damning hopes, their utter impertinences and impending dangers of destruction." The methods of the camp-meeting preachers we have already noted. McGready's camp-meetings ran people distracted and took them from work, according to embittered South Carolinians who wrote him threatening letters in blood and tore away and burned his pulpit. So much for modified Calvinism. The Methodist William Burke "fell senseless to the floor and knew nothing until he found himself on his feet giving glory to God"; and William McFee, a Presbyterian, "would sometimes exhort after the sermon, standing on the floor or sitting, or lying in the dust, his eyes streaming and his heart so full that he could only ejaculate 'Jesus, Jesus.'" About the same time, fumbling approaches were made to the "anxious seat." Preachers would invite those who felt inclined to accept Christ, but did not yet have any assurance, to come up and be prayed for.

Part of the process of persuading them was to have others tell their experiences, thus providing two of the established features of modern revivals. These methods were a new departure and the conservative ministry opposed them with all its power. Asahel Nettleton, Finney's great rival in the 1830's, rejected the anxious seat and refused to call for testimony. "With great solemnity and directness he proclaimed the saving truths of the Gospel. He then followed this up with the inquiry meetings for the anxious . . . and with personal conversations. . . . There was an indescribable awe upon his congregation while he was preaching, making them feel that God was in the house and there was an indescribable charm in his conversations . . . in the 'anxious circle.' " Nettleton's was a decorous method, for the worried soul was not asked publicly to come forward and therefore could not be harried and prodded into a public commitment. The anxious circle consisted of those in the audience who were moved to stay after the exhortation was over. This was considered a superior method by the quieter evangelists and, in the hands of Moody, developed into an extraordinary and elaborate instrument. Its great advantage was that it did not encourage "forwardness, ostentation and rashness." It helped to maintain at least the form of an intellectual questioning in the midst of an emotional upheaval. Daniel Baker, who was like Nettleton a college man, was also extremely cautious in the use of the anxious seat. In spite of references to Christ and Nicodemus, to Philip and the Ethiopian eunuch, the inquiry system seemed always a little like dragooning and those preachers who were finicky always rejected it. Nettleton used his meetings as a psychological check on the progress of the success his revival was making. He was a severe preacher and "never allayed the fears of inquirers," assuring them only that they need not wait for an overwhelming sense of sin, nor go through a protracted period of sorrow or of waiting for the heart to be changed. They had only to wish to be Christians. It was not for them to lay out a plan by which God could change them nor were they to expect any sudden or marvelous change at all. In this he was again on the side of the quiet revivalist and directly opposed to Wesley who believed that all conversions were instantaneous. The opportunities for exhibitionism, for vanity and false conversions is so great in the anxious bench and in all forms of "hitting the trail" that laymen and revivalists alike tend to over-emphasize this picturesque and dramatic episode.

It remains, however, only an episode, an additional touch of melodrama in the real drama of conversion.

In order not to have to return to it again I insert here a description of two inquiry meetings as they were practiced much later. The evolution of trail-hitting is too familiar to need description:

"It is at the close of the Tabernacle service. The anxious had been urged to enter the inquiry room. The merely curious had been specially urged not to disturb the solemn place by their presence. Mr. Moody in opening the meeting assumes there are only two classes present, the seekers and the workers. By a call for the inquirers to rise, he ascertains their number, and at once distributes them in different parts of the room and assigns a 'worker' to each inquirer, or in some cases gathers two or three of similar circumstances and spiritual condition around one judicious and competent teacher. In a few moments the whole room presents a hushed and solemn scene. The Bible, without which no 'worker' is welcome in that place, is freely opened, earnest faces bend together over its pages. In many cases the teacher and the inquirer study its promises on their knees, and then engage in prayer. In almost every case the inquirer is urged to pray for himself, and if unable to form the sentences, the teacher makes the prayer, which sentence by sentence is solemnly repeated. In half an hour Mr. Moody goes to the platform, asks all to kneel while two or three prayers are offered, that the hour may be one of universal decision. 'Now,' says the leader, 'there are many souls here buffeting the waves; let us throw out planks to them. Mr. A., can you tell these people how they may be saved now?' The Christian addressed, in brief words or illustrations, points out the path of life. Another, and then another is called on to throw out some plank from God's Word or his own experience. These testimonies are briefly, rapidly, given while eager souls drink in the counsel they contain. Then Mr. Moody, after explaining the solemn character of the decision to which he has urged the inquirers, calls on those who are ready to accept Christ at once to say so. In various phrases, from all parts of the room, comes the common purpose henceforth to live a Christian life, here from the lips of a child a word of trust in Jesus, here the balanced words of manhood, long tossed on the sea, but now deliberately at rest in Christ, and here the heart-broken confessions of a wanderer, who has once more set his face to his Father's house. While others are hesitating between life and death, Mr. Moody asks all who can sing, 'I will trust Him,' to rise and unite in that chorus. . . . He calls for another singing of the same verse, perhaps changing it thus: 'I do trust Him,' and 'He has saved me' and then the young converts having been earnestly commended to God in prayer, the meeting is promptly closed."

The other inquiry meeting is at the close of a church service. "Mr. Whittle has invited the inquirers and all who were willing to converse with them into the lecture-room. After an opening prayer, he presents three distinct points for the consideration of inquirers: First, that Christ came to save guilty and condemned sinners. Having proven this point from the Bible, he asks all who subscribe to it to signify it by holding up their right hand. Bible statements are incontrovertible and every hand is raised. Second, that all in the room are thus guilty and condemned and need this Savior. Scripture passages proving this point are read, and those who assent to it are asked, as before, to signify their assent. Third, renouncing my sin, I accept the Savior as my Savior. This duty is affectionately urged and illustrated, and all who can assent to this final test are asked to hold up their hands in solemn covenant with God. The path has been made so plain, the inquirer has been so shut in to the necessity of accepting or rejecting the Savior, that very many make it the moment of their supreme choice. Then follow prayers, testimonies and personal counsels and the meeting, without formal close, by the silent retiring of one group after another, slowly dissolves."

§

Out of the ruck of revivalists in the 1820's and 30's there rise three figures; the conservative Nettleton; Lyman Beecher the compromiser; and Charles Grandison Finney, enemy to both, the reputed brigadier-general of Jesus Christ who stormed through the western counties of New York, broke into the citadels of New England, converted millionaires in New York City, and swept westward with unparalleled force until his energy finally spent itself and he rested quietly as a professor at Oberlin College. Finney is not only the great typical revivalist; he is the personification of the whole revivalist spirit of two decades. He is so much more important than any of his rivals that, although it may not be strict justice, one may call him responsible for the madness of religious feeling which later broke out in such diverse movements as Mormonism and Perfectionism and the impostures of Matthias. Finney was not by any means the most violent or the most radical of the revivalists, but he was the only innovator sufficiently trained in logic and doctrine to defend himself. If Beecher and Nettleton had had to struggle only with the Littlejohns and Boyles, they could have wiped out the "new measures" in a day. But when they were driven to condemn the fury of revivalism itself, Finney smashed their attack and triumphantly invaded their own territory.

James Boyle could whip up excitement, could make souls sweat in anguish and then could write to Finney that, three months after he left "a field," he had returned to find the people like dead coals. It was recorded that, although every church in which he worked quickly increased its membership, it as quickly fell into decay. He began as a Roman Catholic, went through most of the congregational sects, and ended, after he had been excommunicated by the latter, as a kind of perfectionist attached to the "infidel abolitionist" William Lloyd Garrison. The almost illiterate Littlejohn was always in trouble on account of doctrinal unsoundness and imprudent conduct. Long after the revivals had exhausted themselves he too was excommunicated. Asa Mahan, after all his labors, looked back and found that, except for Finney and Father Nash, all the evangelists of that period were soon disqualified for their office and that many were vicious and dangerous.

Finney alone combined violence in method with a cool head in argument. A man of sturdy build, he was possessed by an energy which he worked to the point of exhaustion. Then, recuperating, he began again his remorseless trampling of the vineyard. He was threatened with death and excommunication, but nothing daunted him. He was of a granite obstinacy. Two days after his marriage he was called away from home, and, as the work enjoined a revival, he prosecuted it for six months before he returned to his bride. The sculptural lines of his face were all unyielding. The eyes, with which he seems to have exerted some hypnotic power, were cold and deep set. The jutting nose and the firmly held lips give the impression of a hard man and a severe, possibly even an angry one. He was proud of his capacity to face people down.

Finney was born in Warren, Connecticut, in 1792, but when he was a little child the family moved to Oneida county, New York, then a wilderness sparsely populated by emigrants from New England. He was then in the center of his future activities, in that extraordinary little section of country which was to give birth to every variety of cult and fad and movement. He had a common school education, taught school in New Jersey, and was about to found an academy in the South, but was persuaded by his parents to study the law. An orthodox Calvinist perplexed him to such an extent that he began to read the Bible in order to answer his own questions on religion. The first of these was on the inefficacy of prayer. Pursuing the subject to a biblical reply, he came face to face with the question whether he "would accept Christ as presented in the Gospel or pursue a worldly course in life."

§

Finney was self-converted. In his autobiography he describes his labors to break down his pride and tells also of the inward voices which asked him, "What are you waiting for? Did you not promise to give yourself to God? Are you not endeavoring to work out a righteousness of your own?"

"Just at this point the whole question of Gospel salvation opened to my mind in a manner most marvelous to me at the time. I think I then saw, as clearly as I ever have in my life, the reality and fullness of the atonement of Christ. I saw that his work was a finished work; and that instead of having, or needing, any righteousness of my own to recommend me to God, I had to submit myself to the righteousness of God through Christ. Gospel salvation seemed to me to be an offer of something to be accepted; and that it was full and complete; and that all that was necessary on my part, was to get my own consent to give up my sins, and accept Christ. Salvation, it seemed to me, instead of being a thing to be wrought out, by my own works, was a thing to be found entirely in the Lord Jesus Christ, who presented himself before me as my God and my Savior."

Like Edwards he withdrew to the woods to wrestle with his spirit. He was overwhelmed with a sense of his own wickedness and so discouraged that he was almost too weak to stand. Presently he was aware of his difficulty. He had intellectually believed the Bible, but had not known that faith implied a voluntary trust instead of an intellectual state. He addressed himself directly to God and, what with inward voices and passages of Scripture dropping into his mind with a flood of light, we are assured that God directly answered him. "I told the Lord that I should take him at his word; that he could not lie, and that therefore I was sure that he heard my prayer, and that he would be found of me.

"He then gave me many other promises, both from the Old and the New Testament, especially some most precious promises respecting our Lord Jesus Christ. I never can, in words, make any human being understand how precious and true those promises appeared to me. I took them one after the other as infallible truth, the assertions of God who could not lie. They did not seem so much to fall into my intellect as into the powers of my mind; and I seized hold of them, appropriated them, and fastened upon them with the grasp of a drowning man."

A few minutes later he had lost all sense of sin: all consciousness of guilt had departed from him. He struggled to bring it back, but a great tranquillity came over him and he was never afterwards to escape the accusation of dallying with the idea of the sinlessness of the converted man. That evening, "it seemed as if I met the Lord Jesus Christ face to face" and received a mighty baptism of the Holy Ghost. "Without any expectation of it, without ever having the thought in my mind that there was any such thing for me, without any recollection that I had ever heard the thing mentioned by any person in the world, the Holy Spirit descended upon me in a manner that seemed to go through me, body and soul. I could feel the impression, like a wave of electricity, going through and through me. Indeed it seemed to come in waves and waves of liquid love; for I could not express it in any other way. It seemed like the very breath of God. I can recollect distinctly that it seemed to fan me, like immense wings.

"No words can express the wonderful love that was shed abroad in my heart. I wept aloud with joy and love: and I do not know but

I should say, I literally bellowed out the unutterable gushings of my heart. These waves came over me, and over me, and over me, one after the other, until I recollect I cried out, 'I shall die if these waves continue to pass over me.' I said, 'Lord, I cannot bear any more'; yet I had no fear of death."

Notwithstanding this baptism he went to bed without feeling sure that he was at peace with God, but wakened presently on account of the "great flow of the love of God" that was in his heart. This happened several times and, in the morning, the sun poured a clear light into his room and in this light the baptism of the spirit returned. He felt justified by faith. "This was just the revelation that I needed. I felt myself justified by faith; and, so far as I could see, I was in a state in which I did not sin. Instead of feeling that I was sinning all the time, my heart was so full of love that it overflowed. My cup ran over with blessing and with love; and I could not feel that I was sinning against God. Nor could I recover the least sense of guilt for my past sins. Of this experience I said nothing that I recollect, at the time, to anybody; that is, of this experience of justification."

This was the process of his conversion. In its earliest stages he had promised the Lord that if conversion were granted him he would preach the Gospel. The next morning a deacon of the church came to his office and said, "Mr. Finney, do you recollect that my cause is to be tried at ten o'clock this morning? I suppose you are ready?" [He had been retained to attend this suit as the deacon's attorney.] I replied to him, "Deacon B——, I have a retainer from the Lord Jesus Christ to plead his cause, and I cannot plead yours."

He was immediately successful. The story of his conversion spread and the grove in which he had communed with the Holy Spirit was frequented by other anxious souls who imitated him in prayer with equally successful results. When the tides of Spring began to flow and Christian will abated, he would get up before sunrise and make the rounds of the village, calling the brethren to a "precious season of prayer" which they had undertaken to enjoy. His own fervor was again and again sustained by the radiance which poured over him. "One morning I had been around and called the brethren up, and when I returned to the meeting-house but few of them had got there. Mr. Gale, my minister, was standing at the door of the church, and as I came up, all at once the glory of God shone upon and round about me, in a manner most marvelous. The day was just beginning to dawn. But all at once a light perfectly ineffable shone in my soul, that almost prostrated me to the ground. In this light it seemed as if I could see that all nature praised and worshiped God except man. This light seemed to be like the brightness of the sun in every direction. It was too intense for the eyes. I recollect casting my eyes down and breaking into a flood of tears, in view of the fact that mankind did not praise God. I think I knew something then, by actual experience, of that light that prostrated Paul on his way to Damascus. It was surely a light such as I could not have endured long." Mr. Gale, however, in his blind faith had seen no light.

Finney presently discovered that as often as he tried to examine his own feelings, his motives, and the state of his mind, the day would pass without bringing him happiness. He decided this was because he was withdrawn from Christ and thereafter "let his spirit take its own course" which he found "in the highest degree useful." From the very beginning he felt that he must work with professing Christians who assumed themselves to be of Christ without having gone through the process of conversion and repentance, which alone could lead to sanctification. A charming girl "very much enlightened on the subject of religion" remained in her sins and Finney among others tried to convert her, but one day as he was coming to her the girl's sister came out of the room, in her hands a book on Universalism which she had torn in half. The thought that a possible convert had become a Universalist so upset him that he refused to go to her and "could not frame to present the case before God in words but only in groans and tears." Later, however, God spoke to him saying, "Yes, yes." Although he did not think this was an audible voice it gave him great peace and joy. He continued amateur work as a revivalist until he was thirty when he became a candidate for the ministry. Although he intended to be licensed by the Presbytery at Adams, he rejected the strict doctrines of the sect; yet he qualified for the ministry by demolishing the doctrines of the Universalists.

§

Except for his ideas about sanctification, destined to have a profound effect in many ways which irritated Finney exceedingly, his doctrinal teaching developed very little after his student days and can be summed up in the negative statements of what he did not believe. He rejected first of all, the orthodox doctrine of original sin, of the utter moral depravity of the human constitution. Following that, he took the next step and asserted that men are able to repent and to believe; i.e., he denied the Edwardian principle of inability; he denied that men were free to commit evil and incapable of performing any good. He refused to believe that God had condemned men for their sinful nature and that death was the just reward for their transgressions. With an eye already fixed on conversions, he rejected the doctrine that the Holy Ghost acts in a physical way upon the substance of the soul in cases of regeneration. He gave the function of the will a great place and insisted that man should be active, not passive, in seeking regeneration.

In comparison with rigid Calvinism, this was liberal doctrine; in comparison with Universalism, it was strict and reactionary. Actually, Finney's doctrine betrays the able mind of the lawyer, for he cut away from Calvinism precisely those elements which made it vulnerable to the attack of the Universalist.

As a student, he had been warned not to think as thinking might lead him to infidelism. But he persisted and arrived at a composite theology which was remarkably proof against assault from either side. At least it was remarkably successful. For an evangelist it was an almost ideal position since it retained all the elements of terror and threat of the old theology and, at the same time, allowed the preacher to offer every hope. For Christ's atonement had made possible the salvation of all mankind. The popular heresy at the time was that the atonement had not only made possible, but had actually accomplished, universal salvation. In various forms, from the religion of the Sandamanian to that of the Oneida community, this became an essential doctrine, leading its professors to declare themselves incapable of sin, superior to the law, and possessed, in short, of perfection. By avoiding this pitfall, Finney remained orthodox and continued in the church although he rejected some of its cardinal principles. Those who are interested in doctrine can follow his logical attack on the teaching that the guilt of Adam is "imputed" to Adam's children and that Adam's original guilt, and that of his children and then of mankind after him, are both "imputed" to Christ. From this it follows that Christ was deservedly punished and discharged once and for all the debt owed by humanity. The doctrine continues with "imputing" both the obedience and the death of Christ to the elect, who have thereby suffered and paid the penalty in full. This is an argument which Finney used again and again in revivals and, when stated in the usual language of the evangelist, it may have had warmth and persuasion. In cold print it becomes only a syllogism and seems to bear little relation to the actuality of either Finney's mind or his methods.

§

His first commission was from a "female missionary society" in Oneida county, and his work began at Evan's Mills and Antwerp. From the start he was importunate about the things that were God's. After he had preached for a few weeks he called the people together and said to them, "You admit that what I preach is the Gospel. You profess to believe it. Now will you receive it? Do you mean to receive it, or do you intend to reject it? You must have some mind about it. And now I have a right to take it for granted, inasmuch as you admit that I have preached the truth, that you acknowledge your obligation at once to become Christians. This obligation you do not deny; but will you meet the obligation? Will you discharge it? Will you do what you admit you ought to do? If you will not, tell me; and if you will, tell me, that I may turn to the right hand or to the left." He then demanded that they rise up and give pledges to make peace with God immediately. The congregation refused to move and Finney cried out, "Then you are committed. You have taken your stand. You have rejected Christ and his Gospel; and ye are witnesses one against the other, and God is witness against you all. This is explicit, and you may remember as long as you live, that you have thus publicly committed yourselves against the Savior, and said, 'We will not have this man, Christ Jesus, to reign over us.' "

He had stung the congregation into action and, after a few further meetings when the spirit of God came upon him with such power "that it was like opening a battery upon them," he had his first reward. A woman was struck speechless and lay in a sort of fit for sixteen hours after which her "mouth was opened, and a new song was given her. She was taken from the horrible pit of miry clay, and her feet were set upon a rock." There was an additional significance in this first conversion since the subject was a professing Christian and had believed herself saved; but now her hope was annihilated and she knew that she had to come again to repentance. In comparison with such a triumph the conversion of the hotel-keeper, who was the leading Deist of the town, was gratifying, but not important. Nor was the fatal apoplectic stroke of a railer against religion at the very moment of his blasphemy anything more than a sign. What Finney wanted and what, by his own account, he got, were the souls of cold Christians and misled Universalists. It pleased him particularly to see the repentance of the Reverend Daniel Nash who had amazed Finney a year earlier by praying with his eyes open, being then "in a very cold and backslidden state." This was at the meeting which licensed Finney and, a short time after, Father Nash "was taken with inflamed eyes; and for several weeks was shut up in a dark room. . . . He had a terrible overhauling in his whole Christian experience. . . ."

§

It is not necessary to follow Finney through his extraordinary career of revivalism. He stamped up and down the northwestern counties of New York, stopping only at rare intervals to ask God where to go next, turning the cold fire of his eyes on the vain and the hostile, breaking through rigid precedents, making penitents shriek in agony, and establishing himself as a cannoneer in the service of the Lord. His autobiography recounts incident after incident, almost all trivial but mounting into the hundreds, and suggests thousands of conversions besides. The mockers were the first to be converted, the tavern prettily changed itself into a chapel, and the thief made restitution for the Bible she had stolen. At last he became so important that the old guard determined to destroy him. They were dubious about his doctrine and they disliked his methods. "Conversions can be bought at too high a price," cried Lyman Beecher. A few souls may be saved but "the general and more abiding result may be the ruin of a thousand souls." "This is not religion," says another, "it is fanaticism." Startled observers noted strange sights along the trail of the revivalist. Men and women saw visions, assumed the right of prophecy, communicated directly with God. Everywhere the revivalists were insisting that the grace of God would be freely poured. Everywhere they invited all men to exercise their will to repentance. The safeguards of the established churches and the work of the regular preachers were equally jeopardized. Finney was breaking down all discipline, wearing out the spirit of the penitents with importunate demands for immediate repentance and, the moment repentance had come, was exalting the convert with the assurance of eternal grace. It was all extreme and the whole country was nervous with apprehension or hysterical with an unaccustomed freedom and delight. To Lyman Beecher, who had labored long in congregations, occasionally predicting a revival or timidly taking part in one, all of this was offensive. To Nettleton, proceeding in an orderly way, balancing emotion and intellect, refraining from all histrionics, seeking permanent conversions not quick ones, Finney and his co-workers were a peril. The cultivated East stood against the raw West.*

In a vivid chapter in her *Trumpets of Jubilee*, Constance Mayfield Rourke has described the clash of Lyman Beecher and Finney, but not with the same emphasis that Finney himself has given to it. At the head of a band of evangelists, Finney was marching upon New England and Beecher, unable to stop him, summoned such of his friends as he could and met the evangelist at New Lebanon. Finney's account of the conference is full of implications and innuendo. That everybody played politics is perfectly obvious, but it must be guessed from omissions and not from anything Finney says: "We soon discovered that some policy was on foot in organizing the convention, on the part of Dr. Beecher. However we regarded it not. The convention was organized and I believe Dr. Humphrey presided as moderator." The intervals between these sentences, not the words themselves, tell the story. Preliminaries went on with a great deal of jockeying for position. The Westerners refused to be placed in the dock as culprits. They demanded the source of their opponents' information. According to Finney, Beecher replied that "our spiritual dignity forbids us to answer

* Finney always talks of Oneida county, New York, as the West.

any such questions"; and Mr. Nettleton, it seems, "became so very nervous that he was unable to attend several of our sessions." Dr. Beecher had some skill in disputation and moved that the Western evangelists, being parties to the question, should not be allowed to testify as to the nature of their own work. Defeated there, he objected to women taking part in social meetings, but this objection was over-ruled by an appeal to the eleventh chapter of Corinthians. Mr. Nettleton then read a letter which summarized the accusations against Finney. We know that they alluded to the new measures, the use of the anxious bench, to bullying and frightening penitents, to accepting conversions without proof of their reality, the abandonment to hysteria and the other unconventional forms of evangelism. But Finney, in his entire chapter on this subject, never once specifies what these accusations were. He alludes to them only as "these complaints," or "false reports," or "such and such and such." The convention passed a series of resolutions denouncing the excesses of revivalism. The Westerners denying that they ever had been guilty of these excesses, insisted on considering the resolution as a model for future guidance, in which spirit they accepted them. Dr. Beecher and Nettleton persisted in considering the resolutions as a rebuke to their rivals. The parting shot came from Mr. Finney who proposed a resolution against lukewarmness in religion, condemning it as strongly as the other resolution had condemned the excesses of enthusiasm. Dr. Beecher wryly remarked that there was no danger of lukewarmness, "whereupon the convention adjourned"—that is, according to Finney's own account. Miss Rourke, following Beecher's autobiography, says that after nine days of discussion the conference was about to take a fraternal course when Beecher leapt to his feet and, interposing himself between the two groups, cried out to Finney and the opposition, "Gentlemen, you needn't think you can catch old birds with chaff. It may be true that you don't go personally into ministers' parishes, but in the noise and excitement, one and another of the people in the towns want you to come and preach, and you are mighty reserved, and say, 'Ah, no, we cannot come unless the ministers invite us,' and so you send them back like hounds to compel them to call you. Finney, I know your plan, and you know I do! You mean to come into Connecticut, and carry the streak of fire to Boston. But if you attempt it, as the Lord liveth, I'll meet you at the state line, and call out all the artillery, and fight you every inch of the way, and then I'll fight you there."

It is amusing to note that Finney says that he does not remember these words. He quotes only the last three sentences omitting all reference to the sore point of dispute between the stationary and irregular preacher; and he suavely says that as he does not remember the occasion and, as Dr. Beecher does, "let it illustrate the spirit of his opposition."

He can afford to be generous. He claims that Beecher was grossly deceived and ignorant of the character and motives of the revivalist, and that he himself had no design or desire to go to Connecticut or to Boston. Yet, in a short time, that very pressure to which Beecher so angrily alluded manifested itself in Beecher's own congregation. After Finney had undertaken a peculiarly searching work in Providence, he was invited by the Congregational ministers and churches to go to Boston and labor there. He was warned not to bear down too hard, for if he smashed the pretensions of professing (but unsanctified) Congregationalists, the Unitarians would use his arguments against him. But the flail of the Lord was not to be halted. Finney knew that threshing can not be done mincingly. He preached in Beecher's own church and once, at an inquiry meeting there, he tried to show that Christians "were expected to forsake all they had and deliver everything to Christ. . . ." As he paused before calling on the inquirers to kneel, Dr. Beecher rose— according to Finney's account—and said, "You need not be afraid to give up all to Christ, your property and all, for he will give it right back to you." Mr. Finney, without appearing to contradict Dr. Beecher, managed nevertheless thoroughly to correct the impression which the latter had made. At Rochester, where there were no Beechers present to belittle his appeal, a penitent actually handed over to Finney a quitclaim deed in due legal form executed ready for deliverance, "in which he quitclaimed to the Lord Jesus Christ all ownership of himself and of everything he possessed."

After Boston, Finney was successful in New York, at the Chatham Street Theatre * which Lewis Tappan had leased and

---

* The bar-room was naturally changed into a prayer room and it is recorded that one of the penitents cried out, "O Lord! Forgive my sins. The last time I was here Thou knowest I was a wicked actor on this stage. O Lord, have mercy on me!"

fitted up for a church, but he was smitten with cholera which was then epidemic, and presently went abroad. On his return, he delivered a course of lectures which became a standard work on revivals, and began his series of meetings at the Broadway Tabernacle which had been built for him and for which he resigned from the Presbytery, since the Tabernacle was a Congregational church. Later he gave this up to go out to Oberlin College.

§

Here again he crosses the path of Lyman Beecher, who was at that time president of Lane Seminary at Cincinnati. There he had been bedeviled by Theodore Weld, one of Finney's converts and disciples, the apostle of manual labor to the colleges of the country. It was Weld who brought up the question of slavery—and Lane was only across the river from Kentucky. Beecher was not a friend to abolitionists; he despised them as "offspring of Finney's 'denunciatory revivals.'" It may be said in Beecher's defense that abolition was not as popular then as it is now. It was always the work of an extremely small group and a great many of the abolitionists were known to be infidels and suspected of intentions to destroy all discipline, all property, even the family and the home. Yet Beecher acted without any trace of recklessness. He had promised Arthur Tappan, a contributor to the Seminary's fund, that he would never consent to any limitation of the students' right to discuss abolition but, when the trustees of Lane, without consulting him, ordered the faculty to prohibit all public meetings on the Seminary grounds and dismissed the one member of the faculty whose anti-slavery sentiments were marked, Beecher did nothing in particular, in spite of the abolitionists' demand that he resign. Miss Rourke notes that, had he resigned, he could only have become the tail to Weld's kite, since Weld was leading the insurgent students. Beecher temporized and was lost. Just at that time, Asa Mahan invited Finney to come to Oberlin as professor of theology. The particular inducement was that students formerly at Lane Seminary had proposed to come to Oberlin if Weld's master, Finney, would accept the call. Arthur Tappan, on hearing that Finney had held out for admission of negroes on equality with whites, offered his entire income of about $100,000 a year to the new

institution. In the summer of 1835, Finney went to the new college. He brought with him a tent a hundred feet in diameter, and
the streamer which topped the center pole bore the words "Holiness
to the Lord." For several years Finney divided his time between
Oberlin and various revivals. He went again to Boston (where his
wife died) and, if Boston was a bit superior, Finney was positively
arrogant. In his book, when he has to record some great success, he
makes it a point to disclaim any merit. It is for the glory of Christ
that he notes how well his sermons sold. At best he attributes the
wonderful results to a blessed answer to his prayers, but in his
chapter on the second Boston visit, we find an unexpected trace of
intellectual pride:

". . . But in preaching, I have found that nowhere can I preach
those truths, on which my own soul delights to live, and be understood, except it be by a very small number. I have never found
that more than a very few, even of my own people, appreciate
and receive those views of God and Christ, and the fullness of his
free salvation, upon which my own soul still delights to feed.
Everywhere, I am obliged to come down to where the people are,
in order to make them understand me; and in every place where
I have preached, for many years, I have found the churches in so
low a state, as to be utterly incapable of apprehending and appre-
ciating, what I regard as the most precious truths of the whole
Gospel."

He had, without any other trace of mysticism, an absolute conviction of God's special interest in him and, at Auburn in 1826, the
Lord drew near to him and "assured me that he would use and
uphold me; that no opposition would prevail against me. . . ."
With this confidence he had become a reviver of souls, untiring,
astute, sly, and without compassion. His autobiography is full of
professions of kind feelings toward Beecher and Nettleton and his
other enemies, but one can easily feel the shrewd rancor which
persists. He was a hard man engaged in a hard work. He knew no
other pleasure than those floods of light which followed the anguish of his prayers and he trampled upon the pleasures of others
if they interfered with his work. Once, at the very time when he

proposed an inquiry meeting, the church had arranged a sociable, so he broke down the arrangement. At Oberlin, when he was about to harvest a few student souls, he found that secular activities had been arranged. He threatened to resign unless he could control everything and make all pleasures secondary to religious zeal. He was monumentally sincere. The offer of a hundred thousand dollars from Tappan hardly interested him and, when Tappan went bankrupt, Finney lived with his family at Oberlin in such destitution that an unexpected check for $100 was like the opening of heaven to them. There is nothing whatever endearing about his record of himself. There is a great deal that is unctuous and his careful efforts not to appear proud of his work sound faintly hypocritical to one who cannot accept in full his sense of divine appointment. But with the exception of the usual faith in coincidences regarded as miracles, there is nothing trivial about Finney. He was always concerned with a matter which was to him of supreme dignity and superlatively important: the regeneration of mankind through Christ.

§

It was in the final development of his work that Finney broached a doctrine full of danger. I noted at the very beginning the feeling he had on being converted that sin and guilt had fallen away from him. Many years later he began to wonder whether the Gospel did not provide means for life on a higher plane than that which most Christians enjoyed. It is only a guess that he wished to recapture, and in some way make permanent, that feeling of ecstatic sinlessness, which he had once experienced, that entire harmony of the soul not only in its own movements, but in relation to a higher power. As usual he searched his only authority, the Scriptures, and preached two sermons in which he defined Christian perfection and proved that it is in a way attainable in this life. This was his doctrine of sanctification "in the sense that it was the privilege of Christians to live without known sin." It was unfortunate for him that, at the same time, another version of perfectionism was gaining ground, a version which met the moral law with defiance and was associated in the popular mind with licentiousness and immorality. By an irony which Finney does not appreciate, these other perfectionists were his own disciples, following his own theories to a logical, if not human, conclusion. They muddied the pure stream of Finney's doctrine and were so near to the source that, when Finney went to Oberlin, misunderstandings and misrepresentations followed him and that persistent enemy, Lyman Beecher, was the leading spirit in a convention which tried to close Oberlin for its false doctrines. The quarrel about Christian sanctity, or Perfection, went on for many years. Finney hammered his weapons, unwearied and unbroken, escaped from compromising allies, fighting always on two fronts.

We shall come to Perfectionism again in a more interesting phase, not as a theory, but as the astounding practice of John Humphrey Noyes, a happy example of the effects of revivalism on a superior individual.

Revivalism continued long after Finney's time. It is going on to-day. But before we follow its later course and attempt to discover its motives, we can stop to observe the case of Matthias, an example as happy as that of Noyes, but in the opposite sense. In Matthias we see clearly what revivalism could do with a subject naturally unbalanced. Matthias is not a typical figure but, precisely because he is exceptional, he throws the workings of revivalism into the highest relief.

† Fireplaces were beginning to be closed over and, in 1820, the city of Philadelphia used 365 tons of coal. There was gas light in the streets of New York, but rooms were generally without ventilation. † The Erie Canal was opened in 1825 and Chicago had a population of seventy souls. † In New York City 3,000 buildings were in the course of erection in one year and, on one first of May, which was moving day, hundreds of people waited in the parks or slept in jail while their houses were being finished. † Farmers in Ohio complained that oil made their water undrinkable. † Railroads when they entered cities were drawn by horses through the streets and, in 1825, an author wrote "nothing can do more harm to the adoption of railroads than the promulgation of such *nonsense* as that we shall see locomotive engines traveling at the rate of twelve miles per hour." † Philadelphia, Pittsburgh, and Cincinnati were surrounded by "liberties"; in the last of these cities there were, in 1829, sixty lawyers, one to every 5,000 inhabitants. † The distribution of religious tracts, gratis, flourished. † Members of the House of Representatives kept their hats on while they sat. † Between 1825 and the Civil War, the juvenile works of Peter Parley sold 7,000,000 copies. † In 1826, there was a slave hunt in Poultney, Vermont. † Girls worked half naked in factories rather than be servants at twice the wage. † Phrenological societies were founded in the Middle West. † Bed sheets in hotels were considered fresh if used only a few nights. † Among the favorite painters were Washington Alston and Mr. Ingham, because of their mastery over draperies and resemblances. The gallery of antique statues in Philadelphia was open to women as well as to men but at different times. At the Chestnut Street Theatre, Booth played in *King Lear*, and at the Walnut Street Theatre there was a living skeleton. On Sundays chains were stretched across many streets. † At Long Branch it was correct for two girls to go into the water accompanied by one man. † Silk and satin were as often seen in New York City as chintz. † Mrs. Mitford's *Rienzi* was played at the Chatham Theatre in New York City and Forrest appeared in *Damon and Pythias*. † Brownstone was beginning to be used for building houses and there was an abundance of ice for domestic purposes.

# VIII.

## A Messianic Murderer.

IN the fantastic figure of Robert Matthews (who called himself Matthias and let it be known that he was the reincarnation of that Matthias into whom the spirit of Jesus had passed,
or, sometimes, that he was Almighty God, Himself) the sects and
movements following the 1830 revivals of religion in America
provide a perfect burlesque of themselves. The half-dozen men and
women surrounding this incredible impostor exhibit nearly all the
unhealthy varieties of religious experience: mania, delusion, sexual
aberration, hallucination, catalepsy and hysteria of every sort. The
daily lives in this group are full of minor disasters, from reform
movements exploited by scoundrels, to fraud, bankruptcy, and the
imputation of murder. Adultery and sadism were sanctified by the
direct command of God. The characters move in and out of insane
wards and prisons. Matthias, ragged and penniless, stands on the
outskirts of a Finney revival. Matthias, in a coat of green velvet
lined with pink silk and hung with golden tassels, sits in the house
of Joseph Smith, at Kirtland, and discusses theology with his bewildered host before the latter starts the great Mormon trek across
the Mississippi. Into this amazing story not one entirely normal
person enters as a principal. It sums up and parodies, and to an
extent discredits, the whole religious excitement from which it
sprang.

The story is a little complicated at the beginning, for it involves
three sets of characters, two married couples in the city of New
York, and Matthias, a housejoiner, from up-state. The climax of
the story, the trial of Matthias for murder, comes in 1835. It begins, many years earlier, with only a faint premonition, a suggestion
of little cults and backwoods degeneracy, when the minister of the
Anti-Burgher branch of the Seceders, visiting a member of his
flock in Cambridge, Washington county, New York, lays his hands
on the head of Robert Matthews, an orphan living there, and gives
him his blessing. There had been eccentricity in the boy's family.

From the moment he received the clerical benediction, the boy felt that his own fate was to become a distinguished personage.

In pursuit of this ambition, Robert Matthews, as soon as he was grown up, went to New York and learned the trade of joiner. On his return up-state, he became a merchant, failed, and then returned to New York, married (an apparently sensible woman), became bankrupt, and moved from place to place. After trying one occupation after another, he finally settled down as a journeyman joiner in Albany. He had belonged to the Scotch church but after a quarrel with his minister, now attended the services of the Dutch Reformed Congregation. Having been very much moved by a visiting preacher, his excitement about religion grew steadily and reached its climax one evening when he went to hear Charles Grandison Finney and returned home from this particular service in a state bordering upon frenzy.*

Fanaticism laid hold upon him. He underwent all the enthusiasms and became a victim to every fad. He threw himself violently into the temperance movement, asserting that all men would be converted if they would only give up drink. In his own household, he went farther, keeping his entire family on a diet of bread, fruit, and vegetables. The fruit was often only whatever berries chanced to be ripe. Presently, he declared that he had been commissioned to convert the whole city of Albany and began a series of chaotic harangues on the streets. Disappointed in the progress of his mission, he declared, in 1830, that the entire city and all its inhabitants would be destroyed. At this time, he discovered a text which proved that no man who shaved his beard could be a true Christian. One night he aroused his wife and their five children and commanded them to fly with him to the hills, as the city would be destroyed the next day. The mother refused and kept back the youngest child. The eldest daughter also stayed behind. But three little children were dragged for twenty-four hours without stop into the country behind Albany.

This was the beginning of Matthews' madness and, although his condition was recognized, the phenomenon was so common in that age of cranks that very little attention was paid to it. A few

---

* It was generally rumored that Finney had driven several persons mad with his preaching.

years earlier, the anti-Masonic hysteria had run through the whole of western New York. A few years later, the excesses of the Millerites, awaiting the last trump, followed the same course. Two things attacked the incurious, naturally balanced, mind of the backwoodsman: the progress of mechanical arts and the endless series of revivals which devastated county after county with stubble fire and made them, in the common phrase of revivalists, "burnt districts." There was no intellectual make-weight to steady men when they observed the wonders of science. They heard of canals and steam engines and believed them to be the predicted signs of the coming of the Lord. Nor was there an established ritual or disciplined church to direct the religious fervor which wandering exhorters whipped up and left to die down without any permanent object to which it could attach itself. The country quivered and trembled. It was expectant and eager. It was as ready for spiritualism as for Mormonism. Barreled up in the narrow confines of unimaginative lives it was fermenting. The excitement of revivals came to nothing and, on the rare occasions when a revivalist returned, he groaned in spirit to see the "sad, frigid, carnal state into which the churches had fallen." Evangelists arranged men and women in parallel lines and, passing up and down between them, cried out with violent gestures, "Agonize, I tell you. Agonize, why don't you agonize?" Or they prostrated a whole camp-meeting on the ground and crept among them crying, "I am the old serpent that tempted Eve." Violence bred hysteria and, after men and women had shrieked and groaned and fallen into epilepsy before the revivalist, they rose and announced that God had spoken to them, predicted the death of individuals, the destruction of cities, and the damnation of all who did not repent and accept Christ. Lunacy and licentiousness were sown in a fertile field.

This was the background of Robert Matthews who now, rejecting both his name and Scottish parentage and declaring that he was Matthias, the Jew, departed on a grand apostolic tour. Having made his way through forests and prairies and proclaimed his mission as far as the Ozark mountains, he turned back through Mississippi and Tennessee, to the Cherokee country in Georgia where he preached to the Indians. The authorities imprisoned him but, apparently frightened by the curses which he called down upon them, they let him go free. He returned to New York where he could be seen daily promenading along the Battery, his beard unkempt, his nails filthy, his clothes torn, but walking with a majestic gait, shouting his exhortations to loafers and children, or mounted at times on a horse as dejected and scrawny as himself. At this point, the story of the impostor goes back to gather in his disciples.

The background of the cities was more sophisticated. In Boston, a mob might be driven by inflamed religious prejudices to destroy the Ursuline Convent. In New York, the prospect of graft in municipal government was great enough to justify rowdiness and thuggery at the polls. The idea of public schools was still a suitable subject for ridicule, but Boston already was known for its culture and every good college had, or was trying to buy, a philosophical apparatus. The quarrel about Byron's morals was still going on. Noah Webster's dictionary was accepted as standard. The various state governments had appointed official geologists. New York was sophisticated enough to enjoy the dancing of Fanny Elssler. The fruit of revivalism was not so notably seen in excesses of hysteria as in outbursts of moral reform. One of Finney's subordinates, George Cragin, who was later to figure unhappily in the Oneida Community, collaborated with John R. McDowall in "a well-meant, but unwisely conducted work on behalf of the fallen women in New York." This effort was one of hundreds. Timid women met and prayed under the guidance of their ministers and resolved "that while we recognize the obligation to the degraded and perishing heathen, we feel it to be not less our duty to labor for the salvation of those in this Christian land whose character and condition too much resemble theirs." They formed Female Benevolent Societies "for the promotion of moral purity . . . in a way both corrective and preventive." Those who were unhappy formed little sects of their own and dreamed of the miracles of Mesmer and, later, of the spiritualist, Mr. Hume. They also formed societies for educating the children of the poor and sewing circles to make money for converting the Jews. In one group, all ornament was rejected; in another, fasting went on for as much as three days a week.

It was in this borderland of hysteria that the disciples of Matthias, the Elijah Piersons and Benjamin Folgers, passed their

lives. Mr. and Mrs. Pierson were directors of the Magdalene institution. Of the two, he was the more fanatical and the diary he left
of his conversations with the Lord is an extraordinary document in
religious mania:

"Prayed for the harlots at Five Points: asked the Lord to give
us all the ground whereon the soles of our feet had trod, and all the
souls now alive who had heard our voices in that neighborhood.

"Answer. The Lord said, 'You must go and fetch them out.'
The Lord said, concerning the two witnesses, 'Thou art one and
Sarah the other.' "

On another date, the petition is less practical, but the answer is
equally satisfactory:

"O, Lord Jesus! I perceive that I have failed in exercising a
spirit of love, patience, meekness, kindness, and condescension to my
fellows, and especially a spirit of impertinence in disputation. Now,
Lord Jesus, I confess to thee that this has been wrong, and I am
heartily sorry for it, and beg thy forgiveness. O Lord! forgive me,
and cleanse me from these sins: help me hereafter, Lord, to exercise the opposite graces in a double proportion.

"Answer. We have freely forgiven thee and cleansed thee from
this unrighteousness.—Thy petition is granted, and thou shalt have
help from us so as to enable thee to exercise these graces."

On Sunday, the 28th of February, 1830, Mr. and Mrs. Pierson
founded a church which met in their house on Bowery Hill and
included two negresses as members. The physical exertions required
of them by their religious and charitable enterprises were almost
incredible. Throughout the winter they held daily prayer meetings
which seem to have lasted 18 or 20 hours a day. When this rigor
was abated, they spent their time in asylums and rescue missions.
They fasted for long seasons and, when they did not fast, they ate
only the minimum food necessary to keep them alive. By the middle
of June, Sarah Pierson collapsed. On the 18th, her husband fasted
and prayed for her and it seemed to him that the Lord said, "Sarah
thy wife will recover." This was an error, but before the error was
discovered, another more important message came to him, this time
without the interposition of prayer. Mr. Pierson, who was a pros-

perous merchant, was riding down to Wall Street in an omnibus when God spoke to him and said, "Thou art Elijah the Tishbite," and instructed him, in biblical terms, to invite all the members of his church to come together. (It was at this time that the Folger family entered into the sect.)

Mrs. Pierson, regrettably, was dying. Her husband, who was reasonably devoted to her, read to the assemblage "a passage from the Epistle of James, 'Is any sick among you? Let him call for the elders of the church, and let them pray over him, anointing him [with oil], in the name of the Lord. And the prayer of faith shall save the sick, and The Lord Shall Raise Him Up.'" Duly following the injunction, he anointed the body with oil in the name of the Lord. Mrs. Pierson did not recover but, immediately after her death, her husband saw a new sense in the scriptural passage, namely that his wife would die, but would experience immediate resurrection. Before a crowd of friends, he cried out, "O Lord God of Israel! thy own word declares that if the elders of the church anoint the sick and pray over him, the Lord shall raise him up. We have taken thee at thy word; we have anointed with oil, and prayed the prayer of faith, and thou knowest in this faith the dear woman died, and in this faith we thy children live. Now, Lord, we claim thy promise! God is not man that he should lie, and if this dear woman is not raised up this day, thy word will fall to the ground; thy promise is null and void; and these gainsaying infidels will rejoice, and go away triumphing in their belief. Lord God! thou canst not deny thyself. Thou knowest we have performed the conditions to the very letter. O Lord, now fulfill thy promise—now, Lord— O let not thy enemies blaspheme—show that thou hast Almighty power—thou canst raise the dead—we believe it, Lord. Come now, and make good thy word, and let this assembly see that there is a God in Israel!"

A number of women, standing around the coffin waiting eagerly for the miracle, touched the hands and face of the corpse from time to time, expecting to discover signs of returning life. As the prayer ended, a drop of blood issued from the nostril of the dead woman. This was taken for a sign of life, but a doctor present told them that it was the infallible evidence of death, and a token of incipient putrefaction. One of the faithful then interpreted the prophecy to mean that this beloved and lamented Christian shall "rise again—at the resurrection of the just." Mr. Pierson delayed the interment until noon. After the funeral he believed she would be raised at midnight, and not only had her bedroom put in order and nightclothes laid out "as for the reception of a bride," but also sent out to get delicacies that would please her. He continued to postpone the date of her resurrection and, later, he and one of his servants imagined that they talked with the dead woman. Throughout the year, he spoke also to the Lord, asking him what would happen if he gave up his business in order to prosecute the work and asking whether he could perform miracles and how many conversions he should make. The replies were all satisfactory. The usual sacred number of 144,000 was given as the limit of his prospective conversions.

§

Mr. Folger, the other favorite disciple, had suffered a bereavement at about the same time, and he and Pierson, drawn closely together were both peculiarly hospitable to the tall, bearded, and patriarchal stranger who now presented himself to them and declared himself to be God the father (through the spirit of Jesus of Nazareth) with power to forgive sins and communicate the Holy Ghost to those who believed in him. Just as the Piersons were convinced that they were the witnesses spoken of, so Matthias the newcomer, declared himself to be the angel spoken of in Revelations 14. He told them that he had been searching for two years for the true church, and now recognized them as its elders. The kingdom of God on earth had begun with Matthias's public declaration in Albany, June, 1830. By June, 1857, all wars would cease, the judgment of mankind would be passed and the wicked would be destroyed. Coincidence of dates persuaded Pierson that Matthias was indeed the Messiah, for whom he, himself, was John the Baptist. As soon as the men had each recognized and accepted the divine mission of the other, and had washed each other's feet, Matthias settled himself in the Pierson home and became the sole preacher of the church on Bowery Hill. His disciples let their beards grow long and, with Matthias, denounced (according to his somewhat loosely constructed notes):

"All who say that the Jews crucified Jesus.
All who say that the first day of the week is the Sabbath.
All who say that immersion with the clothes on is baptism.
All who say that sprinkling is baptism.
All who say preaching to women without their husbands.
All who drinketh wine in bowls.
All who eateth the Passover in a lower room."

Among other things Matthias preached that the earth and all it contained belonged to him. In any case, all of the earth possessed by Pierson and Folger was now at his disposal. He lived in a luxury and pomp which must have fulfilled his early dreams. "He displayed fine cambric ruffles around his wrists and upon his bosom, and to a rich silken scarf, interwoven with gold, were suspended twelve golden tassels, emblematical of the twelve tribes of Israel. His fine linen night caps were wrought with curious skill of needlework, with names of the twelve apostles embroidered thereon. Thus decked with finery at the expense of his two special disciples, and feasting on the choicest dainties, under pretext of sacraments, he lived upon, and with them."

He prepared, with the money of his friends, to build the new Jerusalem, and went to one of the leading platemakers of New York to have a complete set of silver made with the lion of Judah as a crest. He carried an arm which he called the Sword of Gideon, but from which he failed to delete the *e pluribus unum* of the United States army. He was also provided with a six-foot rule to measure off property in Paradise. His preaching was extraordinary, his utterance was always in sharp sentences without exhortation or appeal. He had a nose for abominations. "They who teach women are of the wicked. The communion is all nonsense; so is prayer. Eating a nip of bread and drinking a little wine won't do any good. . . . Everything that has the smell of woman will be destroyed. Woman is the capsheaf of the abomination of desolation—full of all deviltry. In a short time the world will take fire and dissolve—it is combustible already. . . . When you see anyone wring the neck of a fowl, instead of cutting off its head, he has not got the Holy Ghost. All who eat swine's flesh are of the devil; and just as certain as he eats it, he will tell a lie in less than half an hour. If you eat a piece of pork, it will go crooked through you, and the Holy

it was born, proved to be a girl). Mr. Folger was further persuaded by another argument. If Mrs. Folger had found him lacking in attack, he himself could not resist the promise of a younger mate. Matthias sent him to bring down from Albany the daughter left behind when the prophet began his travels. Folger was prompt in execution of this plan but, on the way back, the daughter of Matthias revealed that she had very recently been married to a Mr. Laisdell. In spite of this, and in spite of the presence of a younger child who made the journey with them, Folger and the daughter of Matthias slept together on the way back to Sing Sing where the family was temporarily residing. Several days after they arrived, the child spoke out. Matthias whipped his daughter crying, "Take death with every stroke," but eventually declared that the adultery which had been practiced nullified his daughter's marriage, and she was therefore wedded to Folger. This was the position of affairs when Mr. Pierson died.

The events preceding his death were eventually looked into by the Grand Jury which discovered that just before the victim's last attack, he had eaten freely of some blackberries in the picking and preparing of which Matthias and—it was hinted—his confederates had something to do. Matthias had eaten no blackberries, nor had Mrs. Folger, as she was not feeling well. Matthias preached throughout the meal and, near the close, Mrs. Folger managed to interject the remark that he had eaten no berries. He thereupon left the table in anger saying that the sons were honored and the daughters blessed themselves in the Father's house, but that the Father did not receive the honor due him. He proceeded to preach with vehemence and severity until a late hour of the night. The next day Mr. Pierson became violently sick. Catherine, another inmate of the house, who had also eaten blackberries the day before, suffered from nausea and displayed all of Mr. Pierson's symptoms with the exception of epilepsy. Matthias denounced Mrs. Folger and a negro servant for encouraging the devil by ministering to the invalids. Mr. Pierson himself had accepted Matthias's idea that disease was the work of the devil and should be exorcised, not cured. For a few days Mr. Pierson was alternately better and worse. (The woman Catherine rested and dieted for a few days, escaping the attention of Matthias, and recovered.) On the following Monday morning,

a breakfast consisting of coffee, bread and shad was taken to Mr. Pierson. It was the last meal the poor man ate. That night he was in great pain. Matthias, engaged in conversation, ordered a warm bath for the dying man, in the midst of which the colored woman, perceiving the symptoms of a fit, slapped Mr. Pierson in the face, saying, "Come out of your hellish sleep." Some time later, Mrs. Folger ventured to say to Matthias that she felt uneasy about Pierson especially as no one had given him water to drink. Matthias thereupon took up a pint pitcher of water and, with the help of the colored woman, from a height of four or five feet, poured it into the mouth of Mr. Pierson. This caused "shocking noises or gurglings in the throat" and Mr. Pierson's fits came in rapid succession. Shortly after one o'clock, Mrs. Folger heard Matthias going into Pierson's room. She followed and met him coming out again. Mr. Pierson, he said, was dead. Even before the funeral, when Mr. Folger spoke of Pierson's death, Matthias said that he would serve all his enemies in like manner, giving Folger to understand that, at a certain moment when Matthias had found Pierson objectionable, he had gone into his own room and made a sign, "as simple as the turn of a spoke of a chair," which had sealed Pierson's doom. Mrs. Folger's testimony before the coroner was too frank to please Matthias and difficulties about the dead man's property, caused an estrangement between them. Mrs. Folger resumed marital relations with her husband, but Matthias continued to live with them and was there on a day when he alone escaped a violent attack of sickness. Mrs. Folger remembered that, on that day, Matthias had refused to drink coffee. From that time, a member of the Folger family superintended the making of breakfast.

Matthias was approaching the end. Once he prayed for the restoration of his decayed teeth, and again that his eyesight might be what it was in his youth. The second of these prayers, he claims, was answered. But his troubles continued. His daughter's husband came to Sing Sing and roused the village to a siege of Matthias, to compel him to give up the young woman. Before a magistrate, Matthias denounced the Lutheran minister who had performed the marriage, on the grounds that the minister was a devil and that the devil could not marry. In spite of his magnificent appearance, hypnotic eye, and princely dress, Matthias was in danger from the mob;

but the authorities protected him and he managed to escape from the village with the loss, a second time, of his beard. He then returned to New York and Folger, now convinced that he had been swindled, began a prosecution. Matthias fled, was captured, and his trunks were examined. "Linen shirts of exquisite fineness, the wristbands fringed with delicate lace, silk stockings and handkerchiefs, kid and other gloves, and a great variety of similar articles filled one of the trunks; while the other contained his gold-mounted cocked hat, an olive cloak of the finest texture, lined throughout with velvet and silk; a new green and brown frock-coat of similar quality, the former heavily embroidered with gold, and the latter with silver, in the form of stars, with a large sun on one breast and seven stars on the other; two merino morning dresses; and other rich et cæteras 'too tedious to mention.' But the rarest articles of all were two night caps, made of linen cambric, folded in the form of a miter, richly embroidered—one with the names of the twelve apostles written around it, and 'Jesus Matthias' adorning the front in more conspicuous characters: the other surrounded with the names of the twelve tribes, the front embellished the same as the other. The whole betokened the utmost extravagance and lavish expenditure of money and labor; and months must have been spent by female hands (probably those of some one or more of his disciples) in ornamenting and making up the apparel of this dainty impostor."

The civil suit against Matthias was not prosecuted, as the Folgers by this time wanted nothing so much as to escape publicity, but Matthias was held for trial on the charge of murder. He had incautiously said to a friend that Pierson would not have died if he had not lost faith in him (Matthias). He had perceived that the spirit of truth was departing from Pierson and, as for the blackberries, he admitted that he had picked them, but having discovered that there was a curse upon them that year had not eaten any himself. He suggested that, in spite of the blackberries, Pierson might have been saved if he had not transferred his faith elsewhere. On the 16th of April, 1835, Matthias was brought to trial and, while in jail, issued a decree commanding all farmers to lay aside their plows, for "there shall be no more sowing in the earth until I, the Twelfth and last of the Apostles, am delivered out of the house of bondage." He also prophesied that the village of White Plains,

where the trial was being held, would sink under the ground if he were convicted. He protested the competence of the courts on the grounds that evidence had been taken in secret before the Grand Jury, and that all secret institutions "are cursed of God and were dissolved five years ago." (He meant his own announcement of 1830.) His raving and gestures were so violent that he was ordered removed from the court room, but, from the door, continued to shriek out the word "dissolved, dissolved, dissolved" until he was carried away.

According to one account, a competent physician found evidence of poisoning in the body of Mr. Pierson, but there was conflicting testimony and a clever lawyer managed to bar the question whether Pierson's death was caused by want of care. The court instructed the Jury which obediently returned a verdict of "not guilty." Judge Ruggles, however, taking up the accusation of brutality to Matthias's daughter, sentenced him, with the name of impostor, to three months in the county jail. He reappears fleetingly in the house of Joseph Smith, the Mormon leader, calling himself Joshua the Jewish minister, wearing a sea green frock coat and pantaloons. To Joseph Smith, already in the possession of the Mormon revelation, Joshua-Matthias spoke even less coherently than to his early disciples. He said "that all the railroads, canals, and other improvements are performed by the spirits of the resurrection. The silence spoken of by John the Revelator, which is to be in heaven for the space of half-an-hour, is between 1830 and 1851, during which time the judgments of God will be poured out, after that time there will be peace."

Eventually, Matthias confessed his identity and lectured to the Mormons. Joseph Smith acknowledged that Matthias made some very excellent remarks, "but his mind was evidently filled with darkness. . . . He tarried until Wednesday, 11th, after breakfast, when I told him, that my God told me, that his god was the devil, and I could not keep him any longer, and he must depart. And so I, for once, cast out the devil in bodily shape, and I believe a murderer. . . ."

From that point on, Matthias is lost in obscurity. The two writers, William L. Stone and Gilbert Vail, who are the chief authorities, finished their work while Matthias was still in jail. His

career made such a sensation in New York that controversy raged about every point and, in Stone's account, many of the important names are veiled by transposed initials or asterisks. Whether he imposed himself on others later in life is doubtful. He had already been the Messiah and suffered a sufficient martyrdom to satisfy his deluded spirit.

Contemporary writers, opposed to the violence and hysteria of religious excitement, used him as a terrible example. His blasphemy and adultery were equally condemned. Stone compared him to Simon Magus and, more closely, to John of Leyden, the leader of the sect of Munster Anabaptists. Here too were found divine commission, the luxuries of dress and table, and oriental versatility in sexual relations. John, like Matthias, condemned all other prophets since the time of Christ and held that he alone could understand the scriptures. A parallel nearer home was found in the career of a discharged army officer named Cochrane who began his imposture by calling himself a clergyman in the hope of getting a night's lodging and a meal. Cochrane was far more deliberate in his impositions and far less deluded than Matthias. His pretension to being a minister was accepted. He soon had a large following in New Hampshire. And even skeptical observers confess to the mysterious power "like animal magnetism," which he exerted. Cochrane, too, believed that he was to be the father of a holy child but, as women continued to attract him, he multiplied his offspring until they became a race of holy men. The women he seduced were many. The story of Matthias is a more complicated record of delusion and imposition, strangely intermingled. The center of it involves five people in the course of only five years, but it exhibits almost in every detail the dangers of religious hysteria when "ancient wisdom and austere control" have departed.

† Among the prominent European authors, were Byron and Tanna-hill, author of *Jessie, the Flower of the Dumbline.* † The death of Marcos Bozzaris stirred the country and public concerts were given to aid the Greek Revolution. Byron's death was reported three months after it occurred, with an account of the destruction of his memoirs by Thomas Moore. † A new novel by Miss Porter, author of *Thaddeus of Warsaw* became popular and also *The Pilot* by the author of *The Pioneer;* the posthumous works of Percy Bysshe Shelley were going through the press, and Samuel Taylor Coleridge announced *The Wanderings of Cain.* † *The Ladies' Magazine* said "love is composed of all that is delicate in happiness and pleasure. . . . It does not appear from the writings of the ancients that they entertained the pure idea which we attach to love." † Three New York doctors made a successful expedition into New Jer-sey and brought back the skeleton of a mammoth. † Mr. Perkins' steam gun to supplant gun powder was patented. † In Memphis men went to hotels for their meals leaving their wives at home. In Cincinnati youths affected curled hair. Nearly everybody suffered from dyspepsia. The fa-vorite amusement was a Chamber of Horrors, and billiards and cards were forbidden by law. † To the annoyance of English travelers, the terms lady and gentleman were freely used without regard to rank. † The appearance of two French dancers in a western theater caused all the ladies to leave and the clergy to protest from the pulpit. † Robert Owen and the Reverend Alexander Campbell publicly debated the truth of all religion for fifteen sittings. † The dance Europeans called quadrille was named cotillion here. † Puddings, pies, and sweets were very popular.
† Pulverized starch was freely used as face powder; and women refused to wear muffs, or boots, or cotton stockings. City women were supposed to have extremely pretty feet but a great "want of tournure." † "The lovers of impassioned and classical numbers" derived gratification from the work of Mr. and Mrs. Brooks. † The prospectus of the Brooklyn Collegiate Institute included Latin through Horace and Tacitus, intel-lectual philosophy, critical reading of Young's poems, hydrostatics, gal-vanism, political economy, Evidences of Christianity, natural theology, treatise on the globes, mineralogy, astronomy, vocal music, and modern languages. † The standing army of the United States consisted of 6,000 men. Heroes of the Boston Tea Party denied that they were disguised as Indians. † In Missouri the only small change consisted of silver dollars cut into halves, quarters, and eighths.

# IX.

## The New Soul.

H IS effect on many types of men, on Tappans, Weld, Matthias, Noyes, and others makes Finney significant; his violence for the Lord makes him personally interesting. The other evangelists of his time and of the period following, lack his essential quality almost entirely. We hear of the Reverend A. B. Earle preaching more than seventeen thousand sermons, but the sample that survives is not particularly interesting. The Brooklyn *Daily Eagle* of the 12th of March, 1858, reports that Neptune Engine Company, No. 7, attended the Second Baptist church in a body to hear Earle preach on the text, "Where the Worm Dieth not and the Fire is not Quenched." "He thought nothing would grieve them more than to meet with a fire they could not put out. They would go home sorrowful at heart should such an event happen to them . . . but he would speak to them of a fire which could never be quenched. . . . That is remorse." Elder Jacob Knapp, a famous Evangelist in his day, seems to have had a readier wit; when a heckler asked, "Who was the devil's father?" Knapp retorted, "Young man, keep your own family record." A typical moderate was the Congregationalist, E. P. Hammond, known as the children's evangelist. He was himself "a child of prayer" and would often repeat the hymn

> "Alas and would my Saviour bleed
> And would my Sovereign die?
> Would he devote that sacred head
> For such a worm as I?"

On one occasion, however, he was suddenly inspired to repeat some less sacred verse—*The Charge of the Light Brigade*. There were those who considered this a bit theatrical, but Hammond was pragmatically justified for, the very next day, one of the survivors of the Six Hundred came to him, converted! He was accused of too great urgency in bringing children to an announcement of their decision for Christ, but he himself maintained that he was careful

to make them intelligent as to their decision and required of each child at least one scriptural reason for loving Christ. It was his intention to "bring a dash of Christian sunlight and a breath of free Christian courage and hope in every sermon."

Some of these evangelists worked in the leaderless revivals which followed the panic of 1857. For several years money and the promise of money had poured out of California. A period of unprecedented speculation and spending set in. Throughout the year 1856, everything in America was booming and statistics were broadcast to prove that it was the most prosperous year in the history of the world. Inflation was excessive. In the summer of 1857, Western business firms began to fail and Eastern banks drained by the West slowly succumbed. On the 14th of October, 1857, the crash came, precipitated by the failure of the Ohio Life Insurance Company. In the state of Maine alone, thirty-seven wildcat banks failed. The new tariff and inflated currency were both blamed. As in the panic of 1837, "shin-plasters" appeared. These were little I.O.U.'s given generally as change in the course of small transactions and ranged in amount from 1 cent to several dollars, redeemable when the banks resumed payment in specie. It was, says a writer of the period, a time of coldness and deadness in the church and Dr. Thompson, the historian of revivalism, noting that times of failure and depression are favorable for the impression of the truth, makes the quaint observation that the "Holy Ghost in his free sovereignty does not despise the help of circumstances." (Finney comments with enthusiasm on this revival but, characteristically, omits all reference to the financial panic.) The business depression was seized upon by a Mr. Lanpheir, pastor of the Reformed (Dutch) church, who proposed noon-day prayer meetings for the business men who were sitting in nervous idleness in their empty offices. These were a great success. Every church in the downtown district in New York held such meetings daily while, by "systematic visitations," an attempt was made to penetrate into every house in the city and discover the religious condition of every family. Although the scrutiny began in the slums, it finally reached the brownstone fronts and "Fifth Avenue itself was not left to be exempt." But there was nothing to shock the fashionable world in this revival. There were no "spiritual jerks" and no fanaticism. From the me-

tropolis, the revival spread through the state. At one time, two hundred towns and cities were holding similar revivals. The seeds were scattered westward so that Cleveland held meetings from six in the morning till nine at night; and some who came to Chicago on business "have become so distressed about their condition as sinners against God that they have entirely forgotten their business in the earnestness of their desire · for salvation." There was "universal unction manifest in Washington." It is also on record that "nearly all the students of Yale college were anxious." During this revival, for the first time, "the Holy Spirit seems to occupy with divine power and glory all the common channels of man's intercourse with man . . . the electric telegraph conveys the thrill of Christian sympathy with the tidings of abounding grace . . ." and, it was reported, without charge.

§

Finney says in his biography that, if he had had a sword in his hand, he could have cut down "the slain" as fast as they fell. The warrior of the Lord was to be followed by the commercial traveler. It was literally as a salesman that Dwight Lyman Moody began his career. "The biggest human," as Drummond calls him, sold more shoes in a Chicago store than any other clerk and a biographer assures us that, had he remained in that business, he might have ended his life as head of a shoe trust. The trust he filled was of a more exalted nature.

Moody was born in a Unitarian family, in 1837, but the decorum and indifference of the Unitarian bodies did not long appeal to this "go-getter," born before his time. In Chicago, he attached himself to a Congregational church and, as the attendance was unsatisfactory, he rented four pews and dragooned enough young men to fill them every Sunday. Then he began to recruit children for the Sunday school and, presently, he founded a school of his own in "the Sands," surrounded by saloons and gambling dens, and established the North Mission. Some ten years earlier, the Young Men's Christian Association had been "organized by a band of active consecrated young men" in New York. It was at first an object of suspicion, but Moody saw it as a beautiful agency and adopted it in Chicago where he became its secretary and sexton. At

that time, it was his habit to let no day go by without stopping at least one person in the street and inquiring about the state of his soul. One night, as he was going home, he remembered that he had not done his good deed for that day, so he spoke to the first passer-by who later said of him, "Moody is doing more harm than any ten men in Chicago." Eventually, however, the man apologized and asked Moody to pray for his soul. When the Civil War began, Moody could be seen, night after night, at Camp Douglas, "going from tent to tent, striving to bring the soldiers under the influence of divine grace." It was as a result of his labors that the first Y.M.C.A. building in Chicago was built. A few weeks later, it burned and, without the loss of a moment, Moody collected enough money for another. His chorister, Bliss, having been killed at Ashtabula ("Heaven's choir needed another sweet voice"), the collaboration of Moody and Sankey began. Together they went to Britain to win ten thousand souls for Christ and, although the Scotch were suspicious of the small harmonium which Sankey used to keep time, suspecting it of being an organ with a devil in every pipe, the Holy Ghost was poured out upon their meetings. They crossed to Belfast, because they wanted Ireland for Christ, and, from March to July, they held meetings in London, where the Earl of Shaftesbury (in a slightly ambiguous sentence) said that "if Mr. Sankey had done no more than to teach the people to sing 'Hold the Fort,' he would have conferred an inestimable blessing on the British Empire."

Sankey's hymns were as well adapted to Moody's melodrama of conversion as "The Brewers Big Horses Can't Run Over Me" is to Billy Sunday's. In spite of reference back to David and the psalms, singing, in Protestant churches, had been called error, apostasy, human tradition, and carnal worship, and Bishop Berkeley's offer of an organ was once declined by a worried church because it was an instrument of the devil. Yet some songs were irresistible:

> Ye monsters of the bubbling deep
> Your maker's praises spout;
> Up from the sands ye coddlings creep,
> And wag your tails about.

After Watt's and the four thousand hymns of Wesley, singing at revivals was fully established and we have records of Philip

Phillips, the singing pilgrim, and of Paul Bliss whose melodeon Edward Eggleston put into a book. Every event and every form of exhortation was used by the hymn writers. "O, mean may seem this house of clay" was written by Gill, "fresh from the contemplation of the anarchy and misery of Shelley's life." "Hold the fort, I am coming—W. T. Sherman," was the source of another hymn, and Sankey put "a sweet, wild melody" to Elizabeth Clephane's *Ninety and Nine*.

In 1875, enthusiasts found four weeks insufficient for one of Moody's revivals, when he preached at Dr. Talmage's tabernacle in Brooklyn; but he had to hurry on to Philadelphia, for John Wanamaker had bought the railroad station at 13th and Market streets and, cannily calculating that his future patrons ought to be made familiar with the new site, offered it to Moody for the Cause of Christ, in which the eminent merchant was a livelong enthusiast. A few months later, Wanamaker and Dom Pedro, the former king of Brazil, were both on the platform of the old Hippodrome in New York which had served successively as a menagerie, as a railroad depot, and as the home of Gilmore's concerts. "Even a great emperor," cried Moody, "cannot save his soul with all his wealth and power unless he bows himself at Christ's feet and accepts him." Dom Pedro, in an audible voice, gave instant and hearty assent. In all, Moody spoke effectively to a million and a half people, in spite of the disconnected and rambling style to which the New York press objected. Favorable accounts also appeared. "Make him the best-read preacher in the world," said one paper, "and he would instantly lose half his power. Put him through a systematic training in systematic theology and you fasten big logs of fuel to the driving-wheels of his engine. . . . We shall not soon forget his incomparable frankness, his broad denominationalism, his sledge-hammer gestures, his profuse diction which stops neither for colons nor commas, his trueness which never becomes conventional, his naturalness which never whines, his abhorrence of Pharisaism and of ecclesiastical Machiavellism, his mastery of his subject, his glorious self-confidence, his blameless life, and his unswerving fealty to his conscience and to his work."

Moody's methods were extremely simple and his comparisons were always to known things in the daily life of his hearers:

"Will you stay to-night and accept this invitation? Don't make light of it. I can imagine some of you saying, 'Well, I never got so low as to make light of religion.' Suppose I get an invitation to dinner from a citizen of Chicago for to-morrow and I don't answer it; I tear the invitation up. Would not that be making light of it? Suppose you pay no attention to the invitation to-night; is not that making light of it? Would anyone here be willing to write out an excuse something like this: 'The Tabernacle, October 29th. To the King of Heaven: While sitting in the Tabernacle to-day I received a very pressing invitation from one of your servants to sit at the marriage supper of the Son of God. I pray you have me excused.' Is there one person in this assembly would take his pen and write his name at the bottom of it? Is there a person whose right hand would not forget its cunning, and whose tongue would not cleave to his mouth if he were trying to do it? Well, you are doing this if you get up and go right out after you have heard the invitation. Who will write this? 'To the Lord of Lords and King of Glory: While sitting in the Tabernacle this beautiful Sabbath evening, October 29th, 1876, I received a pressing invitation from one of your servants to be present at the marriage supper. I hasten to accept.' Will anyone sign it by the grace of God? . . . Are there not some here to-night who will accept that invitation?"

When Moody went to Boston, a Tabernacle was built for him on Tremont Street. Like Finney before him, he felt that Boston had been too daintily handled by revivalists who stood in terror of its reputation for intellectualism and who did not dare to come out, in the full fire of old Christianity, against established Unitarianism. He told the Bostonians that they had the same old nature that all sinners have and brutally confronted them with a God who, he said, "could shake Boston as easily as a mother shakes her child." Evangelism had traveled a long way from the terror and majesty of Jonathan Edwards.

§

A longer way still had been traversed by hundreds of unwearied evangelists before the technique of organizing revivals reached the point to which Moody had brought it. The propaganda in the press began months in advance. Committees of every sort were es-

tablished and people were made at once familiar with Moody's method and expectant of his miracles. Thousands of semi-miraculous instances of conversion were reported and the word NOW in huge letters was prominently displayed. Moody, during the revival at Boston, brought Frances Willard with him to speak at outlying meetings and, when attendance fell off, he appointed no less than two thousand men and women to make personal visitations and bring people to the tabernacle. Seventy thousand families were promptly visited and the attendance picked up again. His energy was exceptional. He preached mornings, afternoons, and evenings, held inquiry meetings, and went out to the crowded corners of city streets to hold prayer meetings for workers in the dry goods and clothing trades, for cabmen, grocers, fishermen, and furniture dealers. He held meetings "for women only." Above everything, he was urgent. "Now, now, now is the time to repent," he seemed to cry. "To-morrow will be too late. To-day is bargain day in salvation. To-morrow the price goes up. Look, it's yours for the asking, but if you refuse it now the price will rocket up. Come in on the ground floor and get your dividends from the first day. This offer may be withdrawn at any moment. It's your big chance." He had to face the demon of evolution. Into the question box which was a feature of each meeting, came the query: "Why do the evangelists know so little about science? Without a moment's hesitation and with an enthusiasm which was positively electric he cried out, 'Because we have something better.' Of course there was nothing left of that question." He had to face the accusation of ignorance and emotionalism. It was said that his revivals lacked those elements of law and conscience which had characterized the earlier ones. He brushed this aside with a story of a man who had been acquitted of a crime, became converted, and confessed his guilt, cheerfully bearing a sentence of three years in a penitentiary. He drowned out opposition with a shout of "harvest-home." He had five hundred singers and thousands of workers. He collected vast sums of money and—to the surprise of a modern reader—it is generally understood that he devoted this money, not to his own purposes, but to the Y.M.C.A. and to the spread of the gospel. When people talked to him of dignity and of doctrine, he replied with a vast spectacular melodrama

of salvation and, at the end of it, amid hoarsely cheering multitudes, he eclipsed himself through a trapdoor on the platform.*

He was, according to a hostile critic, a past master in the art of hypnotism; but, if so, it was hypnotism used as an element in the drama which he staged.

§

After Moody and his immediate successors, the swine ran headlong into the sea. Even if they came within the scope of this study, it would hardly be worth while to continue the record of decline and degeneration. One can only note the stages and wonder what the causes were. For nearly two centuries evangelism has run like a prairie fire—this is the usual revivalist term—over the United States. It has been a blessing or an affliction, as prairie fires may be, but the notable thing to the detached observer is the remorseless falling off of revivalism, not in numbers, but in dignity and in passion. We have noted that revivals had their source in a great intellect and an austere soul. From Edwards as a beginning, we mark the slow degeneration of all his excellent qualities and, as a natural parallel, the growth and exaggeration of all his weaknesses. Whatever is disciplined and calls for ardor and devotion is shuffled out of sight, and the cards that do turn up are either sinister or tawdry. If there was morbidity in Edwards, it was controlled by a severe intellectual discipline. In the later revivalists it breaks into a deliberately evoked hysteria, adopted rather from the bucolic camp-meetings than from the theological thunders of Edwards or Wesley or Whitefield. In the same period the organization of revivalism, the business of creating fervor and frenzy, was perfected. The great tabernacle and the choir and the advertising and whipped-up excitement of the present day have developed in perfect harmony with the intellectual vulgarity and the spiritual barrenness of the later revivalists. In the perspective of time, with Billy Sunday as foreground, Dwight Moody seems a giant of decency and intelligence; but if we compare his characteristic utterances with those of Edwards, the result is pitiful; and from Moody to the present day the decline is headlong and unbroken. The camp-meetings were "a noise and a flash and a sudden flame." Omitting them we can trace the decline of revivalism

* At least once, at the end of the great Chicago revival.

from Edwards to Finney, from Finney to Moody, from Moody to the present day. We find that the Sundays and McPhersons and Uldine Utleys of our own time are the inheritors of the evangelists of the past. They inherit, however, because there are no direct descendants, and what they inherit is only the débris of a great estate. The revivalists of the 1820's and 30's were the last to have any profound effect on the social and intellectual life of the American people. The penitential outbreak in 1857, after the panic of that year, does not appear to have had any serious effect on the progress of Abolition. After that, the revivals besides their personal effects in the lives of individual converts seem to have had no social effects except to encourage whatever was negative and prohibitory in the nature of the American reformer. Out of the 1830 revivals, came colleges and cults; the succeeding ones "make no pretense to intellectual eminence and scholarship sublime." If they created or encouraged a Sunday school league, their object seemed to be fulfilled.

There must be significant reasons for this decline in the quality and in the effectiveness of American revivalism. Obviously, everything in the social history of the country can be claimed as a cause. The change in the racial composition, the changes in economic status; the triumph of the mechanical arts and the slow progress of scientific theory; the very cults which had their source in evangelism; the spread of education and the tremendous impulses to secularism given by press and school; even sports and lithography may have contributed. In a sense everything which has interested the American and occupied his thoughts, everything which has given him pleasure and withdrawn him from the pursuit of sanctity; everything which has fed and clothed and prospered him and removed him from the shadow of fear, has helped to make him irreligious and to make the work of the evangelist harder. But after all these things have been noted, the suspicion remains that some of the causes of its decline were inherent in the nature of revivalism itself. The system changed. It adapted itself to the dominant mood of the country. It became big business. It flung itself into the tabloids. It created its own scandals and tabernacles and radio stations. Nevertheless, some of the old phenomena persisted. The preaching of Uldine Utley parallels the testimony of little girls

at the camp-meetings. The recent outbreak of Pentecostalism in the
Calvary Baptist Church of New York, where the son of the pastor
spoke in strange tongues and men and women writhed in prolonged
agony, calls us back to the very first days of the descent of the Spirit
in America. Yet there is a difference, hidden, internal. To uncover
it one has to disregard the outward manifestations entirely, and inquire into the motives of revivalism, its secret springs and its ob-
scurer meanings.

§

What were they after, these tireless and angry artillery-men of
the Gospel? They themselves would have said that they were working for the regeneration of mankind, for the quick coming of
Christ; but they had a more immediate end in view. With all their
shouting and thumping, with their cries, promises, and threats, they
were trying to effect one of the most delicate of psychological crises
through which the human soul can pass, to bring about a momentous change in the spiritual nature, to overthrow the accepted system of purposes and habits by which men lived and to substitute another. They tried to reproduce in masses and in a single moment of
time the psychological experience which the great saints have gone
through in solitude and after long travail. Purely for the purpose
of contrast, the rapture of the saint and the thrashing and foaming
of the hysterical moron at a Kentucky revival may be accepted as
the two extremes of conversion. The danger in this view is that it
takes a human experience out of the range of the normal human
being. In spite of the grand pioneer work of James in *The Varieties
of Religious Experience,* he is a little unsatisfactory because he has
chosen his examples (for a very excellent reason) at these extremes.
The obstinate agnostic rejoices in this and dismisses all conversions
as manifestations of nervous or sexual disorders. But scientists have
shattered this theory as convincingly as they have broken down the
revivalist's claim of universal inspiration. Neither explanation accounts for the universality of the phenomenon. Conversion has been
found in some form among savage tribes and in the experience of
intellectuals. It has worked on happy sinners and on the morosely
pure. The mechanism of the revival has tended so to debase it that
intelligent people generally look upon conversion as an adolescent

Eng'd by H.B. Hall & Sons, 62 Fulton. St N.Y.

C. G. Finny.

exercise or as a manifestation of that form of virtue which has its source in envy or sterility. But we can understand neither the success of revivalism, nor its terrible abuses, unless we have a more ordinary conception of its crisis. It is a natural thing, a process through which, in one form or another, millions of human beings have passed. What its nature is I propose to indicate neither psychologically nor doctrinally, but by two parallels, both of them extremely obvious. Conversion is a drama. It is also a rather formalized counterpart to a process of psychoanalysis.

James' analysis of conversion reduces it essentially to two elements. First an uneasiness, the sense that there is *something wrong about us;* and second, a solution of this uneasiness, in the sense that we are *saved from the wrongness* by making proper connection with higher powers. The something wrong is interpreted by the doctrinaires of Christianity as a sense of our separation from God and of our guilt before him because of man's first disobedience. The doctrinaires of psychoanalysis interpret it as the lack of harmony between our desires and our ability to express them. James himself suggests that there is lack of harmony between various mental systems which make up our conscious and subconscious lives. In all of these cases, in any interpretation, we may say that the uneasiness is due to a conflict, either within ourselves, or between ourselves and another power; and conflict is the essence of drama. The solution comes when the conflict ceases, when there is harmony within us, when our conflicts have been resolved, when our relations with God or nature or the world are harmonious. Such a solution corresponds with the catharsis of the classical tragedy. It is some momentous turn in the course of the drama of our life. And, when we think of the psychopathic cases, we can say, with a modern sense added to the words of Aristotle, that such a catharsis purges us of pity and terror. The solution of our mortal uneasiness is a deliverance (escape is the favorite word, at the moment) from disharmony and the sense of sin. In the Christian system, it is accepted through the intercession of a power outside ourselves. In psychoanalysis, it is effected by bringing up and releasing certain complexes from the depths of the unconscious. These two symbols are not as far apart as they may seem. James warns us that "it is one of the peculiarities of invasions from the subconscious region to take on objective ap-

pearances." If we are conscious of being blocked in our path by a sense of sin and cry out, "Who shall roll the stone away?", it matters very little in one sense whether Christ or the psychoanalyst is the intermediary.

According to certain divines, no ethical life is possible if we are not possessed by this sense of our own guilt. There are no doubt a happy few so utterly healthy-minded and so fortunately placed in the world that they have no sense of strain or hindrance, no feeling of futility, no frustrations and no expectations which they cannot fulfill. Their bodies live in a perpetual state of animal health and happiness and, if they ever uncover their soul to the eye of any save the most expert psychoanalyst, he is likely to be baffled and, rather·pathetically, to announce that they "have no complexes." At worst such people suffer only from the incorrigible hostility of *things*. They lack money a little, or their mistresses are unfaithful, or the last bottle of wine was slightly "corked." If they have any sin to regret, it is a specific sin. They have failed to attend mass regularly, or were absent without leave, or left town without paying the butcher, or did not marry the girl. But of *Weltschmerz* they know nothing whatever. They have no great abstract "moral hangovers." They may know regret, but hardly remorse. Repentance sits lightly and gracefully upon them. The others, and in northern countries they tend to be overwhelmingly in the majority, have to be "born again." This phrase, the special sense of which James borrowed from Francis W. Newman, is particularly applicable in the phenomenon of conversion. All the Christian phrases point to the same psychological facts. In conversion one is "born again," or regenerated, after having gone through a death of the spirit in sin. The man who feels the need of letting the old Adam within him die out, may approach the matter easily. He may say to himself as Luther did, "Martin, thou shalt not be utterly without sin, for thou hast flesh; thou shalt therefore feel the battle thereof." In this way he may make the best of both worlds and intensify his aliveness by enjoying the struggle between his lust of experience and his desire for purity. Or he may come to this crisis with such an appalling sense of his own ugliness and unworthiness that everything he does seems tainted and corrupt and nothing can save him but the grace of God.

We can see a little more clearly into the matter if we substitute

other words for the sense of sin, and banish from our minds all association with the seventh commandment and the denunciations of moralists. If for the Protestant sense of guilt, we substitute the Hellenic feeling of life as a magnificent contest between man and fate in which man may fight gloriously, but is certain to be defeated; or if we substitute the feeling which many noble and healthy men have had that life is largely made up of woe, that it is all trivial when it is not terrible; or, even the modern tragic sense of life in which we say that, though life is tragic, the tragedy itself gives us deep satisfaction: in any of these cases we still come back to the feeling that, if we could be "born again," we could lose the sense of tragedy and emerge into a happier world. We listen to an extremely successful man, such as Goethe, worshiped by a nation, adored by a sex, and admired by the world, all in his own lifetime, and we hear him say that, at bottom, his life has been "nothing but pain and burden," and he can affirm that "during the whole of my seventy-five years I have had four weeks of genuine well-being." If to Goethe life was nothing more than "the perpetual rolling of a rock that must be raised up again forever," what can it be for the common run of mankind? The observer who withdraws from religious controversy can note with amusement the irony of the last century, in which all the Scriptural authorities for universal damnation were destroyed by scientists at the very moment when science was creating hells of its own: the hell of the struggle for existence, the hell of heredity and, last of all, the hell of the unconscious. The doctrine of predestination goes out and the doctrine of prenatal influence comes in, to check whatever grandiose illusion a man may have of his own freedom. Before there is an end to determinism, we begin to believe that the taboos of our primal ancestors and the sights and sounds of our infancy can create the "immitigability of our mortal predicament." One might as well be damned with Calvin as with Schopenhauer, by Edwards as well as by Freud. We want deliverance. The energetic want only deliverance from difficulties; the feeble, deliverance from sin; the merely neurotic, deliverance from themselves. It remained for a psycho-analyst to assure us that, deep within ourselves, all of us crave, from the day of our birth, deliverance from life itself; that death is not only the end of life, but its purpose and culmination.

§

I suggest these variations on the theme of conversion merely because they have more currency at the moment than the sense of sin. All of them suggest the same conclusion and most of them can be traced to a discovery made centuries ago by religious leaders and fortified recently by psychology, namely that there are more things in the heaven and earth of our own minds than we are aware of. It is to the tangle of emotions lying in the hinterland of the mind that many religions appeal. We are timid and we would like to swagger. We are promiscuous and covet purity. We are austere and dream voluptuously. We are happy and the sadness of mortality overcomes us; we cannot reconcile ourselves to the circumstance that birth lies so close to death. These things lie under the surface of our consciousness and produce discords which we spend our lives trying to resolve.

The return to harmony, the sensation of rightness may be achieved by conversion. The problem is answered, the music returns to its dominant. All this may be a response to our unconscious prayers but, with the intense feeling we have of our own significance, we like to ennoble our sense of deliverance. After we have landed, we magnify the waves which tossed us about. We blacken our sins when we pray for redemption. We thrill to the last-minute rescue. We can only triumph completely if our adversary is strong. If tragedy is to be great, the personality of the antagonists must rise to an absolute pitch of intensity. The action must become so developed that every imaginable force is put into play. Only then can a final impulse give the turn which the drama must take. In conversion this means that the sense of sin must be acute. One must need regeneration and not be able to live a moment longer without it. The triumph of Protestant doctrine is that it encourages precisely this tendency in man. The Catholic church encourages an easy-going and ritualistic absolution. Protestantism emphasizes the other side, and lets it be known that the one sheep that was lost and found again is more precious than the ninety-nine which never strayed. It was for the unrighteous that Christ died. Indeed, without them, his sacrifice would have been empty and men might well cry out, "Now is there nothing serious in mortality." Ignobly conceived, as it usually was in revivals, this doctrine brings us only to the level of the melodrama with the heroine bound to the railroad

track, or to the novel in which things grow impossibly black before
the dawn. But, in essence, it gives a sense of tragedy in which magnificence and dignity are at their highest in the opposition of great
forces, when evil must be all evil and good all good, in a supreme
encounter.

From Jonathan Edwards and his wife, from Finney and others,
we have had reports on the state of bliss which comes when the
struggle is ended. The sense of estrangement is over and, just as
to them inanimate objects seem transfigured, the inner life is lived
on a higher plane of almost rapturous serenity. The old personality
has crumbled away. The stubborn will to remain one's self and not
to yield even to the highest, has at last broken down. The long
struggle is over and the convert, becoming partly a saint, lives in a
new world. I use the term higher because that is how it seems to
the convert himself. He cannot conceive that he could have been
changed except by a miracle, or that he has surrendered to anything less than a superhuman agency. Even if salvation has come
from the depths of his own consciousness, he externalizes it and
throws it like a huge shadow against the background of the infinite.
He cannot allow that it is natural or unimportant. Part of his own
drama is to insist that his personality was altered and sanctified by
a spiritual flash of lightning. Conversion must be instantaneous.
John Wesley himself never knew a single case in which deliverance from sin came gradually. Later revivalists often insisted that,
if you could not say *when* you were converted, you were probably
not converted. That instantaneous flash had to come to strike down
the evil in man and to uplift the good. To pass from an interest in
collecting postage stamps to an interest in collecting books, from one
love affair to another, from selling bonds to selling motor cars, or
to grow gradually less enthusiastic about tennis and more about
solitaire—these are also changes in emotional excitement; but the
change of conversion rejects all similarity with them. In conversion,
the whole life we had denied takes possession of us. We live by a
fresh system of values and everything is new and clean. But it may
be noted that even if the lower self should suddenly rise up, the
resulting freshness and changed habits of living would give a similar exaltation and might cause the victim, particularly if he had not
been consciously working for such a change, to feel that a miracle

had happened. The debauchee and the ascetic, changing places in the night, would each feel that something supernatural had occurred.

In the ordinary meaning of conversion the new self is one to which the convert has aspired. He has been laden with sin and unworthiness and now he is delivered from evil and led no more into temptation. For a moment, the sense of being utterly without sin is dominant, and persuades the convert that his life is for once totally in harmony with a plan of existence nobler than his own. He feels himself in direct communion with the higher power to which he has prayed and which has saved him. In extreme cases he feels that no matter what happens, no matter what he does, he will sin no more. This is where the curtain falls on the completed play. It is the moment when the psychoanalyst dismisses his patient and the preacher gives the penitent a certificate or admits him to the Lord's Supper. He has been born again.

§

What the revivalist made of this delicate and intricate process is something of a miracle in itself. The two terms of James' analysis are still there, uneasiness is represented by our feeling of guilt for the sin of Adam, which is theoretically imputed to all of us. The solution is in repentance and acceptance of Christ as mediator. The Christian argument is closely knit and entirely logical within itself. There can be no other explanation of man's unhappiness than some great sin against the Almighty and there can be no release from this sense of our own depravity by any agency less divine than Christ, or by any sacrifice less precious than his death. The scientific attack on Genesis in the last century was therefore more important than any question of literal truth or divine inspiration. If Genesis falls, the whole system of salvation falls with it, and man becomes infinitely less hopeful than he ever has been in the dourest doctrines of Calvin. If Genesis, on any interpretation, remains and the divinity of Christ is challenged, the position is equally bad. For if Christ is not divine, he could not have taken upon himself the burden of sin from the time of Adam until the time of the Last Judgment. Nor can there be any virtue in Christ's atonement if it did not save us from actual hell hereafter. To be conscious of sin is absolutely the essential step. Without this sense we cannot know the agony of

being separated from God, which means that we cannot know God's power, or his goodness, or his glory. The churches based on ritual make this knowledge of God available to their adherents by way of the scriptures and the fulfillment of individual religious obligations —prayer, reading, and hearing God's word, observing holy days and doing ordained penance—and emphasize, in addition, the necessity of a pious and virtuous life. The evangelizing churches employ the drama of conversion. Being good and being devout are not enough; one must first be nailed on the cross of natural despair and agony, and then, in the twinkling of an eye, be miraculously released. The mystic power to save, which the High Church places in baptism and holy communion, is rejected; its discipline is not considered sufficient and the succession of the priesthood which alone can make it effective is challenged. The terrible example of Aaron Burr is always held up. According to the story, this grandson of Jonathan Edwards was made uneasy by a revival at Princeton and communicated his anxiety to Dr. Witherspoon who assured him that revivals were fanatical and that the established ritual was sufficient:

"Burr proceeded to drink in with avidity the reasonings of the French and English infidels, which were much in vogue at the time. These prepared him for the profligate habits which distinguished him through life, which procured his arraignment at the bar of his country for high treason, which involved him in his fatal duel with Hamilton, and which made him ever after an outcast and a vagabond on the earth. It causes a shudder to think that possibly that deprecating remark as to the revival made him the libertine, the duelist, the plotter against his government, the heartless seducer, and the victim of a supreme selfishness that he was. And it is an illustration of the sad consequences that may follow the utterance of one word against revivals."

Nor is the unaided endeavor of man himself considered sufficient to bring him grace. To the revivalist, crowding the penitents and urging them on to a decision, the spectacle of a man working for salvation and trusting to his own efforts is an abomination; it is setting up his will against the will of God. Whatever means of our own we are conscious of—the strength of our will, the power of our intellect—are the arms of Lucifer. Will and intellectual pride must

be broken down. We must abdicate our own pretense and accept the grace of God. We find the extreme version of this theory in the sects which believe that men must wait passively and never do anything to bring down the blessing of salvation, because whatever they do is an impertinence and casts a doubt upon the omnipotence of God. Other men become aware of the limitations of their intellect, as did John Humphrey Noyes. Some, like Finney, find that even self-scrutiny stands in the way of the holy spirit. But if man's work alone is insufficient, he has still much to do. He must repent of his sins and be willing to put his faith in Christ. The doctrine that man was not able to win salvation which was preached by Edwards was rejected by later revivalists who pounded and shouted and declared that man was able to do whatever God required of him. They only insisted that all he could do was not enough without Christ. They therefore were continually exalting and belittling the will in an alternation of extremes. The one thing they did not do was to control it. It is not surprising that half of the cults which sprang from the revivals were glorifications of the will.

To make the drama of salvation acute, the revivalists insisted upon the utter abasement of man before he could rise to the supreme heights in Christ. They were always holding man at the extremes of his potentialities and naturally they wanted the metal on which they worked to be as ductile as possible. They were well aware that moral regeneration without Christ could occur. The case of John B. Gough, the famous drunkard, has been cited as an example of conversion in which neither Christ nor God is mentioned. But in general such regeneration was dismissed as unsatisfactory. When the emotions were touched, one had proofs in pentecostal shoutings and orgiastic dances. Proofs became extremely important. Young Christians were supplied with little cards on which ten evidences of conversion were listed:

1. A full surrender of the will of God.
2. The removal of a burden of sin gradually or suddenly.
3. A new love to Christians and to Jesus.
4. A new relish for the word of God.
5. Pleasure in secret prayer, at least at times.
6. Sin or sinful thoughts will cause pain.
7. Desire and efforts for the salvation of others.

8. A desire to obey Christ in his commands and ordinances.
9. Deep humility and self-abasement.
10. A growing desire to be holy and like Christ.

And gradually, as revivalism grew in extent and the desire to gather in more and more sheaves became prominent, proofs of conversion grew to be more important than conversion itself.

§

It would be unfair not to mention again the fact that an earnest revivalist seriously believed in his conversions and believed that no matter how a man was brought to confess Christ, his confession was justified. It was a work of God, as Edwards said, greater than the whole seven days of creation. Some of them must really have believed that without hysteria there could be no genuine conviction of sin or regeneration. And yet it is easy to see that, as they substituted hysterical outbursts for the reasoned conversion of the soberer churches, hysteria itself became important without thought of its meaning. The revivalists naturally chose those methods by which they could excite the emotions and bring on crisis upon crisis of hysteria. People were struggling for conviction, their lives were desperately divided by an inner conflict, and they knew that acceptance of Christ gave peace. It is easy to see how they would whip themselves up into a frenzy of anxiety and eagerness and despair to imitate the frenzy they saw about them. The "jerks" themselves became a ritual.

The revivalists were always happy to work with the nervously unbalanced. Finney speaks of converting (curing) an insane woman and, throughout the literature of revivalism, we frequently find the deranged, the maniacal, the slow-witted, and the psychopathic. Such defectives were excellent kindling for the fire, peculiarly susceptible to the stirring up of primal fears in the depths of consciousness and to the imagery which appeals to the visceral centers. The phrases of revivalism seem at times to consist of nothing but reference to food and to sex. In the same way revivalists attacked the young and particularly the adolescent. The period of puberty with its stirrings of unsuspected forces, when the mind is filled with misgivings about the future, the evangelist found extremely receptive to his labors.

§

So much has been made of the parallel between the religious and the sexual impulses that it may be worth while to note a few corrective observations. An obvious one is that conversions are not limited to the period of adolescence. There are notable converts, like the brothers Wesley, who experienced it after thirty. But even if we think of these as intellectual or moral conversions, we have numerous records of emotional crises in full manhood. And there are countless conversions when the dominant motive is probably the fear of death. It is not possible to reject the connection between sexual excitement and religious hysteria; the evidence is too strong. Nor is it entirely an accident that the libertine, Casanova, passed as an abbot. And the Matthiases and Smiths and Cochranes we have met, all found some extreme form of religious excitement easily convertible to the uses of seduction. There is nothing alarming in this connection. It would seem to indicate only that the two emotions lie so close together at the very center of our being, and are both so concerned with tremendous objects, that they often work together and are sometimes interchanged. That at least would be a devout explanation were a zealot ever to admit the connection. A less favorable statement is made by Baring-Gould: "The religious passion verges so closely on the sexual passion, that a slight additional pressure given to it bursts the partition and both are confused in a frenzy of religious debauch." That libertines have used religion as a means, and that the religious have abused the sexual nature, are accepted facts. Yet it is not possible to delimit the phenomenon of conversion, by saying that it is always the result of a sexual disorder. After a long statistical study, Professor Edwin D. Starbuck, a pupil of James, could only formulate the tentative law that conversions are most likely to occur during periods of great bodily growth and suggest that conversion and puberty supplement each other, but do not actually coincide. James summarizes the results of this inquiry which indicates "how closely parallel in its manifestations the ordinary 'conversion' which occurs in young people brought up in evangelical circles is to that growth into a larger spiritual life which is a normal phase of adolescence in every class of human beings. The age is the same, falling usually between fourteen and seventeen. The symptoms are the same,—sense of incompleteness and imperfection; brooding, depression, morbid in-

trospection, and sense of sin; anxiety about the hereafter; distress over doubts, and the like. And the result is the same,—a happy relief and objectivity, as the confidence in self gets greater through the adjustment of the faculties to the wider outlook. In spontaneous religious awakening, apart from revivalistic examples, and in the ordinary storm and stress and moulting-time of adolescence, we also may meet with mystical experiences, astonishing the subjects by their suddenness, just as in revivalistic conversion. The analogy, in fact, is complete; and Starbuck's conclusion as to these ordinary youthful conversions would seem to be the only sound one. Conversion is in its essence a normal adolescent phenomenon, incidental to the passage from the child's small universe to the wider intellectual and spiritual life of maturity."

Starbuck also analyzed the motives of conversion and found that the fear of death and hell was higher when conversions took place in a revival than when they were brought about by other means, and that the non-revival conversions showed altruistic and moral motives more frequently than the revival ones.

§

The severest of preachers, or even the earliest revivalist, could not refuse to suffer little children to come unto Christ, but he exercised due caution and insisted upon delay and deliberation before accepting childish excitement as the equivalent of a true conviction. The cult of the child, which sprang up very early in the 19th century and led to experiments in discipline and education, helped to break down the Calvinist theory of infant damnation and, at the same time, exalted the child as the receiver and transmitter of God's word. To the evangelist the child was always another soul saved, a marvelous medium for jerks and gibberings, another item to be rung up on his cash register of sales. The original objectives and the methods of revivalism were both degenerating and in the process each helped the other to slip down until, at the end, the propriety of revivalism as a method was no longer accepted as self-evident. At a very early time Edwards had written: "It is worthy also of our further notice, that when many profane sinners, and formal professors of religion have been affrighted out of their present carelessness and stupidity by some astonishing terrors approach-

ing them, those religious appearances have not been so durable, nor
the real change of heart so thoroughly affected: many of this sort
of sudden converts have dropped their religious concerns in a great
measure when their fears of the threatening calamity were
vanished."

To this doubt was added the charge of insincerity—that people
went through the form of conversion without feeling its meaning.
Like his father before him, Henry Ward Beecher was suspicious
of sudden outbursts of religious enthusiasm: "My own observation," he says, "has led me to the conclusion that more persons become true Christians without sudden joy and without the consciousness . . . of a great change, than with it," and adds that men
should not "lie in a bath of conviction [of sin] as clothes lie in a
dyeing vat until they are thoroughly stuck through." Calvinism
from the very beginning stressed qualities which the revivalists
tended to ignore. The upright Dr. Chauncy who led his "old
lights" against Edwards, held that conviction of sin is followed by
a real *secret* work of God and that a new Christian character is
shown in a cessation of sin and a high degree of joy and love.
The only means to attain this are the appointed means of grace—
prayer, and the reading and hearing of God's Word—none of
which gratify the instincts of ostentation and all of which tend to
keep a firm discipline on the mind. When he brought charges
against Davenport, Chauncy pointed out the excitement caused by
Davenport's "pretending some extraordinary discovery and the assurance of the very near approach of the end of the world." That
was one way in which normal self-control was broken down for,
if the end was near, one need not go on living in the discipline of
every-day life. This threat was outlawed by the opponents of evangelism from the very beginning. Later, as the conditions of living
grew more secure, revivalists found that our subconscious fears, our
inherited animal phobias, could not be so easily touched. Instead
of appealing to the freer intellect, they began to practice suggestion. Frederick Morgan Davenport, himself a former Methodist
minister, says of the revival: "Its normal tendency is not to
strengthen the intellect and the will, but rather to submerge both
under billows of suggestion and emotion. It is a thing of impulse
rather than of reason. When allowed full sway in a population,

its manifestations become primitive and ultimately so gruesome and grotesque that they can no longer be associated in the thought of earnest men with soundness of method or of mind. Whenever in the past, as has sometimes happened, genuine good has been done in society through the revival, it has been directly in proportion to the control which the reflective processes of individual leaders have exercised over what is essentially impulsive social action."

The bill of accusation against revivalism remains unanswered. Archibald Alexander, a critic of the system who cherished its true fruits, notes that the beauty of a great work of the spirit "will be marred, and its progress retarded by every . . . spurious mixture" of enthusiasm and disorder. "The Church," he continues, "is not always benefited by what we call revivals; but sometimes the effects of such commotions are followed by a desolation which resembles the work of a tornado. I have never seen so great insensibility in any persons as in those who had been subjects of violent religious excitement; and I have never seen any sinners so bold and reckless in their impiety as those who had once been loud professors and foremost in the time of revival."

Excesses of religious excitement break down the will but not always in the sense of rendering it impotent. The will is broken by abasement, but it is afterwards exalted. The release of the subconscious, which runs with every conversion, affords strange fuel for the will to feed upon. This disruption of the will is the supreme danger of revivalism. Even if one grants all its good effects, this black mark remains. The steadiness of human life depends on the balancing of impulses, the expression of some and the subjection of others. In the process of conversion, balance is temporarily lost and, together with the impulse to sanctity, a hundred other desires swim up to the surface. No power of the will remains to sort them and give them precedence and there is every chance that evil desires, long suppressed, will at last be gratified. At the same time conversion, as practiced in revivals, gives encouragement to the wildest mysticism. From the strange sexual theories of Perfectionism to the strange Orientalism of New Thought, we see these effects of revivalism at work.

† *The American Monthly Magazine* published "Room for the Leper! Room!" by N. P. Willis. † Half a million dollars was offered to the owners of White Sulphur Springs for their concessions; ice-cream was served at the hotels there. † It was noted "that people of New England do good by mania." † An American breakfast consisted of buttered toast, hot biscuit, coffee; beef steak, apple sauce, hot potatoes, cheese, butter, and two large dishes of eggs. † It was considered that "all American ladies should know how to clear starch and iron; how to keep plate and glass; how to cook dainties; and if they understand the making of bread and soup, so much the better." † Mrs. Hannah Moore was the most popular British writer in America with Scott, Bulwer, and Miss Edgeworth in high esteem. Wordsworth was deeply respected and *Sartor Resartus*, which was anonymous, was having a great influence. † There was a universal faith in the coming of a great American writer, but although the *North American Review* puffed almost all books, only a few writers made impressions; among them—Irving, Cooper, Bryant, and Judge Hall. † The coeducational college at Oberlin, Ohio, was opening in 1833. A Boston magazine suggested that mild intellectual interests would serve to prevent the decay of female beauty so often remarked by Europeans. There was an excess of women in the East and those who went into the factories found them horrible. † Before 1830 the tenement house had become a problem. † Fannie Kemble noted with horror that women wore bérets when riding horseback. † When the Black Hawk War was over the defeated chief was paraded through the streets. † The death of Goethe, who was called "a distinguished individual," was appropriately noted and Washington Irving had a great reception when he returned to America after an absence of seventeen years.

† N. P. Willis was sending letters from abroad and James Fenimore Cooper complained "that our country is deficient in the materials of society most pertinent to the purpose of the novelist." The *North American Review* defended Washington Irving's predilection for English subjects. † It was announced that Byron's daughter was about to be launched in English society. † The militia went into training twice a year. † After hearing violent anti-catholic sermons a Boston mob, believing rumors that girls were held there by force, burned the Ursuline Convent. † Fresh air, soap, and water were becoming familiar, but baths were far from popular and women complained constantly of weak chests and delicate lungs.

# X.

## The Perfect Communist.

IN the last week of February, 1834, Polly Hayes Noyes, aunt of a future President of the United States, received a letter from her son, who had just begun to enjoy a license to preach at New Haven. It was before the days of cheap postage and letters often meant bad news. Mrs. Noyes did not stop to use the kitchen towel. Holding the letter in her wet hands she read it through and exclaimed to her daughter, "What *does* John mean?"

He meant that he was perfect. He meant literally, seriously, and religiously that he was then and forever free from all sinfulness and that, no matter what he did in the future, he would still be without sin. His mother was an imaginative woman. In her self-examinations she was conscious of dreadful shortcomings. She had joined a Congregationalist church, in spite of the cool indifference of her husband, because that church accounted for sin and gave some hope of future forgiveness. It is no wonder that the announcement from her son surprised her. She read:

"The burden of Christian perfection accumulated upon my soul, until I determined to give myself no rest while the possibility of the attainment of it remained doubtful. At last the Lord met me with the same promise that gave peace to my soul when first I came out of Egypt: 'if thou wilt confess with thy mouth the Lord Jesus and shalt believe in thine heart that God hath raised him from the dead, thou shalt be saved.' By faith I took the proffered boon of eternal life. God's spirit sealed the act, and the blood of Christ cleansed me from sin."

His mother had not been the first to hear of John Humphrey Noyes' perfection. To her he wrote in the accepted words of doctrine, but to a student of divinity at Yale, he had expressed himself so curtly and drastically that the student went off to spread the news: "Noyes says he is perfect." Before the day had passed, it was common knowledge in New Haven that "Noyes is crazy."

If he was, it was the strangest madness among all the afflictions of the stammering century. For Noyes put his belief into action and, before he was through, had founded the most successful of American communities, had built up a great business organization which can still make frequent appearances on the back cover of the *Saturday Evening Post*, had practiced a form of and probably originated the term "free love," had done a great deal for the progress of eugenics in connection with a sexual practice which was called abominable, had enlisted the support of Garrison and Greeley, and had startled and horrified the entire country. With penetrating intelligence, he had discovered the weakness in all previous communities and avoided it. A student himself, he engaged in industry and manufactured the best steel trap in the country, so that the path to his door at Oneida was beaten by the footprints of thousands of visitors every year. He put his peculiar ideas into practice with great caution and, although he was an extremist, he cannily managed to avoid being swept away by the other fads and cults of his time. He practiced vegetarianism, and studied Spiritualism and phrenology, but always kept his own theories free from entangling alliances, so that he could be judged by them alone. He passed through three phases and, perhaps because a supreme harmony of character gave them unity, he surpassed in each of them the other prophets who spent their whole force in any one of the three. He began as a religious leader, and built a community on his idea that the Second Coming of Christ had already taken place and that, therefore, man can be perfect in this life. He carried the community forward until it became an experiment in sexual relations with spiritual wives, a kind of regulated promiscuity, eugenics, and a new method of cohabitation, all interwoven and all related to the idea of perfection. On the foundation of his religious and sexual innovations, he built an industrial organization, abolishing private property and wages. Combining the three, he created the perfect communism which, he asks us to believe, banishes Death. The conception is grandiose; its architecture is amazing; and the man behind it most amazing of all.

§

The family tradition is that Noyes is an English corruption of the name of William Des Noyers, a Norman baron in the army of

William the Conqueror. A dissenting rector of a church in Wilt-shire, in 1585, heads the actual genealogy. There is a strain of noble blood in the family tradition coupled with dissent from ecclesiastical orthodoxy. Perhaps these facts, according to the popular concept of heredity, account for two of the dominant strains in the life of the American descendant. The sons of the dissenter came to America, presumably not on the *Mayflower* since they settled in Medford. In 1635 they moved to Newburgh. A century later a ship-building grandson was living in that vicinity. In 1795, John Noyes was graduated from Dartmouth and began teaching in that college. When his son, the Perfectionist, was a student at Dartmouth a distinguished alumnus said to him, "Young man, I wish I could do as much for you as your father did for me." But it is not on record that Daniel Webster ever did do anything for John Humphrey Noyes. The elder Noyes tried the ministry, but his health failed. He was in Congress for one term. At forty, being then a clerk in a store at Brattleboro, he married Polly Hayes, aunt of Rutherford B. Hayes. The next generation was a distinguished one. Of the nine children, one founded Oneida; one became the mother of Larkin Mead the sculptor, of William Mead (of the firm of McKim, Mead, and White), and of Elinor Mead, who married William Dean Howells; one became a successful banker; and three devoted themselves to their brother's community.

When he was sixteen, a thoughtful and imperious boy, he was told by his mother that she had never seen anyone so improved as Henry Smith who had returned to Putney, where the Noyes family then lived, after having been converted in one of the early revivals of the new preacher, Charles G. Finney. Henry and his brother Hervey were ideal converts for they promptly started a revival themselves, using all of Finney's methods and astonishing the little town by the force and directness of their attack. John Humphrey withstood them; but he did not forget them. The ideas they absorbed from Finney, particularly Finney's experience of sin-lessness at his conversion, moved the boy deeply. But he was going to Dartmouth. He was going to be a lawyer. And one year later, when he had already begun the study of law, he deliberately resolved "to indulge the lust of the eye and the pride of life for the present, and risk the consequences; in short, to jump the life to come." He was just twenty, but the springtide he felt in his

blood was not yet to rise. His determination to be a voluptuary is pathetic. He tells us with the sincerity which marks all his confessions, though not as bluntly as usual, that he had lived a pure life. His roistering at Dartmouth was not vicious. In his senior year, he passed through a period of doubt and change at which he himself marveled. He was still virginal, but he decided to give himself to lust. Four weeks later, he had given himself to Christ; had, like Finney, abandoned the law for divinity; and had become a student at Andover Theological Seminary.

What had happened? He tells us: "After a painful process of conviction, in which the conquest of my aversion to becoming a minister was one of the critical points I submitted to God and obtained spiritual peace. With much joy and zeal I immediately devoted myself to the study of the Scriptures, and to religious testimony in private and public. The year of 1831 was distinguished as 'the year of revivals.' New measures, protracted meetings, and New York evangelists had just entered New England, and the whole spirit of the people was fermenting with religious excitement. The millennium was supposed to be very near. I fully entered into the enthusiasm of the time; and seeing no reason why backsliding should be expected or why the revival spirit might not be maintained in its full vigor permanently, I determined with all my inward strength to be 'a young convert' in zeal and simplicity forever. My heart was fixed on the millennium, and I resolved to live or die for it. Four weeks after my conversion I went to Andover and was admitted to the Theological Seminary."

Taken in connection with the text he quoted three years later in his letter to his mother, this account, while it leaves obscure the spiritual change in Noyes and its psychological reasons, gives us an insight into his mental processes. He had breathed the exciting air of revivalism. As a little girl, Frances Willard had been terrified merely by reading Finney's orations. Noyes was not frightened. In the mêlée of pentecostalism he drove directly at the one thing to which he was to cling for ever after: the idea that by accepting Christ he could attain perfection. The only shortcoming in this first conversion was that, when he accepted Finney's experience of being sanctified, he also accepted his idea of the Second Coming—that it was an event of the future. By the time the Millerites with their

millennium, in the 1840's, had made this a dogma, Noyes had come to reject it entirely.

A miracle (of a minor order) advised Noyes to quit Andover and go to New Haven where he entered as a student, was soon licensed to preach and established a Free Church. Again a revivalist influenced him for, in 1834, Noyes invited James Boyle to preach to his congregation and this fellow-worker of Finney's gave them doctrine which, a year later, was to lead the Presbytery to suspend him from the ministry. The inter-relation of Boyle and Noyes is hard to determine. Noyes invited Boyle because the latter was reaching toward the same sort of Perfectionism that he, himself, was seeking. Later, when Noyes had outstripped Boyle in audacity of thought, Boyle allowed himself to be converted by the younger man to outright Perfectionism.

Slowly Noyes worked away from the idea that perfection is merely a possibility, and toward his final position that it is an accomplished fact. The light dawned in 1834, on February 20,—a date which Oneida Community considered as the "high tide of the spirit." The antipodal date, August 20, was considered the high tide of the flesh and annually, on that day, special precautions against temptation were taken.*

§

It had always been orthodox doctrine that man would be wholly redeemed from sin at the Second Coming of Christ. By close application to the Scriptures, Noyes discovered that this event had already taken place, in the 70th year, at the time of the destruction of Jerusalem. This, the crucial point in his whole mechanism of salvation, is an obvious reaction against Millerism. It is a healthy

---

* In one of the Oneida publications of 1850, the significance of the two "tides" is marked by an appropriate essay on capital punishment: "Our almanac for this season, always shows stormy, tempestuous weather on the spiritual main. After about this date, the weather begins to clear up,—the flesh tide ebbs rapidly—navigation becomes safe and easy—enterprise starts with new life, and we find ourselves sailing buoyantly on the calm, open sea of spirituality about the last of winter. This climax of the flesh the present year, could not be signalized more appropriately, than by the execution of Webster, the 'Supreme Scoundrel,' and special representative of sensuality. Our community unanimously consent to this judgement of the flesh, and rejoice that there is a Commonwealth and executive power, that can show so much sympathy with God's indignation against the workers of iniquity."

refusal to be stampeded by one of the wildest excesses of religious frenzy. Noyes would ascend no mountain in a white shift to be that much nearer to Christ in the month of October, 1843. For him the last judgment of the Jewish Dispensation had already come. Those who now accepted Christ were without sin forever. Once he had succumbed to the hysteria of religion. If hysteria occurred again, he would be in a position to create it, not to suffer from it. On the 16th of April, 1834, the Association which had licensed Noyes to preach met at New Haven. "Mr. John H. Noyes at the request of the Association, made a statement of his peculiar opinions respecting the doctrine of Christian perfection; whereupon, on motion of Dr. Taylor, the following resolution was adopted:

"Whereas, Mr. Noyes had adopted views on the doctrine of Christian perfection, which in the opinion of this Association are erroneous, unscriptural, and inconsistent with his usefulness as a preacher of the gospel, and such as in his opinion are inconsistent with his retaining his license,

"Therefore, Resolved, that without impeaching the Christian character of Mr. Noyes this Association do hereby recall his license to preach the gospel."

He stayed on for a time at New Haven, expounding his doctrine, and his letters home during this period are admirable pictures of his state of mind. He was, at heart, a radical pioneer. It was only the possession of a disciplined intelligence which kept him from becoming a fanatic and a faddist. He writes: "I had not only lost my standing in the Free Church, in the ministry, and in the college. My good name in the great world was gone. My friends were fast falling away. I was beginning to be indeed an outcast: yet I rejoiced and leaped for joy. Sincerely I declared that 'I was glad when I got rid of my reputation.' Some persons asked me whether I should continue to preach, now that the clergy had taken away my license. I replied, 'I have taken away their license to sin, and they keep on sinning; so, though they have taken away my license to preach, I shall keep on preaching.'"

And to his mother, "As you desired to know my plans, I have told you all I know at present. Perhaps before to-morrow everything will be changed. I live by no sure rule of calculation except the faithfulness of God. Therefore, if you would have peace so

far as I am concerned, you must make no calculations other than
that. . . ." And, more violently, to his sister: "Am I a boy or a
man? Am I sane or crazy? Am I a wretch or a servant of God? If
you think me a boy, or crazy, or reckless apostate, I commend your
course, and only ask you to use care in forming your opinion of me.
After that, use persuasion or force to bring me home or consign me
to a hospital. But if you think me a man . . . I pray you believe
. . . that I can best manage my own matters. . . . If this be so,
if you are waiting for results (whether Perfectionism will prevail)
and not looking at truth, nothing but sorrow is before you. . . .
Let me say now for your special notice, that family considerations
have become with me subordinate to my relations to God and, if
there is any conflict between them, the first will be sacrificed without
faltering. . . . I want it [money] not. . . . I know full well, if
this letter does not cure her [his mother] it will trouble her. I
commit the result to the Lord." He had refused money from
friends, but accepted a little from his father. Even this he rejects,
unless it comes with grace: "I have not received money because
my father has supplied me. What you have given I have received
as a gratuity with thankfulness both to you and to my Father in
heaven. If you are not interested in the object for which I live, I
cannot ask or expect you to assist me."

§

The theory of Perfectionism is at the root of all Noyes did,
but it sounds so incredible that the best way to approach it is from
its worst side. It was, as Noyes knew, being embraced by libertines,
"not because they loved holiness, but because they were weary
of . . . restraints. Perfectionism presented them a fine opportunity
of giving full swing to carnality . . ." and, although Noyes condemned this licentiousness, he was the chief exponent of the religion on which it rested, and was held responsible. Perfectionism
appeared simultaneously in many forms. His was New Haven
Perfectionism, disciplined and directed; the others were New York
and Massachusetts Perfectionism. It was out of the latter varieties
that the first scandal came. Simon Lovett and Chauncey E. Dutton
in the 1830's were circulating through New England as missiona-
ries of Perfectionism, and their early theory, according to common

report, was opposed entirely to intercourse between the sexes. Another leader, Dr. Gridley, boasted that "he could carry a virgin in each hand, without the least stir of unholy passion." At Delphi, in Central New York, Lucina Umphreville, a fascinating Perfectionist, had been teaching that "carnal union was not to be tolerated even in marriage." Then, just as Noyes was beginning his labors, a regrettable event occurred. According to Hepworth Dixon, a mocking English reporter of Noyes' *Spiritual Wives,* Noyes claimed that "at Brimfield, Mary Lincoln and Maria Brown visited Simon Lovett in his room; and they came out of the room in the innocence of Shakerism." But Noyes' own account of his flight from Brimfield and what happened after he left, is quite different. The young man who, a few years earlier, had decided to gratify the lust of the eye, was dismayed by a single kiss. The man who was shortly to claim that your wife is the bride of Christ, and so every man's bride, struggled for twenty-four hours through the snow of a New England winter to put sixty miles between himself and— was it temptation? The case of Noyes is exceptionally complicated. His naturalness and common sense about sex are bounded on one side by an exceptional timidity: on the other, by an equally exceptional audacity. The two boundaries are often found together, but without the middle term; the ascetic is the inverted libertine. In Noyes we have the ascetic and the libertine and the common sensual man, all in one. In the Brimfield affair, which had grave consequences, the Puritan is uppermost:

"I was so near being actually present at this affair," Noyes writes, "and so liable to be thought responsible for it and implicated in it, that I must now tell more particularly how and why I left Brimfield. From my first contact with the Massachusetts clique of Perfectionists at Southampton I had been aware of a seducing tendency to freedom of manners between the sexes. The expressions 'brother,' 'sister,' 'beloved,' 'dearly beloved' were in common use. One young woman kissed Simon Lovett the first time she ever saw him. At Brimfield there was a group of handsome, brilliant young women, and manners were equally free. By my position as preacher of the doctrines which had taken all by storm I was the object of attentions, which were seemingly innocent but

which I soon began to suspect as dangerous. Finally one evening at a social gathering around William Tarbell's fire his daughter, Hannah, in the midst of the general cheerfulness seemed downcast. I asked her what made her sad. She replied that she imagined I had no confidence in her. Thereupon I took a seat beside her and put my arm around her. As we separated she kissed me in token of recovery from her distrust. That night, while on my bed in prayer, I got a clear view of the situation, and I received what I believed to be 'orders' to withdraw. I left the next morning alone, without making known my intentions to anyone, and took a bee-line on foot through snow and cold—below zero—to Putney, sixty miles distant, which I reached within twenty-four hours."

The affair he alludes to was the same visit referred to by Dixon to the attractive Lovett's room. The two girls went with a purpose "by no means carnal"—in fact they were seeking a crowning demonstration of the spirit triumphing over the flesh. But, says Noyes sadly, "as usually happens in such presumptuous experiments . . . the flesh triumphed over the spirit." A terrible scandal broke, and its first effect upon one of the victims affords another instance of the religio-sexual hysteria of the time, a parallel to the cases of Matthias and his friends. Shocked by the failure of her faith and possibly by the tumult of sexual inhibitions suddenly broken down, and whipped by the scandal she had caused, Mary Lincoln had a vision of God destroying the whole town of Brimfield with fire from Heaven and called all true believers to flee to the mountains. Only one young woman, Flavilla Howard, went with her. Tramping through mud and rain in the night, the girls, as they approached the peak, cast off their clothing as they ran until, naked on the mountain top, they prayed God to stay the avenging bolts. "As a result of their intercession, they afterwards said, the city was saved." The news from Brimfield quickly reached Delphi, New York, where, at the same time, Erasmus Stone was gratified by a disturbing vision. The combined impact overcame the Platonic prejudices of Lucina Umphreville, who was joined in "spiritual union" with Jarvis Rider, a Perfectionist preacher. Presently the other heroine of Brimfield, Maria Brown, visited Delphi, and

Noyes tells us that soon the Platonic friendships became anything but Platonic.

It is the exceptional interest, and merit, of John Humphrey Noyes that, unlike most other prophets and reformers, he had in him a great capacity for growth. He could be as uncompromising as the stars in their courses; but he was not a fanatical radical, ridden by a theory to which facts must conform. It is characteristic of him that when Darwinism struck the world aghast with what seemed to many an untempered materialism, he went to the poetic root of the matter and accepted in Darwin the great idea of the plasticity of living forms. He was adaptable. Whatever happened to him gave change and development to his ideas. So it was with Brimfield. Psychologically, he was unprepared to accept fornication. He had not yet discovered sufficient sanctity. The Brimfield episode taught him, rapidly, to modify his Perfectionism until it became distinct from the more licentious forms, and to give it a discipline. Clearly, he wanted to keep his doctrine in his own hands. Whoever pushed it farther than himself was to be outlawed. One of the few traces of sectarian anger in his writings occurs in his final comment on Brimfield: "I confess that I sympathized to some extent with the spirit of the first letters that came to me about this affair, and sought to shelter rather than to condemn the young women who appealed to me against the storm of scandal which they had brought upon themselves. But in the sequel, as the irregularities continued and passed on into actual licentiousness and finally into propagandism, I renounced all sympathy with them, and did my best in subsequent years to stamp them out by word or deed."

§

In Brimfield, the hysteria of Perfectionism had answered the hysteria of the religions of sin. At Putney, to which Noyes returned toward the close of the 1830's, deep called again to deep, this time by way of miracles. These two episodes, Brimfield and Putney, are, as I have said, the worst manifestations of Perfectionism. They are noted first because they connect the new doctrine with the old and because, out of the excesses of the practice, we can arrive at some reasonable estimate of the theory. At Putney, Noyes founded, not an actual community, but a group of believers. He was not yet

ready for a great organization, but had experienced the disasters of an impulsive gathering of disciples. "At this time," he says, "I commenced in earnest the enterprise of repairing the disasters of Perfectionism, and establishing it on a permanent basis, not by preaching and stirring up excitement over a large field, as had been done at the beginning, nor by laboring to reorganize and discipline broken and corrupted regiments as I had done at different places, but by devoting myself to the particular instruction of a few simple-minded, unpretending believers, chiefly belonging to my father's family. I had now come to regard the quality of the prose-lytes of holiness as more important than their quantity; and the quality which I preferred was not that meteoric brightness which I had so often seen miserably extinguished, but sober and even timid honesty. This I found in the little circle of believers at Putney; and the Bible School which I commenced among them in the winter of 1836-7 proved to be to me and to the cause of holiness the beginning of better days."

Hostile critics imply that sexual irregularities in Noyes' group offended the neighboring Vermonters, but when we recall that by this time persecution had driven the Mormons across the Mississippi and killed their prophet, we may assume that Noyes kept a firm hand on his disciples and that the mere nature of his doctrine was offensive enough to cause the indignation meetings that were held by the good Christians of Putney. Noyes was always sensitive to the opinion of the churches. On a later occasion, he gave up an essential of Perfectionist practice in order to save the rest from ecclesiastical persecution. But to the criticism of his townsmen at Putney he reacted pugnaciously. On the first of June, 1847, he startled his followers with this question: "Is not now the time for us to commence the testimony that the Kingdom of God has come—to proclaim boldly that God in His Character of Deliverer, Law-giver and Judge has come to this town and in this Association?"

The essential word is "testimony." A witness was needed for the Lord, and that presently. This was in keeping with Noyes' own idea of his church—that its only affiliations were with the primitive churches of the early Christian Era. It also fitted in with his very mildly expressed belief in his own personal relation with Divinity. In his proposal of marriage he had written that he had the "per-

mission and goodwill" of God in making his offer. Without claiming direct inspiration, he obviously felt that, since he had found the secret of Sanctification, God was very close to him. A miracle was needed as proof.

It was needed also as a warning. Shrinking from the sexual debauches of Brimfield, Noyes could only discover one reason for them: that the Brimfield Perfectionists were not perfect, not entirely sanctified. He could not read them out of the church, for one of the principles of Perfectionism was the independence of each unit and of each individual. But he could cry out woe "unto him who abolishes the law of the apostasy before he stands in the holiness of the Resurrection"; that is, woe unto him who assumes the liberties of the sinless soul before he has actually accepted Christ. When one has really accepted Christ, it is Christ who acts, not the mortal alone, and so sin is impossible; but if one has not partaken of Christ, sin is inevitable. It is only in the Kingdom of God that utter freedom is granted; and Noyes, looking for that degree of freedom, needed proof that Putney was, at that moment, God's Kingdom.

His need was fulfilled with gratifying promptness. It was made known on the first of June and, three weeks later to a day, the miracle occurred in the mystical healing of Harriet A. Hall, a chronic invalid. In many ways this is a more unhappy episode than the Brimfield seductions. It deeply implicates Noyes himself and shows a weak strain in an unexpected place—in his intellect. It associates him with the least impressive phenomena of revivalism. The healing power was exercised by Noyes and Mary Cragin and the testimony of the invalid is all that could be required. It reads more like a testimonial than like a testimony. "From a helpless, bed-ridden state, in which I was unable to move, or even to be moved without excruciating pain, I was instantly raised to a consciousness of perfect health. I was constrained to declare again and again that I was perfectly well. My eyes, which before could not bear the light, were opened to the blaze of day and became strong. My appetite was restored, and all pain removed."

Noyes' explanation is also according to rule. The woman, he says, "was completely bed-ridden, and almost blind, lying in nearly total darkness. . . . From this state, she was raised instantly, by

the laying on of hands, and by the word of command, into strength which enables her to walk, to face the sun, and ride miles without inconvenience, and with excessive pleasure. . . . The cure of Mrs. Harriet Hall, is as unimpeachable as any of the miracles of the primitive church." The difficulty here is that of all faith-healing: the cure took place, but we are not acquainted with all the particulars of the disease. It may have been one of the many which are properly treated by psychotherapy. The internal evidence is, however, unfavorable to Noyes. "The miracle is," says Professor Warfield, "as obvious a sham as any of the thousands and thousands of sham miracles which disgrace the annals of the church, and not of the church only but of every popular religious movement throughout the world—differing only from other sham miracles in bearing on its brow the brand of fraud, as many of them do not. The part taken by Mary Cragin in this miracle—and others—is so barefacedly that of a play-actor, that one wonders that so shrewd a man as Noyes permitted the details to be made public." There are two circumstances supporting this view, and one of them—the character of Mary Cragin—is fully analyzed by this critic. She was the wife of George Cragin, and their coming to join Noyes was considered a capital event. Cragin, as noted before, had been a revivalist under Finney and an active moral reformer in New York City. His wife shared his enthusiasms and was herself a zealous revivalist. Both eagerly accepted the Perfectionism of Noyes, for which their association with Finney had prepared them, and were converted to the new religion, going to live in the house of another ardent disciple, Abram C. Smith, at Rondout, where Mrs. Cragin became the spiritual wife, i.e., the mistress, of Smith. (The parallel to the unlovely story of Matthias and the Folgers is startling.) Noyes rebuked profligacy at Rondout as at Brimfield and the grateful, if not dignified, Cragin came with his restored wife to Putney.* To the outside world she seemed at the time a discredited witness. To us it still seems that she must have been an exceptionally prejudiced one. The best one can say of her is that her own spiritual excitement might well have worked on the excitement of the invalid.

* Later, until her death by drowning in the Hudson, Mrs. Cragin acted as matron of the Oneida Community.

The second circumstance to challenge the miracle is that Noyes never insisted upon it and that, after the Community went to Oneida, miracles were never again of primary importance. Possibly Noyes understood that, by claiming the highest proof, he was putting himself in the class of thousands of charlatans and was inviting a criticism having little to do with the genuine miracle of sanctification which he believed in. Or possibly the growth of his ideas and of his industries made further calls for proof unnecessary. The Perfectionists continued to believe that prayer was effective in curing disease, but they did not despise medical aid and accepted all the usual scientific measures for health. The affair at Putney was a desperate expedient, and an unsuccessful one. It not only diminishes Noyes' intellectual stature, it is a rare mark of practical instability in him. The believers at Putney were, perforce, convinced, but the skepticism of outsiders was aggravated. Again there is a slight discrepancy in the accounts. Hinds says that no personal violence was offered to the group at Putney, but that Noyes and his followers considered it prudent to move. The exceptionally documented essay by Professor Warfield suggests the contrary: "Other miracles followed in rapid succession; and not content even with these, others still, alleged to have been wrought previously, were now brought forward and made public. But it was all in vain. The people were obdurate; and, having refused to believe Noyes and his followers, would not believe though many rose from their beds. Vigorous action was begun to rid the town of the scandal. Indignation meetings were held. The courts were set in motion; civil suits for damages were brought; the Grand Jury found a true bill and in the indictment thus made Noyes was arraigned on specific charges of adultery and held for trial on heavy bail. The result was, happily, the destruction of the obnoxious community at Putney. The suspension of the publication of the community's journal—*The Spiritual Magazine*—was compelled. Immunity in the courts was bought at a heavy cost; the civil suits were satisfied by money payments out of court; before the criminal case came on, Noyes broke bail and fled beyond the jurisdiction of the court. The community itself began to scatter and in a year or so it was gone."

§

Noyes and his followers went, at the invitation of Jonathan Burt, a land owner, to Oneida, in Madison County, New York, where they were to attain a great success and to practice freely the system of industry and the methods of sexual relations which Noyes was developing. In the first ten years of his leadership, Noyes was primarily a prophet of a new religion, the doctrines of which we have seen in their least attractive phases. While the colony broke ground, starved in horticultural simplicity, and was saved from disaster by a steel trap, the doctrines grew to maturity. For a moment we can leave Noyes and his band clearing swamps, farming a little, building log cabins, using an attic for a sleeping apartment, living on an enforced diet of bread, milk, potatoes, and beans, because they had nothing else and Noyes' principle was "pay as you go," so that only occasionally could they buy a pound of sugar at the grocery. In a barn without pulpit or chairs, they held their Sunday gatherings, and here Noyes began his extraordinary home talks in which the full glory of Perfectionism was unfolded.

§

That glory breaks upon us in diminished splendor. What is hard to understand is not the doctrine itself, but the fact that anyone could believe it. Yet it did not spring sourceless into existence. The eighteenth century had given birth to at least two ideas which are its ancestors: the idea that man is naturally good and that society is the source of crime, and the idea of infinite progress to perfection. Both of these ideas were abominated by Calvinists who believed man naturally depraved and perfection attainable only in Christ. But Noyes combined the hostile articles of faith and made Christ the solvent of man's present evil and the source of his immediate good. It was the immediacy of Perfectionism which offended. In the hereafter we could be saints, all or a few of us, in accordance with various modifications of Calvinism; but Noyes said that in this life, in the pursuit of our daily functions, man *is* perfect if he only chooses the way to perfection. And being perfect he is superior to the restraints placed by imperfect men upon their imperfect brethren. The new covenant of pure Perfectionism "gives liberty from external law." The system likewise "disclaims all obligation to obeying the moral law" for "believers by fellowship

with Christ in His resurrection, are released from the beggarly elements and carnal ordinances of that worldly sanctuary which they have left," and any impulse of a true Perfectionist—since Christ is really its author—is legitimate and praiseworthy. There were Perfectionists who went beyond Noyes and he was at pains to mark the differences between himself and them. It is properly of the more radical Perfectionists that contemporaries were thinking when they said, with Asa Mahan, himself a mild Finneyite Oberlin Perfectionist:

"1. Perfectionism in its fundamental principles, is the abrogation of all law. . . . (2) In abrogating law, as a rule of duty, Perfectionism abrogates all obligation of every kind. (3) Perfectionism is a 'rest' which suspends all efforts and prayer, even for the salvation of the world. (4) Perfectionism substitutes the direct teaching of the Spirit, falsely so called, in the place of the 'word.' (5) Perfectionism surrenders up the soul to blind impulse assuming that every existing desire or impulse is caused by the direct agency of the Spirit and therefore to be justified. (6) Perfectionism abrogates the Sabbath and all the ordinances of the Gospel, and, in its legitimate tendencies, even marriage itself. (7) Perfectionism by abrogating all law, abrogates all standards of conduct and accordingly demoralizes man. (8) Perfectionism, in short, in its essential elements, is the perfection of licentiousness." Or, with Henry Cowles, Perfectionism "supposes the Christian to receive Christ within him, in such a way, that henceforth Christ only acts within him; and whatever himself seems to do, Christ really does. Some even suppose their own individual being to be absorbed or merged into Christ, so that themselves, as distinct persons, have ceased to exist, and all that was themselves is not Christ. . . . It either avowedly or virtually annihilates personal agency and responsibility. . . . As a consequence, mental impressions supposed to be from the Spirit of God, are deemed perfect truth and law, paramount even to the Bible itself. . . . These principles lead more or less extensively, as the case may be, to the rejection of all Gospel ordinances, the disuse of prayer, and to all manner of licentiousness."

Noyes himself shows no timidity in the early expression of his doctrine. By communing with Christ and "apprehending . . . his victory over sin and death . . . and the spiritual reconciliation of God with man . . . believers are brought into fellowship with Christ's death and resurrection, and made partakers of His divine nature and His victory over the evil one." And "faith identifies the soul with Christ, so that by His death and resurrection the believer dies and rises again, not literally, nor yet figuratively, but spiritually; and thus, so far as sin is concerned, is placed beyond the grave, in heavenly places with Christ." We are actually living, according to Noyes, in the Resurrection state, and are as free from law as we are from sin. William Lloyd Garrison wrote him a letter expressing identical views: "There is nothing more offensive to the religionists of the day than practical holiness; and the doctrine that total abstinence from sin in this life is not only commanded but necessarily obtainable they hate with a perfect hatred, and stigmatize entire freedom from sin as a delusion of the devil! Nevertheless, 'He that is born of God cannot commit sin,' 'He that committeth sin is of the devil.' . . . 'There is therefore now no condemnation to them who are in Christ Jesus, who walk not after the flesh, but after the spirit. For the law of the spirit of life in Christ Jesus hath made us free from the law of sin and death.' "

Noyes was not slow to see that out of his doctrine there might rise fundamental difficulties with the statutes. He did not want one of his Perfectionists to be haled into court for nonpayment of debt or murder and defend himself by saying, "My religion tells me I can do whatever I please, that I cannot sin, and that I am not subject to your law." * At the same time, he saw that Perfectionism, carried to any extreme, would ruin Oneida, for some sort of authority had to exist in industrial relations. Under this pressure his Perfectionism was remolded and refined. Unity, organization, and self-improvement were exalted against the individualism, chaos, and licentiousness of all other brands of Perfectionism and Noyes drew up a table showing his position between the strict legalist and the type of Perfectionist opposed to all restraints. One makes law

* Yet in 1837 before Oneida had been founded, he renounced his allegiance to the United States. He alludes to this in a letter to William Lloyd Garrison quoted on page 246.

the paramount factor, the other freedom from law; Noyes makes "God's leadership exercised through Christ by love without law" supreme. He carries the contrast through. The legal type has action with insufficient faith. The antinomian has faith with insufficient action. The true Perfectionist (Noyes) has "faith which accepts God's leadership and brings forth corresponding action." So the Perfectionist alone cultivates the intellect as a guide to faith and action, whereas the others either disparage it or use it without purpose. The one finally results in impotence; the other, in irresponsibility. Only Perfectionism leads to salvation from sin. Noyes' table is an extremely neat argument in which not a single point in the first two columns would be admitted by anyone except a Noyesian. The significant thing is that Noyes did succeed in founding a community on the basis of Perfectionism, that he imposed a strict and, in some respects, inhuman discipline and that, to the very end, he escaped the hand of the law. We may say that his theory was all too obviously created to fit his special facts. It will appear more likely that the theory was developed in order to regulate events, to be prepared for "facts" in human nature. In any event, it worked amazingly.

§

On all these theories, Noyes founded a community considerably less sanctimonious, much better managed, and far less dreary, than most of the others of the century. The second period of his life of leadership was concerned with the workings of his practice in the "ascending fellowship" or "complex marriage." It was only in the third that industry became a dominating motive. But it was external hostility to his sexual theory which eventually made him depart from his industrial community. It was only after industry was well under way that he placed the keystone of eugenics in the arch of his marriage theories. For that reason we can reverse his chronology and look at Oneida as an industrial community before examining its extraordinary basis of sexual intercourse.

The early struggles of Oneida are like those of every other colony. For a long time the communists did all their own work and attempted to live on the proceeds of their farms and fruitlands. On the title page of their first publication appeared a banner read-

John Humphrey Noyes

ing "Horticulture the Leading Means of Subsistence." The chief mechanical aid they had was a sawmill.*

Excellent jams and preserves left the colony with a growing financial burden from which they might never have escaped without the invention, by Sewall Newhouse, of a steel animal trap instantly recognized as superior to the German traps which had previously held the American market. Noyes was too intelligent to pour the baby out with the bath. He was opposed to the wage system and to private property, but he was not opposed to the advantages of industry which wages and property could create. The sacredness of the land, on which so many other communities broke, left him indifferent. He recognized America as an industrial country and knew that Oneida, in order to survive, must be an industrial community.

Newhouse had improved the Soligen and Elberfeld traps by making one lighter in weight, simpler in form, and more certain and deadly in its spring. Within a few months, the German traps were unsalable in the state of New York and, within a few seasons, the Oneida trap had captured the entire market. In one year the profit on these traps alone amounted to $80,000 and, even after scores of imitators had cut into the industry, it remained a highly profitable one. When a visitor suggested that traps for killing animals were a strange source of daily bread in a terrestrial kingdom of heaven, a communist replied gravely that the earth is lying under a curse of which vermin are a consequence and that the Oneidists do well to destroy them and thus help to perfect the earth. Steel chains were presently manufactured for use with the traps. When the community was seven years old, an extensive canning industry was started. Some ten years later, they began the manufacture of sewing and embroidery silks. They made traveling bags, and invented labor-saving machinery, and built their own machines for the silk factory, afterwards producing silk-making machinery for sale. Eventually, the community added hardware and the famous community silver. When the time came to transform the community into a stock-company, an issue of $600,000 was made. By the year 1900, without any serious deviation from the methods of the founders, the corporation had doubled the capital stock, with

* Noyes later noted that the sawmill crops up in nearly every American community.

factories in many cities and annual sales, at that time, of two million dollars, most of the enterprise remaining under the direction of men who had been born in the community.

This exceptional achievement was accomplished almost without friction and without the shadow of regimentation. The communists of Oneida had an almost fanatical horror of forms. They would move from place to place and, when a second community was founded at Wallingford, Connecticut, the two populations were within reason interchangeable. They would deliberately avoid scheduled functions, change the number of meals from three to eight a day and back to three, and vary the hours at which they ate. Every communist worked at several trades. In particular, the disagreeable tasks of the community were never performed by the same person for longer than two months.

The organization of the business was entirely democratic. The heads of the industrial departments gathered every Sunday morning to discuss business and these sessions were open to any member of the community. On Sunday evening, the minutes of the morning session were read and criticized by the entire group. Before the great annual meeting, which determined plans of campaign for the year, all the members were asked to make suggestions. It was the ideal of Oneida to attempt nothing without the general consent of all the members, and those having preferences in work were indulged to the greatest possible extent. The hours of labor were not long and, when the community was matured, a large number of outsiders were hired to do whatever was pure drudgery. There was no bell ordering the communists to work, but a large board with pegs indicated the whereabouts of each person, and the community never had any difficulty with idlers. The men dressed in ordinary clothes; but the women, who worked with the men and frequently superintended whole factories, wore a dress "consisting of a bodice, loose trousers and a short skirt falling to just above the knees." Although they bobbed their hair, and the younger women usually gave it a curl, Charles Nordhoff, who visited them in the 1870's, found the dress of the women "totally and fatally lacking in grace and beauty." But Hepworth Dixon, the English observer, whose reports caused Noyes so much pain, found that in the Oneida dress "a plain woman escapes much notice, and a pretty girl looks bewitch-

ing." He says that this is not part of Noyes' plan, "but for my own poor self, being only a Gentile and a sinner, I could not help seeing that many of his young disciples have been gifted with rare beauty, and that two of the singing girls, Alice Ackley and Harriet Worden, have a grace and suppleness of form, as well as loveliness of face and hand, to warm a painter's heart." He adds, however, that the total sum set aside for each woman's dress for a year was $33 and that this included shoes and hats.

Whenever a man needed a suit of clothes he went to the tailor, who made it for him, and there was a functionary known as "incidentals" who met unforeseen expenses for the colonists and supplied the younger women with breastpins, their only ornament. A committee for watches—there were twenty-one committees in all—was appealed to when anyone needed a time-piece. The community ate in one large hall, the table consisting of a stationary rim and a revolving center, the rim for one's own plate and the center for the food. The meal was not served in courses but in the "old-fashioned domestic style," the principal dishes, sauces, bread, and butter, and condiments all being put on when the meal started, and the dining plates and knives and forks only changed when shortcake appeared. The excellence of the Oneida meals was famous and perhaps accounted in part for the six thousand visitors, who outnumbered the communists three to one during an average summer. The upbringing of the children was extremely careful. They were well fed, properly dressed and almost continually in the open air until an hour or two after dinner, when "they come in and sit down for half an hour and have a little meeting in which they listen to Bible stories, repeat their little verses and confess Christ all around," after which, with a bath twice a week, they were put to bed. The children were in their mothers' care only until they were weaned. They then went into the nursery. It was a particular point of pride with Noyes that the children were especially healthy and intelligent and that parents loved the children of others as much as their own.

Although he concentrated on a theory of sexual relation, Noyes also cared deeply about the social relations of his people. His communism, it must be remembered, was Bible communism. It was equally opposed to the infidel communism of Owen and the transcendental communism of Brook Farm. "I tell you," Noyes is

reported as saying, "they have all failed . . . because they were not founded on Bible truth. Religion is at the root of life; and a safe social theory must always express a religious truth. Now there are four stages in the true organization of a family: (1) Reconciliation with God; (2) Salvation from sin; (3) Brotherhood of man and woman; (4) Community of labor and of its fruits. Owen, Ripley, Fourier, Cabet, began at the third and fourth stages; they left God out of their tale, and they came to nothing." Oneida was actually a part of the restoration of primitive Christianity. What was more, if Perfectionists could not love one another, the whole system was challenged; and, in the back of his mind, Noyes probably also knew that harmony between the communists was the only certain basis of financial success. He had therefore to prevent jealousies, rivalries, gossiping, and intrigue. He was not fool enough to think that calling men Perfectionists would instantly erase these stains on human character. In sexual relations an iron theory of "ascending fellowship" governed. For all other relations he instituted the extraordinary system of mutual criticism. At frequent meetings the members of the community would criticize one another in public, a certain number of them appearing before the rest for criticism each time. These criticisms were afterwards printed and a few samples show how direct they were:

"J.'s whole manner is sensational. He talks for effect and walks for effect, he flourishes his handkerchief for effect; takes out his letters and watch for effect. When he talks at the table it is not for fellowship, but to make an impression on the whole table. A little simplicity would improve him very much. His business character is excellent. We never had a young man in his place that did better, and he is thoroughly loyal. He is very fond of liberty—likes a great sweep, but I never heard of his wanting to leave the Community."

"I am bored sometimes with his making a long conversation about a little matter that could be disposed of with a few words."

"I have heard him express some discontent that he was not sent to college; he thinks he has not had the opportunity for education that he should have had. I think he has had a great deal of oppor-

tunity that he has not improved. He is not a natural student; he loves active life and a thousand excitements that interfere with study. C. will get an education here in our library and not ask any favors of the colleges, because he loves books."

"J. has naturally a good deal of what I should call the high-toned Southern tendency in him. It is one of the hardest elements in the world to take criticism and surrender itself to the meekness and gentleness of Christ. It is masculinity carried to excess. There is not woman enough about him."

Criticism at Oneida represented the organized force of public opinion and it was based on another of Noyes' wise principles, that of sympathy. There was no check in general social relations on what a communist could do but, if he wished to do it at Oneida, it had to fall in with the general wish. The group was considered higher and, in a sense, more perfect than the individual. Thus if one wished to change his occupation, or another to take a holiday, or a third to have a new hat, he made these wishes known through the proper channel and, if his wish was sympathetic to the general good, it was gratified. In most cases the committee would have no need to refer the question beyond themselves. In order that perfect sympathy should be uninterrupted, the little irritations of life had to be swiftly put out of mind; there could be no injuries and no rasping of one man's nerves by the tics and idiosyncrasies of another man's character. Mutual criticism improved the victim, made each man more subtle in estimating his fellows, and provided relief for the critic's emotions. The victim never replied until the following meeting and then only in writing. The young Sydney Jocelyn having been somewhat severely criticized for laziness, sensuality, sauciness, and ostentation, and moderately defended for certain good qualities, addressed the community on the following evening as follows:

"I take this occasion to express my thanks for the criticism and advice I received last evening, and for the sincerity that was manifested.

"I wish to thank Mr. Noyes for his sincerity, especially in

regard to times long past. I well remember when I felt very near him and used to converse freely with him; and I consider those my happiest days. . . .

"I confess Christ the controller of my tongue and a spirit of humility."

On one occasion at least the system of criticism was used in a special way—to cure a cold. The psychology of the cure is excellent. "The operation was not particularly agreeable—there is no method of cure that is; but it was short and speedily efficacious. One secret of its efficacy is, it stops the flow of thought toward the seat of difficulty, and so tends directly to reduce inflammation. At the same time it has a very bracing invigorating effect. In the present case, it went right to the cause of the disease, which was discovered to be a spirit of fear, throwing open the pores and predisposing the subject to the attack. S. P. had been brought up in a bad habit in this respect, expecting with every exposure to take cold—and then expecting to have it go on to a serious cough, and so on—fear realizing itself. Criticism stopped this false action, and not only made her well in the first instance, but by breaking up this fear it has given her comparative security against future attacks. It requires some fortitude and self-denial in the patient, when he thinks he needs sympathy and nursing, to take criticism instead; but it is well known that to rouse the will to strong exertion is more than half a cure. The criticism remedy professes to be universal, and is recommended for trial to all the afflicted."

There was a decided tendency toward faith healing, religions of the will, and spiritualism in the Oneida community. Noyes himself was interested in animal magnetism and said of one practitioner, whose experiments he recommends as "not differing in kind from Christ's miracles," that "Dr. Buchanan . . . will never approach equality with Christ, as a practical neurologist, until he establishes communion with God, the great vital energy . . . so long as mere human life is the fountain of magnetic influence its effects will only be proportionate to the weakness of human nature." And he considered that when such a man as Greeley gives serious attention, and at least qualified endorsement, to the spiritualism of the rapping Fox sisters, "it is a thing in favor of the kingdom of God." Dr.

Theodore R. Noyes, the eldest son of the founder, was a trained
scientist. He was therefore considered the most appropriate man to
investigate spiritualism in the community and it was under his direction that séances were held with mediums who had been brought up
at Oneida from childhood "and were of such character that there
was no possibility of deception." The results differed in no essential
from any other séance. After the death of the founder, some of the
mediums received communications from him, but they were generally discredited in the community. In fact, all the vagaries of the
time were practiced indifferently at Oneida. They used Graham
bread but were not Grahamites and, although meat was sparingly
used, they were not vegetarians. Tea, coffee, tobacco, and liquor were
not used and it was a trial to the communists when visitors came and,
in accordance with the custom of the country, spat. "The 'Bees'
descended as the Vandals had left and soon not a spot of tobacco
juice remained in all the mansion to tell a tale of filthy invaders."
The Perfectionists of Oneida took most things calmly; they did not
dissipate their forces in a hundred fads and fanaticisms. Instead,
they concentrated them in one elaborate and fundamental experiment—the experiment of complex marriage.

§

It is obvious that in his complex marriages, Noyes created a
system which corresponded to his own social and sexual needs; he
tells us so himself in regard to some particulars, and the others are
subject to parallel columns. He was sexually timid and his system
broke down certain reserves while it raised new barriers against
promiscuity. It exalted desire and put a check on lust. He was
capable of exceptional restraint, and the full development of his
system called for an exceptional continence. He had passed the hot
flush of youth and his system was the ideal of all middle-aged men
and women, since it supplied them with lovers young in years and
without experience. He was tremendously virile and a born varietist,
and his system allowed almost infinite change of lovers. He was un-
sentimental and sentiment was the one thing, after licentiousness,
which complex marriage did not tolerate. At its simplest we see
a tall pale man, with sandy hair and beard, extremely impressive,
dominating without ever being domineering, with gray dreamy

eyes and a firm mouth, a high light on his temples, a fine forehead, looking rather like the familiar pictures of Carlyle, but unlike that tortured soul, successful with woman. And around him we see his disciples—men and women—living under a sexual régime which is eminently satisfactory to the master and is imposed on the others by religious mummery.

This picture is largely false. There is no question that Noyes worked out a sexual relation pleasing to men and women, that they accepted it with eagerness and continued to practice it until outsiders managed to interfere. These outsiders tell us that there was much unhappiness, that many of the Bible Communists resented the necessity of complicating their love affairs; but nothing in the history of Oneida justifies this charge. In the community, Noyes' version of free love was a success. It stood somewhere between ordinary marriage and polygamy and, strangely enough, its religious basis was almost exactly the same as that of ascetic Shakerism. The temperament of the hysterical Ann Lee, brought up in Toad Lane in Manchester, a victim of convulsions and hallucinations, married in childhood, bearing four children in quick succession and seeing them almost as quickly die, worked on the same hypothesis—that Christ had become one with human beings. But she created, by a logical revulsion from all that concerned sex, an ascetic cult, which reasoned that, as men are born in sin, there can be no sin if none are born and so, out of distaste for birth, rejected the union of the sexes. The commotion of sexual impulses which came with the revivals brought converts and money to the Shakers. The same revivals sent disordered souls to follow Joseph Smith whose undisciplined temperament had brought him, with a parallel religious bias, to polygamy. Noyes having the hard temper of the common man and the discipline of intellectual energy, avoided all excess; at the same time, he gave a peculiar exaltation to the sexual nature of man.

Like many theorists of the supremacy of sex, Noyes was always a little uneasy about it. When Dixon accused him of drunkenness and wantoning in the flesh, Noyes gave his own account of one unhappy winter in New York, when he "descended into cellars where abandoned men and women were gathered and talked familiarly with them about their ways of life, beseeching them to believe in

Christ, that they might be saved from their sins. They listened to me without abuse. One woman seemed much affected. I gave her a Bible. To another I gave a Testament. Sometimes when I had money, I gave that to the wretches whom I found in those dark places. These were the only dealings I had with them." At Brimfield, he fled from a kiss of peace. All familiarity made him uncomfortable until his religious ideas had sanctified the relation. It was his concept of perfection which released his sexual energy and saved him from debauchery and from abhorring his own impulses. To the end, he remained in equilibrium between his two fears: license and frigidity; and he recognized them as two forms of the same thing. He detested the purity which comes of impotence or fear, as much as he detested unbridled passion:

"Animalism in the sexual department works in the two extremes of action and reaction. On the one hand, it is sensual and fiery, and on the other, dead. Both these forms are equally disgusting. The second form of animalism, that of amativeness in its reactive state, is considered a high state of grace in the world. There is a seeming continence in it, which actually passes for virtue. But it is repulsive to real purity. It is antagonistic to the spirit that makes truth supreme. A person under its influence is virtuously horror-struck whenever sexual matters are alluded to. His mind revolts from the study of an important branch of human nature, and the Spirit of Truth can not be at home with him.

"This reactive form of amativeness, so much commended, is really a disease. A person can not be in health who has lost the natural activity of amativeness. The devil's oxidation is at work in him.

"Fix your attention on animalism, and don't be deceived with regard to the identity of these two forms of it, but learn to hate it in both forms. Abhor this touchy kind of virtuosity that the world is so full of, as much as you abhor the sin of harlots. It is the same thing in another form. . . . The trouble is that we cannot talk on sexual matters without making the waters turbid. We must be able to think on this subject and speak of it in a way that is really natural. We can judge what is natural by little children; their minds are full of curiosity about sex. This subject is the vital center of

society. It is the soul of the fine arts. It will be foolish for us to undertake to cultivate music or poetry or painting or sculpture, until we set the center and soul of them in its place."

In this sense, Noyes accepted sex as a fundamental natural impulse. He rejoiced in his cohabitative strength, and he found "nothing very horrible in the idea" of sex and its gratification existing among the angels. But in his composition there was totally lacking the feeling of selection. That a man should cleave to one woman, should love her exclusively, was a displeasing thought; or perhaps it was displeasing only that a woman should give herself exclusively to one man, and so deny herself to another—to him. He rebelled against the idea that one man could possess a woman and forbid her to others. He meant to keep for himself the theoretical possibility of being the lover of every woman who would have him. In the imagination behind the theory we find a Vermont Casanova; in practice, rather a patriarch.

Ten years before complex marriage had been given a fair trial, and a year or so before his own marriage, Noyes, having "walked in the ordinances of the law blameless," wrote a letter which became notorious. It is known as the Battle-Axe letter from the name of the journal in which it first appeared:

"I will write all that is in my heart on one delicate subject, and you may judge for yourself whether it is expedient to show this letter to others. When the will of God is done on earth as it is in heaven, there will be no marriage. The marriage supper of the Lamb is a feast at which every dish is free to every guest. Exclusiveness, jealousy, quarreling, have no place there, for the same reason as that which forbids the guests at a thanksgiving dinner to claim each his separate dish, and quarrel with the rest for his rights. In a holy community there is no more reason why sexual intercourse should be restrained by law, than why eating and drinking should be; and there is as little occasion for shame in the one case as in the other. God has placed a wall of partition between the male and the female during the apostasy, for good reasons which will be broken down in the resurrection for equally good reasons; but woe to him who abolishes the law of apostasy before he stands in the

holiness of the resurrection. The guests of the marriage supper may have each his favorite dish. I call a certain woman my wife— she is yours; she is Christ's, and in Him she is the bride of all saints. She is dear in the hand of a stranger and according to my promise to her I rejoice. My claim upon her cuts directly across the marriage covenant of this world, and God knows the end."

For ten years following he developed his theory, and out of his marriage grew complementary doctrines. The story of his marriage is a queer one. Dixon in his *New America* and in *Spiritual Wives* accuses Noyes of marrying Harriet Holton, in 1838, for her money alone, and of using it freely for his own experimental purposes. His proposal was by a letter which Dixon and Noyes both print; the versions differ, but nothing in the enemy's account is inconsistent with Noyes' teaching. He asks his "beloved sister" not to call his proposed partnership a marriage before he has defined it, and then proceeds to define free love in such terms as are hardly lover-like in any accepted sense:

"At first I designed to set before you many weighty reasons for this proposal; but upon second thought, I prefer the attitude of a witness to that of an advocate, and shall therefore, only suggest briefly, a few matter-of-fact considerations, leaving the advocacy of the case to God, the customary persuasions and romance to your own imagination, and more particular explanations to a personal interview.

"1. In the plain speech of a witness, not of a flatterer, I respect and love you for many desirable qualities, spiritual, intellectual, moral, and personal; and especially for your faith, kindness, simplicity, and modesty.

"2. I am confident that the partnership I propose will greatly promote our mutual happiness and improvement.

"3. It will also set us free, at least myself, from much reproach, and many evil surmisings, which are occasioned by celibacy in present circumstances.

"4. It will enlarge our sphere, and increase our means of usefulness to the people of God.

"5. I am willing at this particular time, to testify by example, that I am a follower of Paul, in holding that 'marriage is honorable in all.'

"6. I am also willing to testify practically against that 'bondage of liberty' which utterly sets at naught the ordinances of men, and refuses to submit to them

even for the Lord's sake. I know that the immortal union of hearts, the everlasting honeymoon which alone is worthy to be called marriage, can never be made by a ceremony; and I know equally well that such a marriage can never be marred by a ceremony. William Penn first bought Pennsylvania of the British King, and then he paid the Indians for it, 'Thus it becometh us to fulfill all righteousness. . . .' "

It is after this that, in Noyes' own version, he acknowledges having God's permission and good will in the business. In Dixon's longer version we proceed to a sentimental quotation about the watchman, after his wanderings, "hieing himself to his quiet home."

The letter with its allusion to the torments of the flesh, its frankness about an extended sphere, and its honesty, was effective. Harriet married Noyes and was one of the great workers of the community. Her unhappy experiences in child-bearing resulted in Noyes working out a system of voluntary parenthood which was neither exactly contraception, nor abstention, and which he neatly worked into his complete sexual system.

§

The purpose was to "make love safe and edifying," and the first step was in the "ascending fellowship." Perhaps memories of his own adolescent fervors and qualms accounted for Noyes' tenderness about virginity. Perhaps the absence in his youth of a great passion led him to underestimate the force of young love. Perhaps the reason I have already suggested, that he had passed the first flush of young manhood, is to be held responsible. In any case, Noyes laid down the principle that the introduction to sexual love ought to be confided to an elder person of the opposite sex. The girls, especially, were instructed to regard their first sexual experience as more momentous than that of men, and to seek, as companions, elder men, under the discipline of self-control, who would "elevate them with the consciousness of having innocently exercised a pure and natural function on the spiritual plane" (and avoid impregnation), whereas the hot ardor of youth might make their entrance into sexual experience a mere exercise in the gratification of lust and lead to "unplanned" offspring.

Behind this was the fixed idea of Noyes that love can be not only controlled, but guided to its proper object. He rejected the

whole idea of spontaneous affinity in love. He was as distant as he could be from the Fourierite idea of natural pairing and parting. Young people might "fall in love with" one another, but the procedure was neither encouraged by a vast literature of love, nor was it in "sympathy" with the social system. There were no trysts, no dear secret vows. If a man desired a woman for a mate, the proposal was made in the presence of a third party, the older women of the community usually acting as the intermediaries. No proposal which was offensive had to be accepted; but it seems clear that certain proposals—of young men to young women—might have been made if the force of public opinion had not prevented. By this system, the unspiritual and inexperienced were prevented from mating, and marriages being impermanent, as a man or woman grew older the prospect of younger lovers still remained. The young enjoyed the benefit of intercourse with the more instructed and subtle. The old rejoiced in the somewhat formally offered fire of the young.

He had said that "my wife is yours, is Christ's, and so is the bride of all saints" and, at Oneida, this bold saying was boldly lived. It is hard to say to what extent Noyes and the Community interfered with any tendency to be monogamous. The natural point of separation between lovers would be an acceptable proposal from another man. But there was no compromise in the theory, and probably very little in action. Noyes was creating a Bible Family in the patriarchal sense and would tolerate no suggestion of private attachments. "We do not believe," he says, "in ownership of persons at all, either by spiritual claim or legal claim. We give no quarter to the 'marriage spirit,' or to 'special love,' or to any other fashion of idolatry and appropriation that takes folks out of the family circle of heaven and dedicates them to one another. How much should we gain for Social Communism by merely shifting from legal marriage to spiritual marriage? Such a change would only make matters worse, in proportion as spiritual ties are stronger than legal. Swedenborgians believe in eternal monogamy; Spiritualists believe in mating by affinity; and fanatics generally . . . adopt one form or another of . . . dualism, involving more sentimentalism and in the end worse slavery than common marriage. But the Oneida Community instead of training in any of these companies,

has always fought them, and maintained that the only true foundation is that which Jesus Christ laid when he said that in the good time coming there will be no marriage at all."

§

With the ascending fellowship (from young to experienced, from uncouth to spiritual) and with directed love, Noyes had become a tyrant compelling his followers to be promiscuous—so his enemies said. He was to take a further step—and to succeed. In the first eight years of their married life, Harriet Noyes had borne five children to her husband, four of them prematurely and with appalling agony. Only one of the five children lived. This experience "under God," says Noyes, directed his studies to the subject of sexual intercourse:

"After our last disappointment I told my wife that I would never again expose her to such fruitless suffering. I made up my mind to live apart from her, rather than break this vow. This was the situation in the summer of 1844. At that time I conceived the idea that the sexual organs have a social function which is distinct from the propagative function; and that these functions may be separated practically. I experimented on this idea, and found that the self-control which it required was not difficult; also that my enjoyment was increased; also that my wife's experience was very satisfactory, as it had never been before; also that we had escaped the horrors and the fear of involuntary propagation. This was a great deliverance. It made a happy household. I communicated my discovery to Mr. Cragin. His experience and that of his household was the same. In the course of the next two years I studied all the essential details and bearings of the discovery. In 1846, we commenced Community life. In 1848, I published the theory of Male Continence. This is the only true account of the origin of that theory."

Whatever Noyes wrote on the subject is sober, rather severely expressed, and emphatic. But as it describes a means of preventing unwanted children from being born, I am not permitted, under the laws of the United States and under the eye of The Society for the Suppression of Vice, to quote him. What he means by saying that

the sexual organs have a social function is that the early stages of coition have a spiritual quality and a richness of emotion which is dissipated by the physical excitement of the later, propagative, stages. What he proposes is to prolong this early pleasure of presence and communion, and to "refrain from furious excitement." "If you say that this is impossible," he cries after an almost lyrical outburst on the sweetness and nobility of the first moment of intercourse, "I answer that I *know* it is possible—nay, that it is easy."

It was a system of moral restraint and self-control—it differed from every method of birth-control known at that time. It was freely published. Noyes debated its merits in print with doctors and laymen. He denied that it caused debility in men and women and his figures at Oneida proved that he was right. He himself had eight children after he was fifty-eight years old.

§

But he did not stop at Male Continence because it lacked relation to his whole edifice of theory. He had spoken of the act of sex with frankness and freedom—and his own words lack the unhappy air which surrounds their restatement above. He was now to speak of cohabitation in regard to breeding, and to be as audacious in eugenics as he had been in marriage. To use the briefest and most shocking terms, Noyes asserted the necessity of incest and in-breeding, if man is to produce a superior race.

For a generation, Oneida Community had held about two hundred and fifty souls; it is obvious that unless the society scattered, or attracted an overwhelming number of new adepts, in-breeding and incest, within an unusual, if not unnatural, degree of blood-relationship, must result within the next few generations. So a defensive theory was needed. Noyes lifted it out of the class of apologies by a combination of fervor and logic. Characteristically he stretched out his hands to touch patriarchal Israel with one, and modern science with the other. First he announced that "scientific generation is a business second in importance only to regeneration" (which in his terminology means accepting Christ, becoming a Perfectionist, and living in the ascending fellowship). He even goes so far as to suggest that "regeneration and all other forms of education depend for their success on right generation. By the grace of God,

men and women can be taught to enjoy love that stops short of propagation" and to go in for scientific selection. (It will be noted that this proposal in eugenics gives moral purpose to Male Continence and brings it completely into the structure of Perfectionism, the religion, and Bible Communism, the practical system of life.) The vital center of sociology, he asserts, is the science which presides over reproduction, and adds (in 1873), "It is becoming clear that the foundations of scientific society are to be laid in the scientific propagation of human beings." He had read his Darwin; from Galton he took the idea of hereditary genius; he was himself ready; and the children of his later years all came after the attempt at scientific propagation had begun. In the course of four years, twenty-four women and twenty men cohabited four times a month for the purpose of propagating "proportionately to the average family's capacity to have children." It is as well to anticipate a question raised by critics at the time. The answer is, "No idiotic, deaf and dumb, blind or deformed children have been born in the community," and the ratio of nervous diseases among infants and adults was about half that of New England and New York.

Noyes begins with the usual argument from the stock-breeder. It is useless to perfect an individual if we cannot reproduce him; i.e., blood must precede training as it did in the half dozen or so famous stallions who have sired nearly all the supremely fine horses in the United States. In breeding animals we get quantity from the female, quality from the male. What prevents the application of this obvious rule to humanity?

"Though it must be conceded that, in the present state of human passions and institutions, there are many great difficulties in the way of our going back to the natural simplicity of the Hebrew fathers or forward to the scientific simplicity of the cattle-breeders, yet it is important to know and remember that these difficulties are not physiological, but sentimental. As the old theologians used to say, our inability to obey the law of God is not natural, but moral. We are too selfish and sensual and ignorant to do for ourselves what we have done for animals, but we have surrounded ourselves with institutions corresponding to and required by our selfishness and sensuality and ignorance. But for all that we need not give up

the hope of better things, at least in some far-off future. If the difficulties in our way were natural and physiological, no amount of science or grace could ever overcome them; but as they are only passional and institutional, we may set the very highest standard of thorough-breeding before us as our goal, and believe that every advance of civilization and science is carrying us toward it."

Having brought in scientific propagation to give dignity to his sexual system, Noyes uses it as another argument against marriage:

"Undoubtedly the institution of marriage is an absolute bar to scientific propagation. It distributes the business of procreation in a manner similar to that of animals which pair in a wild state; that is, it leaves mating to be determined by a general scramble without attempt at scientific direction. Even if the phrenologists and scientific experts had full power to rearrange the pairs from time to time according to their adaptations, there would still be nothing like the systematic selection of the best and suppression of the poorest, which is perfecting the lower animals. How much progress would the horse-breeders expect to make if they were only at liberty to bring their animals together in exclusive pairs?

"As we have already intimated, marriage ignores the great difference between the reproductive powers of the sexes, and restricts each man, whatever may be his potency and his value, to the amount of production of which one woman, chosen blindly, may be capable. And while this unnatural and unscientific restriction is theoretically equal for all, practically it discriminates against the best and in favor of the worst; for while the good man will be limited by his conscience to what the law allows, the bad men, free from moral check, will distribute his seed beyond the legal limits as widely as he dares."

[He then proceeds to the question of incest]:

"As the general law of marriage forbids breeding from the best, so the special law and public opinion against consanguineous marriages forbids breeding in and in. And as there is no sure line of demarcation between incest and the allowable degrees of consanguinity in marriage, the tendency of high-toned moralists is generally to extend the domain of the law of incest, and so make all approach to scientific propagation as difficult as possible. Thus

there have been movements in various quarters within a few years to place marrying a deceased wife's sister under the ban of law; and the State of New Hampshire has quite recently forbidden the marriage of first cousins as incestuous."

[And, characteristically fearless, he defends polygamy and libertinage]:

"It is curious to observe that while the law of scientific propagation on the one hand thus criticizes some of the holiest institutions and sects, on the other it finds traces of good in some of the vilest forms of existing society. For instance, polygamy, so far as the fact of obtaining and supporting many wives implies that a man is superior to his fellows, is an approximation at least to nature's wild form of breeding from the best, which is more than can be said of monogamic marriage. Again, slavery is always more or less a system of control over propagation; and so far as the interest of masters lead to selection, like that practiced in animal-breeding, it tends to the elevation of the subject race. Probably the negroes have risen in the scale of being faster than their masters, for the same reason that horses and cattle under man's control rise faster than man himself. Even common licentiousness, cursed as it is, is sometimes not without compensations in the light of the propagative law. It is very probable that the feudal custom which gave barons the first privilege of every marriage among their retainers, base and oppressive though it was, actually improved the blood of the lower classes. We see that Providence frequently allows very superior men to be also very attractive to women, and very licentious. Perhaps with all the immediate evil that they do to morals they do some good to the blood of after generations. Who can say how much the present race of men in Connecticut owe to the numberless adulteries and fornications of Pierrepont Edwards? Corrupt as he was, he must have distributed a good deal of the blood of his noble father, Jonathan Edwards; and so we may hope the human race got a secret profit out of him.* Such are the compensations of nature and Providence."

* It is possible that the persistence of the legend that ministers' sons are all wastrels can be traced back to the careers of Aaron Burr and Pierrepont Edwards. I have made no special effort to unearth the details of the latter's life. In the literature of the period following his death there are many references like the one above; and even encyclopedias speak of his dissolute habits, but obscurely and without references to sources.

Surprisingly, for the man who imposed such tyranny over the affections, he states the first qualification of the institutions which are to supplant marriage, whoredom, and casual breeding: "They must not lessen human liberty." It is hard to see what he means by that.

§

With scientific propagation Noyes had completed his work. He had made perfection permanent by making it transmissible. He had banished Death by abolishing the elements in human society by which Death was caused. The trace of mysticism is evident, but Noyes was not speaking mystically when he said that "the death system must be abolished." He was merely summing up his earthly labors. In the preceding account of religious beliefs, it was noted that the Perfectionist, being identified with Christ, partakes of Christ's victory over Death. At first Noyes claimed only that the believer dies and rises again spiritually. Later he added the mystical idea that the believer, although he may "pass through the form of death," will not really die. Professor Warfield calls this a "sad concession to the appearance of things," but Noyes would not have held it so. Partaking of Christ's nature was a reality to him. The death through which Christ passed is one of the limitations of earthly law which cannot touch those beyond death. To abolish death utterly: "First we abolish sin, then shame, then the curse on woman of exhausting child-bearing, then the curse on man of exhausting labor," and so, by the religion of Perfectionism, by the ascending fellowship and free love, by Male Continence, and by communism in labor and property, are removed all the antecedents of death and "we arrive regularly at the tree of life." The syllabus is re-stated: "Reconciliation with God opens the way for the reconciliation of the sexes, emancipates woman, and opens the way for vital society. Vital society increases strength, diminishes work, and makes labor attractive, thus removing the antecedents of death." It is a grandiose structure. It accounts for itself in every particular. It satisfies certain essential needs of man and sets him into relation with the Infinite. The success of Oneida is to be admired, not to be wondered at.

§

It is no belittlement of that success to record the practical end
of the Community. It had become, by the end of the 1870's, an
extremely prosperous business concern with a reputation for integrity such as the Rappites had in their day. Materialistic critics have
pointed out the many ways in which Noyes' theories adapted themselves to the typical American life of making money. In his own
book on *American Socialisms*, Noyes singled out eight communities
whose organization he praised. Every one of them rejected marriage and, although he complicated instead of rejecting it, he still
held firm to the great principle of forbidding private attachments.
The canalized love of young people, the constant pressure of
steadier elements, the absence of private ownership, the communal
care for the education of children, the acceptance of these children
into full membership so that there could be no cares for their
future—all these made for a strongly knit unity of life, for a single
ambition, the good of the community, which was interpreted as the
success of the workshops. Even the two final principles, continence
and selective propagation, served the community, by limiting the
number of children born and by improving the stock of the future
owners of Oneida. (Actually only a few unplanned-for children
were born.)

Writing a dozen years after the colony changed its system, Anita
Newcomb McGee said that one-fourth of the adult communists were
living in pairs for weeks and months at a time, had children, and
were inspired with "the Spirit of Monogamy"—the old solidarity
vanished "and each desired a mate." This is hardly credible, for the
colony held together until outside forces broke down its marriage
system; then only it dispersed.

For six years, Professor John W. Mears of Hamilton College
had been tirelessly demanding legislative action against the community. He led a committee of seven, appointed by the Presbyterian Synod of Central New York, "to confer with other religious
bodies" on "further measures" against Oneida; and lectured on
the subject before other organizations, winning resolutions condemning the community and agitating a public opinion which was
at best skeptical of Oneida's morality. In 1879, forty-seven hostile
critics, including Mears and Bishop Huntington, were gathered at

Syracuse. As they entered the hall of their deliberations a printed statement was handed to each. In it Noyes made these points:

"The Communists had always been peaceable subjects of civil authority no seditious act ever having been charged upon them; that they had never proposed to carry out their peculiar principles in defiance of the laws or of the public opinion of their neighbors; and if special legislation should be obtained unfavorable to them they would still be faithful to their record in submission to 'the powers that be.' In all this the Communists, it affirmed, were the very antipodes of the Mormons, as they also were in their social theory and practice, there being more analogy and more practical sympathy between them and the Shakers than between them and the followers of Joseph Smith."

On the 26th of August—six days after the "high tide of the flesh"—the Community, in full assembly, read and accepted the following proposals of their founder: "I need hardly remind the Community that we have always claimed freedom of conscience to change our social practices, and have repeatedly offered to abandon the offensive part of our system of communism if so required by public opinion. We have lately pledged ourselves in our publications to loyally obey any new legislation which may be instituted against us. Many of you will remember that I have frequently said within the last year that I did not consider our present social arrangements an essential part of our profession as Christian Communists, and that we shall probably have to recede from them sooner or later. I think the time has come for us to act on these principles of freedom, and I offer for your consideration the following modifications of our practical platform. I propose:

"1. That we give up the practice of complex marriage, not as renouncing belief in the principles and prospective finality of that institution, but in deference to the public sentiment which is evidently rising against it.

"2. That we place ourselves not on the platform of the Shakers, on the one hand, nor of the world on the other, but on Paul's platform which allows marriage but prefers celibacy . . . To carry out this change, it will be necessary first of all that we should go into a new and earnest study of the 7th chapter, 1 Cor., in which Paul fully defines his position, and also that of the Lord Jesus Christ,

in regard to the sexual relations proper for the Church in the presence of worldly institutions. If you accept these modifications, the Community will consist of two distinct classes—the married and the celibate—both legitimate, but the last preferred.

"What will become of communism after these modifications, may be defined thus:

"1. We shall hold our property and businesses in common, as now.

"2. We shall live together in a common household and eat at a common table, as now.

"3. We shall have a common children's department as now.

"4. We shall have our daily evening meetings, and all of our present means of moral and spiritual improvement.

"Surely here is communism enough to hold us together and inspire us with heroism for a new career. With the breeze of general goodwill in our favor, which even Professor Mears has promised us on the condition of our giving up the 'immoral features' of our system, what new wonders of success may we not hope for in the years to come?

"For my part, I think we have great cause to be thankful for the toleration which has so long been accorded to our audacious experiment. Especially are we indebted to the authorities and people of our immediate neighborhood for kindness and protection. It will be a good and gracious thing for us to relieve them at last of the burden of our unpopularity, and show the world that Christian Communism has self-control and flexibility enough to live and flourish without complex marriage.

"J. H. Noyes."

Complex marriage was at an end. "From the present date," says the resolution, "the Community will consist of two classes of members, namely, celibates, or those who prefer to live a life of sexual abstinence, and the married who practice only the sexual freedom which strict monogamy allows. The Community will now look for the sympathy and encouragement which have been so liberally promised in case this change should ever be made."

It is said that, with infinite contempt for the legal marriage relation, Noyes led his flock into their great hall and lining the men and women up on opposite sides of the room, ordered them to

count off. When the count was concluded, he paired the corresponding numbers and so satisfied the claims of a monogamic society. On somewhat better authority, I have heard that one woman was unpaired at the end of Oneida and resented it for the rest of her life. With the end of community in persons came an end to communism in property. Oneida was skillfully translated into a joint stock company. Some of the members stayed. A few followed Noyes to Canada. The others scattered. In 1886 the perfect Communist, who founded a great American business and abolished death, died self-exiled from his community, but undisturbed in his faith.

† Until 1834 every citizen of Massachusetts had to contribute to the support of some religious sect. Ministers with unsure livings were afraid to support unpopular causes. † The drift to the cities became marked in the 1830's and one of the attractions of New York was the Siamese Twins. † People said, "Don't you take?" in the sense of "get the point?" † Silver forks came in and also the balanced knife handle to keep the blade off the cloth, "a little thing, but very promotive of cleanliness." † The reaper was perfected and the first horticultural society was founded. † In 1832, Frederick Tudor was sending ice from Massachusetts to the southern states, Brazil, and to Calcutta for Lord William Bentinck and the nabobs of the India Company. † Railroad construction gangs were made up chiefly of Irishmen paid from forty to seventy-five cents a day, with their meals and six drinks of whiskey daily. † In 1836, Lovejoy was killed by anti-abolitionists at Alton, Illinois. † In the same year there was a mad speculation in building lots in Manhattan, many of them known as "water lots."

† The city of Lowell, named after a manufacturer of cotton, was built as a complete factory town and, before it was paved, 5,000 young women and a thousand men were already at work. † In Ohio there was an "utter aversion to ministers trading in horse flesh" and settlers there united to do violence to land speculators. † In 1832, a steamer landed troops in Chicago and, eight years later, the first Cunarder, the *Britannia*, arrived in Boston. † In 1835, Colt's rotating chambered gun breech was patented. † In 1829, a scandal was caused in New York by the public examination of a girl in the subject of Geometry, "the clergy, as usual, prophesying the dissolution of all family bonds." † In 1835, was circulated the first petition for property rights for women; the marriage by contract of Robert Dale Owen was sneered at, and the phrase "committed matrimony" was in use. † The "backwoods" were no longer known by that name and "eastern exquisites" visited Lexington and Louisville. The country suffered a flood of European critics. † The American business man was already tired—of making money. † By 1832 "The campaigns against Black Hawk and Madame Trollope are over, and both have ceased to be objects of editorial concern. And there are no new Lions—The steam engine— march of mind—spirit of the age, above all 'the West'—'the Far West' —'the great West,' those standard topics of newspaper paragraphs, have had their praises exhausted, and 'delight no more.'" † Mr. Barnum was exhibiting Tom Thumb.

# XI.

## Reformer and Radical.

IN the autumn of 1840, Emerson wrote to Carlyle, "We are all a little wild here with numberless projects of social reform. Not a reading man but has a draft of a new Community in his waistcoat pocket." It was the great era of criticism and of change. It began when William Miller was predicting the immediate end of the world, and seven years later, just as Mr. Greeley's London correspondent was writing "Workers of the World, unite! You have nothing to lose but your chains," most of the experiments had ended. "Mad-men, and women, men with beards, Dunkers, Muggletonians, Come-outers, Groaners, Agrarians, Seventh-day Baptists, Quakers, Abolitionists, Unitarians, and Philosophers" were seen by Emerson in those catch-alls of radicalism, Reform Conventions. He held aloof; he reproved; he disliked their enthusiasm for helping everybody and changing everything but themselves; and he was, in a strange way, their inspiration. Whatever broke from the established order could justify itself by some sentence from his rattling essays. He thought that Fourier was magnanimous * and inspired; but he refrained from joining the great experiments at his very door, benignly sending blessings to the esthetes at Brook Farm and to the philosophers at Fruitlands, or paying an austere, friendly visit, and returning to Concord to write coldly in his journal about ideas without hands or feet. The experimenters admired him, envied him, wanted him with them, and reproached him for his indifference. The eternal injustice of man to man left him unmoved, and only some salient act of ungenerosity, some ignobility in human dealings, could stir him to action. When he finally spoke, as he did on slavery, his utterance was momentous but, in the

* Fourier was magnificent. Not satisfied with creating a new type of communal life, he imagined a world-state, with its capital at Constantinople, and an entirely new cosmogony. He foresaw the time when the earth would bask in perpetual spring and when the salt waters of the sea would turn into an ocean of lemonade, with whales and dolphins acting as beasts of burden. His influence on American communities was great; Horace Greeley and Albert Brisbane were his chief disciples and dozens of phalansteries were founded. An accurate and entertaining account of the Fourierite enthusiasm is given in Miss Rourke's *Trumpets of Jubilee.*

general run of events, he stood aside because his mind was occupied with other things. The radicals about him professed their indifference to wealth and social position, and were infuriated by poverty or snobbism; Emerson managed to be indifferent to both. To the reforming enthusiast he said, "Why so hot, my little man?" To the altruist, asking contributions, he wanted to say, "Are they my poor?", and to withhold his dollar. If wealth was not important, as they all agreed, how could the lack of it signify greatly? There were more pressing obligations on the true man than the duty to amass coin or the necessity of preventing poverty. To know the moral order of the universe was one of these graver tasks, to come into harmony with it, to turn inward and to trust one's self. The kindest word he has is for Alcott, who believed that all social and political changes were fruitless, since they shifted evil from one place to another, and that personal reform, a change in the individual, bringing him closer to the order of Nature, alone could eradicate evil.

Emerson, consequently, is the prophet of the next generation of reformers: the prophets of the will; the priests of the sinless religion based not on Christ but on self; the mind healers, and optimists, and teachers of self-confidence in fourteen lessons; the mystics of success. When we come to them, we see how, out of the vast range of Emerson's ideas, and out of his high conceptions of the gentleman and the man, they managed, by skillful selection, to create the bounder with an aggressive ego and how, out of a lofty mysticism, they drew a silly one. From that, at least, the radicals of his own time were deterred by his severe presence and by his hostility. They drew from him a single encouragement: to trust themselves against society. In some of his most impressive sentences he spoke of divine justice: "It is impossible to tilt the beam. All the tyrants and proprietors and monopolists of the world in vain set their shoulders to heave the bar. Settles for evermore the ponderous equator to its line, and man and mote, and star and sun, must range to it, or be pulverized by the recoil." That type of retribution they understood, for they all believed themselves instinctively at one with nature, and privy to its secret intentions. They could trust themselves, because they—and they alone—trusted nature.

§

The radicals of the 1840's and after created the type-radical of our own time. The changes which words undergo have confused us somewhat for, in 1840, the radical was called a reformer and, in 1928, the reformer is not a radical and the radical is called a Red. In 1914, before Prohibition and Bolshevism had blurred the picture in the back of our minds, the radical was, in our imagination, a comparatively harmless crank, given to fads, strolling about in white garments, eating nuts, talking of love and beauty. He was, in reality, already turning into something harder and more dangerous to settled convictions, but the cartoonist lagged a little behind the fact, and we still thought of the radical as he was in 1840. The reformer, meanwhile, had undergone another transformation. In 1840, that name was given to the lofty soul who, at the risk of martyrdom, was ready to lay the ax at the root of every human institution:

"The trump of reform," wrote the *Dial* in 1841, "is sounding throughout the world for a revolution of all human affairs. The issue we cannot doubt; yet the crises are not without alarm. Already is the ax laid at the root of that spreading tree, whose trunk is idolatry, whose branches are covetousness, war, and slavery, whose blossom is concupiscence, whose fruit is hate. Planted by Beelzebub, it shall be rooted up. Reformers are metallic; they are sharpest steel; they pierce whatsoever of evil or abuse they touch. Their souls are attempered in the fires of heaven; they are mailed in the might of principles, and God backs their purpose. They uproot institutions, erase traditions, revise usages, and renovate all things. They are the noblest of facts. Extant in time, they work for eternity; dwelling with men, they are with God."

So he stood, ax uplifted, at the threshold of the Gilded Age, and the age paralyzed his arm. In 1863, when the Emancipation Proclamation was signed, the radical-reformer—the ultraist as he was called—had reached the end of his tether. In that notable success was the seed of his failure, for it meant that the most extreme of radical measures had succeeded without destroying society, and without much aid, even, from the radicals. Until 1860, the infidel, the suffragist, the Perfectionist, the experimenter in Communities, all were somehow tolerated by society provided they were not also

Abolitionists. Abolition was the Bolshevism of that time in the North as well as in the South. The opponents of slavery avoided Garrison because he prejudiced their cause, their compromises, their projects for restoring the negro to Africa. Our school histories have given us the picture of a North of Abolitionists and a South devoted to the "peculiar institution." We reject the bitter facts that neither Lincoln nor his party was in favor of abolition; that both might have made slavery permanent to save the Union; that New England mobbed anti-slavery meetings; that liberals of all types avoided the taint of Abolitionism; that Lovejoy was not killed by a true southern mob; that only a pitiful handful of fanatics voted for an abolitionist president; that Quakers and New England Congregationalists supported slavery; that to all right-thinking people John Brown and William Lloyd Garrison were anathema; and that a good Bostonian shrank from being seen even with so eminent a negro as the orator, Frederick Douglass. The Abolitionist was the arch-enemy of established society. When his cause was carried by the accident of a war which he did not inspire, all other causes were shaken. It should not have been so: one triumph should have led to others, and might have done so if the field of operations had not changed. Causes went into politics. After the Civil War we see a succession of third parties with programs of social reform. And as the scandals of the age rose out of economic exploitation protected by politics, the reformer, too, had to shift his ground.

Beginning with the '70's, the personal reform of temperance was transformed into the political reform of prohibition, and the radical-reformer of the 1840's reappeared, a decade later, as the protagonist of honesty in politics, to be followed closely by the muck-raker and eventually by the Progressive. The radical element in the reformer had separated out of the composition. By fissure, the man of the 1840's had become two: the radical attached to abstract ideas, the reformer attached to politics. The return of Roosevelt to orderly Republicanism, the liberal enthusiasm for Wilson and the Peace, put an end to that type of reformer. But, in the meantime, another had risen, antipodal in every superficial respect to the reformer of 1840, yet psychologically close to him. The key-word of 1840 was "abolish"; of 1900 "improve"; of 1926 "prohibit." At the moment it seems that only the last was successful.

PICTURES OF PROGRESS.

"Come along and help dig them Taters!"
"Why, you must be a new comer in this Phalanstry, or you would know that I belong to the Eating Group."

The early radical-reformer was, strangely enough, a sympathizer with the supposed motive of the modern prohibitionist; that is, he usually disliked liquor in all its forms. What he would have despised utterly is the prohibitionist's method; for the 1840 radical was not a legalist, and his way of banishing liquor was a transcendental kind of local option. Association was another key-word of the time (Alcott preferred Con-sociation); and when an association was made, a colony founded, the members could banish liquor and tobacco if they chose, and any new member would naturally accept the laws of the Community in that respect as he did in respect to property or wives. The radicals corresponded in time to the Washingtonian Movement, the great effort to impress temperance on Americans through the testimony of reformed drunkards. This movement was as personal as the Anti-Saloon League was impersonal. It required a moral conversion, and it offered individual happiness, invoking no law but the moral law, appointing no bureaucracy, and carrying on no lobby. This was the typical movement of the time, trusting to moral suasion, appealing to the individual, and involving no compulsion. It wanted to abolish the drunkard without abolishing the drink. The communist experiments of the same time wanted to abolish private property and unequal wages —for themselves. The vegetarians desired an end to the universal wrong done to animals, but their chief aim was to persuade people to stop incorporating the flesh of beasts into their own bodies. The suffragists demanded the right to vote; they did not try to take that right away from any man. Only the Abolitionist pure and simple attacked a right or a privilege and he, too, worked on the basis of equality, for he did not propose to let the black man keep the white man as slave. To abolish a pernicious institution, and then to leave men and women to their own devices, was the ideal of the libertarian radical, and whatever institution he founded or approved was one which protected liberty.

Contrasted with the sour figure of the modern Prohibitionist, the reformer of 1840 is a happy and generous person, trusting human nature in its "natural" state, eager to allow every liberty to mankind, and never happy himself so long as injustice and unkindness remained on earth. In that view, the radical comes to our mind in the same group-picture with the martyrs of liberty, the saints,

and the prophets. We imagine the contempt an Alcott or a Greeley might have had for the tyrannical practice and mean devices of a censor of literature, or an Anti-Saloon Leaguer, or a Tennessee legislator of to-day, and it seems to us that a miasma of intolerance has spread over our own time, choking our finer sensibilities and stunting the growth of great spirits.

For the sake of convenience, we may take the period 1800-1840 (roughly) as the one in which the revivalist worked on the radical-reforming temperament and created communities; and the period from 1840 to our own day as the one in which the radical-reformer turned into the prohibitory-reformer. Stated even in these terms, the marks of degeneracy become plain. It would be premature to stress the point. But it may be noted now that the degradation of radical doctrine is probably due in part to the vast failure of radical movements when they founded communities. At that point, they touched America with the sharpest edge: they challenged the system of production, of capitalism. Had they made any success for themselves there, they might have developed more happily, with the respect which America (and possibly Europe) pays to whatever establishes itself. But they failed, conclusively. Except for the Shakers and the Rappites of an earlier, religious day, only one community gave any indication of success. This was Oneida, and it, too, was based on a religion. Many years later, Zion City seemed successful, came close to bankruptcy, and was saved, but it was not a true community.

The others, the communities founded on faith and hope perished without grandeur. Several records exist, most of them based on fragments of a manuscript written by a forgotten Scot whose practical mind seems to have been fascinated by all these impracticalities. On one side is a list of lovely names, names of abstract virtues, of philosophical ideals, of pious devotion; on the other side is the deadly record of bankruptcy and dispersal. One wishes they had been as intelligent as they were gallant, as beautiful as they were fanatic. But making all reservations, these communities still have a touch of human dignity, and it seems hard that they should have struggled and perished and left their name to be exploited as bait for bad furniture and limp leather books.

In the period of the '40's, the most famous experiment was

Brook Farm; the most numerous experiments were the Fourierite phalanxes. The stories of these colonies are so well known that I have preferred to choose two others: Ballou's Hopedale, which in its meekness and dullness exhibits all the lesser vices of communities, and Alcott's Fruitlands, where every idiosyncrasy flourished and all the absurd impracticality of the reformer when cultivating the land was exposed.

† The West was being cultivated by the Bible, Mission, Tract, Sabbath School, Temperance, Education, and Seamen and River Men's Societies. † In the novel *Home*, a family was described as spending Sunday morning in church and the afternoon in religious conversation on a sailboat. So much offense was taken at this frivolity that the edition was withdrawn and the sailboat deleted. When Italian opera was proposed in Boston, the name was considered daring, and "lectures on music with illustrations" were offered as a substitute. † The mayor of New York denied that he had violated the Sabbath by entertaining visiting nobility on a Sunday. † Baldwin built a locomotive which ran sixty-two miles an hour. † After 1830 fruit crops for the first time appeared in agricultural statistics. † The parade celebrating the election of Jackson was described by a visiting Frenchman as a grotesque version of the Kermesse. † The Appellate Court decided that a free black woman was not entitled to the privileges of the ladies' cabin on a steamer in Massachusetts. † Official geologists were appointed by many states. † In 1837, "a wagon load of girls for the western market lately passed through Northampton, Massachusetts." † "The Americans are always in a hurry," says a visiting Frenchman. † Democratic Protestantism was favoring the exaltation of the lower classes, and Frenchmen and Englishmen alike found that all Yankees were cast in the same mold. † The gospel of salvation by manual training was being vigorously taught. † The beard was an object of mockery.

# XII.

## An Apostle of the Newness.

"THE most refined and most advanced soul we have had in New England" had been lecturing for several months in the Middle West; his subject was the New England mind as represented by Greeley, Garrison, Webster, Theodore Parker, Greenough, Margaret Fuller and, most illustrious of all, the man whose superlative opinion has been quoted, Ralph Waldo Emerson. The seven were included in six lectures, and the price for the series was three dollars. On a cold, black, February night, the lecturer returned to his home in Concord with exactly one dollar in his pocket. "He looked," wrote Louisa Alcott, his daughter, "as cold and thin as an icicle, but as serene as God." It was Bronson Alcott's habit to face his own failures with serenity. On the one occasion when he turned his face to the wall, it was Nature, whom he trusted, and human nature, which he did not understand, that had failed: he himself had been true.

He had been true, in fact, to the most absurd collection of fads and principles that ever occupied the mind of one man. Nothing radical was alien to Bronson Alcott and there was no departure from the accepted ways which he did not take. In the disastrous experiment at Fruitlands, he and the two families which, with a few followers, made up the community, created a complete world of ineffective radicalism. All the types were there, all the idiosyncrasies, a sufficiency of chaotic genius, a touch of selfishness, a trace of madness and more than a trace of heroic patience. In all, there were at Fruitlands about a dozen adults and four or five children on a farm, between the towns of Harvard and Still River, twenty miles away from Concord. Of the children, four little girls were Alcott's, and they and their mother became familiar to millions of American children when Louisa Alcott put them into her books. With Mrs. Alcott, who destroyed herself with the work of bringing some equilibrium into an unbalanced household, correcting the errors of her erratic husband, and gathering in the crops which the men left to rot in the fields, there was but one woman at Fruitlands and she

was of no great help. All the vagaries, the foolish and pathetic ideas, came from the men. One of them seemed possessed by a hatred of cattle, for the farm was never polluted by a cow's foot and neither flesh, nor milk, nor any product of milk, entered into the diet of Fruitlands. Another allowed weeds to grow in the vegetable patch because they had as much right to be there as corn or cucumbers. Another would eat no vegetable which pushed downward into the ground, instead of aspiring nobly into the sun. Another, whose name was Abram Wood, indicated his independence of common forms by insisting on being called Wood Abram. Another chose to go as nearly naked as possible. Alcott himself did not allow the land to be manured—"a base and corrupting mode of forcing nature"—and tried to render palatable the bread he himself made of unbolted flour by shaping the loaves into animals and other attractive forms.

His chief collaborator was the Englishman, Charles Lane, who owned the property upon which Fruitlands stood—that is, he had paid for it, but Emerson held it as trustee, since the ownership of property was outlawed in the community and Fruitlands was always referred to as "liberated from human ownership." On an unproductive farm, in an uncomfortable house, with a diet of vegetables and water, Charles Lane wrote, "To me our mode of life is luxurious in the highest degree." He had come from England only a short time before, following the admired Alcott, with the purpose of founding a New Eden. He had first gone to visit Brook Farm and that comparatively simple and uncomfortable community had inspired in him a feeling almost of nausea. When he saw Brook Farm, "where there are eighty or ninety persons playing away their youth and day time in a miserably joyless frivolous manner," he felt that he must remove Alcott as far as possible from its softening influence and from that of Emerson, its absent inspiration, in particular. The sight of "no less than sixteen cows besides four oxen, a herd of swine, and a horse or two" displeased him intensely. Brook Farm was a community of taste and he did not care for it. He wrote back to friends in England asking them to urge youthful men and women to come to Fruitland, saying, "There is now a certain opportunity for planting a love colony the influence of which may be felt for many generations and more than felt; it may be the be-

ginning of a state of things which shall far transcend itself." What the austere Lane and the mystic Alcott meant by a love colony must remain forever obscure; the colony they did found was hardly a home for the voluptuary.

§

The meeting of Lane and Alcott was the result of that part of Alcott's life which time has made most honorable to him. He was one of the earliest of modern schoolmasters putting into practice, in 1826, theories of child education which still inspire modern experiments although they made Alcott a target for abuse and contempt in his own time. He began by abolishing the backbreaking form-benches customary at that time, and gave each child a chair and a desk. He improved blackboards. He brought works of art into the schoolroom and touched off the imagination of his pupils by allegory and fiction. He was a pioneer in the use of gymnastic exercises in public schools. These innovations aroused only criticism. When he went further and established a school discipline based on free courtesy and understanding and left his school for a whole day to the self-government of the pupils, he began to be considered a menace. Given his character, it could only be a matter of time before he offended everyone. The occasion for all his work to be attacked was when he published a series of *Conversations with Children on the Gospels*. Against the advice of Miss Peabody (whose sister later married Nathaniel Hawthorne), he left in the book a few passages relating to birth and was promptly accused of being obscene and blasphemous. His whole method of teaching was now called into question. The Boston *Daily Advertiser* complained that "on the most important questions this teacher, while he endeavors to extract from his pupils every thought which may come uppermost in their minds, takes care studiously to conceal his own opinions" except where he gives principles of questionable soundness. To this accusation, which the modern pedagogue would consider the highest praise, was added the damning indictment that Alcott believed childhood to be a type of divinity. The *Courier*, at the same time, so abusively demanded a trial for blasphemy that Emerson was moved to protest. But Emerson could not deny Alcott's literal belief that children come trailing clouds of glory and it is, in modern

eyes, infinitely to Alcott's credit that he did everything in his power to keep the shadow of the prison house from falling across his pupils. He really believed that "infant education when adapted to the human being is founded on the great principle, that every infant is already in possession of the faculties and apparatus required for his instruction, and that, by a law of his constitution, he uses these to a great extent himself; that the office of instruction is chiefly to facilitate this process, and to accompany the child in his progress, rather than to drive or even to lead him." In a time when people believed seriously in infant damnation, Alcott could not be popular and, although the temper of the community was shown when wells near by were polluted and school houses attacked because of the presence of negro students, Alcott deliberately invited a young negress into his school. The school broke up.

§

Harriet Martineau, the distinguished English visitor, had bent her receptive ear trumpet to catch words of praise for Alcott's Temple School. On her return to England, although she, herself, was not enthusiastic, she gave such an account of Alcott's methods that a group of mystic Englishmen, who were then interested in Pestalozzi, began a correspondence with Alcott and eventually founded, in England, a school on his principles and bearing his name. In 1842, Alcott sailed for England on their invitation and, having conceived the idea of a New Eden, brought back Charles Lane and a few others to assist in laying its foundation. This was the beginning of Fruitlands.

Many years later, Louisa Alcott wrote a lightly romantic account of Fruitlands under the title of *Transcendental Wild Oats*. She was not particularly generous to Charles Lane, but she was fairly accurate, and the opening picture of the departure for the earthly paradise is typical:

"On the first day of June, 1842, a large wagon, drawn by a small horse and containing a motley load, went lumbering over certain New England hills, with the pleasing accompaniments of wind, rain, and hail. A serene man with a serene child upon his knee was driving, or rather being driven, for the small horse had it all his

own way. A brown boy with a William Penn style of countenance sat beside him, firmly embracing a bust of Socrates. Behind them was an energetic-looking woman, with a benevolent brow, satirical mouth, and eyes brimful of hope and courage. A baby reposed upon her lap, a mirror leaned against her knee, and a basket of provisions danced about at her feet, as she struggled with a large, unruly umbrella. Two blue-eyed little girls, with hands full of childish treasures, sat under one old shawl, chatting happily together.

"In front of this lively party stalked a tall, sharp-featured man, in a long blue cloak; and a fourth small girl trudged along beside him through the mud as if she rather enjoyed it.

"The wind whistled over the bleak hills; the rain fell in a despondent drizzle, and twilight began to fall. But the calm man gazed as tranquilly into the fog as if he beheld a radiant bow of promise spanning the gray sky. The cheery woman tried to cover everyone but herself with the big umbrella. The brown boy pillowed his head on the bald pate of Socrates and slumbered peacefully. The little girls sang lullabies to their dolls in soft, maternal murmurs. The sharp-nosed pedestrian marched steadily on, with the blue cloak streaming out behind him like a banner; and the lively infant splashed through the puddles with a ducklike satisfaction pleasant to behold.

"Thus these modern pilgrims journeyed hopefully out of the old world, to found a new one in the wilderness."

The editors of the *Dial* had already received a statement of principles from Lane and Alcott and various other periodicals published similar documents. From these we gather that Fruitlands was not a social or political or spiritual experiment, so much as a personal one. While other communities held that the evils of life are due to political and social organization, Alcott turned inward and declared that only a personal reform can eradicate these evils. He and Lane inclined to approve of the asceticism of the Shakers and, "as to property, we discover not its just disposal either in individual or social tenures, but in its entire absorption into the New Spirit, which ever gives and never grasps."

The new apostles objected to trade and wages, but their passion seems to have been to rid the world of cattle. "Our ultimate aim is

to furnish an instance of self-sustaining cultivation without the sub-
jugation of either men or cattle, or the use of foul animal manures;
we have at the outset to encounter struggles and oppositions somewhat formidable. Until the land is restored to its pristine fertility
by the annual return of its own green crops, as sweet and animating
manures, the human hand and simple implement cannot wholly
supersede the employment of machinery and cattle. So long as
cattle are used in agriculture, it is very evident that man will remain a slave, whether he be proprietor or hireling. The driving
of cattle beyond their natural and pleasurable exertion; the waiting upon them as cook and chamber-maid three parts of the year;
the excessive labor of mowing, curing, and housing hay, and of collecting other fodder, and the large extra quantity of land needful
to keep up this system, form a continuation of unfavorable circumstances which must depress the human affections so long as it continues, and overlay them by the injurious and extravagant development of the animal and bestial natures in man. It is calculated that
if no animal food were consumed, one-fourth of the land now used
would suffice for human sustenance. And the extensive tracts of
country now appropriated to grazing, mowing, and other modes of
animal provision, could be cultivated by and for intelligent and
affectionate human neighbors. The sty and the stable too often secure more of the farmer's regard than he bestows on the garden
and the children. No hope is there for humanity while Woman is
withdrawn from the tender assiduities which adorn her and her
household, to the servitudes of the dairy and the flesh pots. If the
beasts were wholly absent from man's neighborhood, the human
population might be at least four times as dense as it now is without raising the price of land. This would give to the country all
the advantages of concentration without the vices which always
spring up in the dense city.

"Debauchery of both the earthly soil and the human body is
the result of this cattle keeping. The land is scourged for crops to
feed the animals, whose ordures are used under the erroneous sup-
position of restoring lost fertility; disease is thus infused into the
human body; stimulants and medicines are resorted to for relief,
which end in a precipitation of the original evil to a more disastrous
depth. These misfortunes which affect not only the body, but by

reaction rise to the sphere of the soul, would be avoided, or at least in part, by the disuse of animal food. Our diet is therefore strictly the pure and bloodless kind. No animal substances, neither flesh, butter, cheese, eggs, nor milk, pollute our table or corrupt our bodies, neither tea, coffee, molasses, nor rice, tempts us beyond the bounds of indigenous productions. Our sole beverage is pure fountain water. The native grains, fruits, herbs, and roots, dressed with the utmost cleanliness and regard to their purpose of edifying a healthful body, furnish the pleasantest refections and in the greatest variety requisite to the supply of the various organs. The field, the orchard, the garden, in their bounteous products of wheat, rye, barley, maize, oats, buckwheat, apples, pears, peaches, plums, cherries, currants, berries, potatoes, peas, beans, beets, carrots, melons, and other vines, yield an ample store for human nutrition, without dependence on foreign climes, or the degeneration of shipping and trade. The almost inexhaustible variety of the several stages and sorts of vegetable growth, and the several modes of preparation, are a full answer to the question which is often put by those who have never ventured into the region of a pure and chaste diet: 'If you give up flesh meat, upon what then can you live?'

"Our other domestic habits are in harmony with those of diet. We rise with early dawn, begin the day with cold bathing, succeeded by a music lesson, and then a chaste repast. Each one finds occupation until the meridian meal, when usually some interesting and deep-searching conversation gives rest to the body and development to the mind. Occupation, according to the season and the weather, engages us out of doors or within, until the evening meal,—when we again assemble in social communion, prolonged generally until sunset, when we resort to sweet repose for the next day's activity."

There was a great deal more to this manifesto. The last paragraph of it is put in Alcott's mouth in his daughter's story and it has the unmistakable ring of his style:

"In these steps of reform we do not rely as much on scientific reasoning or physiological skill, as on the Spirit's dictates. The pure soul, by the law of its own nature, adopts a pure diet and cleanly customs; nor needs detailed instruction for daily conduct. On a re-

vision of our proceedings it would seem, that if we were in the right course in our particular instance, the greater part of man's duty consists in leaving alone much that he is in the habit of doing. It is a fasting from the present activity, rather than an increased indulgence in it, which, with patient watchfulness, tends to newness of life. 'Shall I sip tea or coffee?' the inquiry may be. No; abstain from all ardent, as from alcoholic drinks. 'Shall I consume pork, beef, or mutton?' Not if you value health or life. 'Shall I stimulate with milk?' No. 'Shall I warm my bathing water?' Not if cheerfulness is valuable. 'Shall I clothe in many garments?' Not if purity is aimed at. 'Shall I prolong my dark hours, consuming animal oil and losing bright daylight in the morning?' Not if a clear mind is an object. 'Shall I teach my children the dogmas inflicted on myself, under the pretense that I am transmitting truth?' Nay, if you love them intrude not these between them and the Spirit of all Truth. 'Shall I subjugate cattle?' 'Shall I trade?' 'Shall I claim property in any created thing?' 'Shall I interest myself in politics?' To how many of these questions could we ask them deeply enough, could they be heard as having relation to our eternal welfare, would the response be 'Abstain'? Be not so active to do, as sincere to be. Being in preference to doing, is the great aim and this comes to us rather by a resigned willingness than a willful activity;—which is indeed a check to all divine growth. Outward abstinence is a sign of inward fullness; and the only source of true progress is inward. We may occupy ourselves actively in human improvements;—but these unless inwardly well-impelled, never attain to, but rather hinder, divine progress in man."

"A mild snore seemed to echo the last word," says the undutiful daughter. But Alcott talked on. He was to talk on to the end of his life.

§

Characteristically, Fruitlands, which relied implicitly upon nature's promises, refused to conform to nature's system, for Miss Alcott is not romancing when she notes the date. It was actually at the beginning of June that Alcott and Lane went to Fruitlands, much too late for the early planting. They had agreed that "ordi-

nary secular farming was not their object." According to one who knew them, they intended to "evolve orchards out of their inner consciousnesses"—but it is quite impossible to parody an enterprise which is always a parody of itself. "Chaste supplies for the bodily needs" and ample manual occupation were to be afforded by assiduous attention to fruit, grain, pulse, herbs, and flax, and "consecrated to human freedom the land awaits the sober culture of devout men. . . . This enterprise must be rooted in a reliance on the succors of an ever-bounteous Providence, whose vital affinities being secured by this union with uncorrupted fields and unworldly persons, the cares and injuries of a life of gain are avoided. The inner nature of every member of the family is at no time neglected. A constant leaning on the living spirit within the soul should consecrate every talent to holy uses, cherishing the widest charities. The choice library is accessible to all who are desirous of perusing these records of piety and wisdom. Our plan contemplates all such disciplines, cultures, and habits as evidently conduce to the purifying and edifying of the inmates."

There were a few halcyon days when everyone worked and was well, when long summer twilights let Mrs. Alcott sew without bringing in the pernicious oil lamp which offended Lane's sense of justice, when three mulberry trees had been planted—so close to the front door that the growing roots eventually threatened to undermine the foundation—and fruit trees were set out—just where they could not thrive—and "they all had gotten their linen suits designed by Mr. Lane: loose trousers, tuniced coats and broad-brimmed linen hats like Southern planters'. The Alcott girls, Anna, Beth, Louisa, and three-year-old baby May were in linen bloomers, and so were Mrs. Alcott (protesting!) and poor Miss Page, who was summarily dismissed from Fruitlands for having eaten fish."

It was hardly fish that poor Miss Page had eaten—only a little bit of the tail. She was stout and mature and sentimental and lazy and wrote verses and yearned for the unknown and, having been a school teacher, believed herself fitted for a higher sphere. She wanted to sleep and eat and dream of writing poetry. The idea of helping Mrs. Alcott with washing or cooking or harvesting never entered her head. Like all the other adults at Fruitlands she took a turn at instructing the young, adding her bit to the chaos in their

minds, but she could not help slipping out of Fruitlands and borrowing a glass of milk or a bit of cheese from a neighbor and, when her transgression was reported home, Lane was inexorable. The consumers of flesh meat (which oddly included fish) nourished the wolf or tiger in their bosoms and Anna Page, having sinned, was banished from the community.

It seems only proper that she should have gone, for her fancies lacked imagination. She left behind a strange group. Samuel Larned had lived one whole year on crackers and the next exclusively on apples. One Fruitlander believed that clothes hindered spiritual growth and that the light of day was pernicious. Another crowed like a cock at midnight if a happy thought struck him. One, holding that words only betrayed the true spirit, greeted the rest with "Good morning, damn you." Samuel Bower went into the wilderness to walk naked and eat huckleberries. When the communists of Fruitlands dined out they discussed the horrors of "shambles," ate nothing but apples and bread, and advised their hosts to serve "bowls of sunrise" and "solar seeds of the sphere." At the spare dining table at Fruitlands, there were vegetarian wafers to encourage the fainting flesh. Some of them have been saved for us. They were in Alcott's own style, a little mysterious, but brief, and dramatic. First the practical Yankee:

> Vegetable diet
> and sweet repose.
> Animal food and
> nightmare.

Then the uplifted lover of animals:

> Pluck your body
> from the orchard;
> do not snatch it from
> the shamble.

Surprisingly the moralist appears:

> Snuff is no less snuff
> though accepted from a
> gold box.

And the fanatic who sees in his single remedy the universal panacea:

> Without flesh diet
> there could be no
> bloodshedding war.

And finally the crackbrained mystic:

> Apollo eats no flesh and has no beard;
> his voice is melody itself.

§

The reference to beardless Apollo is an instance of shocking ingratitude, for a certain Joseph Palmer who was a martyr to his beard was a friend in need to Fruitlands. In an age of ingenious safety razors, when the game of beaver lasts only a fortnight, it is hard to understand the passion which beards aroused in the 1830's and '40's. Just as Matthias, the prophet, lost his beard to a mob, Joseph Palmer, a sober Yankee farmer, lost his freedom when he defended his beard against lawless attacks upon its integrity; he was actually jailed. His epitaph reads, "persecuted for wearing the Beard." But meanwhile he remained bearded and sensible, continued to live in an unclaimed spot, which lay between two townships and was therefore named "No Town" and, when Fruitlands was abandoned, bought land and buildings from Charles Lane. Later, although tempted, he avoided joining Lane and the naked-going Samuel Bower in founding a new community.

Palmer and his wife Nancy were perhaps the most obscure of American communists, for their house was their community which had no name and no permanent recruits. But there were always two iron pots, one of baked beans and the other of potatoes, and any passer-by was welcome to partake of them and stay as long as he pleased. On account of his beard, he was called "old Jew Palmer" and neighbors said his house was a refuge for tramps. The last earthly view we have of him is on the day after a heavy snow storm when he started to shovel a path to the highway. The right of way crossed a neighbor's farm and, as soon as Palmer cleared the path, the neighbor shoveled the snow back again. All day long the two obstinate and angry old men tossed the snow about and, in

the dusk, had to send for Ralph Waldo Emerson to settle their dispute with his transcendental wisdom. Palmer was much too hard-headed to be a Fruitlands communist. He had those rules of thumb and instinctive feelings about farming which the true peasant has and, although, as we shall see, he was always coming to the rescue of Fruitlands, he knew that the experiment was destined to failure.

§

Whenever there was work to be done at the farm, the spirit moved the men residents to attend a reform convention where they might meet Spiritualists, and Muggletonians, and Abolitionists, and Perfectionists, and the followers of every fad. They would start out penniless and get on a train or boat and offer to deliver a short talk to the passengers in lieu of paying their fare. Once when Lane and Alcott both talked on a steamboat, a collection was taken up for them, but this they refused and "went serenely on their way with their linen blouses flapping airily in the cold October wind." Their way was anywhere except to Fruitlands when work had to be done. In the planting, they had refused to have a plow because that in-volved beasts of burden, but after the hoe had worn through Lane's tender hands, a compromise was effected and Joseph Palmer came over from No Town with an ox and a cow yoked together. But no provision had been made for the harvest and the Oversoul had not reckoned with an easterly storm. Mrs. Alcott hitched herself, her three eldest girls, and Charles Lane's son to clothes-baskets, and with these got in the grain. "Mrs. Alcott," wrote Lane, "has passed from the ladylike to the industrious order, but she has much in-ward experience to realize. Her pride is not yet eradicated and her peculiar maternal love blinds her to all else—whom does it not so blind for a season?" She was to blame, according to him, for the failure of others to come to Fruitlands and whatever she did an-noyed the philosophers. The lamp she insisted upon contained ani-mal fat and was offensive but, one after another, the philosophers came out from their dark rooms and joined her where she sat sew-ing. The days were drawing in and there was not enough food to meet the winter. "What shall you do?" Mrs. Alcott asked. And Lane answered that he would wait until the way had been made clear to him, inasmuch as being was the great aim in life, not

doing. With the first frost, Lane found the way; it led him to the more successful Shaker colonies near by.

"Then the tragedy began for the forsaken little family. Desolation and despair fell upon Abel.* As his wife said, his new beliefs had alienated many friends. Some thought him mad, some unprincipled. Even the most kindly thought him a visionary, whom it was useless to help till he took more practical views of life. All stood aloof, saying: 'Let him work out his own ideas, and see what they are worth. . . .'

"Deep waters now for Abel, and for a time there seemed no passage through. Strength and spirits were exhausted by hard work and too much thought. Courage failed when, looking about for help, he saw no sympathizing face, no hand outstretched to help him, no voice to say cheerily,

" 'We all make mistakes, and it takes many experiences to shape a life. Try again, and let us help you.'

"Every door was closed, every eye averted, every heart cold, and no way open whereby he might earn bread for his children. His principles would not permit him to do many things that others did; and in the few fields where conscience would allow him to work, who would employ a man who had flown in the face of society, as he had done?

"Then this dreamer, whose dream was the life of his life, resolved to carry out his idea to the bitter end. There seemed no place for him here,—no work, no friend. To go begging conditions was as ignoble as to go begging money. Better perish of want than sell one's soul for the sustenance of his body. Silently he lay down upon his bed, turned his face to the wall, and waited with pathetic patience for death to cut the knot which he could not untie. Days and nights went by, and neither food nor water passed his lips. Soul and body were dumbly struggling together, and no word of complaint betrayed what either suffered."

This was the end of Fruitlands, but not the end of Alcott. Hawthorne, so merciless at Brook Farm, could not resist this visionary. In his *Hall of Fame* he wrote:

"Here also was Mr. Alcott, with two or three friends, whom his

* Abel is Louisa's name for Alcott in *Transcendental Wild Oats*.

spirit has assimilated to itself, and drawn to his New England home, though an ocean rolled between. There was no man in the enchanted Hall whose mere presence, the language of whose look and manner, brought such an impression as this mystic innovator; so quiet in the utterance of what his soul brooded over, that one might readily conceive his Orphic Sayings to well up from a fountain in his breast which communicated with the infinite Abyss of Thought. 'Here is a prophet,' cried my friend, with enthusiasm,— 'a dreamer, a bodiless idea amid our actual existence. Another age may recognize him as a man; or perhaps his misty apparition may vanish into sunshine. It matters little; for his influence will have impregnated the atmosphere, and will be imbibed by generations that know not the original apostle of the ideas which they shall shape into earthly business. Such a spirit cannot pass through human life, yet leave mankind entirely as he found them.' "

§

Alcott was a much greater person than the experiment at Fruitlands might indicate. When Anthony Burns, a runaway slave, was held by the authorities under the Fugitive Slave Law in Boston, the greatest northern bulwark of the slave power, a mob gathered to free him but was driven back from the courthouse. Alcott arrived then and said calmly to the ringleader, "Why are we not within?" He was told that the mob would not follow. Thereupon he walked deliberately up the steps alone with his cane in his hand and, when a revolver was fired at him as he came to the highest step, he looked about for supporters and finding none walked deliberately down again. Thomas Wentworth Higginson who was there says, "It was hard to see how Plato or Pythagoras could have done the thing better." In all his crankiness, in all his passing from one cult and one fad to another, Alcott remained incorruptibly true to himself. "He makes all other souls appear slow and cheap and mechanical," wrote Emerson. And Ellery Channing said of him, "I never see that man without being cheered." Thoreau, whom he most resembles, calls him "the best-natured man I ever met," and characteristically adds, "The rats and mice make their nests in him." Isaac Thomas Hecker, who was at Brook Farm and Fruitlands both and, finding that they did not concern themselves sufficiently with eter-

nity, became a Catholic priest, makes the only disparaging remarks about Alcott's character. He thought that Alcott wanted him at Fruitlands because he had money and says that "he was unquestionably one of those who liked to sit upon a platform." These comparative trifles exhaust his censure on a man whom others thought easily the peer of Emerson.

Alcott was a true radical and his dealings with individuals and groups were always inspired by his singular sense of confidence in nature. This made him an impossible citizen and a strange husband and father. Although Lane complains that "constancy to his wife and inconstancy to the Spirit have blurred over his life forever," no one who knew "Marmee" Alcott could imagine that her hardworking and devoted life was an easy one.

It is extraordinary how Alcott managed to put from him all trace of Yankee smartness. He was born in the house of his grandfather, a poor Connecticut farmer, just before the new century began. At fourteen, he was an apprentice in a clock factory and afterward traveled through North Carolina and Virginia as a peddler with almanacs and trinkets. Later, he was a school teacher and, after experiencing contact with a fine spirit, that of the Reverend Samuel A. May, placed himself at last "in the still more favored position of Emerson's footnote." Emerson was already famous but, according to Thomas Wentworth Higginson, "it suddenly made itself clear to the old Concord circle that there was not one among them so serene, so equable, so dreamy, yet so constitutionally a leader as this wandering child of the desert." It never seems to have entered his head that he ought to make money, and his dealings in which money was involved are almost incredible. A notorious swindler asked him for the loan of five dollars. The impoverished Alcott happened to have only a ten dollar bill, so lent that without even asking the borrower's name. Half a year later the money was returned with an offer of interest. From his diary there has been quoted a passage which recounts in mystic phrases a typical financial transaction on the Alcott model:

*Mammon*

April, 1839, Thursday, 18th—

"Things seems strange to me out there in Time and Space. I am not familiar with the order and usages of this realm. I am at home in the kingdom of the Soul alone.

"This day, I passed along our great thoroughfare, gliding with Emerson's check in my pocket, into State Street; and stepped into one of Mammon's temples, for some of the world's coin, wherewith to supply bread for this body of mine, and those who depend upon me. But I felt dishonored by resorting to these haunts of Idolaters. I went not among them to dig in the mines of Lucre, nor to beg at the doors of the God. It was the hour for business on 'Change, which was swarming with worshipers. Bevies of devotees were consulting on appropriate rites whereby to honor their divinity.

"One of these devotees (cousin-german of my wife) accosted me, as I was returning, and asked me to bring my oblation with the others. Now I owed the publican a round thousand, which he proffered me in days when his God prospered his wits; but I had nothing for him. That small pittance which I had just got snugly into my fob (thanks to my friend E——) was not for him, but for my wife's nurse, and came just in time to save my wife from distrusting utterly the succors of Providence. I told my man, that I had no money; but he might have me, if he wanted me. No: I was bad stock in the market; and so he bid me good day. I left the buzz and hum of these devotees, who represent old Nature's relation to the Appetites and Senses, and returned, with a sense of grateful relief, from this sally into the Kingdom of Mammon, back to my domicile in the Soul."

He was at home in the soul and the object of Fruitlands was to make a home for the soul of mankind. One fancies that Alcott alone could be comfortable in any place so removed from actuality. He had a strange communication with the spirit of things and occasionally the thoughts which he drew from nature expressed themselves in odd ways. He was always holding conversations, rivaling Margaret Fuller in his capacity for talk at any length on any subject, for his conversations were only broken monologues and, even when James Russell Lowell and the bright Fredrika Bremer were present, he swept over interruptions and discoursed on any topic he

A. Bronson Alcott

chose. In the house of a friend in Boston, he developed his favorite theory that a dark complexion indicated the remainder of a brutish nature:

"The Greeks held that a brown complexion betokened courage, and those who had fair skins were called children of light and favorites of the gods. And the gods themselves were demonic or divine, as tempered by darkness or light,—the gods Infernal, the Midgods, the Celestials. So Christian art has painted Satan dark and Christ fair. And late experiments on the sunbeam showed that dark substances imprison the rays, these absorbing more and delivering less. The more of sun, so much the more of soul; the less of sun, of passion more, and the strange fire. He [Alcott] fancied black eyes were of Oriental descent,—were tinged less or more with fairer hues in crossing West. People of sandy hair and florid complexions were of Northern ancestry. The fusion of the various races was now taking place, blending all, doubtless, into a more harmonious and beautiful type. He asked if there did not lurk in the fancy, if not in our atoms, a persuasion that complexion, like features, voice, gait, typified and emblazoned personal traits of their possessors,—if the rhetoric of morals and religion did not revel in like distinctions. 'Handsome is that handsome does.' Beauty was the birthright of all, if not their inheritance. It was shame that brought deformity into the world. Every child accused he knew not whom for any blemish of his. 'Why not mine the happy star, too?' Still some trait was insinuated and stamped upon the embryonic clay. Ebony, alabaster, indigo, vermillion,—the pigments were all mingled as purity or passion decreed. Types were persistent, family features standing strong for centuries, and perpetuating themselves from generation to generation. Place the portraits of a long line of ancestors on the walls, one's features were all there, with the slight variations arising from intermarriage, degrees of culture, calling, climate."

This is a typical transcendental mode of thought. "The more of sun so much the more of soul; the less of sun, of passion more, and the strange fire"—set that sentence before the student of American literature and unless he knows Alcott he will say Emerson, and wonder a little that the first half of the sentence should have

the sharp quality of Emerson's style and the second a dying fall which Emerson rarely achieves. In the whole passage we find leading ideas of the time, curiosity about nature and a sense of the correspondence, the implicit relationship, in all of nature's movements; the presumption of a moral order underlying all the phenomena of nature, the arrangement of branches on a tree, the patches of color on a wooded upland, the turn of the seasons and pigment of the skin. He had the old romantic feeling of contrast, as Hugo had it, in his continual struggles between light and dark and between love and death. "Antipodal" was one of Alcott's favorite words as "polarity" was one of Emerson's favorite ideas. And as to the other romantics and the transcendentalists, the moment came to Alcott when his communication ceased to be in the ordinary mode, when he drew out of Pythagoras, Boehme, and other philosophers a totally mystical conception of life. Until his death, he wanted to publish a mystical manuscript called *Psyche*. From an earlier manuscript we get something of its spirit. He had written out several series of questions and we guess from them the turn of his mind.

"Which is the older, the memory, the thing remembered, or the person remembering?

"Can you remember when you did not remember?

"Which is predecessor, Time or the memory?

"Are moments born of the memory, or memory of the moments?

"How old is your Person?

"What measures age,—the memory of times or of eternities?

"Are the veils hidings or findings?

"What discovers us?

"Is the doubling in all things around singles, or the singling around doubles . . . ?

"Is the single content and complemented without the double?

"Which feeds the curiosity and draws us on to discovery?

"Which is the pursuer, which the pursued?

Before these questions he quotes a characteristic quatrain of Emerson at which a physicist might smile, but not a mystic:

"Through a thousand voices
Spoke the universal dame:
'Who telleth one of my meanings,
Is master of all I am.' "

He was a sage and he was a saint; one of the singular people who instantly took possession of the friendship of others; more far-reaching in his thought and often more far-seeing than Thoreau, but much less inspiring than Emerson because he had so much in him of the fabled Diogenes with his lantern and his tub. Yet Thoreau adored him:

"Then may I wait, dear Alcott on thy court
Or bear a mace in thy Platonic reign!"

and Lowell wrote an ode to him calling him "less of iconoclast than shaper."

In an odd way, Alcott was justified of his faith. Sheer desperation had driven Louisa to write, and good fortune at last came to the Alcott family. Alcott could now talk as much as he wished and began again to publish books. In all, he was the author of ten, and Louisa wrote nearly thirty. The name of Alcott had magic and, almost thirty years after his disastrous lecture tour, he went West again at the age of 81. For eight months, he lectured or held conversations at least once a day and, although many of them were free, he returned to Concord with a thousand dollars. He was no longer cold as an icicle, but his serenity remained. For seven years longer, he was associated with the Concord School of Philosophers and only a few traces of orthodoxy in the rather narrow Calvinistic mode, and an old man's gratification at being the center of interest, marred the picture of his last days. He remained what he had been and he knew that the words success and failure are much too hastily applied. Long after the disaster at Fruitlands he wrote his epitaph:

"That is failure when a man's idea ruins him, when he is dwarfed and killed by it; but when he is ever growing by it, ever true to it, and does not lose it by any partial or immediate failures,— that is success, whatever it seems to the world."

† Thirty-nine thousand persons were bankrupt and $741,000,000 were lost in the great panic. † Four hundred railroad stocks were listed and the express business was started by Adams. † Brooks and Company and Lord and Taylor were lining Broadway with marble and nearly 50,000 strangers came over the ocean and passed through New York each year. † Johnson's Negro Brass Band was very popular in Philadelphia. † School books began to be covered with cloth. † The preaching of the Reverend Mr. Douglas, a Negro, was highly thought of, and Francis Scott Key, a lawyer in Washington, was extremely doubtful about the advisability of abolishing slavery. † President Van Buren was interested in steam navigation, O'Connell's progress in Ireland, and the Chartist rising. † Wise travelers sat as far away as possible from the stove in each railway carriage. † It was generally understood that John Quincy Adams was the only man who had saved money out of the presidential salary. † There was threat of war with England over the Maine boundary and the standing army consisted of 12,539 men of all ranks. † American doctors complained that our women were hypochondriac, had too little fresh air, too many pastries and no exercise. Bath-tubs existed but Americans, "from some misapprehension of their influence, do not remain long enough in them to enjoy their full benefit." † The West was stricken with ague. † In March there was eighteen inches of mud between Easton and Philadelphia. † A duel between two rival editors at Vicksburg was witnessed by a thousand persons who laid bets on the outcome. † The wages of day laborers were higher than those of school teachers. † Nearly everybody lectured in New England, for $40 or $50 a lecture, and, in Boston alone, 6,000 men and women attended lectures each winter.

† There was one fire every two days in New York City. † Firemen brayed on a tin trumpet as they ran and often rival engine companies would brawl over the possession of a hydrant while houses burned; zinc was being used on roofs to insure safety from sparks. † Ten thousand dollars was the highest life insurance written. † The *Great Western* sailed from Bristol to New York in twenty-three days and the trip by rail from New York to Philadelphia took six and a half hours except when the Delaware was frozen and passengers walked across. † The scavengers of New York streets were swine and it was no part of the police duty to hunt for criminals; no newspapers could be sold on the streets on Sunday. † The Tontine system of insurance left its mark in the name of hotels and halls.

# XIII.

## Sweetness and Light.

THE name of Adin Ballou, who founded the Hopedale Community, links the middle of the nineteenth century with an earlier era of reform. Mathurin Ballou, an ancestor of Adin, was associated with Roger Williams in the beginnings of Rhode Island. Liberal theology was, thereby, assured in the family. The Ballous became the royal line of Universalists; so that it seems unkind of the young preacher, Adin, to reject one of their doctrines. He did this in a sermon delivered in April, 1830. The actual heresy it involved does not seem important. Ballou rejected the particular type of Universalism which teaches that death suddenly transforms all men into angels and preached, instead, the doctrine of a final restoration at an appropriate time. This departure caused a temporary break in the ranks of Universalism but the Restorationists managed, before they died, to insinuate their chief tenets into both Universalism and Unitarianism. Ballou was from that moment a man marked for courage and for heresy. Within a month after he had organized his sect, he was dismissed from the church at Milford; but it was not his fate ever to suffer physically for his beliefs. Within the week of his dismissal, he was installed as minister in the first parish of Mendon with a higher salary, $400 a year. At the end of ten years at Mendon, Ballou gathered some thirty people into Fraternal Community Number One and, within a short time, bought the Jones farm, called the Dale, at Milford. "This estate they named Hopedale—joining the word 'hope' to its ancient designation, as significant of the great things they hoped for from a very humble and unpropitious beginning." By that time, Ballou had become an ardent propagandist for temperance; had helped to break up his own Restorationist following by a declaration in favor of abolition; and (after twelve years of service as chaplain to a militia brigade) had begun to advocate the doctrine of Christian Non-resistance and to urge non-coöperation with any government which employed force. When spiritualism swept over the country, he embraced it and spoke and wrote in its behalf. It

coincided with his restorationist ideas of life after death. He remained, however, essentially a Christian, believing in all seriousness that there was but one duty for every man and that it could only be fulfilled in "an order of Human Society based on the sublime ideas of the fatherhood of God and the brotherhood of man as taught and illustrated in the gospel of Jesus Christ." Hopedale was an attempt to create in the world, "under the limitations of time and sense," the scriptural ideal of the kingdom of God on earth.

The organization of Hopedale was simple. "We are all here in one household, professionals, mechanics, farmers, ordinary laborers, male and female, agreeing alike to serve the Community if able, eight hours per day for fifty cents, and to pay for our board, lodging, etc., one dollar per week. Also to pay cost prices for clothing, livery, and other necessaries not included in the above."

At the end of a decade, there were thirty-six families of adults at Hopedale and a total population of about 175, living on 500 acres of land, in some thirty houses, with mechanics, shops, a chapel and school, and the other necessities of life. Particularly, there was Ebenezer D. Draper, who was originally in charge of the farming and eventually became the industrial genius of Hopedale. The external life of the community as a whole is almost without interest. It struggled, it improved, and Draper and his brother, who controlled the majority of the joint stock, eventually turned it into a business enterprise. But internally, Hopedale is a tragi-comedy, not dismal and not exalted, but a little heartbreaking. The brothers Draper established the Hopedale machine works and, after a time, developed the famous Northrop loom for spinning cotton. As they became more interested in this work and less in Hopedale, the community lacked management and, from year to year, sank more capital into its small affairs. When Ebenezer Draper had bought up three-fourths of the stock and still saw no hope of improvement, he told Ballou that "this thing must not go any further." Draper paid the debts of the community and so it ended. Ballou remained for a long time as minister of the Hopedale parish, and the manufacturing community, which succeeded the "Universal Religious Moral, Philanthropic and Social Reform Association," was long known as an exceptional experiment in industrial relations.

§

In the small community of Hopedale, Ballou promulgated no theoretical dogmas and insisted upon no ceremonies. It was in practical Christianity that he was strict. No man was to work ill to another man and there was to be abstention from every word or deed which did not honor God. In Hopedale, there was to be no unchastity, no intoxication, no taking of oaths, no holding of slaves and no compromises with slave-holding, no preparation for war and no support of war, no capital or other vindictive punishment, and no violence. It aimed, as so many other communities did, at a restoration of the conditions of primitive Christianity. Its method was moral suasion, not militant temperance, or violent anti-slavery, or belligerent pacifism. It rejected tobacco and was, both in theory and practice, based on the equal rights of women. From time to time, Ballou and Draper would announce "a call to the friends of social reform in New England . . . to cheer each other's hearts by taking note of the advance of the social scheme discovered by Charles Fourier." Occasionally, they would go into Associational conferences with delegates from Northampton and Brook Farm, with which communities they exchanged statistics and information. Sometimes they, with James Boyle and George Ripley and William Lloyd Garrison, would respond to a call published in all the reformatory journals, "to the Friends of a Reorganization of Society that shall Substitute Fraternal Coöperation for Antagonistic Selfishness; a Religious Consecration of Life and Labor, Soul and Body, Time and Eternity, in Harmony with the laws of God and Life, instead of Fragmentary, Spasmodic Piety."

Meanwhile there were other activities at Hopedale. A water cure was established at the cost of $600.00 and, at the rate of from $4 to $5 a week exclusive of laundry, patients were accepted under the care of Dr. Butler Wilmarth. Ballou also founded a juvenile community of which "The great desideratum was to exclude all enervating frivolity, all unseemly vulgarity, all rough and brutal conduct, and to so combine physical, intellectual, and moral exercises and gratifications as to promote and not subvert the great ends of personal improvement and social order. We succeeded in this particular fairly well; not as perfectly as we wished, but about as we did in other departments of activity pertaining to our comprehensive undertaking." And in the interest of morality, all parents

and guardians were required to see that the children refrained from profanity and obscene utterances and that "they retire from their sports to their respective homes by eight o'clock P.M." In 1848, there was a May Day festival, "as innocent as any meeting and far more improving and Christianizing than those in which a pro-war, pro-slavery brutalizing religion is instilled into men's minds and hearts." The children, dressed in white and carrying bouquets in their hands, sang the verses and the congregation sang the chorus of a hymn written especially for the occasion:

### WILDWOOD FLOWERS

"We've been in search of wildwood flowers  
In Hopedale glens and shady bowers,  
And gathered each a fair bouquet  
To celebrate this festal day.

#### CHORUS

"And why should we not love the flowers  
That grow about this Dale of ours?  
Sweet tokens they will ever prove  
Of our dear Father's precious love."

In 1854, Ballou was dreaming of a confederacy to affiliate the many communities then in existence and had drafted a constitution for the "Practical Christian Republic." By 1856, Hopedale had passed into the hands of the Drapers.

§

There is no doubt that the failure was the direct result of amateur Christian financing, but other causes were also at work. Ballou did not call upon the law in his dealings with other men and, although he was warned that his principles of non-resistance would make him the victim of every rowdy and thief in Massachusetts, he never lost more than a few chickens and a sack of potatoes. But, from the time Draper turned his energy to private affairs, the countless irritations and the conflicting personal interests which he had to adjust overcame Ballou. The sweetness of Christianity was corrupted by lust and the light of Communism was dimmed by greed. In the early days, when a northeaster would imprison the colonists

in the large hall, Brother Gifford would examine heads in accordance with the principles of phrenology, and try to put a member to sleep by animal magnetism. The Community would agree that children should not take lights to their room unless attended by one of their elders. Ballou would discuss the great spiritual revelations of Andrew Jackson Davis in which he firmly believed. Or the communists would drive out to hear the Hutchinsons, "the tribe of Jesse," sing "We Pitch Our Tents on the Old Camp Ground." But "as the tinsel of novelty wore off and the hard actualities of our uncomfortable domestic situation began to overtax our nerves, we lost a portion of our spiritual enthusiasm, firmness, and patience. Our religious natures no less than our physical suffered for want of needed solitude and repose, as they did for lack of wholesome nurture and stimulus to holy aspiration and endeavor. Social, secular, and financial matters engrossed so much of our attention and energy that our higher faculties were partially starved. . . . As a consequence, every temptation that assailed us was less resistible than would otherwise have been the case."

Most grievous of all was the damnation of the flesh. With an eye on Oneida and other experimenters in sexual relations, Hopedale "resolved that with our views of Christian Chastity, we contemplate as utterly abhorrent the various 'Free Love' theories and practices insidiously propagated among susceptible minds under pretext of higher religious perfection, moral exaltation, social refinement, individual sovereignty, physiological research, and philosophical progress; and we feel bound to bear our uncompromising testimony against all persons, communities, books, and publications which inculcate such specious and subtle licentiousness."

The unhappy story of what actually happened is best told in Ballou's flat, but earnest style:

"But notwithstanding our vigilance, and in utter contravention of our solemn declaration concerning chastity and of our well-known adherence to the principle of monogamic marriage, there arose in our midst during the year 1853, a case of marital infidelity and illicit intercourse that caused great unpleasantness, perplexity, and scandal, and that required, at length, Community intervention.

"The story is simply this: One of our male members, the head

of a family, became enamored of a woman, also a member, who had for some time resided in his household, and proportionally estranged from his faithful and worthy wife. Suspicions of something wrong arose among outsiders, causing considerable talk of a scurrilous nature, though nothing was absolutely known or could be proved to that effect. At length the unhappiness of the wife was revealed, and the cause of it, upon investigation, made public. The matter then very properly received attention from the Council, who summoned the delinquents before them for examination and discipline. Upon being questioned and confronted with proof of misconduct, they acknowledged culpability, professed regret, and penitence, and promised amendment. But these professions proved insincere, or at least, transient, and the parties were again called to account. They then did not deny or attempt to conceal their criminality, but rather justified it on the ground that it was consonant with the principles of the new philosophy touching personal liberty, sexual relations, and the conjugal bond, which they had embraced—in a word, they openly and unhesitatingly avowed themselves to be Free Lovers, from conviction and in practice also. Having taken that position they could not do otherwise than withdraw from the Community membership and leave the locality where both their theory and their action were held in almost universal derision and abhorrence."

The delinquents, it may be noted, joined "a settlement of Kindred Individual Sovereigns" in the free-love Community on Long Island called Modern Times. A little righteous indignation Ballou could summon up; there were bound to be unregenerate ones in every Community. But worse was to befall him. A "ministering brother" named Lamson, from whom nothing but the best had been expected, turned all-too-human and well-nigh broke Ballou's heart. Brother Lamson's proposals were reasonable enough. In the fundamental law of Hopedale a common nursery for babies had been guaranteed, but it had not yet come into existence. Lamson only suggested that, in these circumstances, the Community ought to pay nursing mothers at least as much per hour as was paid to any other person doing useful work. The only excessive suggestion he made was that they be paid for sixteen hours a day which would give them exactly twice as much as any other member in the Community

earned. "Some of us," Ballou writes, "were hardly in a mood to accept such an interpretation of the principle of justice"; and they were all the less so inclined when they remembered that, by a co-incidence, brother Lamson's wife was at the moment nursing a child. The sacredness of motherhood obviously inspired Lamson for, after the nursing mothers were allowed the usual fifty cents a day, Lamson suggested that, whenever a minister from the Com-munity drove out, it should be his obligation to take a mother with him. As Ballou was the most active of the ministers, this suggestion of "neglect of duty and violation of solemn pledges of fraternal interest" hurt him deeply and he protested that his cares and labors and anxieties were taxing his strength to the utmost limit.

Nor was brother Lamson alone in the sudden uprushing of human instincts. Some new buildings had been erected, much more comfortable than the old, and the Community naturally wished to know who was to occupy them. From the outside, the criticism had often come that the shiftless and the unworthy would claim every advantage if there was no system of merit and reward; and it was said then, as it is now, that generosity to the lazy and incompetent would only make them more exacting. Ballou had brushed aside these criticisms "as an imputation on the better impulses of human nature and upon the Christian spirit of brotherhood in the human soul." He was therefore surprised and shocked to find that a con-siderable number of Hopedale communists declared that the prin-ciples and constitutional pledges of the group bound them to give the new houses, with all their advantages, to the poorest and least efficient, and that the talented and responsible members should be the last to enjoy prosperity. Certain familiar precepts were quoted, among them: "He that is chief among you let him be the servant of all"; "It is more blessed to give than to receive."

What distressed Ballou was not so much the outcropping of hostility as the significant circumstance that Lamson and the others who were so earnest in behalf of the undeserving, were precisely the people who would move into the new houses if their argument suc-ceeded. And Ballou was "disappointed and made heartsick at the thought that the hostile critics of the Christian Community were justified." In the end, a dozen disaffected Communists seceded. Lamson himself joined the Shakers, and sent back letters (which

Ballou honorably published in his newspaper) praising the true
Christianity of that denomination and insinuating that Hopedale
was neither practical nor Christian. It is, however, not without a
grain of satisfaction that Ballou notes that Lamson eventually
"withdrew from these eminent practical Christians" and, after returning to ordinary society, which he had condemned for its un-
christian character, was heard of no more.

§

From the *Practical Christian*, which Ballou published for many
years, we get a cross section of the character of Hopedale and interesting side lights on that wave of reform which characterized
the period. The motto of the weekly was broad enough: "Absolute
Truth, Essential Righteousness, Individual Responsibility, Social
Reorganization, Human Progress, Ultimate Perfection." And all
subscriptions payable in advance "unless by indulgence of publisher."
The *Saturday Courant*, of Clinton, Masachusetts, had published
an attack on Hopedale from which one can gather the opinion of
communal establishments held by outsiders. The Hopedalers were
accused of having "peculiar and perhaps eccentric tastes" and offended against the common opinion because they were not engaged
in the business of accumulation of property. They were "a company
of people tired of the distractions of fashion, ambition, and business," and were now "comforting each other with a little model of
an earthly paradise . . . dawdling away life in a religion of sentiment and esthetic culture." Ballou's retort gives an excellent account of the nature of Hopedale and its differences from other
communities:

"Now the Hopedale people have never been distinguished for
peculiar or eccentric tastes. They have never been governed by
tastes, nor by mere sentimentality. They never had an associate that
would be considered literary or esthetic, in the elegant sense of those
terms. They are a plain, practical people, and, so far as regards
taste, education and manners, are very much like the middle class of
New Englanders generally. Not one of them ever graduated from
any University or College. Not one of them ever belonged to any
coterie of fine-spun sentimentalists, or moved in any genteel sphere

of life, or figured among the world's fashionables. Whether this be to their credit or discredit, so it is. Wherein they differ from other people of their general grade in society, they do so in a plain way, from conscientious obedience to acknowledged divine principles; and in respect to these, it were better for them to be more unlike other people than they actually are. They are far enough from being 'perfect as their Father in heaven is perfect.'

"It seems to be taken for granted by our Clinton friend that we are Communists, or a kind of Shakers. This is altogether a misapprehension. The Shakers are very exemplary and worthy people. We will not compare Hopedale with their orderly and admirable societies, because we are not like them in any important feature of our social organization. We do not reject marriage nor dissolve the natural family, nor receive any of their distinguishing theological, theocratical, or ecclesiastical fundamentals. Communists, properly so called, deny the natural right of man to individual property, or at least contend that in a true order of society all property must be public and common. There are several classes of them, differing widely from each other, yet all agreeing in this distinctive matter of common property. But the people of Hopedale belong to no class of Communists. They hold the right of individual property to be inherent, essential and inviolable. In all the four kinds of Communities proposed in their social system: viz., Parochial, Rural, Joint Stock, and Common Stock Communities, the absolute natural right of individual property is held sacred. . . . This is not Communism."

The *Practical Christian* published news of all other American experiments in Communism, encouraging the Icarians and noting that a thousand people had abandoned the oligarchy of Brigham Young. It attacked the morals and theology of the Oneida Community. But it was violent only on one subject—tobacco. "A word from a spirited lady," objected to tobacco juice being squirted on her dress when she took a journey in the cars. And "three young men formed a smoking club and they all died within two years." Unprovoked by any specific news item we have an editorial exclamation:

"What! puff the cigar in the cars, these beautiful railroad cars! Smoke and chew, and chew and smoke, and spit this dirt all about? What avail laws, rules and regulations, unless enforced? Can't help it!, indeed! Ladies and gentlemen are annoyed, painfully annoyed! Even that tobacco smoke at the head of the cars passes directly through the whole train, diffusing a stench intolerable." And on another occasion a poem:

### LITTLE ROBERT REED

"I'll never use tobacco; no,
  It is a filthy weed;
I'll never put it in my mouth,
  Said little Robert Reed.

"Why, there was idle Jesse Jones,
  As dirty as a pig—
He smoked when only ten years old,
  And thought it made him big.

"He spent his time and money, too,
  And made his mother sad;
She feared a worthless man would come,
  Of such a worthless lad.

"O, no! I'll never smoke nor chew,
  'Tis very wrong indeed:
It hurts the health, it makes bad breath,
  Said little Robert Reed."

The paper supported Catherine Beecher's propaganda for simple food, and the movement for dress reform, and whatever else was liberal and Christianizing. Its tone was always earnest, but there was no energy behind it. Except for his acceptance of fake spiritualists and a somewhat too open hospitality to reform movements, there was nothing silly, and there was certainly nothing vicious, in the communism of Adin Ballou. He was not lacking in moral courage, for when one of his great objectives—the abolition of slavery— became entangled with one of his great abhorrences—the war system—he sacrificed most of his friends and his authority by holding out against the war. His communism, nevertheless, was that of a weak saint. His disappointment was that of a man who did not

know and did not learn much about human nature. Toward the end of his life, he began a correspondence with Count Leo Tolstoi, who called him the greatest of American writers but, in Tolstoi, too, he was somewhat disappointed. He ended his life writing genealogies of his family and autobiographical works, with a great deal of indulgence for his enemies, without more than a slight trace of the sanctimonious, and totally lacking in power.

† Extreme publicity concerning Harrison during his campaign shocked delicate souls and his enemies compared him to Bolivar "corrupted and ruined by ambition." † On canal boats, bed-linen was promiscuous. Pittsburgh was becoming an oil center. † The rocking chair was in. † A bath at the Saratoga hotel cost half a dollar and dinner in Boston was at three o'clock with a few glasses of wine and conversation until six. Snobs dined at six. † Children in public schools sang, "I love my native land the best" and, in South Boston, formed "an association for the suppression of profanity." The fare from Boston to New York, six hours by rail and over night by steamer, was seven dollars. † "To swartwout" meant to abscond with public money, after the name of the Collector of Customs at New York. † Joseph Buonaparte was toasted in Philadelphia as "once a king, still a sovereign and always a philosopher."

† The centenary of the fire companies at Philadelphia was celebrated in 1839 by a parade of engines one mile long. † Eight thousand persons in the same city visited Mr. Dunn's Chinese Museum in a week. † Sully's portrait of Queen Victoria became notorious because the painter insisted on exhibiting it and charging admission after he had been paid a thousand dollars for the picture. † Rembrandt Peale had painted an equestrian portrait of General Washington; Mr. Trumbull was also making historical paintings. † At Laurel Hill Cemetery there was placed a group of Sir Walter Scott, Old Mortality and his pony. † A mob burned down a public hall in Philadelphia because it was used for abolition meetings and the fire companies made no effort to save the building. † Big Gothic type was used in advertisements and, in the *Public Ledger*, Madame Dusar announced that "she will be happy to solve all questions relating to dreams, marriages, journeys, losses, gains, and all other lawful business, sickness, death, etc., etc." Mrs. Louisa Kraft of Chrystie Street and Mrs. Theresa George Medier of Orchard Street, New York, were visited by plain clothes men who had their fortunes told for fifty cents. † "Baltimore was called the monumental city because it possessed two public monuments" and, in Washington, the Capitol was "painted white to resemble marble." † America Vespucci came here to solicit from Congress a grant of land in return for the name which her ancestor gave to this country. The Senate rejected her plea. † Mr. Charles Matthews published a book entitled *How Do You Like Our Country?* and Massachusetts, New York, and Pennsylvania established state lotteries and forbade the sale of lottery tickets from other states.

# XIV.

## A Saint.

WHEN the time came for Major Anderson to raise the Stars and Stripes again over Fort Sumter, in April, 1865, one of those who, with him, were guests of the Secretary of War on board the *Arago* was William Lloyd Garrison. The symbolism of the event was perfect, for the man who first met the onset of secession, and the man who above all others had preached Abolition, were united in the ceremony which marked the triumph of freedom and of Union. As they were escorted through the principal streets of Charleston, negroes extemporized a triumph, singing "John Brown's Body lies amould'ring in his grave." No doubt the military man and the editor of *The Liberator* congratulated each other and, in the general sense of a happy outcome, the difference in status between them was not emphasized. It was, however, significant. For Anderson represented the North, the victorious armies, the faithful defenders of the Union; for him, it was an act of pious restitution to run up the flag his own hand had hauled down four years earlier. Garrison represented the lunatic fringe, the despicable "infidels" and "anarchists" of five years before, the enemies of society. To him, a grateful country, which had cursed his talent and virtually set a price on his head, was now making atonement, promising him, by that gesture, a deserved immortality among American fighters for liberty.

§

As an abolitionist, Garrison was a great man. The purpose here is to mark his association with a variety of other movements, from temperance to spiritualism, and to pass his single claim to greatness by. He is an illustration of the effect of radical cults on a great spirit. We can take for granted the long, heartbreaking struggle for abolition, except where it touches upon those other "ultra" ideas to which Garrison was so receptive.

In the major activity of his life, in his dominant impulses and his moods, Garrison *was* great: it is, in fact, his greatness which

illuminates the workings of radicalism in his time. There were tones in his voice and looks in his eye which no other man had. The phrases we associate with his name have a quality of sincerity and noble indignation which are rare in a self-satisfied age. He called part of the law of the land "a covenant with death and an agreement with hell" and, when cautious colonizers or gradual emancipators begged him to moderate his insistence upon unqualified immediate abolition, he cried out, the moment he had issued from a Baltimore jail and was his own master, "I am in earnest—I will not equivocate—I will not excuse—I will not retreat a single inch—*And I will be heard.*" If we think of him as being surrounded by enthusiasts and defenders and shouting defiance to the miserable South, such words are silly braggadocio; but he was alone. Taking up the work of Abolition with the slight, nervous, gentle Quaker, Lundy, Garrison became a solitary figure as soon as he was recognized as the great power he really was. A thousand temptations beset him to desert his cause, to compromise on buying out the slaves and settling them in Hayti, to be satisfied, as almost all liberals were, with restricting slavery to the South. He not only kept on; he carried the struggle into the real camp of the enemy—New England, where the murderers of Lovejoy were exalted, where the prospect of a college for negroes in the neighborhood of Yale caused a mass meeting of protest, over which the Mayor of New Haven presided and to which the whole faculty of Yale gave tacit approval. He took the cause of abolition to the anti-slavery champion, Lyman Beecher, a colonizationist, who coldly replied, "I have too many irons in the fire already." Beecher believed that if the slaves were freed, permission for them to stay in America would be permission to starve, and he begged Garrison to give up his "fanatical notions," promising him that, if he did, the clergy "will make you the Wilberforce of America." He preferred to be its Garrison.

He went to jail, he faced mobs, he starved. And he lacked the heroic figure for such deeds—a man of middle size, bald and shaven, "a phrenological head illuminated," as Alcott said, with large hazel eyes beaming behind glasses. Only a strong nose and firm mouth suggested a fighter. The lips were always smiling benevolently or twisted with a slight sardonic humor. He moved his body briskly, erect, through the slushy streets of Boston, making his way

among enemies to the obscure hole with dingy walls and small windows spattered with sticky, black, printer's ink where his bed, and his table, and his composing room, and his one-man copy desk (littered with exchanges), and all he possessed and cherished were assembled. For a year he had no bills to pay at grocers or butchers; a single bakery provided his food. And all this time, he was not only happy in his struggles; he was enchanted by life, uplifted.

"What could you do with a man like this?" asks his distinguished grandson, Oswald Garrison Villard. "You threw him in jail and he liked it immensely and utilized the opportunity to strike off his best bit of verse. You put a price on his head and he gloried in it. You threatened him with death and dragged him through the streets with a rope around his waist and he showed his courage by failing even to be excited, and then went home to utilize your outbreak against him in a most effective sermon against the thing you were trying to uphold. You ridiculed him as a nobody and he calmly admitted it and went on preaching his gospel of liberty. You tried to close the mails to him, to undermine his influence, to destroy his reputation, his judgment, and his sanity, and he went on pounding you, convicting you out of your own mouth and printing in his column in *The Liberator* headed 'The Refuge of Oppression' telltale happenings which portrayed at its worst the institution you were seeking to defend. And then when in despair you sought the aid of the law and of the officials of his State to prosecute him you found that he so walked by day and by night that you could not even indict him for running an underground railroad station, which he was careful not to do because of his conspicuousness.

"You called him an effeminate fanatic because he would stand up for the cause of women in a day when there were fewer suffragists than Abolitionists, and he went calmly insisting that his platform was not occupied unless women stood upon it. You called him crack-brained because he crossed the ocean to plead for the slave and then declined to speak for what was dearest to his soul because the women delegates with him were not admitted to the Convention. You denounced him as the friend and ally of Susan B. Anthony and Lucy Stone, yes, of Mary Walker, and Garrison's hopelessly addled brain took it all as a compliment and gloried in these spiritual alliances which some would have dubbed his shame. How

could you keep patience with a man like this—one who would not only let loose the savage negro on the community, but believed that every walk of life, every sphere of intellectual activity should be open to the despised sex and actually preached that women, not men, should decide what place women should occupy in modern society.

"And he always insisted upon being happy, no matter what you said or did to him. His heart was the heart of a child even when he denounced a whole class in language of complete immoderation. It did not affect that heart when you assured him for the five-thousandth time that he had thrown away his influence by his vituperation and his denunciation of good men and women who did their duty by their slaves like Christians, or by taking up the despicable cause of those masculine females who wished the ballot. You certainly can not wage polemical warfare with an antagonist like this. He will not play fair; he does not follow the rules of the game. He enters the combat in such a shining armor of happiness and personal righteousness and complete unselfishness as to make it impossible for the point of your sword to enter at any point. And all the time he is belaboring you with his heavy broadsword with the utmost of calmness and most annoying vigor. . . ."

John Jay Chapman has said that, in a cold age, Garrison burned with a spiritual fire. We can measure his greatness in another way: the martyrs of Abolition are Lovejoy and John Brown, but who are its great men? Not Lincoln, who was an Emancipator, but not an Abolitionist fighting, as Garrison fought, forty years for the cause. Lincoln made little of the raid at Harpers Ferry, and used emancipation as a war measure; used it gladly, because he hated slavery, but cautiously because two years earlier he had believed other solutions adequate. In June of 1862, Congress had gone only as far as to abolish slavery in the territories. The announcement of the great proclamation, in September of that year, gave the Confederate states until January 1, 1863, to lay down their arms and return to the union *with their slaves*. The Proclamation is not the work of an Abolitionist! With Lincoln assured of immortality elsewhere, who stands beside Garrison? Good men and women; inspiring men and women; Lowell, Whittier, Lucretia Mott, Lucy Stone, Theodore Parker, Wendell Phillips, Alcott; but few of them, even, gave their

whole energy to the cause, and none would be remembered by that cause alone. After them come men still more definitely of the second order. Garrison stands alone.

§

What was he doing in the gallery of cult-leaders and Communists? Briefly, he was accepting every one of them as at least a potential messiah. There is something magnificent in his appetite for the radical ideas, the reforms and delusions of his time. He underwent the anti-Masonic hysteria which followed the disappearance of William Morgan and, although he considered the abduction of one man trifling in comparison with the slave-trade, he remained "utterly and irreconcilably opposed to the institution of Masonry." As a youth, he shared the great American ambition to go to Greece and fight for Marcos Bozzaris, adored Lafayette, and declared that "of all conceits that ever entered into the brains of a wise man, that of marriage is the most ridiculous." Putting away these childish fancies he found time, in a manhood seriously devoted to the great object of abolition, for woman's suffrage, temperance, non-resistant pacifism, Prison Reform, justice to the Red Man, and attacks upon state lotteries, and had radical ideas on education, spiritualism, keeping the Sabbath holy, and the sinlessness of humanity. He was, moreover, unwilling to sacrifice any of these to the cause of abolition. And the whole turmoil of his life, between 1831 and 1860, was as much due to dissensions he caused among orthodox abolitionists as to battles with hostile mobs.

In education, he rejected "the tinsel, the frippery, and the incumbrance of classical learning, so called" and favored the practical education sponsored by his fellow-abolitionist and mild Perfectionist, Weld. His spiritualism, an additional offense to orthodoxy, was not a mastering influence. He read a great deal of the testimony which was so common in the Forties, and was persuaded of its truth. Presently, he received a number of messages from the spirit world and, although he knew that his acceptance of spiritist phenomena would prejudice his more serious activities, he announced and earnestly defended his belief. In regard to the Sabbath he went further. He was engaged in a bitter struggle with numerous clergymen whose support was needed if *The Liberator* was to remain the great organ of abolition yet, in the midst of it, he wrote a poem in which,

among other infidel doctrines, he advised keeping "not one in seven, but all days holy." This was the worst kind of Perfectionism, and the clergy, in their Protest, said, "We confess that from the moment of Mr. Garrison's attack upon the Sabbath, we have entertained suspicions of *The Liberator*." From their point of view, they had good grounds.

For Garrison was, in essence, a Perfectionist. Except for plural marriage, he seems to have adopted the whole of Noyes' teaching, and the letter quoted in connection with Noyes * proves him a valuable disciple. The two men met infrequently, but their correspondence indicates an extraordinary sympathy. They had both lived through the same religious experiences, from 1825, when missionary, tract, and Bible Societies began to evangelize the world with true millennial ardor, to the most intense of Finney's revivals, which took place in 1831, the year *The Liberator* was founded. Noyes had acquired his Perfectionism by working on the experiences of Finney and developing the theology of Asa Mahan. Garrison turned to more typical New Englanders: through him we see New England liberalism linking itself with Perfectionism. We find Garrison's ideas repeated by the liberal theologian, Channing, in the hot terms of antinomianism: "The liberation of three millions of slaves is indeed a noble object; but a greater work is the diffusion of principles by which every yoke is to be broken, every government to be regenerated, and a liberty more precious than civil or political is to be secured to the world." And of the cardinal principle of Perfectionism, "the unutterable worth of every human being," Channing writes sympathetically: "I am not discouraged by the fact that this great truth has been espoused most earnestly by a party which numbers in its rank few great names. . . . The less prosperous classes furnish the world with its reformers and martyrs. These, however, from imperfect culture, are apt to narrow themselves to one idea, to fasten their eyes on a single evil, to lose the balance of their minds, to kindle with a feverish enthusiasm. Let such remember that no man should take on himself the office of a reformer whose zeal in a particular cause is not tempered by extensive sympathies and universal love."

And even Emerson gives comfort to the Perfectionist when,

* On page 173.

mocking at small reforms, he writes: "Society gains nothing whilst a man, not himself renovated, attempts to renovate things around him." This statement is pregnant with all the cults of the ego, but the Perfectionist was justified in thinking that his way of renovation was suggested. So it is not surprising to find Garrison and Noyes at one. Noyes traces Judaism "and its successor, Popery" in nearly every form of Protestantism and Garrison exclaims, "Oh, the rottenness of Christendom! Judaism and Romanism are the leading features of Protestantism." Noyes abandons the Sabbath, and Garrison will not keep it holy. In 1834, Noyes is "landed . . . in a new experience" and has "new views on the way of salvation," and, three years later, in the spring, he calls at the Anti-slavery office in Boston, and finds Garrison, John Greenleaf Whittier, and other abolitionists, talking politics. "I heard them quietly," he says, "and when the meeting broke up I introduced myself to Garrison. He spoke with interest of *The Perfectionist;* said his mind was heaving on the subject of Holiness and the Kingdom of Heaven, and he would devote himself to them as soon as he could get anti-slavery off his hands. I spoke to him especially on the subject of government, and found him, as I expected, ripe for the loyalty of heaven." On that ripeness he presumed sufficiently to write Garrison an extraordinary letter which influenced the recipient profoundly:

"Newark, N. J., March 22, 1837.

Dear Mr. Garrison: In addressing you, I use the liberty which ought to exist between every member of a race which God made of one blood. Moreover, the fact that I was once most heartily engaged in the cause you advocate, and am now separated from it only by devotion to a kindred object, entitles me to call you brother, with a peculiar emphasis. When I saw you in Boston, we spoke of the Kingdom of God, in its relation to the kingdoms of the world. I rejoiced to find in you a fellowship of views and feelings on this subject which has long been a rarity to me. I proposed to show you a written declaration of my principles, but was prevented. I write now to fulfill that proposal.

"I am willing that all men should know that I have subscribed by name to an instrument similar to the Declaration of '76, renouncing all allegiance to the government of the United States

and asserting the title of Jesus Christ to the throne of the world. . . ."

Noyes proceeds to call the American government "a bloated swaggering libertine," and wants to know, "What have I, as a Christian, to do with such a villain? . . . I cannot make myself a partaker of their ungodly deeds by mingling in their counsels or assisting their operations."

Garrison never threw off Perfectionism and, when scandals issued out of Putney, they were promptly put upon Garrison by his enemies. One former adherent withdrew because he felt that Garrison's abolitionism was not meant to stop with slavery; that all property, all law, and all government would next be attacked. The seceder was willing to work with all who held to the fundamentals of Christianity, but to him a Perfectionist was as bad as Fanny Wright or the blasphemer, Abner Kneeland. A friend wrote to Garrison that the Reverend Daniel Wise had "said that a man in Putney, Vermont, had written something which you had commented on with approbation" and "lately, the same person (he had forgotten Noyes' name), had written something in a newspaper carrying out the non-resistance doctrines to the alarming consequence intimated by him. The idea was a promiscuous cohabitation of the sexes, which he stated, as near as he could recollect, thus: that a man had no more exclusive right to one woman than, when a number sat together at their dinner, consisting of different dishes, one man had exclusive right to the whole of one dish. He had had the article, but he had lent it to a person to copy, and it was not now in his possession. So, because you had commented favorably on one article, it followed that you endorsed what he published afterwards." The reference is to the Battle-Axe letter of Noyes, and, although the logic is not good, since Garrison praised Noyes in some respects and blamed in others, it indicates the trend of popular feeling. In 1841, Garrison was moved to write in self-defense: "If what we have heard of the sayings and doings of the perfectionists, especially those residing in Vermont, be true, they have certainly turned the grace of God into licentiousness, and given themselves over to a reprobate mind." But, he adds, "Whatever may be the conduct of these perfectionists, the duty which they enjoin, the ceasing from

all iniquity, at once and forever, is certainly what God requires, and what cannot be denied without extreme hardihood and profligacy of spirit. It is reasonable and therefore attainable. If men cannot help sinning, they are not guilty in attempting to serve two masters. If they can, then it cannot be a dangerous doctrine to preach; and he is a rebel against the government of God who advocates an opposite doctrine."

This is a quixotically fair defense. Garrison would not throw over a doctrine he held, even if it led to excesses he abhorred, even if it imperiled his life-work. The unfounded charge of countenancing "spiritual wives" was enough to make the Evangelical Anti-slavery Society wish that Garrison would not become a member. His belief in human sinlessness made him, in orthodox eyes, a danger to the cause of Abolition. And when he headed "infidel Conventions," he drove thousands of would-be abolitionists into the societies for colonization. He reached the position of non-coöperation with governments by extending his principle of non-resistance. Ideally he meant that the abolition of government is ultimately desirable. Noyes reached the same antinomian position through his theology, his doctrine of "holiness" based on his idea that Christ had already come to earth. But people made no distinction. In essentials they found Noyes and Garrison identical; hostile to organized Society, hostile to Christianity, and dangerous to common morals. When they heard of Garrison talking to spirits, violating the Sabbath, prospering the cause of women, declaring against the sovereign right of government to make war in self-defense, they knew him for Anti-Christ.

To us he appears singularly Christ-like in the bold outline of his character; but the waywardness of his mind alarms us. Why did he have to take up so many causes? Why be so anxious to redeem mankind in so many ways? The answers lie deep in the motives of radicalism. For the moment, we need only note that all these causes were common in Garrison's time and that, like many lesser men, he succumbed to them. We can easily rectify any error we are inclined to make about the incidence of radical cults. In the 1840's, at least, they were not limited to the intellectual underworld for their recruits. The good and the great fell under their influence as easily as the unbalanced and the weak-minded.

† The *United States Gazetteer* considered "revolting" a lecture establishing the connection between beauty in the proportions of the figure and health; the word leg was not mentioned before women, and Mrs. Gove's lectures on physiology were scandalously misrepresented in the *Morning Herald*. † Fire departments began to be "a convenient apology for . . . indulging in irregular habits."

† The word obey was occasionally omitted from the marriage vow as being unconstitutional. † There was no anti-semitic feeling in Philadelphia and intermarriage was frequent; omnibusses ran on Sunday, and Negro chimney sweeps "yoddled" in quest of employment. † Religious instruction was being gradually barred from public schools and the University of Pennsylvania had over nine hundred students. † Messrs. Harper omitted three paragraphs of Franklin's autobiography, those dealing with his amours. † "The Americans take a great interest in Queen Victoria and forgive her royalty in consideration of her youth and sex." † The fiftieth anniversary of Washington's inauguration was celebrated by William Cullen Bryant's Ode which ended:

> "That noble race is gone; the suns
>     Of fifty years have risen and set;
> The holy links these mighty ones
>     Had forged and knit, are brighter yet.
>
> Wide—as our own free race increase—
>     Wide shall it stretch an elastic chain;
> And bind in everlasting peace,
>     State after State, a mighty train."

† In New York the following societies all held meetings in one week: "the New York Marine Bible Society; the New York Female Moral Reform Society; the American Seamen's Friend Society; the New York and American Sunday-School Union; the Foreign Evangelical Association; American Tract Society; Second American Health Convention; American Home Missionary Society; New York Colonization Society; Central American Education Society; American Moral Reform Society; New York City Temperance Society; American Board of Foreign Missions; New York Academy of Sacred Music."

# XV.

## The Winsome Heart.

THREE great reform movements of the 19th century were fulfilled, sooner or later, in amendments to the Constitution: abolition, prohibition, and equal suffrage. This seal on their propriety almost takes them out of the catalogue of cults and fanaticisms with which this book has been dealing; but not entirely. Two of these reforms were libertarian, the abolition of inequalities. The third also looked forward to an equality, but entirely in the negative sense. It was, as its name indicated, prohibitory. Theoretically, under prohibition, all men are equal—in not having the privileges of liquor.

The early years of the Prohibition movement and its outstanding personalities show how Temperance rose out of the same soil that fostered vegetarianism and communism, Perfectionism and New Thought. They show also, in the most obvious and striking way, how a reform as personal as that which Alcott or Noyes intended became a powerful force of negation; how the reformer of 1840, who was nearly an anarchist, became the embittered bureaucrat of to-day.

§

Even in the 1690's, Cotton Mather recorded in his diary a fear lest the flood of excessive drinking should drown out Christianity. In the year of the Declaration of Independence, the Reverend Ebenezer Sparhawk told his congregation that intemperance was a sin against the Lord and wasted money. After the Revolution and Doctor Rush's famous *Inquiry into the Effects of Ardent Spirits*, the first temperance society was founded (in 1808) by the pastor of a Congregational Church. Four years later, Lyman Beecher was protesting against the use of ardent spirits by the clergy. The Methodist and Baptist churches joined to lead the cause of temperance. And the religious revivals, both of 1800 and 1830, directly inspired temperance work.

"The reform," says John Allen Krout, a recent historian of pro-

hibition, "took on the attributes of a great revival. . . . Temperance workers were evangelists preaching a new gospel, and they stated its dogmas in the pulpit phraseology of the day. Persons who responded to the powerful appeal and signed the pledge were known as 'converts.' For the programs of the societies into which the 'converts' were gathered the evangelical prayer meeting served as a model. Appropriate verses, set to familiar gospel tunes, were sung with all the fervor of religious exaltation. The emotional appeals of the speakers and the 'testimony' of the pledge-signers strongly suggested the revivals of the evangelical sects. Indeed, the most effective propagandist for temperance was usually the Protestant clergyman who devoted a large proportion of his sermons to denunciation of the liquor traffic, indicating intemperance as the great barrier in the way of the church militant as it marched on to become the church triumphant. . . . Methodist and Baptist conferences, Presbyterian and Reformed synods passed resolutions commending the temperance reformation, encouraging ministers to support the movement and exhorting church members to abstain from all connections with the liquor traffic. Camp-meetings in the South and West were turned into seasons of pledge-signing, and converted drunkards were admitted into Christian fellowship as evidence of the power of temperance principles to save souls."

The names of the leaders of the early Temperance Movement are also the names of the founders of Bible and Tract societies and of anti-slavery organizers. In temperance, as in Fourierism, association was considered the only successful method and, behind temperance, there was the religious call to salvation and the moral call to a more perfect life. Since drink visibly insured the damnation of its victim, signing the pledge was a step toward salvation. Intemperance had to be destroyed as the great enemy which retarded the coming of Christ. The *Temperance Manual* of 1836 said: "The Holy Spirit will not visit, much less will he dwell with him who is under the polluting, debasing effects of intoxicating drink. The state of mind and heart, which this occasions, is to Him loathsome, and an utter abomination. Not only does it darken the understanding, sear the conscience, pollute the affections, and debase all the powers of the soul; but it counteracts the merciful designs of Jehovah, and all the overflowing kindness of an infinitely compassionate Saviour,

for its deliverance; binds the soul in hopeless bondage to its de-
stroyer; awakens the 'worm that dieth not, and the fire which is not
quenched,' and drives the soul away in despair, weeping and wail-
ing, to be punished with everlasting destruction from the presence
of the Lord and the glory of His power."

And "to Lebbeus Armstrong, who had labored diligently since
the formation of the first society at Moreau, temperance seemed
to have been sent by Providence for the salvation of men. It had
been foretold by the prophets of old and was a part of God's plan
for blessing the world. From the beginning the movement had been
attended by signal manifestations that some supernatural agency
was controlling it. Every sign pointed to the hand of God working
through men to exterminate the use of ardent spirits and drive the
curse of intemperance from its strongholds."

This was the religious background. Morally, the temperance
worker shared that enthusiasm for progress and perfection which
inspired reformers from Owen to Noyes. In doctrine, the religious
reformers were like the Rappites or the Perfectionists, restorers of
primitive Christianity learnedly arguing the question of alcoholic
content in the wine used at Cana. In method, the great majority of
them were libertarian, appealing to the individual to abstain and
not to the law to forbid.

In 1838, the failure of most temperance societies—that is the
failure of the methods of enlightenment and persuasion then in
use—was confessed in hundreds of petitions and memorials to the
legislatures of many states asking that legal approval be withdrawn
from the liquor traffic. In 1839, in Georgia, prohibition candidates
were nominated and their defeat was the signal for a tremendous
protest against all forms of appeal to the law. In the next year,
faith in legislation was swept away by an hysterical outburst which
paralleled in every respect the religious revivals then coming to
an end.

§

On the second of April, in 1840, the Reverend Matthew Hale
Smith delivered a lecture in a church close to Chase's Tavern in
Baltimore. The lecture by every account was in no way remarkable.
At the Tavern, that evening, was a group of average individuals

who met there frequently in a loosely organized "mechanics' drinking club." For some reason, unexplained, these two commonplaces came into contact and their meeting struck an electric spark.

In the drab church, a group of enthusiasts had gathered to be fortified in their faith; in the bright lights of the tavern, the mechanics sat around a rough table, shuffled cards, drank hot rum or wine, and let their bodies relax and their tongues run. They speculated idly on the peculiar people who preferred a temperance sermon in a dreary church to a comfortable tavern; their humor was high and they determined to see for themselves. At least, they appointed a number to invade the meeting, in a friendly way, and to bring back a true report. This was done, without any overwhelming enthusiasm for temperance. The deputies returned to the pothouse and a long discussion of temperance followed, accompanied by their usual temperate drinking. There was never a more strictly logical beginning for a fanatical movement. Persuaded by their own arguments, six men decided to sign the following pledge which one of them wrote out:

"We, whose names are annexed, desirous of forming a society for our mutual benefit, and to safeguard against a pernicious practice which is injurious to our health, standing, and families, do pledge ourselves as gentlemen, that we will not drink any spiritous or malt liquors, wine or cider."

The names signed were William K. Mitchell, David Anderson, Archibald Campbell, John F. Hoss, James McCurley, and George Steers.

Thus was formed the Washingtonian Society, the founders of which took the name of the "six reformed drunkards of Baltimore." They were presently joined by John H. W. Hawkins, another reformed drunkard, who became "the St. Paul of the Washingtonians." Within nine months, the Society had made 1,000 converts in Baltimore, all of whom were drunkards reformed by reformed drunkards. The meetings consisted of the recital of personal experiences on the model of the testimony at revivals. From Baltimore the movement spread and, in the spring of the next year, Mitchell and Hawkins started a revival in New York.

The crowds overflowed the churches in which the first meetings were held. They overflowed the largest halls. Whenever Hawkins spoke, he was interrupted by the cries and groans of those who pressed forward to sign the pledge at once. Finally, the crowds grew so great, and so excited, that a meeting was held at City Hall Park. Hawkins and Mitchell stood on rum-kegs to tower over the four thousand men and women pressing around them and, while they spoke, agents passed through the multitude and enrolled nearly half of the audience in the first Washingtonian Society of New York. The same year Hawkins advanced on Boston and the *Daily Mail* of that city thus reported his success:

"The Odeon was filled to its utmost capacity, last evening, by a promiscuous audience of temperance men, distillers, wholesalers, and retail dealers in ardent spirits, confirmed inebriates, moderate drinkers, lovers of the social glass, teetotalers, etc., to listen to the speeches of the famous 'Reformed Drunkards,' delegates from the Washington Temperance Society of Baltimore, who have excited such a deep interest in the cause of temperance in other places. . . . Mr. Hawkins, of Baltimore, was the second of the 'Reformed Drunkards' introduced to the meeting. He was a man forty-four years of age—of fine manly form—and said he had been more than twenty years a confirmed inebriate. He spoke with rather more fluency, force, and effect, than his predecessor, but in the same vein of free and easy, off-hand, direct, bang-up style; at times in a simple conversational manner, then earnest and vehement, then pathetic, then humorous—but always manly and reasonable. Mr. Hawkins succeeded in 'working up' his audience finely. Now the house was as quiet and still as a deserted church, and anon the high dome rang with violent bursts of laughter and applause. Now he assumed the melting mood, and pictured the scenes of a drunkard's home, and that home his own, and fountains of generous feeling, in many hearts, gushed forth in tears—and again, in a moment, as he related some ludicrous story, these tearful eyes glistened with delight, sighs changed to hearty shouts, and long faces were convulsed with broad grins and glorious smiles."

Reformed drunkards went out in teams on evangelizing circuits and, to the eloquence of Hawkins, was added the dramatic

vehemence of John Bartholomew Gough whose conversion, like
that of the original six, was accomplished without the intervention
of religion.* Gough's life had been strange and wild and his description of his delirium tremens became a set piece of American
oratory, although the printed page totally lacks the vehemence and
fire which his delivery gave it. Gough even fell from grace without losing his influence. He had gained over 15,000 signatures to
the pledge in four years when, on a visit to New York, he went on
a long debauch ending in a bawdy house where he was found by
his friends. As soon as he recovered, he explained that he had met
an acquaintance, whose name he did not know, and this man had
suggested a drink of soda water in a drug store. The implication
was that an *agent-provocateur* of the liquor interests had drugged
Gough and caused his downfall. Gough's youth and humility carried
him through, but other backsliders soon gave the Washingtonians
an unsatisfactory reputation. In spite of their revivalist enthusiasm,
Washingtonians were accused of infidelity; they were, in fact, non-
sectarian. The older temperance societies were annoyed by this outburst of emotion, which addressed itself exclusively to the dregs of
society and which brushed aside entirely all questions of restraint
on the manufacturer and vendor of liquor. At the end of ten years,
the moral fervor of the Washingtonians had died entirely away
but, before that time, it had had one significant effect. It had caught
the emotions of women. The temperance agitators of a later date
issued a romantic booklet reporting a supposed speech made by the
young Abraham Lincoln when he was a Washingtonian. The historian of temperance pays more attention to the fact that one Josiah
Willard transmitted to his daughter the Washingtonian enthusiasm
and thus connects the outburst of 1840 with the calm, shrewd,
highly organized, and eventually successful work of the Women's
Christian Temperance Union and the Anti-Saloon League.

§

By the middle of the century, the Temperance Movement had
made its first successful step toward prohibition. On the second of

---

* Gough is, in fact, a classic example of non-religious conversion. In his case, a
waiter in a temperance hotel stood in the place of the revivalist and Gough was brought
to conviction of sin, to repentance, and to conversion with sobriety and not sanctity as
the object.

The Women's Crusade

MATTHIAS.

formed a miracle in driving out a devil of fever from Mrs. Folger and he now proposed that she should abandon her husband and marry him. The method was simple. In as much as Christian marriages were performed by ministers who confessed themselves sinners, they were in themselves illegal and it was in Matthias's power to dissolve them. He went to live with the Folgers, richly promising them salvation, but it would seem that there were drawbacks. "He always took the meal time to preach, and generally preached so long that it was very difficult to find sufficient time to get through the duties. He often detained the breakfast-table until ten or eleven o'clock in the morning—say three to four hours; he would spend several hours at the dinner-table; and the supper (as the third meal was always called) table until eight, nine, ten, or eleven o'clock at night."

Among the other peculiarities of life at the Folgers was Matthias's habit of getting into a barrel of water, thereby sanctifying it, and from it sprinkling the naked women of his sect who stood by. His feeling about bathing was deep. He used to assist Mrs. Folger at her bath, she returning the courtesy for him. He followed the Folger family when they removed to Mount Pleasant and Pierson and Folger were preparing to give him a house in Greenwich Village when Folger when bankrupt, owing about $220,000. Matthias, who was not directly responsible for this turn in Folger's affairs, promptly argued that, since all the property in the world belonged to the children of God, no true believer could owe anything to the Gentiles. Mr. Folger, however, persisted in thinking that what remained of his estate should go to satisfy his creditors. In the summer of 1834, Mr. Pierson, who was still solvent, began to suffer from peculiar fits, and Matthias exercised his power by making him arise and walk while still under the influence of epilepsy. Regaining consciousness, Mr. Pierson seemed gratified to hear of the miracle vouchsafed him.

By this time the relationship of Matthias and Mrs. Folger had been regulated. The husband, reluctant at first, was finally convinced that his wife and the Messiah were "matched spirits" and, by some ingenuity of logic, Mrs. Folger persuaded herself that she was a virgin, although she had borne children. This was necessary as a holy son had been promised to her and Matthias (the son, when

Ghost will not stay in you, but one or the other must leave the house pretty soon. The pork will be as crooked in you as the rams' horns, and as great a nuisance as the hogs in the street." *

Mr. Pierson at the same time continued to converse with his dead wife:

"Sunday, June 24, 1832. Second anniversary of the morning when I went to Sarah's bedside, and in the name of the Lord, bid her arise and walk.

"She gave me her hand, arose from the bed, and walked round the room, and laid down again.

"It appeared to me this was a pledge of her future resurrection. . . . [I asked] suppose I felt as a husband ought, in point of office. She said, I have peace, my Lord. Again, thou hast power, and this shall be a sign unto you that these things were real. It was according to her word. These things appeared real, except bodily presence."

Matthias meanwhile revenged himself on the mocking crowds of a few years ago, by appearing at the Battery gate in a superb coach with a fine pair of horses. Sometimes walking to and fro, he would cause his friends to follow him at a reverential distance. His great height, his long wavy hair, his coarse curly beard and mustaches, and his green coat, figured vest and black pantaloons, with a sash of crimson silk around his waist, made him one of the most striking figures in the New York of the early Thirties.

Presently, friends of another disciple broke the harmony of the church and managed to have Matthias committed to the hospital for the insane at Bellevue. Here his beard was cut; but a relative got him out of Bellevue and he returned to the Pierson household. As crowds followed him to the door, he would mount to the steps and preach to them. If the negro servant Isabella annoyed him over some household economy, he would remain at home and preach to her the whole day. In March of 1833, Mr. Pierson received a disastrous order from the Lord. It was to give no more money to Matthias. Without breaking off relations with Pierson, Matthias, thereupon devoted himself to the Folger family. He had per-

---

* This violence about hogs occurs again in John Alexander Dowie, a prophet on a larger scale. See page 391.

June, 1851, John Hubbard, governor of Maine, put his signature to a bill forbidding the manufacture and sale of intoxicating liquors in that state. That law was the work of Neal Dow.* But the Maine law was far ahead of the times. It was prohibition, while the majority of the foes of liquor were still advocating temperance. They were fundamentally opposed to the exercise of civil power. They wanted the morality of the church and not the menace of the law to persuade people to temperate habits. The Washingtonians not only opposed statutory prohibition, but even defended liquor dealers. A restrictive, but not prohibitory law had been repealed in Massachusetts, after a trial lasting but two years and similar measures ran only for short terms in other states. At the most, in 1850, the country and the temperance workers were ready for local option. Essentially, they were still making a single appeal: to the drunkard, not to drink; to the moderate drinker, to abstain entirely. Temperance in America was still individualistic. On the whole, it still protected human rights. It was in nature a counterpart to the entire libertarian movement for the freedom of women and the freedom of slaves. The twenty years which followed the passage of the Maine law continued the struggle between local option and no license, between the legalist and the moralist. In 1873, an event occurred in a little Ohio town which in many ways parallels the reformation of the drunkards in Baltimore. A year later the W.C.T.U. was founded.

§

It was at this time that Frances E. Willard first became a worker in the cause of Temperance. From 1874 to the end of her life, this cause was her mastering impulse; at its service she placed the mind of a statesman, the spirit of a sentimental saint, and a demonic energy. She is the typical prohibitionist of a time when for a woman to be a prohibitionist, lecturer, traveler, and politician, virtually meant ostracism from good society. So far as she put herself under this social ban, Frances Willard was a radical. If we examine merely the logic of her activity we find her as radical as Alcott, crying out with him "Abstain, abstain." In Alcott's case, abstention was from meat and manure and money, from intoxicants,

* Among his fellow-lecturers in the campaign was P. T. Barnum.

sedatives, and clothes. In Miss Willard's program, one abstained from wine, and loose women, and finery of clothes, and ornaments, and the theater, and nicotine; and one went in for a little phrenology, and perhaps Graham bread, and the water cure (because water was sacred to Temperance), and perhaps a touch of Perfectionist sanctification. The objects are different, but the attitude is very much the same. This is the more surprising because, essentially, Frances Willard had the habits of mind of a bourgeoise reactionary. She should never have been a radical, and the reason that she became one is a pretty problem in psychology. To the psychoanalyst she offers, deliberately, a mystery, saying in her autobiography that the real romance of her life must remain hidden but, apart from private reasons, there were enough things in the temper of the time to account for the turn of her activities.

Her father had, in the early days of revivalism, started an outpouring of grace—as usual in northern New York—inconsiderately but symbolically choosing the harvest period for his labors. Frances was born at Churchville, near Rochester, New York, in 1839, and her mother used often to say to her, "Frank . . . thank heaven you were a welcome child." When she was two, the family moved to Oberlin which was presently to become known for its type of perfectionist theory and for the many ultraisms which, under Finney and Mahan and Weld, were encouraged there. The general atmosphere of the Willard home may be guessed from a little incident Mrs. Willard relates about Frances. "It was a tiresome journey, for we went by carriage. She often put her little arms around my neck, laid her head upon my shoulder and said, 'Mamma, sissy's dress aches!' It rejoices me to believe that she intuitively recognized the fact that it is not one's real self that is ever tired, but only this dress of mortality that aches sometimes."

In her third and fourth years, says her mother, "She used often to go with me to church where President Finney usually preached. She said his great light eyes, white eyebrows, and vigorous manner were to her like a combination of thunder and lightning; lightning in his look, thunder in his voice. I am sure her impressionable spirit became somewhat frightened by the thought of Christianity as administered by that great orator, who was very much given to rehearsing in our hearing the pains and penalties of the condemned."

She was called "mother's little infidel" and, for many years, merely reading Finney's sermons terrified her. She read the *Sunday School Advocate* and the *Slave's Friend* and, at the age of eleven, wept over *Uncle Tom's Cabin* but, throughout her life, she grieved sadly "to have missed the helpfulness and sweetness of nature" which she might have learned from *Little Lord Fauntleroy:* "Happy children of the present, do not fail to read it everyone!" She spoke pieces in public and, at an early age, sent a composition to the *Prairie Farmer* in Chicago:

"An autumn zephyr came sighing through the branches of a noble elm, which stood like a protecting giant over my cottage home. It shook, half regretfully, I thought, one tiny bough; and down through the gnarled branches of the grand old tree, fell one, two, three, dark crimson leaves.

"The sight, though insignificant, was a sad one to me, then. It reminded me of the similitude existing between leaves and mortals. Both wake to being in a bright beautiful world; both live their appointed season, enjoy their allotted share of happiness, die their inevitable death, and are, alike forgotten. This is the epitome, the simple story of everything that ever existed, save the Eternal God. We all begin life with bright hopes and eager expectancy. In time we leave the stage of action with one conviction—that all is vanity. . . ."

At the age of ten her favorite poem for public recitation was that which ends:

> "In vain, alas! in vain, ye gallant few,
> From rank to rank your volleyed thunders flew;
> Hope, for a season, bade the world farewell,
> And Freedom shrieked, as Kosciusko fell!"

Her father and her mother were both studying at Oberlin and the calisthenics practiced there took the place of dancing which "of course," as good Methodists, they would not learn. She was sensitive because she had red hair, which her mother thoughtfully alluded to as "bright-colored," and she was always annoyed when the misspelling of her name suggested that she was a boy, although, throughout her life, her intimate friends called her Frank. In her chaotic autobiography she sums up her life in seven main divisions: "a welcome child, a romping girl, a happy student, a roving teacher, the tireless traveler, a Temperance advocate and organizer, and a woman in politics." She tells how the children played Indian. On Sunday, her father would not shave, or black his boots, or read a letter, or look up a word in the dictionary, and she could not use her slate on Sunday unless she promised to draw nothing but meeting-houses. The actual religious training in the home was comparatively slight. Mr. Willard had been much influenced by the hydropathist, Dr. Jennings, at Oberlin and "If we had sore throats, a cold water compress was put on; when I stepped on a nail, and might easily have had locked-jaw, mother lifted me into the kitchen-sink and pumped water over the aching member; when on a summer morning Oliver's leg was broken by an ugly ox, his mother sat beside him, attending to the cold-water bandage by night and day for a week. And yet, in the twelve years of our farm life, 'The Happy Five' (as I was wont to call them) knew almost nothing about sickness. Our golden rules were these, worthy to be framed beside the entrance door of every home:

"GOLDEN RULES OF HEALTH

Simple food, mostly of vegetables, fish and fowls.
Plenty of sleep, with very early hours for retiring.
Flannel clothing next the skin all the year round; feet kept warm, head cool, and nothing worn tight.
Just as much exercise as possible, only let fresh air and sunshine go together.
No tea or coffee for the children, no alcoholic drink or tobacco for anybody.
Tell the truth and mind your parents."

Frances wrote little poems on the "felling of the favorite oak" and with her brother and sister, learned to love nature, and was instructed in the patriotism and dignity of their ancestors, some of whom had helped to found Concord where "Emerson, Hawthorne and other literati live." At the age of fourteen, she made a very pretty sampler. She was then, as always, passionately devoted to her brother and questioned whether it really was God's will that he should leave home and go to college. She herself was solicitously educated. Some of her relatives taught in Catherine Beecher's Female College at Milwaukee. She read much, but very few novels.

Once when she was reading a work by the "lonesome-hearted genius" Charlotte Brontë, a long shadow fell across the threshold and her father took the book from her hand. " 'Never let my daughter see that book again, if you please, madam,' he said to the lady of the house, who, not knowing his rules, had hardly noted my proceedings; the book was taken from me, and to this day I have never finished reading *Villette*."

§

In 1859, she had already begun to teach and was reading the *Memoirs* of Margaret Fuller Ossoli whose views she found "so essentially correct," adding that she thinks "Margaret Fuller Ossoli would have been, could have been, was, so far as she went, the greatest of reviewers." John Halifax was her ideal gentleman and she admires Humboldt, whose death she records in her diary. The girls of her school got autographs from Greeley and Lincoln and a verse of *Excelsior* by Longfellow; but their request to Queen Victoria failed to get an answer. Frances had already heard Elder Knapp at a revival meeting, but had not "come out." She had been reading Emerson and she was beginning to believe that, if the Bible was opposed to "known facts," the Bible was to be rejected. The principal of a woman's college at Evanston asked prayers on her behalf and she wrote him an extraordinary letter:

"Professor—I thank you very much for the interest you manifested in me and at the same time I feel very guilty.

"I do not think you know how hard my heart is, how far I am from feeling anything. I see I have no excuse to offer for my conduct. Three facts stand out before me as facts, nothing more. I view them calmly, coldly. They are these. I am a great sinner; it is a sin greater than I can comprehend to doubt God, or to refuse submission to him, for a moment. I have no excuse for delaying to become a Christian. The third fact is, I am as cold as an iceberg, as unconcerned as a stone. I am not proud of it, I am not ashamed of it. I view it simply as a truth. I disconnect it from myself. I seem to think that all these things concern others, but do not concern me. You will say that I shall feel in hell (a hard word); I shall see that these things did concern me, when I come to die. I acknowledge it. If there is a God, a heaven, a hell, a devil, then I am un-done. I have been taught to think that all these exist, yet from childhood I have doubted.

"I have been told that man feels a lack, a longing for something not possessed, when away from God. Candidly, honestly, I feel no lack, no want. I would not ask for more happiness than I have al-ways had, if by asking I might obtain it. You will say I ought to be thankful for this to God. I am thankful to something, thankful to whatever had thus blessed me, and I wish I was as sure that a good Spirit ruling the universe had done this, as Christians are.

"If I were to pray, I should say, if I were candid, 'O God, if there be a God, save my soul, if I have a soul!'

"It is humiliating for me, the child of pious parents, for whom a thousand prayers have been offered up, to confess this. I had thought no human heart should be permitted to look so deeply into mine. But I think it just that you should know.

"And now, in view of all these facts, I ask, respectfully, yet earnestly, ought I to go to the altar, to kneel before the Chris-tian's God, to hear the Christian's prayer, careless and unconcerned? Soon it will be expected that I speak in church. Congratulations will be numerous, that I have 'returned to the fold,' and my dark, wicked heart alone shall know how far I have wandered, how hypocritical I am.

"I am willing to attend church, though it interferes very much with my progress in science. I am willing to go, if you think it will do any good, but until I feel differently, I dare not go to the altar again. When I do I will go unasked. I am,

"Gratefully and respectfully yours,

"FRANCES E. WILLARD."

She was then not twenty. Wayland's *Moral Science*, however, persuaded her to say from her heart, "I believe that there is a God and that he is my father."

Toward the end of her college career she became ill with ty-phoid and a voice spoke to her saying, "My child, give me thy heart." Another voice urged her to hold out, but the voice of God was triumphant and she called her mother into the room and said that, if God let her get well, she would try to be a Christian girl.

The following winter, there was a revival at Evanston and, for fourteen nights in succession, she went to the altar rail and was finally baptized in 1861. To the end of her life, the doctrine of the trinity worried her. A few years after her acceptance of grace, she had an experience resembling the sanctification of which Finney spoke, "The conscious emotional presence of Christ through the holy spirit held me," she says, and she intuitively knew what was right to do; but she went to teach at a school where holiness was not discussed and, at the end of a few months, the rapture of her soul passed away. For the rest of her life she was a good Christian.

She intended always to be a teacher and took a district school near Chicago shortly after she graduated from Evanston. Her progress was rapid. In a short time, she had become head of the Women's College of the University at Evanston, and was much admired. But presently a question of authority had to be met. Miss Willard, champion, in her way, of women's rights, developed strong tendencies to tyranny. For the good of the University she demanded restrictions on the free movement of women students. It did not seem right to her that girls should freely go walking with young men. She proposed restraints and worried with honor-systems: she loved honor. The merits of the question were obscured by another: was she, as head of the Women's College, subordinate to the University? She said no. And as the University would not uphold her, she resigned. This was in 1874 and another event of greater importance to Miss Willard had been taking place at the same time in the neighboring state.

§

At Hillsboro, Ohio, toward the end of 1873, Diocletian Lewis delivered a lecture.

This was the "beautiful bran-eating Dio," who desired his name to go down to posterity as the inventor of the gymnastic ring, the wooden dumb-bell, and the beanbag. He was a pioneer in gymnastics with wands and rings and Olympia Brown, an early woman preacher, reports that his Boston school gave very pleasing and graceful exercises. He preferred calisthenics to dancing because of the "mischievous concomitants" of the latter and explained how to have a capital table for ten cents a day. He wrote a famous paper in the *North American Review*, on corsets, knew the value of night air, and opposed rockers. He invented the spirometer to enlarge the lungs and wrote, "a clean tooth never decays." He discussed halitosis, which was then known oddly as bad breath, with a great deal of frankness; and his book on *Chastity, or Our Secret Sins* is extraordinary. In this work he is particularly interested in means to combat lascivious fancies and lewd thoughts. He advises the use of a card on which ten key words, each representing an interesting topic, are written. The moment a voluptuous revery began, the victim was to grasp this card and interest himself in the ten subjects in order until his "subjective incontinence" had passed away.

By a strange combination of circumstances this man was to become the main spring of the successful prohibition movement. Everything that had gone before looked toward Temperance. Dio Lewis himself advocated Temperance. But carried away by his enthusiasm, the women of Hillsboro made an astonishing Christmas gift to the Nation. The preacher had said simply that "if the women would go to the saloons they could soon close them up for ever." Under the leadership of Mrs. Judge Thompson they went! Carrying their knitting and zephyr work, or embroidery, they first held a morning prayer meeting and then advanced in a long procession to the saloons. Some of them did not even known what saloons looked like. They believed "that those second-rate looking places were barber shops." The women of Hillsboro asked permission to enter the saloons and to offer prayer there. Miss Willard, who was teaching at the time, followed the movement with interest. Her own ecstatic style is suitable to the event:

"Women gave of their best during the two months of that wonderful uprising. All other engagements were laid aside; elegant women of society walked beside quiet women of home, school, and shop, in the strange processions that soon lined the chief streets, not only of nearly every town and village in the state that was its birthplace, but of leading cities there and elsewhere; and voices trained in Paris and Berlin sang 'Rock of Ages, cleft for me,' in the malodorous air of liquor-rooms and beer-halls. Meanwhile, where were the men who patronized these places? Thousands of them signed the pledge these women brought, and accepted their invitation to go back with them to the churches, whose doors, for once, stood open all day long; others slunk out of sight, and a few cursed the women openly; but even of these it might be said, that those who came to curse remained to pray. Soon the saloon-keepers surrendered in large numbers, the statement being made by a well-known observer that the liquor traffic was temporarily driven out of two hundred and fifty towns and villages in Ohio and the adjoining states, to which the Temperance Crusade extended. There are photographs extant representing the stirring scenes when, amid the ringing of church-bells, the contents of every barrel, cask, and bottle in a saloon were sent gurgling into the gutter, the owner insisting that women's hands alone should do this work, perhaps with some dim thought in his muddled mind of the poetic justice due to the Nemesis he thus invoked. And so it came about that soft and often jeweled hands grasped ax and hammer, while the whole town assembled to rejoice in this new fashion of exorcising the evil spirits. In Cincinnati, a city long dominated by the liquor trade, a procession of women including the wives of leading pastors, was arrested and locked up in jail; in Cleveland, dogs were set on the crusaders, and in a single instance, a blunderbuss was pointed at them, while in several places, they were smoked out, or had the hose turned on them. But the arrested women marched through the streets singing, and held a temperance meeting in the prison; the one assailed by dogs laid her hands upon their heads and prayed; and the group menaced by a gun marched up to its mouth singing, 'Never be afraid to work for Jesus.' The annals of heroism have few pages so bright as the annals of that strange crusade, spreading as if by magic, through all the Northern States, across the sea and to the Orient itself. Everywhere it went, the attendance at church increased incalculably, and the crime record was in like manner shortened. Men say there was a spirit in the air such as they never knew before; a sense of God and of human brotherhood."

The crusade failed. In one or two cities it lasted through the winter, and Miss Willard herself entered a saloon in Pittsburgh, in the spring of 1874, and prayed in the sawdust. A week later, she was president of the Chicago Women's Christian Temperance Union which she calls "the sober second thought of the Crusade." For seventy years men had been organizing temperance work and had addressed themselves to drunkards trying to effect a personal reform and to restore backsliders. With the Women's Crusade, the Temperance movement changed its objective. It attacked not the drinker, but the drink. It threw itself against the saloon. It changed, in fact, though not in name, from temperance to prohibition.

§

It was her enthusiasm for the Crusade which led Frances Willard to accept an unsalaried position as a Temperance worker at the very moment when she was offered the post of lady principal in an elegant school for young women at a salary of $2,400 a year. Her choice of life work is a decisive event in the social history of America, for she alone is responsible for the two great changes in tactics which eventually lifted prohibition from the status of fanaticism. Overcoming incredible obstacles, Frances Willard compelled the W.C.T.U., of which she soon became the dominant figure, to adopt suffrage as a means and to support the Prohibition Party.

The rightness of suffrage came to her by divine inspiration. She was secretary of the national, and president of the Chicago, W.C.T.U. when, one Sunday morning in Columbus, Ohio, the call came to her: "Upon my knees alone, in the room of my hostess, who was a veteran Crusader, there was borne in upon my mind, as I believe, from loftier regions, the declaration, 'You are to speak for woman's ballot as a weapon of protection to her home and tempted loved ones from the tyranny of drink.'" But when she offered to speak on the "Home Protection Ballot," permission was withheld by the head of the W.C.T.U. In the autumn of 1876, she made a complete declaration at the end of which the presiding officer said, "I wish it clearly understood that the speaker represents herself and not the W.C.T.U., for we do not propose to trail our skirts through the mire of politics." What the rank and file felt may be judged by one story:

"One of these women, quiet and gray-haired, sat silently listening all through the speech and when it was over and the people were going away, she suddenly burst into bitter crying. With the spirit of friendliness that pervaded the conventions, Hannah Whit-all Smith went up to her to console her and asked her to tell the trouble and be comforted. But the poor convert could not be comforted. 'Frances Willard has just convinced me that I ought to want to vote, and I don't want to.' Nothing could help her. She was convinced, and could not escape it, and she didn't want it, and could not escape that, and so there was no comfort to be given her."

The utmost demand in women's rights was embodied in a petition to Congress asking that, in territories, the sale of liquor should be legalized only when a majority of men by their votes, and women by their signatures, should so request.

Frances Willard joined Moody's Boston revival. She then went on a lecture tour, working as a free lance for Temperance, and helped to collect 2,000,000 names in Illinois to a petition for local option in which "women of lawful age shall be privileged to take part . . . when voting on the question of license." In 1879, she was elected president of the national W.C.T.U. and, with her election, it became certain that the organization would indorse Woman's Suffrage. In her first annual address, she predicted the coming of Suffrage "and then America, beloved Mother of thrice grateful daughters, thou shalt find rallying to thy defense and routing the grimy hosts that reel about thee now, an army of voters which absenteeism will not decimate and money cannot buy." At the same time, she foreshadowed her more significant work by a friendly allusion to the Prohibition Party.

To those familiar with later events, the connection between the W.C.T.U. and the Prohibitionists seems an entirely natural one. But as late as 1882, Frances Willard herself doubted it. The stumbling block was the Republican Party.

The W.C.T.U. existed at that time almost exclusively in the North. It was composed of women whose fathers had been called "barn-burners" and "free-soilers," who had suffered to bring the Republican Party into being. Their brothers had fought and died in the War which the Republican Party had waged to preserve the Union. The Great Martyr, who had delivered an address to the Washingtonians and was claimed as a Temperance man, had been a Republican. The Republican Party had saved the Union and freed the slaves, and was now reconstructing the South and restoring sound currency. It was "the party of moral ideas." Regrettably, it feared the beer-drinking German vote and was sold to the liquor interests. Miss Willard, for many years, felt that her only possible course was to work upon the Republican Party from within. Patiently and heroically, she braved the fumes of nicotine in committee rooms at the great conventions and made brief logical addresses to the delegates preparing platforms. Usually there was no effect but, once in a while, the Republican Party declared itself in favor of "the virtue and sobriety of the people and the purity of the home," and expressed sympathy with "wise and well-directed efforts for the promotion of Temperance and Morality." And these sops encouraged those members of the W.C.T.U. who were eager to support the Republicans.

The organization had in fact been unanimous in endorsing Garfield, whom the leaders had known as a brotherly Disciple preacher of the Campbellite persuasion but, after the election, Garfield met them coldly and they came to see that the liquor interests "held the balance of power."

In the meantime the Prohibition Home Protection Party was beginning to appear "as women's answered prayer." It was, almost from the start, enthusiastically in favor of woman's suffrage. "To-day," said Miss Willard in 1883, "that party is Endymion, the unknown youth, who by the friendship of Diana, the clear-eyed queen of heaven, shall make for itself friends everywhere, until it becomes regnant, and the two reign side by side." In 1884, Democratic and Republican Parties both refused to adopt a prohibition plank and, although the Prohibition Party gave up the name of Home Protection which Miss Willard had found so winsome, the W.C.T.U. gave that party its endorsement. On the 20th of November, 1884, Miss Willard could look back upon the election and ask her followers not to gloat over their defeated adversaries. For the party of moral ideas had, for the first time since 1861, been defeated and by such margins that the mugwumps were without dispute guilty; not only political mugwumps, but those natural-born Republicans whom women had diverted from the true path to vote for Prohibition. The Republican papers were furious and called the W.C.T.U. a political party. The Prohibition candidate for President, ex-governor John St. John of Kansas, was burned in effigy. When the W.C.T.U. was about to meet at the Central Methodist Church in St. Louis, the leaders were asked whether they would promise to avoid politics. They refused and Miss Willard said, "We can give up the high-toned churches, but not our high-toned ideas." After the Republican defeat, the churches turned bitterly against the W.C.T.U., but Miss Willard held firm and was able to defeat a resolution to make the Union non-partisan. From that time on, the Republican Party was considered the great enemy of Prohibition.

It is not precisely true that the Prohibition Party gave the 18th Amendment to this country. It never had a great leader and it saddled itself with too many social and economic theories ever to be successful. The Prohibition Amendment was ratified in the Middle West by people who believed in Prohibition, not by members of the Party; and these were the people to whom the W.C.T.U. appealed. Until it exerted a political influence by breaking down the series of Republican victories, the W.C.T.U. was considered harmless and insignificant but, from that time, it never ceased to gain in power, at least so long as Frances Willard remained at its head. Behind her action in pushing her organization into politics, there lay a statesmanlike concept. While the wives of Republicans and Democratic leaders went in for Temperance they still pretended to find some difference in essential things between the two parties. Miss Willard brushed these differences aside. She made it clear that social and moral reforms of any scope could only be accomplished by cutting across party lines. Like most Americans, she believed heartily in political action. The personal appeal had failed with the Washingtonians and the Crusaders, and Miss Willard went in for organization and the law—that is, for political action. For that reason, she demanded the Suffrage and, for that reason, too, she supported the Prohibition Party. To her, they were essentially the same; both were only political means to her moral ends. Both of them cut diagonally across the existing political organization. Miss Willard was actually helping to form a party, really national, and expressed her statesmanship in a pun on the initials of her own society, "We Come To Unite." Particularly, she wished to unite the North and the South, letting a great moral wave flow over and obliterate the rancor of the war.

She was responsible for the morality of Prohibition, for the emotions which the movement expressed. She withdrew the energies of women from the trivial and fruitless reform of individuals and directed them to a reform of society. She was too good an American to inquire whether society really could be reformed by law.

Miss Willard's work was carried on by the Anti-Saloon League which was founded, in 1895, exactly where one would expect it to be founded—in the town where Frances Willard spent her early childhood, the middle western center of reform, Oberlin, Ohio. The Anti-Saloon League went much further than the W.C.T.U. The women's organization still trusted to a degree in moral suasion and still was happy at the thought of a signed pledge and a great petition. The League had but one object, divided into two parts: the abolition of the saloon wherever it could be abolished, and the ultimate amendment of the constitution to destroy the liquor trade entirely. The Women Crusaders of 1873 had attempted to abolish a single saloon by prayer. They discovered that the drunkards went elsewhere and converted barkeepers had a tendency to backslide, but they had pointed the way. And although Miss Willard never dropped moral suasion—and thereby kept alive the emotions to which the Anti-Saloon League ultimately appealed—she foreshadowed the whole politico-legal movement which was eventually successful.

§

She was to be followed by one of the rare comic figures of the American reforming movements—Carry A. Nation. But before Miss Willard passes from the scene, it is worthwhile to record some of her other thoughts and activities. For example, one is pleased to note that she drank wine, under doctor's orders, and twice, once in America and once in England, she went to the theater. She allowed Nelson Sizer the phrenologist to examine her head, and liked Walt Whitman whom she thought a genius. In conversation with Harriet Beecher Stowe, they agreed that "pens and voices are constrained from on high." She went to a water cure and to a spiritualist. She once asked Henry Ward Beecher to explain the scriptural significance of "it is good neither to eat flesh nor to drink wine."

She at one time published the Chicago *Post* and always liked newspapers and newspaper men, wishing only that they would not drink and smoke so much. The editor of the *Atlantic Monthly* could not tell from a sample of her writing whether her work would be acceptable. It surprised her when a "great beak-nosed unmistakable Jew" helped her out of a slight difficulty in a New York bus. Her dog was named Prohibition. She deplored the prevalence of French dolls and denied that dolls are needed to "develop or cultivate" a mother heart suggesting that boys might better play with dolls and develop the fatherly instinct. She called her secretary Little Heart's Ease. She disliked the pleasures of the table almost as much as the pleasures of the glass.

She was of course deeply interested in marriage and her horror at the arranged marriages of Europe, with love left unfulfilled or unsanctified, was very great. On other questions concerning sex she spoke with a certain freedom up to a point and then involved herself in vagueness. When she was nineteen "a young woman who was not chaste came to the college . . . not knowing her degraded status I was speaking to her, when a schoolmate whispered a few words of explanation that crimsoned my face suddenly; and grasping my dress lest its hem should touch the garments of one so morally polluted, I fled from the room." She attributes this to a healthful instinct, but thanks God that, with the years, she became mellowed. Yet it was not till long after other groups in the W.C.T.U. had added a crusade against vice to their activities, that she lifted the White Cross, a crusade to pledge men to purity, and the White Shield, a work for penitent prostitutes. In the *Advocate for Moral Reform*, she had read a story which haunted her more than any other except *Uncle Tom's Cabin:* "It was brief but it was tragic, and the lovely young girl was left at the close in a madhouse, while of the man, I remember this sentence, 'I see him often, passing to and fro in his elegant carriage. Beside him sits his wedded wife, around him are his happy children, and he is a candidate for the state legislature.'"

At the age of thirty she kept in her house a servant girl who had been seduced, but all improprieties of the animal nature made her uneasy. In an essay entitled, *Is Marriage a Failure?* she discusses property rights and co-education and monogamy and the right of a woman to her own name and then proceeds to this astonishing climax:

"Last of all and chiefest, the *magnum opus* of Christianity, and Science, which is its handmaid, the wife will have undoubted custody of herself, and, as in all the lower ranges of the animal creation, she will determine the frequency of the investiture of life with form and of love with immortality. My library groans under accumulations of books written by men to teach women the immeasurable iniquity of arresting development in the genesis of a new life, but not one of these volumes contains the remotest suggestion that this responsibility should be at least equally divided between himself and herself. The untold horrors of this injustice dwarf all others out of sight, and the most hopeless feature of it is the utter unconsciousness with which it is committed. But better days are dawning; the study by women of heredity and prenatal influences is flooding with light the Via Dolorosa of the past; and the White Cross army with its equal standard of purity for men and women is moving to its rightful place of leadership among the hosts of men. I believe in uniform national marriage laws, in divorce for one cause only, in legal separation on account of drunkenness, but I would elevate and guard the marriage tie by every guarantee that could make it at the top of society, the most coveted estate of the largest-natured and most endowed, rather than at the bottom, the necessary refuge of the smallest-natured and most dependent woman. Besides all this, in the interest of marriage . . . men who, by bad habits and niggardly estate, whether physical, mental, or moral, were least adapted to help build a race of human angels, should find the facility with which they now enter its hallowed precincts reduced to the lowest minimum."

Almost equally vague is Miss Willard's record of her love affairs, as a prelude to which she records all her childhood and schoolgirl infatuations, with girls in school and women teachers. About men she says very little. At Evanston she had an inamorata—it is her word—and told her mother that she had written to Maggie, "I love you more than life, better than God, more than I dread damnation," to which her mother ambiguously replied, "Oh, Frank! Pray

Heaven you may never love a man." It seems likely that the prayer was answered. "I was almost nineteen," she says, "before the slightest token of interest came to me from beyond the mystic line that a virtuous woman's glances may not cross." This token was a polite invitation to go to a students' entertainment. She makes a peculiar point about even slight intimacies insisting that "the most delicate approach in deeds" must be accompanied by those self-committing words that women always expect to hear in the connection, and says, " 'hands off' is the golden maxim for every genuine girl and each true gentleman. All this I say out of a heart that suffered once and to help those yet untried." For nine months she was engaged to be married and, of this episode, she would say no more during her lifetime. She was by the nature of her work always closer to women and seemed to be happy in that intimacy, yet still wondered why she missed "life's crowning joy . . . love's delirium of delight." Her explanation of friendship between women betrays her own bewilderment, for she "pondered much" why "the loves of women for each other grow more numerous each day." She cites the example of the two maids of Llangollen who withdrew from their lives of wealth and position to live secluded together, and speaks of women, unfortunately married, joining in business and taking each other "for better or for worse." She tries to believe that drink and tobacco separate men from women and, just as she wandered from the subject of birth control in the excerpt above, she wanders now from this troubling subject to say that the men advocating women's advancement do not use tobacco or drink. The trouble, however, is still in her mind and she returns to it: "The friendships of women are beautiful and blessed; the loves of women ought not to be, and will not be, when the sacred purposes of the temperance, the labor, and the woman movements are wrought out into the customs of society and the laws of the land."

She was always sentimental, but she was not sanctimonious, and it is astonishing how much charm there is in her autobiography into which in six weeks she threw nearly half a million words consisting of diaries, reminiscences, petitions, addresses, and letters until even her devoted organization had to protest and shorten the book by nearly a half. She had working habits which would have made her an intolerable person to live with. She woke early, wrote on trains, could travel 20,000 miles a year, visiting every state in the Union in twelve months, and giving at least three hundred lectures a year. Yet she seems to have been driven by conviction and not by fanaticism. One regrets what she accomplished. By her methods she aided the most unhappy turn in the character of the American reformer, but her spirit remains faintly attractive. The pendant to her portrait is Carry Nation, the perfect fanatic, who shares with her the position of prominence in the history of American prohibition.

# XVI.

## A Moral Hijacker.

IT is fairly obvious that Carry A. Nation was a freak, slightly deranged. She claimed that the drunkenness of her first husband was responsible for her imbecile child, but her own mind was definitely unbalanced at the end of her life and nothing in her career suggests health or equilibrium. She was a moralistic hijacker born a little before her time.

"I never saw anything that needed a rebuke, or exhortation, or warning," she writes, "but that I felt it was my place to meddle with it." She meddled! Her extraordinary autobiography, which she modestly called *The Use and Need of the Life of Carry A. Nation,* is a bizarre record of meddling as practiced by "Your Loving Home Defender." She would not allow her name to be spelled "Carrie," for she considered that, as it stood, it was an imperative from on high to "carry a nation"—the United States—into prohibition and out of what she considered another danger as great as drunkenness—the influence of Masonic and other lodges, which gave men a pretext to absent themselves from their wives in the evening.

She was so violent, so conspicuous, that she probably has given to our time its most definite mental picture of the fanatic and reformer. She was always right. When she was teaching school she preferred a pronunciation not countenanced by the local trustees, and she resigned rather than change. She was still quite young when her first husband died and, one gathers from her own account, she prayed that a true mate be pointed out to her. Upon which, and immediately, she met the man whose name, taken with her own, makes such a happy English sentence. She went to live in Medicine Lodge, Kansas, and worked as the Jail Evangelist of the Women's Christian Temperance Union, exhorting the prisoners and wringing confessions from them that they would have remained upright, prosperous citizens if it had not been for liquor. Kansas was dry. Neither liquor nor the paraphernalia for dispensing it had any legal right to exist: it could hardly be called property. In place of a license to operate a saloon, Kansans paid a monthly fine. The saloons, openly flourishing, were called "joints" and, in addition, "sneaking, degenerate druggists" sold beer and whiskey. Mrs. Nation began her crusade in the traditional manner. Dressed in shining black alpaca, her heavy face lit with enthusiasm, her stocky figure planted as a rock, she stood at the door of a "joint" and sang:

> "Touch not, taste not, handle not,
> Drink will make the dark, dark blot."

The song, in a dozen verses, was ineffective and the singer turned to a monitor she had long known. For three days she enjoyed "a heavenly rapture" in which "my Savior was my constant companion." Presently, she heard a voice ordering her to "go to Kiowa," a neighboring town. Arming herself with stones and other missiles, wrapping them in paper and carrying them in the crook of her arm, she went into a "joint" and flung the first of these "smashers" into the mirror behind the bar. She hardly noticed the fury of the joint-keeper, or the surprise of the drinkers for, in the mirror, appeared by magic the figure of President McKinley—whom she had always identified with the liquor interests. Her second smasher struck his chair; her third, his head. Finally, the whole mirror crashed and the President with it.

After she had smashed five saloons, she became aware of her false tactics. A stone, however effective, could only be used once; when she ran out of ammunition she had to retreat, unless she could find, as happily she once did find, a billiard ball handy. So she armed herself with a hatchet and crossed into the town of Enterprise. Quietly she went to breakfast at the home of the Mayor's father. Soberly she attended prayer meeting at two in the afternoon. At three, she went down the street. Saloon-keepers, warned of her presence, had locked up, but she was not dismayed. With a terrific blow she smashed a plateglass window and, climbing through the jagged edges of glass, hammered a great mirror to pieces, swept bottles and glasses from shelves, emptied cases of liquor, and smashed the bottles one by one. She was unhurried and thorough, but finally the city marshal pushed his way through the cheering crowd and led her away.

Carry A. Nation

A shout of ribald joy rose in the land, and a cry of pain from the Kansas joint-keepers. Mrs. Nation was jailed for disturbing the peace, but no law could touch her for destroying property which did not legally exist. She went to Chicago, to consult with prohibitionists, and Chicago trembled but, for the moment, Mrs. Nation was concentrating on states where liquor traffic was forbidden. She toured the country, carrying little hatchets with her as souvenirs. She smashed when she could and, when she could not smash, she shouted. Or prophesied. She was denouncing a saloon in New York when a man jostled her. "Never mind," she cried, "Never mind, you beer-swelled, whiskey-soaked, saturn-faced man. God will strike you." And without any particular show of pride she adds, "In six weeks from that time this man fell dead in the streets of Coney Island."

She had a style in writing as in action. Her published work suggests a childish infatuation with words. She throws in a few extra adjectives, without specific regard for their meaning, just to give her sentence a swing. Of a Bangor hotel keeper she says, "This Chapman was a noted dive keeper, a rummy, and ran a representative, rum-soaked Republican hotel," making her five R's roll like the rumble of thunder. When she spoke in cheap vaudeville houses, or between the acts at burlesque shows, she was never embarrassed by the jeers and catcalls of the rum-soaked audiences. She faced them and, if she did not make them listen, she claims that she did. She was reproached for exposing herself in such desperate sinks of iniquity and responded that they needed her most. She was certainly nobody's fool. Howls of laughter did not deter her, because she knew she was making her propaganda dramatic. If governors and Presidents refused to see her, it could only be because they were suborned by the whiskey interests. This she knew, because she was pleading the cause of American wives and mothers. "Conspiracy and Treason!" she shouted from the balcony of the Senate chamber during a debate, to make that august body listen to her, and then tried to wreck their private bar. She refused to pay fines and wrote, usually without rancor, of the jails she had visited. But in the end, she was able to dicker with lecture agencies for respectable fees, to contribute money to weeklies supporting the crusade of hatchet-ology, to plan a home for the wives of inebriates, and to go abroad to England so that *Punch* could have fun with her and the valor of her ax.

She hated love-making; it was one of the things which most "needed a rebuke, or exhortation," and she never failed to give it. Even if she caught a boy and girl spooning, she would threaten their future peace of mind and, when she heard of a seduction, her energy was endless. She made it a personal matter to see that justice was done, and once when suicide followed her interference, she recorded it as an entirely natural and desirable result. In her autobiography, she accuses everyone, high and low, because she was seriously incapable of believing that any honest person, anyone of good will, could be on the other side. If they were against her, they must be slaves to rum or slaves to rum's money.

At Harvard, she had seen professors smoking, but at Yale the boys became her special pets, for they appealed to her to come and put an end to the way the college authorities were debauching the young by forcing them to eat ham with Champagne sauce. She quotes, with perfect equanimity, the broad spoofing letters which students wrote, and her heart breaks for the boy who had "brandy so strong on the food it made his head dizzy." She was a remorseless enemy of every other movement or individual that attracted public attention and wrote attacks on Dowie, on Weltmer's Mindcure Treatment, on Christian Science, and on theosophy. She had some very clear ideas on the profession of advertising; particularly, she pointed out that makers of whiskey so often used an animal as a trade-mark, because they wanted to associate something dignified, healthy, and clean with their ignoble product.

She was appallingly reckless in her accusations. Daniel Webster, she said, was so drunk that he had to hold on to the railing when he argued cases before the Supreme Court. Theodore Roosevelt, because the train on which he crossed dry Kansas had liquor on board, was a dive keeper. His successor was "Taft, of the noted Taft cigar." McKinley would have recovered "but his blood was bad from nicotine." She quarreled with Roosevelt's secretary because she wanted to make a public protest against Alice Roosevelt's cigarettes. She was a comic figure, with a certain drastic common sense, and, in spirit, she was much closer to the prohibition of Wayne B. Wheeler than Frances Willard was. Miss Willard, one fancies, wanted the world to be sober so that it might be happy. Carry Nation wanted it to be sober so that it might not be happy. Miss Willard had, therefore, a little of the older tradition of reformer which includes pious idealists, warm lovers of humanity, and visionaries. Carry Nation is the new order, a fanatic and a crank, hating whatever joy it is given to others to experience. Like most other women reformers, Carry Nation was ultimately successful. But it seems rather a pity that her crazy figure should not have lived on to become the apostle of direct action in prohibition enforcement. Somehow, the milieu of bootleggers, corrupt revenue officers, hijackers and night-club speak-easies, seems to call for her presence.

† Carriages drove along the Bloomingdale Road in clouds of dust, and "they were filled with parties driving for pleasure." † It was held against Newark, New Jersey, that whips for floggings slaves were manufactured there and the mayor of that city presided at a meeting which resolved that the subject of slavery and the question of its duration or abolition belonged exclusively to the slave states. † Horses on tread-mills turned the paddles of steamers at times and nobody seemed to be willing to pay 12½ cents for the use of a book from the steamer's library. † The leading literary lights of the country—Irving, Cooper, Bryant, Bancroft, Willis, and Prescott—were all Democrats. † There was an excitement about rearing silkworms and James P. Espy was granted a sum of money and offered a bonus to experiment in rain-making by means of a great artificial fire. The New York *Evening Star* objected because the "proposition savors of blasphemy." † The schooner *Amistad* bearing slaves who had rebelled on the high seas and killed the captain came into territorial water. The abolitionists defended them and in Boston they were considered as pirates. Eventually the courts decided that the Negroes should be set free but exported to Africa.

† A hundred votes were cast for Mrs. Maria Ann Chapman for governor of Massachusetts. † About fifty Americans settled annually in Cuba and the slave states wished that island to become a state of the Union. † There was a revolt against the patroons of northern New York; in New York City it was noted with dismay that the number of stock brokers had risen to eighty-six. † Female education was accused of an anti-domestic tendency "and to this we may trace the restless craving for excitement and public pleasures, which so strikingly characterize the aggregate of female society at the present day"; Lucy Stone and her friends did their own cooking and laundry at Oberlin College and helped to pay tuition fees by washing for the male students. † Abolitionists considered Boston the center of pro-slavery feeling. † The Negro quarter in New York was dreary and squalid beyond description. † When the famous violinist, Ole Bull, visited Washington, a Congressman asked him to play *Hail, Columbia,* and when an appropriation of $25,000 was suggested for Morse's telegraph, another Congressman proposed that half of that sum should be spent on mesmerism and still another suggested Millerism for the other half. † On the Erie Canal boats, corns were cured between stops at fifty cents for the first corn and less in quantity. † "Mr. Daniel Webster, the greatest political character of Massachusetts, is not rich."

# XVII.

## Some Women Reformers.

THE success of women reformers in America is extraordinary. While men were founding colonies and going bankrupt, or founding religions and going crazy, women threw themselves into great political and social movements and inscribed their purposes in the laws of the land. Like most other reformers, they were reviled and ridiculed but, in their case at least, martyrdom may be considered as proof of the ultimate righteousness of the cause. When the Constitution was being framed, Abigail Adams wrote to her husband ironically assuming that the new nation would recognize the equal rights of women. But long into the next century, the woman who married was legally dead, without rights or privileges, and popular prejudice sustained the legal status. Socially, the majority of women were privileged to be as coyly attractive to men as they desired; but this was the ideal of the town and the city. In the backwoods, there was but one right: the right to bear children abundantly. The woman who wrote, or painted, or thought, was a freak; the woman who demanded the right to hold her own property was an anarchist.

The actual history of the woman's movement, which changed all this, does not come within the scope of this book: some of its connections and a few of its leaders do.

§

The hidden spring of Suffrage as an actual political movement is, oddly enough, in Prohibition. From 1800 to 1860, a very few women wanted to vote, but a much larger number wanted to vote against slavery. For half a century longer, although the desire for the ballot *per se* increased, the majority of women still wanted to vote only against the saloon. The Temperance Convention which met in Rochester, in 1852, was led by Susan B. Anthony, Elizabeth Cady Stanton, Lucy Stone, and Mrs. Bloomer—the leaders of Woman's Suffrage. All of them were temperance workers and all were hampered by the lack of the ballot in their efforts to destroy the demon

Rum. Thirty years later, Frances Willard and the women of the W.C.T.U. went through the same experience and, for the same reason, became workers for Woman's Suffrage. It was many years later that suffrage became an end in itself, and that the emancipation of women came to include not the right to stop men from drinking, but the right of women themselves to drink. In the early days, nearly every item in the program of woman's rights was approached on that side which bore a relation to drink. Women wanted to hold property so that the drunken father might not ruin their children. They wanted divorce made easier so that the virtuous wife might elude the drunken husband. They wanted to speak in public, to be lawyers and doctors and bankers, so that the drunkard in delirium tremens, or in his grave, might not leave the wife and mother penniless. They were interested in phrenology, and diet, and dress reform, and participated in most of the other movements of the time, but above everything was the dominating desire to destroy the demon Rum. Had there been a prohibition amendment in America in 1800, the suffragists might have remained for another century a scattered group of intellectual cranks. Temperance gave to Suffrage an emotional overtone and a moral fervor which the movement never lost even when free lovers and intellectuals began to be influential in the Party. Mrs. Stanton wrote, "Let women's motto be 'no union with drunkards.'"

One reason for the success of women reformers is their extraordinary guile. In small things and in great they were easily the equals of the experienced political males. "On the fifth day of November, 1872, Miss Susan B. Anthony was a woman" as the indictment said and, being a woman, exercised certain rights she claimed as a citizen: she voted for a candidate for Congress. Knowing that she would be tried for this crime, Miss Anthony took the precaution to vote the Republican ticket and so mollified the Republican prosecutor, judge, and jury. Miss Willard's veiled threats to the major parties of the influence of women in critical states, where a few thousand persuaded husbands could swing a national election, were made with great dignity, but with the political astuteness of a ward boss. In a whole century of radical endeavor, women for the most part kept their heads. Rarely, a Fanny Wright attempted to combine half a dozen unpopular causes. As a rule,

women went forward to a specific object and only took up side issues
if they were compelled to. When their first convention met in 1848,
—in upstate New York—they skillfully avoided a direct demand
for the ballot for fear that this might prejudice outsiders against
"more rational" demands. Even the eccentric among women were
not unbalanced. Of these, two may be taken as fair examples.

§

The syllables of Mrs. Bloomer's father's name, Ananias Jenks,
and of Gloriana, the pen-name she used, carry us back to a day
remote from our own. The omission of the word "obey" from
her marriage vow brings us on to the year 1927, in which the Established Church first countenanced this change in ritual. Another event
of the day of her marriage strikes the balance. Her modest husband,
Dexter C. Bloomer, relates it with a becoming appreciation of his
wife's superiority:

"Mr. Bloomer had many friends in the town, and on the evening of his arrival with his bride they filled Mr. Fuller's room to
welcome the newly wedded couple to their new home and new
life. With them came many members of a fire company of which
Mr. Bloomer was a member, accompanied by a band of music, and
all went merry as a marriage bell. Refreshments were, of course,
served, and among them a plentiful supply of wine, for in those
days this was the almost certain accompaniment for all social gatherings. All, or nearly all, partook of it; and just then occurred an
incident which told most instructively of the moral character and
firmness of the young and happy bride. Glasses were filled with the
sparkling beverage and one of them was presented to her by the
bridegroom himself, but she firmly yet pleasantly declined to accept it. 'What!' he said with the greatest earnestness. 'Will you not
drink a glass with me on this joyful occasion? Surely it can do you
no harm.' 'I cannot! I must not!' A crowd of guests standing around
could but admire her great self-denial and devotion to principles;
and ever after, to the end of her days, she was a firm and consistent
advocate of Temperance and the unceasing enemy of strong drink
in all its varied forms."

One follows the sensible and energetic Amelia through her full and interesting life with a sense of recapturing the whole of American history. She fell under the influence of the Washingtonians. She became a contributor to her husband's newspaper and assistant postmaster at Seneca Falls. Then she began to edit her own magazine, *The Lily*, thus being virtually a pioneer in her field, as most other women editors had not owned their magazines. Quite casually she adopted a "sensible costume" created by a neighbor, a Mrs. Miller. It never occurred to her that her name was to be for ever associated with this particular costume. With some excitement, she first took the New York and Erie Railroad steam cars to visit New York and, among her visits in the metropolis, was one to the home of the great phrenologist, L. N. Fowler (it will be noted that the other great dress reformer, Dr. Mary Walker, shared this enthusiasm for phrenology), and another to the home of Horace Greeley. The gentleness, the perfume, the waywardness, and the energy of the time, all come out in her account of a soirée at Greeley's:

"At the latter place we met about a dozen of New York's literati. Of these I only remember Charles A. Dana, then on the *Tribune* staff; Mrs. E. F. Ellet, a prominent story-writer at that time; and Alice and Phœbe Cary, the poet sisters. I remember the latter as dressed with very low necks and arms bared to the shoulders, while their skirts trailed upon the floor. Around their necks were hung huge boas, four feet long, the style of that day, as a protection, I suppose, from the cold. These, being heaviest in the middle, were continually sagging out of place and kept the wearers quite busy adjusting them. I confess to a feeling short of admiration for this dress display at a little social gathering in midwinter, and my estimation of the good sense of the Cary sisters sank accordingly. And I never read of them to this day but that those bare shoulders and necks and trailing skirts appear before me. They, no doubt, were as much disgusted with my short dress and trousers which left no part of the person exposed. Tastes differ, that is all; and I was not used to seeing women in company half dressed."

The Bloomers went West, Mrs. Bloomer continuing to edit *The Lily* whenever they rested long enough to get out an issue.

At one of these stops, she brought from the East a woman type-setter and, in a masterly fashion, put down the resulting strike of annoyed male coworkers in her establishment. In March, 1850, she reports that the legislature of Tennessee "have in their wisdom decided, after gravely discussing the question, that women have no souls" and, presumably as a consequence, "no right to hold property."

Against such attacks, against divorce laws which tied frail but sober women to property-holding and soul-endowed drunken males, she lectured in the backwoods. As she proceeded from Chicago to Alton, she noted deer and other game along the railroad tracks. At St. Joseph her lecture was announced by bell ringers. On the way to Iowa, carrying "choice shrubbery and fruit grafts" to make glad the wilderness, she met Kit Carson on a stage-coach and was apparently interested in, but not favorably impressed by, his buckskin coat with fringes. When she arrived at Council Bluffs, the Omahas were dwindling away and she saw one of the last transfers of this vanishing race to a reservation. The city of two or three thousand inhabitants in which the Bloomers settled was a collection of log houses, and paths, through fields of sunflowers, served for sidewalks and streets. Cottonwood boards on the outside and muslin tacked to the logs within made the cabin warm and, if Amelia suffered, it was only with a nostalgia for civilization:

"Situated as we are three hundred miles west of the railroads connecting the Mississippi with the cities of the East, we, of course, neither hear the shrill shriek of the locomotive nor see the trains of cars dashing through our streets with a velocity that outstrips the speed of the light-footed deer; but we are living in full expectation of the day when these things will be familiar to us as they are now to my Eastern readers."

But the West was to become the real pioneer in suffrage, and Mrs. Bloomer was happy there. She wrote, she spoke, and she participated fully in the life of the times. When the Civil War broke out, she was a loyal Federalist but, almost unique among women pioneers, she was not actually an abolitionist. It was her duty to present a flag to the infantry leaving Council Bluffs and she did it with her customary dignity and enthusiasm:

"Soldiers: We cannot part with you without a few words of counsel and warning. In the new and dangerous path you are entering upon, let us entreat you to guard well your steps and keep yourselves aloof from every vice. Avoid, above all things, profanity and the intoxicating cup. The latter slays annually more than fall on the battlefield. The hearts of mothers, wives, and sisters go forth after you. Many tears will be shed and many prayers offered in your behalf. See to it then that you so conduct yourselves that whatever may befall you in the service of your country, you will return to gladden the hearts of the loved ones you leave behind and to enjoy the peace you will have conquered—that no sting will pierce their hearts, no stain rest on your fair name. Go forth in your sense of right, relying on the justice of your cause, seek peace with God, your Savior, that you may prepare to meet His summons should it come suddenly, or to enjoy life should it please Him to spare you for many days."

She was interested in everything that concerned women and she was apparently right in all her predictions. Inspired by a famous invention, she wrote: "It will be no strange thing to see, within a few years, women merchants, bookkeepers, jewelers, booksellers, typesetters, editors, publishers, farmers, physicians, preachers, lawyers. Already there are some engaged in nearly or quite all of these occupations and professions, and as men crowd them out of their old places, the numbers will increase. . . . It is well that it is so. Woman has long enough stitched her life and health away, and it is merciful to her that sewing machines have been invented to relieve her of her toilsome, ill-paid labor, and to send her forth into more active and more lucrative pursuits, where both mind and body may have the exercise necessary to health and happiness. Men are aiding to forward the woman's rights movement by crowding women out of their old places. Women will be gainers by the change, and we are glad to see them forced to do what their false education and false delicacy have prevented them doing in the past."

§

It was a full life and, except for the absence of children, a happy one. In it the part played by dress reform was extremely small and, serious as she was about it, Mrs. Bloomer would hardly have cared to be known by her costume alone. That costume was an entirely logical development. The dress of women in Mrs. Bloomer's time was fantastic in appearance, dangerous to health, and appropriate only to a type of woman which was definitely dying out. In his *Social History of the American Family*, Arthur Calhoun notes that, by 1830, the domestic type of woman was being displaced not by the active professional type but by giggling triflers; "fashionable females had nothing to do but harass servants and gouge money out of husband and father." A double revolution in the status of women was taking place. The ideal good wife was changing on one side into the idealized and silly lady and, at the same time, in other economic conditions, into a factory worker or a member of the learned professions. The former was supposed to be typical; she was socially dominant:

"The delicacy of American women during the first half of the nineteenth century was to some degree the realization of an ideal. Woman was supposed to be of finer clay; and this 'finer-clay' fragility, futility ideal was already pretty well established at the end of the eighteenth century. In American periodical literature of the early part of the nineteenth century, girls languishing of broken hearts . . . were an immensely popular theme, especially in ladies' magazines. Women up to the War and beyond were nourished in the cult of female delicacy and refinement. Of course this theory was capable of complete application only in leisure-class circles; but it helps us to understand the neglect of physical training for girls and also to appreciate the remark of a physician of the first quarter of the nineteenth century who said that not one woman in ten enjoyed perfect health. At a much later date Catherine E. Beecher 'made enquiries into physical health of American females and . . . among her immense circle of friends and acquaintances all over the union, is unable to recall ten married ladies in this century and country who are perfectly sound, healthy, and vigorous.' "

These were the women who could wear the clothes against which working women rebelled. Elizabeth Cady Stanton, after changing to the new costume, wrote that it was a positive joy to go "running up and down stairs with my hands free." The girls in factories were almost naked to the waist and wore short skirts to keep out of the way of machinery. Every new free activity of women demanded some change in their style of dressing. The first change was made to a peculiarly unattractive costume which almost defeated its object. Before she went West Mrs. Bloomer had lived, like so many other reformers, in upstate New York where she became acquainted with the severe garb of the little sects and communities about her. From them, and from the least advanced women in the world, the slaves in the harem, came the Bloomer costume.

Her own description of it is so unattractive as to suggest that she took that "grim satisfaction in dreariness" which a reformer has called the characteristic of the time:

"We would have the skirt reaching down to nearly halfway between the knee and ankle, and not made quite so full as is the present fashion; underneath the skirt, trousers made moderately full, in fair mild weather coming down to the ankle, not instep, and there gathered in with an elastic band, the shoes or slippers to suit the occasion; for winter or wet weather the trousers also full, but coming down into the boot, which should rise at least three or four inches above the ankle. This boot should be gracefully sloped at the upper edge and trimmed with fur or fancifully embroidered, according to the taste of the wearer. The material might be cloth, or morocco, moose skin, and so on, and made waterproof if desirable."

But the New York *Tribune*, describing her at one of her lectures, presents a much more attractive picture: "Mrs. Bloomer was attired in a dark brown changeable tunic, a kilt descended just below the knees, the skirt of which was trimmed with rows of black velvet. The pantaloons were of the same texture and trimmed in the same style. She wore gaiters. Her headdress was cherry and black. Her dress had a large open corsage, with bands of velvet over the white chemisette in which was a diamond stud pin. She wore flowing sleeves, tight undersleeves, and black lace mitts. Her whole attire was rich and plain in appearance."

§

*Amelia Bloomer*

Several generations later the bicycle brought the bloomer a new lease of life—a second blooming as it were—but, by that time, another dress reformer had gone farther and fared worse. Dr. Mary E. Walker was a fanatic. She had a few interests outside of dress reform and she expressed herself on all matters violently, but she seemed to believe that if women wore men's clothes almost all the evils of life would be abated.

She dedicated her book on dress reform on four successive pages; first to her parents, then to her professional sisters "of whatever school or pathy"; then to the great sisterhood of women suffering "trials and worries that God has not given men the power to comprehend." But finally and above all, the book is dedicated "to the practical dress reformers: The truest friends of humanity, who have done more for the universal elevation of woman in the past dozen years than all others combined. You who have lived the precepts and principles that others have only talked about. You who have been so consistent in your ideas of the equality of the sexes, by dressing in the manner to fit you for the duties of a noble and useful life. You who have written and spoken and been living martyrs to the all-important principles involved in a thoroughly hygienic dress, and thus given to the world an indisputable proof of your unflinching integrity. . . . To you, in a word, who are the greatest philanthropists of the age, this . . . Dedication is made."

She had put on men's clothes because, being a qualified physician and a first lieutenant on the surgical staff in the United States Army, she could not do field work during the Civil War in the usual costume of women. She was captured and spent some time in Libby Prison. She won a medal of honor, and the right to dress as she pleased was confirmed to her by a grateful Congress. Her own costume was not at all striking. More than twenty years ago, I saw her driving a buggy over a country road, sitting very erect and forbidding, and apparently unconscious of the jeers of small boys who ran after her carriage. She was dressed then in rather dingy black with an ordinary white shirt and black tie. But when she appeared in the court of St. James's, she wore black silk trousers with velvet side stripes and a loose black silk coat with velvet bands on the pockets. This was not, however, the "American Reform Dress" that she offered to women with an earnestness and vehemence almost unique in the history of women reformers:

"The dress is made with high neck and loose waist, and whole drawers, and long sleeves with waistbands attached; thus making a complete undersuit in one garment. The drawers are folded over the ankles and the stockings adjusted over the drawers, thus keeping the ankles warm and also keeping the stockings arranged without elastics or other bands, or any troublesome or injurious arrangement, most of which impede the circulation and produce varicose veins and weariness in walking.

"The pants are made like men's, and are either buttoned to the waist of the undersuit or are arranged with the usual suspenders. The dress is made to hang free of the body, the waist and skirt of one piece like a sack coat, and falling to the knees to prevent its being stepped upon when descending stairs, or of becoming soiled on rainy days; but principally because of a needed relief to women from its shortness. Thus for general wear but three garments are required.

"Woolen and cotton, flannel and silk may be made the same as the ordinary linen suits—with the exception of waistbands—when the season makes more clothing necessary, and these can be worn either under or over the linen; thus giving the required amount of warmth without expenditure of vitality to carry the clothes about, or of money to purchase them. The time is coming when every woman will dress in this style, for the advantages are too evident to be much longer overlooked."

She never persuaded her own sex, who used to set bulldogs on her in the public streets. She was even unpopular with advanced Suffragists because she held that being a woman, and hence a citizen, she already had the right to vote—and considered it hardly worth having. A great many women in the Suffrage conventions were dress reformers, but they were turned back by the monomaniac vehemence of Dr. Walker's arguments:

"So much of the nervous energy is expended on Dress and dressing and carrying the burdensome stuff that a morbid sensibility is induced which women cannot prevent. At the exhibition of this, men lose their patience, believing there is no necessity for a woman ever to be nervous and easily annoyed at such matters. Not only does the husband and father suffer from this continuous irritation, but the children that are, and those that are to be, partake of the same. . . . The greatest sorrows from which women suffer to-day are those physical, moral, and mental ones that are caused by their unhygienic manner of dressing! The want of the ballot is but a toy in comparison."

One reform she accomplished; the back collar-button on the ordinary man's shirt chafed her neck and, with a solitary outburst of domestic inspiration, she created the inside neckband which, by the insertion of a strip of linen, prevents the metal from touching the skin. Yet the grateful male can hardly rank her among the saints, for Dr. Walker, comparatively indifferent to drinking, was a violent enemy of nicotine, expressing herself in her usual ejaculatory manner:

"Many a lady has married a 'mild Tobacco user' who was not herself aware of the depth of her disgust for the weed until she found the restraints of society thrown off by her husband, and Tobacco used freely by him! . . . The Wife's eyes are often dim with tears as she says half aloud: 'Oh! I wonder if the men are all so selfish that they will smoke when they know how sickening it is to their wives? His breath is so bad, and his clothes are all full of the odor, and even in the washtub and in the ironing room, one cannot pass the door without catching something of the odor! Oh! If he would only not smoke, or if I could only endure it! But my heart is broken. He, yes, he promised so faithfully that he would not smoke any more! And now, when I am married to him, and must stay, I am to be tormented all the rest of my life with Tobacco! Oh, dear, dear, what would I give if I were only single again, and at my own home, where I would be out of all traces of Tobacco!"

She had one other interest—literary expression—and by this, too, she intended to make domestic life happier. She would gladly have cut down a ten-hour working day to eight hours of labor and two of literary composition. "Who will not say that the marriage relations would not be made much happier if the laborers had time to think and write, for as it affords me happiness in expressing my ideas, and makes me more noble, so it would another human being. Every noble expression adds a title to one's own soul's nobility. There are branches of labor where one cannot stop and pen the burning words that rush out of the brain and demand paper to rest upon and a pen to hold them there. But if they labor a fewer number of hours they would not be so weary that they would forget how to clothe their beautiful ideas. . . . Many a laborer has listened to such appeals with a sorrowing heart, knowing that his or her want of time to clothe would result in the interment of the neglected gems, and they could only attend the funeral, for that takes but little time, and so everybody can attend funerals. The immortal Tupper, in the following words, has beautifully expressed the necessity for clothing the 'naked' ideas as soon as they are called for:

'Hast thou a thought upon thy brain
   Catch it ere it fly
Or other thoughts will intervene
   And it will soon take wing.' "

She prefaces her book with a few remarks about herself but, recalling that it is not considered decent for women to use the personal pronoun, she says, "Next to self is the phrenologist," and quotes one on her capacities. She believes sincerely in work and alludes with contempt to the "shoddyocracy" who look down upon labor. She worked for the reform of marriage laws and, with Mrs. Stanton, believed in a woman's right to keep her own name after marriage.

§

Dr. Walker had herself no opportunity to be a "Lucy Stoner," as she never married; the odd thing is that Lucy Stone herself could hardly be called one. Like Frances Willard and Mrs. Stanton, Lucy Stone believed in the right of a married woman to keep her own name. Mrs. Stanton had said: "A woman's dignity is equally involved in a lifelong name, to mark her individuality. We cannot overestimate the demoralizing effect on woman herself, to say nothing of society at large, for her to consent thus to merge her existence so wholly in that of another." Lucy Stone agreed and, in accordance with the principles of psychoanalysis and of common sense, she kept her name and put the right to do so out of her mind. It was very far from being her major interest in life and it was certainly not an obsession. When, on May Day, 1855, the Rev. Thomas Wentworth Higginson married Lucy Stone and Henry D. Blackwell, the high contracting parties issued a joint protest of which Doctor Higginson so approved that he had copies made and sent them to other clergymen. It was a protest against the injustice of the marriage laws by which "the legal existence of the wife is suspended during marriage." The two signers agreed that, in case of dispute between man and wife, it would be preferable to choose an arbitrator, rather than trust oneself to the courts, for every law relating to marriage was in favor of the male. This protest does not mention the preservation of the maiden name, and, in fact, one of Lucy Stone's journalistic supporters, publishing the protest, referred to her as Lucy Blackwell. Yet all her work for education, abolition, temperance, and suffrage is nowadays forgotten in favor of the incidental circumstance that she kept her maiden name.

§

The Jemima Wilkinsons and Ann Lees of an earlier day were much more peculiar than the women who became so conspicuously successful in the history of American reforming movements. Most of the latter are much too intelligent to be "typical radicals"; if they do not rise to philosophic intensity they manage, at least, to avoid idiosyncrasy. Catherine E. Beecher was not precisely a radical reformer, but she was an intelligent woman, associated with every reform movement, interested in every improvement in the status of women, in diet reform, and in health; and we find her writing with the utmost common sense, the common sense of her time, this prophecy of the future of women:

"Woman has never waked to her highest destinies and holiest hopes. She has as yet to learn the purifying and blessed influence she may gain and maintain over the intellect and affections of the human heart. Though she may not teach from the portico, nor thunder from the forum, in her secret retirements she may form and send forth the sages that shall govern and renovate the world. Though she may not gird herself for bloody conflict, nor sound the trumpet of war, she may enwrap herself in the panoply of heaven, and send the thrill of benevolence through a thousand youthful hearts. Though she may not enter the list in legal collision, nor sharpen her intellect amid the passions and conflicts of men, she may teach the law of kindness, and hush up the discords and conflicts of life. Though she may not be clothed as the ambassador of heaven nor the minister of the altar of God; as a secret angel of mercy she may teach its will, and cause to ascend the humble but most accepted sacrifices."

That is the moderation of the theorist; in practice, women were energetic, were devoted, were tireless—but immoderate. Few of them founded colonies and sects; but they effected moral reformations of the first order, they were definitely in the current of American progress; and this is almost equal to saying that they were against the current of American radicalism. It is dangerous to use one key in deciphering the whole of a nation's history; but it is possible to say that, looked at with a partial eye, the first hundred years of the American Republic are a history of the distribution of political power with its economic consequences. At the beginning, the male white property holder was almost unchallenged in command. There followed, first the emergence of the male white citizen, then of the male citizen and, finally, of the citizen regardless of sex or color. Two great reforms accomplished the last two of these changes in power and both of these were ably supported by women. At the same time, the economic stream led to greater holding of property and never to the abdication of the wage system; yet it was against property and wages that most of the men reformers fought. If it is a proof of intelligence to choose a favorable terrain for a battle, the women reformers of America prove themselves infinitely superior to the men. But if it is a proof of idealism to fail, men reformers are the saints, and women for all their high ideals, remain as realistic, and unsaintly, as business men.

# PART II

*"There is nothing too stupid for intelligent people to believe."*

† Arsenic was the base of many quack medicines. † The popular novelty was rounce, a kind of whist with dominoes. † An editor inquired what the age was characterized for and answered, "dollar magazines—shilling lectures—shilling theaters—shilling concerts—penny papers—beggarly office-seekers—rascally politicians—unprincipled bankers—cutthroat financiers—doubtful saints—miserable Wall Street editors—and fine women." † At the Park Theatre in New York was offered, "the drollest, the oddest, the funniest, the queerest, the most curious, the most novel, the most unpronounceable amusement" called concerts *à la Musarde*. An orchestra of eighty played and the thousand young men patrons walked about, beat time to the Zampa Overture, and made eyes at a few dozen gay ladies in the boxes. In Philadelphia *Norma* was playing simultaneously at two theaters. † The *Garland* waltz was popular and the Methodists of Ohio petitioned the legislature to "protect them from intemperance at camp-meetings." † Invoking divine guidance, the Reverend Mr. Taylor and eleven other men at Oberlin whipped with a rawhide the writer of some improper letters. "Sabbath schools and Bible classes have, in a peculiar manner, been filled with that solemnity, which, turning the soul from the hot pursuit of pleasure and sin leads it . . . to unfeigned repentance and faith in Jesus Christ." † On the third of May, 1840, a lovely Sunday, Fanny Elssler landed in New York and for two weeks cleared $500 a night in spite of the sneers of the *Herald*. In December, the *Petersburgh Intelligencer* noted that the dancer was "modestly attired in a short skirt which barely reaches below her hips" and by that time Forrest, Booth, and Welch and his giraffe were all failing in the theaters of New York. † "The republic of Texas . . . is beginning to loom large among the nations of the earth." † Ventriloquism was a popular art; and the social ideal of the time was to be "a distinguished financial agent in Wall Street . . . wearing elegant *mustaches* . . . driving a pair of bloods . . . and keeping a beautiful *cottage ornée* at Bloomingdale where he gives elaborate *dejeuner à la fourchette*." † Mr. Niblo was conducting *concerts d'hiver* with increased gaslight. † The *Ladies' Book*, conducted entirely by women, published the best engravings of the time.

# XVIII.

## "The Coming of the Prophets."

CONCURRENTLY with the rise and fall of social experiments in the nineteenth century, there appeared in the United States a series of prophets. Either as a promise or as a threat, the immediate advent of the Messiah had been preached since the time of Jonathan Edwards and, when the emotional atmosphere became favorable, the Messiahs appeared, in numbers. None of them was acceptable to the evangelists. They seemed to be not Christ, but Anti-Christ. In various ways, they labored to destroy the religion which the revivalist preached. Yet they were specifically in the great messianic current, in the tradition of the Messiah as Healer.

The source of this tradition is, of course, in the story of Christ's ministry with its climax in raising Lazarus from the dead. From the Middle Ages to our own time, cults and churches, pretending to the purity and power of Early Christianity, have always held that curing the sick is the supreme test of authority. The American prophets went farther. To the astonishment and sometimes to the delight of Europe, they passed beyond the conception of cures as proof of religious purity and made the cures a religion in themselves.

§

The interrelations of quackery, medicine, mind-cures, and spiritualism are so complicated that sign-posts are advisable. In the following pages, it has been impossible to preserve a strict chronological order. Movements overlapped, drew together, separated. Individuals embraced seemingly incompatible doctrines. A discredited science of the beginning of the century returned to scientific favor at the end. In this chaos, an order of development has seemed more important than an order of time.

The development, roughly, is this: Medical quackery, based on distrust of scientific medicine, leads back to magic and the religions of superstition. It had a period of efflorescence at the beginning of the nineteenth century and presently came into enlivening contact with mesmerism. This was a decisive event, for mesmerism was the first great system treating disease through mental channels which did not claim religious authority. Quacks, hitherto limited to the invention or concoction of physical aids to health, now turned to the soul. At about the same time, phrenology was brought to the United States and added a preoccupation with moral ills to the business of curing the body. Three of the most significant of the new prophets derived their powers from mesmerism and phrenology. All of them were engulfed in the flood of spiritualism which began in apparent independence of any other movement, but was, in actuality, closely connected with every movement from revivalism to bump-reading. Spiritualism, communication with the dead, became the universal solvent of quackery. In it all things found place and out of it rose the two movements in which the spiritual history of the nineteenth century culminates: Christian Science and New Thought. With these movements the circle is completed. They are the result of which Jonathan Edwards was the cause and, as often happens, the end precisely inverts the intention of the beginning.

The history of the prophets becomes clearer when they are seen against their proper background. We are to consider them as seekers for perfection and as fellow-workers, in that sense, of the revivalists, the social experimenters, the faddists, and the radicals. The methods were different, but the object was identical. For Edwards there could be but one perfection—in the freedom of the Will—and it could be enjoyed only by God. Human perfection, although unattainable, was foreshadowed in a sort of ecstatic communion with the Holy Ghost. With Finney, perfection becomes something more specific. It was a kind of sanctification in the person of Christ, a barely attainable state of being in which man is so graced by God that he has no more will to sin. In the doctrine of John Humphrey Noyes we come almost upon the mystic utterance of St. Augustine that, if you but love God enough, you may safely follow all your inclinations. At the same time, the perfection of the order of nature is a leading idea in Emerson and the other trancendentalists. We have only to become aware of the workings of this order, to submit ourselves, and we become one with perfection and one with God.

Radicalism found other ways to perfection. In the spirit of the true fanatic, like Mary Walker, something close to perfection is promised to women if they adopt men's clothes. In the deranged mind of a Matthias there is the promise of universal salvation if men give up liquor. Perfection is attained in the ascetic colonies of the Shakers and of Rapp by abstention from the great sin of procreation. It is arrived at in the Phalanstery by mutual love and the abolition of property. It triumphs even over death in the ingenious combinations of the Oneidists. Further without touching upon sex, or property, or salvation, the advanced faddist of diet promises health and longevity which make man almost perfect because he is almost immortal. The single idea that man can and must be perfect runs, therefore, through the activities of a century, and only toward the end degenerates into the less vaulting ambition to make man healthy, cultured, and terribly rich. The fundamental idea of perfection through improvement characterized equally Finney and Emerson and Orison Swett Marden, the physical culturist and the developers of memory and self-confidence. This idea is not a firm binder, not powerful enough a magnet to attract all these doctrines and vagaries so that we can say that they are essentially one; but it does give them a center, and a line drawn from any one of them through this center is certain to touch another. The differences between them are great and the most marked is that the early perfectionists are essentially Christian; the later ones, either unorthodox or oriental. The early ones intended the perfection of the spirit; the later ones, the perfection of the body and of the mind. The emphasis of some is on God and, in others, on nature. But in all of them, there is the idea of man rising to perfection by uniting himself with a higher power or submitting to a higher order.

It was only after mesmerism had come to America that quackery rose from mean streets and country byways to become part of the intellectual movement of the time. Presently, quackery was to come to the crossroads between science and religion. One division chose science and, never forsaking quackery, created patent medicines, electric belts, and manipulative systems. The other chose religion and created peculiar cults with miracle-working Messiahs. Transcending quackery, passing into the realm of established religions, come no less than three great systems of mental healing: the Emmanuel movement, Christian Science, and New Thought.

† Divorces by private statutes in state legislatures existed and, in Rhode Island, mutual consent was admitted if man and wife lived apart for two years with propriety after declaring their intention. † In 1846, the liberals in America hailed the advanced ideas of the new Pope and Greeley and the transcendental *Harbinger* welcomed him. In the latter publication appeared the work of Lowell, Dana, William Wetmore Story, Thomas Wentworth Higginson, Parke Goodwin, George W. Curtis, Albert Brisbane. † In 1848 the democratic revolutions broke out in Europe and German liberals made their way to the Middle West. A year later the gold rush began. † In magazines of the early '40's, we find stories in which girls who study science nevertheless make good wives, and women urging their daughters to marry fools who would let them have their own way. † In 1843, the extension table was patented and a few years later aluminum was invented.

† The foulness of the factory system was one of the things which the Millerites managed to adduce as proof of the end of the world in 1843. † The 1840's brought in anesthetics, hydropathy, daguerreotypes and cheap postage. † The works of Eugene Sue were widely read. † Owing to an accident in France, 10,000,000 feet of tricolor silk were sent to America and nearly all gentlemen's sleeve linings were in those colors for a year. † The Mexican War was fought. † In 1843, William Cullen Bryant heard some negroes in a tobacco factory singing spirituals and this reminded him of one of Dr. Johnson's favorite stanzas:

"Verse sweetens toil however rude the sound,
All at her work the village maiden sings,
Nor, while she turns the giddy wheel around,
Revolves the sad vicissitudes of things."

The spiritual, however, he did not record.

# XIX.

## The Forerunners.

TO the skeptic all unorthodox ways of treating disease complete the circle by which medicine, beginning in magic, returns to magic, ironically sneering at the centuries of science which have intervened. To the orthodox physician, there is little difference between the savage putting ointment on a spear in order to cure the wound which the spear has made and the mental healer curing tuberculosis or cancer by "absent treatment." A less partial observer, with no tendency to believe, finds himself confronted at the very beginning of his investigation by the actuality of cures—cures proclaimed by the healers and not rejected, only explained away, by their enemies. From Mark Twain to Hugo Münsterberg, critics of Christian Science have been compelled to admit that the Scientists have cured. Their only reservation is that the maladies have been curable by suggestion. To this the Scientist usually replies that they have not been curable by any other means. In this case, to say that a cure is only a fancied cure is to beg the question, for an imagined illness is often as disastrous as a real one and the distinction between them, we may take it from psychoanalysis, has to be finely drawn.

The success of most unorthodox cures is due to distrust of the science of medicine. When medicine was all priesthood and magic, the death of a patient was easily explained as due to the intervention of a hostile God or the anger of an omnipotent one. In the age of reason, however, the doctor was compelled to confess his own fallibility. He wrapped himself in the obscurity of a learned tongue, gave himself the solemn air of a master and, when he failed, looked deplorably like a mountebank. Keeping step with science at every point, there seems to be a superstition or a mystic science. We find Galileo and Keppler turning from astronomy to draw up horoscopes on pure astrological principles, not believing in them, but practicing that science which the world still believed. We find Berkeley concocting a tar water which, according to him, cured gout and fevers, pleurisy and erysipelas, asthma, indigestion and hysterics, hypochondria, liver disease and dropsy and, in addition to this, was an excellent preservative for the teeth and gums; in fact, to this idealist philosopher who denied the reality of matter, "tar water was everything and the material universe was nothing." This was a remedy not in the pharmacopœia, but the "theriac" which, for two hundred years, was sold by every pharmacist in Europe, was considered equally effective for at least as many maladies and its composition was as little inspiring. It was, in fact, the druggist's slop-jar into which he tossed medicines for which he had no future use, compounded prescriptions which had somehow spoiled in making and whatever odds and ends remained in bottles on his shelves. Yet the pharmacist was trusted, presumably because he knew less than the physician. In the time of Cromwell, when there was no king to touch the scrofulous, one Valentine Greatrakes flourished as a stroker and cured not only the king's evil and nearly everything later listed by Berkeley, but lameness, palsy, consumption, and at least a dozen minor ailments as well.

The quack, when he does not invoke the sanctity of religion, has a habit of basing his cures on science—that is, every science but that of medicine. The simplest and possibly the most successful fraud in American history was the invention of a physician, a graduate of Yale named Elisha Perkins. In Walsh's *Cures* it is noted that Perkins used suggestion on himself. He was over six feet tall and had tremendous strength and, when he was tired, "five minutes of rest made him a new man, a minute more did away with the good effect and he felt the worse for it." The science which diverted Perkins from his ordinary profession was his own interpretation of the discoveries of Galvani and of Franklin. The existence of positive and negative forces, the fact that an electrical discharge, through the medium of two different metals, would set a frog's legs twitching, suggested to Perkins a brilliant idea. He prepared two metallic rods in each of which a number of metals, including a little gold, were fused and, placing these two together in order to call out their electrical virtues, he would draw them over the skin of a patient suffering from any malady, and effect a cure. These rods, which were called tractors, were sold for fifty dollars—in the 1790's an enormous sum of money—and thousands of invalids gave testimony to their miraculous powers. The sick were made whole and the bent walked upright. It was essential that the tractors should be drawn downward and all the benefit of days of "tractation" might be lost if a nervous person were stroked upward. The tractors made Perkins rich and took his fame abroad. In London, a Perkinian institute, under the auspices of members of the nobility, was founded with Perkins' son as chief. By public subscription it instantly surpassed in endowment all of the hospitals then existing in London. As in Copenhagen and in Berlin, favorable reports on the Perkins treatment were drawn up in London by doctors both of divinity and medicine, and testimonials came from at least eight professors in four different universities, twenty-one regular physicians, nineteen surgeons, and thirty clergymen. A sardonic British physician named Haygarth put an end to this patronage by preparing two ordinary pieces of wood painted to resemble tractors, persuading his patients that they were tractors and had electro-galvanic-magnetic powers, and effecting thousands of cures as promptly as the tractors did. This did not put an end to the tractors; for that nothing short of an epidemic was necessary. In 1799, yellow fever descended on New York to make the ultimate test of Perkins' invention. He had the courage to go into hospitals and apply his tractors in person, but was himself smitten with the fever and, in spite of his tractors, died of it. The tractors were a type of cure which, in the form of electric belts (to restore virility) and various compositions of metal and rubber, still exist.

A generation after Perkins died, a totally uneducated rustic of New Hampshire, Samuel Thomson, took his place with an entirely different practice. His knowledge of medicine had been gained by watching old women prepare concoctions of herbs. With that as a basis, he developed an entire system of therapeutics. He made the great discovery that man was composed of earth, fire, water, and air. Earth and water were the substances of the machine, and fire and air gave it motion. Heat, he said, is life, and cold is death. The stomach is a sort of fireplace, or stove, and is liable to get foul or clogged and need cleaning. "All disease," said Thomson, "is caused by some filthy accumulation and the art of curing consists of removing this undesirable detritus." The obvious way was to chew lobelia which has a strong emetic power and, by use of other herbs, to keep the passages of the body clean. Thomson published a pamphlet on his discoveries and developed a most ingenious scheme for making money out of it. He sold the pamphlet with the right to use the preparations described in it for $20 and this sum gave the owner the right in perpetuity, but only for himself and his family. In addition, Thomson instructed practitioners, and he and his disciples formed Free Botanic Societies all over the country and sent delegates annually to great Botanic Conventions. Thomsonist practitioners numbered about two thousand in the 1840's and constituted a vast majority of all irregular practitioners who made any pretense to science. Occasionally, a disciple died. Once Thomson was indicted for murder, but the judge having charged that there was no malice aforethought, Thomson was acquitted. True believers cried out that he was being persecuted as Harvey and Jenner had been and, by some occult logic, suggested that, as Thomson shared the fate of these discoverers, he was worthy to share their glory.

Thomson is important because he was the most successful of the nature-curers and, although he was ultimately discredited, his influence was powerful. When communists, and vegetarians, and other radicals, erected their systems of nature worship they took over the essential idea of Thomsonism, that nature in her primal state can cure all earthly ills.

Ten years after the beginning of Thomsonism, Dr. William Turner imported the theory and practice of Chrono-Thermalism which was originated by Samuel Dickson in London and was flourishing in France and Germany, Sweden, Prussia, and Denmark. The essential doctrine of this quackery is unusual. Most other quacks provide a single cure for all diseases, but Chrono-Thermalism discovered the great Unity, which transcendental politics and religions were also seeking, not in a panacea, but in disease itself. Dickson announced, in short, that the human race is subject to one disease, to wit, ague or intermittent fever, and that all other morbidities were only conditions of this single ill. At the end of twenty years, there were still three hundred Chrono-Thermalists practicing. There were, at the same time, three times as many homeopathists although they had been subjected to years of ridicule. Hahnemann, it is said, claimed that the true science of medicine began with him. His followers were classed among the *Humbugs of New York* in a book bearing that title and were ridiculed for the absurdity of

believing that an infinitesimal dose of common table salt is capable
of producing 895 serious and dangerous forms of drug sickness, and
for prescribing the smell of a cork of a bottle containing salt and
sugar in milk pellets as a cure. There remained, however, in spite
of ridicule, the attractiveness of the homeopathic theory. There
seemed a moral righteousness in having like cure like.

In addition to practitioners in specific systems, such as these,
there were eclectics who chose bits from various systems, omitting
orthodox practice and combining the herbs of Thomsonism with the
waters of Hydropathy, and adopting simultaneously the theories
of Homeopathy, Isopathy, and Chrono-Thermalism. The same
thing exists to-day and suggests that there must be a large number
of people to whom any eccentricity is attractive, and who are willing
to combine the most incompatible elements, so long as none of them
is orthodox. The same tendency can be observed also in politics
and morals and religion, and a "debunker" of almost a century ago
seems to have observed it very competently. Mr. Mencken could
hardly withhold approval from these sentiments taken from *Humbugs of New York: Being a Remonstrance Against Popular Delusion; Whether in Science, Philosophy, or Religion:*

"But it were an endless task to enumerate the half of similar
impostures which our city has witnessed; and if it were even done,
it would be fruitless. While the reign of humbug continues, our
citizens have neither eyes nor ears; and experience itself seems to
have been lost upon them, though bought so dearly. Every year, and
indeed almost every month, brings to our city some imported
mountebank; some foreign or domestic humbug; each of which in
its turn is greedily swallowed while the rage of novelty lasts, until
another more clamorous, or more showy, succeeds it. Meanwhile,
however, each of these acquires proselytes; and as fanaticism is
constitutional, the same individuals, in many instances, deliberately
swallow them all. Indeed there are gentlemen and ladies in this city,
who have been successively gulled by Matthias, Fanny Wright, the
moon story, and the Crawcours. They have taken the pills of foreign
and domestic quacks by the thousand, with Lobelia, Cayenne pepper,
and vapor baths. They have swallowed Maria Monk, abolitionism,
and homeopathia; and are now equally busy in bolting down Phre-

nology and Animal Magnetism. These several humbugs having been disposed of, the same persons, and thousands more, will be prepared for still farther experiments in gullibility, ad infinitum."

The general psychology of the medical quack and his victim is not specifically our concern. The points which have to be noticed in connection with blue glass cures, and rattlesnake oil, and sarsaparilla and whiskey tonics, and a thousand nostrums since driven under cover by belated legislation, are first their unorthodoxy and second the implication of miracles. The first point is connected with the breakdown of authority which went on in other fields. The connection is not so close as that between phrenology and the degeneration of Calvinistic doctrine; but it is at least illuminating to note that the criticism which attacked authority did not spare the learned professions. Among the intellectuals, lawyers and doctors were as suspect as divines, and more than one community signalized its departure from convention by refusing the services of doctors, and either established an unconventional system of curing diseases or "lived in accordance with nature" and needed no physician.

The belief in miracles, a superstition in a country preëminently Protestant, is itself a point of interest. The Catholic Church jealously guards its miracles,* and makes them the property of saints but, again and again, we find Protestants in unorthodox sects proving, by the occurrence of miracles, that their religion contains the whole truth of primitive Christianity. As the great miracle is the raising of the dead, the next greatest and most easily accomplished must be the cure of the sick. We constantly find this claim among the impostors. Because the miracle proving saintliness is so often the cure of the sick, any cure which is not performed by scientific methods soon comes to be considered a miracle and a proof of divine inspiration. From this idea, it is only a short step to religions which are based entirely on the cures themselves.

§

* To avoid those which cannot be proved, and to escape false miracles arranged by its enemies for future exposure. A French couplet of the time of the Jansenists runs:

"De par le roi, Defence à Dieu,
De faire miracle en ce lieu."

The significance of Friedrich Anton Mesmer lies precisely in this: that he was the first healer who never claimed any special sanctity for himself. In his own estimation, he was not a prophet inspired by God: he was a scientific discoverer. He was not a fanatic, but a man of the world.

The science with which Mesmer began was magnetism. Like Perkins he used magnetic plates. He was accused of stealing the idea of these plates from a Jesuit, Father Hell, and it is quite possible that Perkins had heard of these when he created his tractors. Trouble about these plates persuaded Mesmer to leave Austria, and, in February of 1778, he appeared in Paris as "the famous Viennese physician" and took lodgings near the Place Vendôme, charming a growing circle of friends with his wit, his beautiful piano playing, and his skill on the new harmonica. He charmed them also with a catchword as potent in its time as "inferiority complex" is in ours. Mesmer's phrase was "animal magnetism" and, although it was never itself fully explained, it explained everything else.

Mesmer cured. A committee of famous scientists investigated his work and refused to give him their approval. But modern investigators, although certain that his claims were exaggerated, cannot deny that cures did take place. Actually, Mesmer made a contribution to therapeutics with his discovery of the uses of hypnotism. He wrapped it up in an involved theory which assumes "a mutual influence existing between the celestial bodies, the earth, and all living beings," and suggests the existence of a magnetic fluid passing through time and space from the healer to his patient. Nor was the mechanism of Mesmer's cure calculated to inspire respect in the mind of a Lavoisier or a Franklin. But as the scientists repudiated Mesmer, the multitude, rich and poor, intelligent and brutish, flocked to him. It became impossible for him to magnetize, or hypnotize, each patient individually and he had recourse to a peculiar system called the *baguet*. In a setting of stained glass and dark draperies, with soft music, dim lights, and strange fragrances, Mesmer would place his patients in two concentric circles. In the center stood a large oaken tub full of bottles of water resting on layers of powdered glass and of iron filings, the whole covered with water. Each bottle of water had been previously magnetized by Mesmer. Each patient held a little iron rod, and all were bound together by a cord which looped around the body and passed back to the tub. The whole thing was a travesty of the galvanic cell but, as Mesmer and his assistants passed around the circles, directing rods to the point where disease was supposed to rest, or applying their magnetic hands to obstinate cases, patients cast away crutches, proclaimed themselves cured of cancer and other diseases, and often went into such fits of hysteria that a special *salle des crises* had to be provided for their recovery.

The cures of Mesmer were not, in themselves, influential on the course of American mind-healing. Hypnotism was. Mesmer had actually put subjects into a trance and, after the decline of Mesmerism in Europe—he undertook to explain his method in 1815 and quickly dropped from sight—Charles Poyen and other disciples made their way to America to exhibit hypnotic trances.

Oddly enough, skepticism in this country fixed upon the one thing which science was later to uphold, for the opponents of animal magnetism refused to believe in the genuineness of the trance. With Mesmer, the nineteenth century stood upon the threshold which it hesitated to cross—the threshold of the unconscious. It began an examination of the mind which was not to end until the unknown, the unconscious, was raised completely to the position of ascendancy. In its time, Mesmerism was largely a fad. The trances were often not real and the clairvoyance, fortune telling, location of missing objects, and prescriptions for cures, were humbug. As a piece of quackery, Mesmerism is chiefly interesting because it is a good illustration of an almost universal law, namely, that education, and even the possession of intellect, form no bar to the ravages of superstition provided it sounds scientific. In Providence, Rhode Island, factory girls, quack doctors, and unsuccessful grocers, not only believed in Mesmerism; they quickly learned how to duplicate its phenomena and how to draw in the yokels at county fairs at a dollar a head. But a contemporary report also assures us that one French professor of animal magnetism in the same city "seems to have gained over the faculties of physick and divinity"; and that, at Schenectady, the president and faculty at Union College "seem to have swallowed the humbug whole—some of whom have committed themselves in writing." It was, in fact, Colonel William L. Stone, editor of the *New York Commercial Advertizer* and one of the analysts of the impostures of Matthias, who was most responsible for the welcome given to some of the most obvious charlatans among the Mesmerists. Toward the end of the 1830's, New York was having at least two public exhibitions of Mesmerism a day and magnetic séances were being held "for the accommodation of private parties."

§

Mesmerism, as a fad, ran a comparatively short course. Its decline is an illustration of H. L. Mencken's thesis that no quackery is ever rejected by the American public until a more scientific sounding, but inherently less plausible, quackery is ready to take its place. In rejecting the hypnotic side of Mesmerism and turning to the bump theories of phrenology, the general public was as wrong as it possibly could be. It was as wrong, in fact, as George Eliot, and Richard Cobden, and Alfred Russel Wallace, and Abbott Lawrence, and Horace Greeley, and Henry Ward Beecher, and Metternich, and thousands of other men of education and achievement, all of whom believed, not indeed in the theory of bumps, but in the much better sounding theory of "faculties." Among these were Amativeness and Adhesiveness and Ideality and Vitativeness, and Pneumativeness (or the tendency to take in air), Parentiveness and all the other fantastic categories of phrenology which have been utterly discredited by science.

Like Mesmerism, Phrenology was an importation into the United States. When the ecclesiastic authorities had put an end to the lectures of Franz-Joseph Gall in Vienna, in 1802, he and his pupil, Johann Caspar Spurzheim, began to spread the doctrines of Phrenology over the rest of Europe and, after the lapse of thirty years, which period seems to have been required in those days for a sensation to be made ready to cross the Atlantic, Spurzheim arrived in America and was received with a great deal of respect by intellectuals of Boston. "The course of lectures," wrote Nathaniel Bowditch, in November, 1862, "was attended by a more brilliant company than have listened here to any other lecturer upon any subject whatever." The death of Spurzheim was considered a loss to the intellectual life of America. His work was taken up by George Combe, a Scottish Phrenologist, who spent three successful years

308 The Stammering Century

explaining the theories of his masters (and afterwards published one of the most entertaining and intelligent books ever written about the United States).

The scientific pretensions of phrenology were mingled with an extraordinarily unscientific method. Gall, who ranks well in the history of anatomy, especially for his localization of the speech centers, observed that monkeys loved their young and that the superior occiput in women slopes backward like the monkey's, whereas in the male it is not so recessive: on this evidence alone he localized the maternal instinct. In fact, most of his discoveries were guesses, and had been made, as he himself says, "in a moment when the mind was favorably disposed." Both he and his pupil, Spurzheim, would observe the actions and temperaments, either of their friends or of total strangers, and associate them with peculiarities in the structure of the head. When the skulls of Burke, the body-snatcher, and two or three other notorious murderers coincided at a certain point, the position of the brain corresponding to that point was promptly marked on the phrenological chart as the seat of the organ of destructiveness. The Phrenologists proceeded from the known to the unknown, but so rapidly that their deductions were almost always guesses. When Spurzheim, for example, found a lack of Ideality and a strong organ of locality in the perpetually wandering idealist Samuel Taylor Coleridge, the guess was obviously not a good one. Yet it was claimed for Gall and Spurzheim that they did as much for the science of mind as Copernicus and Newton for the sciences of matter.

The principles of phrenology are extremely simple. Departing from Aristotle, who believed that the function of the brain was to temper the heat of the heart, the phrenologist assumed that both the mental powers and the sentiments of man can be analyzed into a number of natural "faculties." Each of these faculties is seated in a specific portion of the brain. According to others, each faculty is located in two places and the difference in distance between the two is the measure of strength. The bump theory is of course rejected by all scientific phrenologists, but the line of cleavage between the scientist and the faker is very hard for the average mind to follow. We do not know quite what to say of the statement that "the heart . . . is recognized in the chin; the lungs each side of the nose; . . . the stomach the center of the cheek; . . ." and wonder whether it differs essentially from

> "Just here the bump appears
> Of innocent hilarity;
> And just behind the ears
> Are faith and hope and charity."

At the beginning of the twentieth century, Alfred Russel Wallace, looking back on the decades in which he had shared with Darwin the honor of propounding the doctrine of evolution wrote, "In the coming century phrenology will assuredly attain general acceptance. It will prove itself to be the true science of mind. Its practical uses in education, in self-discipline, in the reform treatment of criminals and in the medical treatment of the insane will give it one of the highest places in the hierarchy of the sciences; and its persistent neglect and obloquy during the last sixty years will be referred to as an example of the most inconceivable narrowness and prejudice which prevailed among men of science." But on the 21st of April, 1927, Dr. John B. Watson, the behaviorist, wrote, "Phrenology passed out of the interest of scientific men many, many decades ago. Neurology is the science which has taken its place. . . ." Between the forecast and the epitaph it is hardly necessary for the unscientific layman to judge. There have been efforts to reconcile phrenology, usually under another name, to modern science but, on the whole, phrenology is now practiced almost exclusively on the boardwalk at Atlantic City and in obscure villages among the ignorant and the deluded.

Yet phrenology has some points of exceptional importance. It is one of the few pseudo-scientific cults which has possessed vitality enough to change with the years so that, in a variety of disguises, it exists and flourishes to-day. The readers of personality from photographs, the advisers on personality who examine complexion, the graphologists and other psychological fakers who guess at vocations and aptitudes, are all the descendants of phrenology. This practical use for phrenology was one of its earliest claims. The name of "the employment consultant, Theophrastus of Eresos," who flourished 372 B.C., is drawn into the controversy. And in the 1840's, advertisements like the following from the *New York Sun* were by no means uncommon: "An apprentice wanted—a stout boy not over fifteen years of age of German or Scotch parents to learn a good but difficult trade. N.B. It will be necessary to bring a recommendation as to his abilities from Messrs. Fowler and Wells, Phrenologists, 131 Nassau Street, New York. Apply corner West and Franklin Streets."

Combe emphasizes the practical value of phrenology by pointing out that banks could avoid engaging clerks whose organ of Acquisitiveness overbore the organ of Cautiousness. Another Scotch phrenologist demanded that judges should be chosen for the size of the phrenological development in Conscientiousness. The problem of educating children could be solved by discovering to a fraction their various faculties and tendencies. Here phrenology touched on a subject which was particularly attractive at the time for, in addition to discovering the proper faculty which each individual ought to make his mastering impulse, phrenology also announced its own version of the doctrine of "self-help." Action, according to the phrenologists, is the great means of strengthening every peculiarity in our nature; "self-made or never made" is the motto of O. S. Fowler and, according to Dr. Bartlett:

"This is strictly true of every intellectual power, and it is as true of the animal instincts as it is of the knowing faculties. The love of children is made strong and fervent by loving children. Hate becomes a burning and ferocious passion only by hating. And, furthermore, as strictly true as this is of the intellect and the instincts, is it of all the higher sentiments. Hope can be nourished only by its own ambrosial food,—the bright colors, the ever-blossoming flowers, the fairy enchantments of the future. Conscientiousness, that deep-seated sentiment of right and wrong, the stern monitor within us, can be crowned with the supremacy which it was designed to possess, only by our being just. Ideality,—the versatile power,—constituting, as it may be said to do, the wings of the spirit, can acquire strength and freedom only by soaring aloft into a pure and celestial atmosphere, and by visiting, in the heavens and on the earth those scenes of beauty and sublimity and order, those manifestations of the perfect, the excellent and the fair, which have been created for its gratification. Benevolence can be quickened into a divine and soothing sentiment only by our being compassionate and humane."

Retreating from this flight, we find other phrenologists a little more practical in developing the same theory. There was moral imbecility, a disease which phrenology made famous in connection with murders a century before it appeared in our Sunday papers. Through phrenology this was to be recognized before it led to crime. The sufferer was then to be taken to a moral reformatory where the opposite faculty of conscientiousness, and other desirable traits, were to be exercised until an equilibrium was established in the brain and the potential murderer was changed into a good citizen. The phrenologist established a hierarchy of the faculties and objected to contemporary education because it developed only the intellectual powers and omitted the exercise of moral and re-ligious feelings. These, according to his theories, needed only to be put in use, by a sort of gymnastics, to make them dominant. Combe was particularly interested in education:

"One general defect in the mental condition of all of us is, that in ten instances we act from impulse and habit for once that we do so from reflection. This arises from imperfect training in youth. Our impulsive faculties, being early developed, and possessing great natural energy, are constantly liable to err, and to lead us into evil, when not controlled and directed by enlightened intellect. One object, therefore, in teaching the young, should be to communicate knowledge, and another to train the propensities and sentiments to submit to the control of the intellect. . . . Reflection, when founded on knowledge, produces habits of self-denial, self-re-straint, and obedience. The want of this practical training and dis-cipline is seen in the males, in the recklessness with which they dash into speculation and adventure, pursuing their leading impulses at all hazards; and in the females, in the pertinacity with which they adhere to practices which they know to be injurious to health, and in their deficiency of mental resolution to submit to the tem-porary sufferings which always accompany a change of evil habits."

Phrenology condemned free love and vindicated marriage, which was, of course, to be regulated on phrenological principles. The dangers of unscientific mating are vividly described by Nelson Sizer in *Thoughts on Domestic Life; or Marriage Vindicated and Free Love Exposed* (1857):

"Phrenology opens the only direct avenue to the feelings, and the hidden under-current of passion, that give tone to the character. These, being suppressed during courtship, gather strength by confinement. As volcanic fire, long smothered in the bowels of the earth, bursts forth with redoubled fury, covering whole cities with its burning flood; so, a smiling swain, may be all kindness and condescension till the Rubicon be passed, and she is made his own, when casting off his borrowed character, he assumes his native ferocity, causing the doating wife to 'curse the day that made them one, and wish the priest speechless, who knit the knot.'"

In the thirty odd faculties, that of Amativeness is usually placed first, but phrenologists warned even those whose Amative faculty was over-developed to indulge this feeling only "in pure love and virtuous wedlock," as to which, says another:

"Phrenology would be of blessed use in forming that most important and dear of all earthly ties, the marriage relation. Gentle maiden, study it; study it, as you value your peace, as you would mate yourself into a happy home, and especially as you would train yourself to make that home a paradise to the chosen of your heart. This is no laughing matter, although you may mirthfully read it. Could you see with the Perceptions our science would put into your power, you would infinitely prefer life-long singleness in your native abode, or severest toil among strangers, to the hand which otherwise might crush you, body and spirit, to uttermost misery.

"Young hopeful man! the same doctrine will apply to you. With our science, you would often find beauty as but ashes, aye, ashes with fire in them, too. On the altar of wedlock they would shoot up the flame of sacrifice indeed—the sacrifice of a husband's peace. Wisdom, enshrined in Phrenology, calls aloud to both sexes: 'Come unto me and learn. Get understanding; it is better than rubies, whether in the casket of manhood, or on the countenance of woman!' "

Another one of its leading theories was that there should be no punishment for children; instead, the organ counteracting the one responsible for misdeeds was to be exercised and developed.* At this point, we begin to see that phrenology was undermining not only the Calvinist theory of damnation, but the common principle of human responsibility. This was one of its chief contributions to the stream of liberal ideas which eventually wore through the bedrock of Calvinist prejudice but, before we come to it, there is a single, almost ludicrous, circumstance which needs to be mentioned. For as the phrenologists found themselves on the defensive before medical science, they embraced as proof the very quackery which they had supplanted, to wit, Mesmerism. At Barnum's Museum, Mr. Peale gave exhibitions of phreno-magnetism and the Reverend La Roy Sunderland, of New York, claimed to be the first to apply magnetism to phrenology with scientific objects. Mr. Sunderland, in the presence of phrenologists whose organ of Cautiousness was highly developed and who were ready to reject all unorthodox principles, magnetized the organ of Adhesiveness, "appertaining to that exquisite tenderness and blending of soul with soul which should exist and be prominent in the marriage relation." The subject "immediately began to express the strongest attachment to an individual. 'Who is he?' was the inquiry. At first, with the most natural but unaffected delicacy, she declined answering, but at length confessed that it was a little boy she knew many years ago. She was asked his name. This she would not divulge at first, but, on being solicited, gave it. The witness then suggested to the magnetizer to influence Hope, which he did. She immediately expressed the most gladdening anticipations of again seeing her earliest love. But when the witness informed her that he knew several of that name, and saw them every day, and would inquire if one was not the individual in question, she became almost frantic with the joyfulness of hope. 'Will you, will you?' exclaimed she, her countenance kindling into an intense glow of pleasure, even ecstasy, which no art could possibly counterfeit.

* The connection with the moral theories of Robert Owen is notable.

"As in this description we would somewhat observe the order we have followed in our work, we will here state that at a third and different place Philoprogenitiveness was magnetized, and the lady expressed the most intense desire for a child to caress and pour out her affection upon. A shawl, rolled up, was placed in her lap, and she was willed by the magnetizer to believe it a child. She enfolded it in her arms, pressed it to her bosom, and kissed it over and over, as if she had been a mother who, after months of separation, had been permitted to embrace her babe. We may remark, as we pass, that the organ doubling with Philoprogenitiveness is one producing affection for pets." *

§

From these and similar experiments it was deduced that every living being has a peculiar magnetic nature, that magnetic forces are the means of motion and sensation, that the magnetic forces in the different organs terminate in the face and may be excited separately by magnetism and, finally, "that this magnetic nature is governed by laws peculiar to itself, and may be communicated from one person to another." This is still in the region of orthodox phrenology heavily weighted with orthodox mesmerism; but there were of course tangents even to these eccentric sciences. Etherology, in which Prof. J. S. Grimes tried to combine the philosophies of mesmerism and phrenology, announced that "There is a material substance occupying space, which connects the plants and the earth, and which communicates light, heat, electricity, gravitation, and mental emotion, from one body to another, and from one mind to another." This the author announces merely as an inference; and it is interesting to note his type of monism, which identifies as etherium the substance which quickens material objects and communicates mental phenomena. He says however that etherium is an exceedingly "subtile and elastic substance." Etherium is evolved from the blood in combination with oxygen, and Submissiveness, Kindness, and Credenciveness (among other faculties in the horrible jargon of the phrenologist) produce etheropathic phenomena "which have never

* Whereas it is a commonplace of amateur psychoanalysis (our current substitute for phrenology) that affection for pets is a certain symptom of suppressed murderous desires.

heretofore been understood, even by phrenologists themselves." *
Motions of etherium transmitted from the operator to the medium
cause clairvoyance, and etherium itself accounts for the most amazing phenomena of phreno-magnetism. A Dr. Engledue reported the
magnetization of a young woman whose forehead was gently rubbed
at the required spot and who cried out, " 'It makes me know what
time it is,' and then told the time with almost perfect accuracy. The
organ called wit or mirthfulness being excited she very soon began
to laugh involuntarily," although the mesmerizer remained very
grave. This particular operator had a faculty not often mentioned
by others; he could paralyze an organ as well as excite it.

In spite of these fancies to which the incautious abandoned
themselves, phrenology had a great vogue. Like mesmerism, it attracted people of intelligence and position as much as it did the
ignorant, and again warns us against the assumption that only "the
boobs" support superstition and quackery. We find the name of
Spurzheim falling into place in one of Emerson's categories of great
minds with Locke, Lavoisier, and Bentham. Combe examined the
head of the Prince of Wales, at the request of Albert and Victoria, and Julia Ward Howe found phrenology of great assistance
to her in educating the blind, deaf, and dumb Laura Bridgeman.
It was used as an argument against drinking, since it proved that
alcohol aroused and stimulated only the lower faculties while it
weakened the higher and moral powers. John Brown's cranium was
read by Sizer and, although the phrenologist never saw his patient's
face, he declared that "this man has firmness and energy enough to
swim up the Niagara River and tow a 74-gun ship, holding the tow
line in his teeth." James A. Garfield, as a young man, was advised
to exercise his combativeness until it was as great as that of Stephen
A. Douglas so that he might become Chief Justice. General George
A. Custer called at Sizer's office in 1875, when he was en route to
Phil Sheridan's wedding in Chicago. Walt Whitman and Greeley
frequented the same phrenological depot and, on the boardwalk at
Atlantic City, you may still see Henry Ward Beecher's statement,
"All my life I have been in the habit of using phrenology as that
which solves the practical phenomena of life."

§

* Cf. page 368.

As a science, phrenology was ultimately discredited. But it was also a vague philosophy, a way of approaching moral problems. At first, it seemed only a scientific restatement of the principle of determinism; we are damned by our faculties as surely as we are damned by our God. But especially in the self-confident, pushing, acquiring, self-improving society of America, the doctrine of developing the faculties corrected the excesses of Calvinistic dogma. Phrenology was, therefore, subject to attack on the ground of being utterly anti-Christian and of destroying all sense of responsibility. One judges from the following onslaught (in the 1850's) that people went to the phrenologist as they now go to the psychoanalyst and that, rightly or wrongly, the same motives were ascribed to them:

"The moral aspect of phrenological doctrines is that, however, which renders the humbug the most mischievous and deplorable. Multitudes go to the science *for the purpose of easing a loaded conscience,* by learning that their delinquencies and vices are constitutional, and depending wholly on organization. Such find a false peace,—an imaginary comfort in the doctrine, that virtue and vice are alike the result of organs implanted by the Creator, and thus persuade themselves into the disbelief of human accountability. And learning, as they do, that they are irresistibly under the influence of their propensities to which the animal organs impel them, they despair of reformation, notwithstanding its necessity is so obvious to themselves and others. And here they are taught to regard the lascivious man to be prompted by the organ of 'amativeness' formed by muscles of the neck;—the liar to be driven by the development of 'secretiveness'—the thief by that of 'acquisitiveness'—the desperado by 'combativeness'—the drunkard by 'alimentiveness'—and the murderer by 'destructiveness.' While on the other hand, the virtues of charity, truth, honesty, peaceableness, and brotherly kindness are the results either of the absence or diminished size of these organs, or the counteracting influence of others. Hence a man is religious, or otherwise, by reason of a physical necessity, since the prominence, or the depression of the top of the head, where the organs of veneration, theosophy, and marvelousness are located, must irresistibly result in one or the other character. But we must not call this materialism or fatalism, else a hue and cry of persecution is raised, as though the sympathy of heaven and earth should be moved in behalf of this precious humbug."

The phrenologist tried to square his doctrine with Christianity and, to avoid the taunt of materialism, declared that his system was the most moral in the world because it taught that happiness is derived from the exercise of certain faculties and misfortune from the over-indulgence of others. But no such concession could break down the hostility of the devout Christian who still asked, "What has become of sin?" It gives us an insight into the progressive decay of the strict Calvinist doctrine, to read a letter written by a Dr. Taylor, a moderate divine, and then to note the comments of an intelligent phrenologist. Dr. Taylor writes:

"I do not believe that the posterity of Adam are, in the proper sense of the language, guilty of his sin; or that the ill-desert of that sin is truly theirs; or that they are punished for that sin. But I do believe, that, by the wise and holy constitution of God, all mankind, in consequence of Adam's sin, become sinners by their own act.

"I do not believe that the nature of the human mind, which God creates, is itself sinful; or that God punishes men for the nature which he creates. But I do believe that sin, universally, is no other than selfishness, or a preference of one's self to all others,—of some inferior good to God; that this free voluntary preference is a permanent principle of action in all the unconverted, and that this is sin, and all that in the Scriptures is meant by sin. I also believe, that such is the nature of the human mind, that it becomes the occasion of universal sin in men in all the appropriate circumstances of their existence; and that, therefore, they are truly and properly said to be sinners by nature."

This is very far from Puritan doctrine and it partially satisfies Combe who says:

"The phrenological doctrine, that every faculty is manifested by a distinct organ; that the Creator constituted the organ, and ordained its functions; that therefore each is good in itself, and has a legitimate sphere of action; but that each is also liable to be

abused, and that abuse constitutes sin . . . approaches closely to
Dr. Taylor's views . . . as expressed in the preceding letter. There
is a general opinion abroad that Dr. Taylor is still progressive in his
opinions, and that he will announce further modifications of Calvinism. Those who embrace liberal opinions in theology say that
they expect him still farther to purify the faith of Connecticut;
while those who adhere to the ancient creed express their fears that
the extent of his backslidings is not yet fully developed."

The full phrenological doctrine of responsibility, according to
Combe's confession, makes necessary a new interpretation of the
scriptures. It divides men into three great classes depending on the
proportionate size of the moral organs and the organs of the propensities. Where the former are great we have good and wise men
with the power to know what is right and to do it. These "are justly
liable to be punished by the law if they do what it proclaims to be
wrong." In the second class, the moral faculties and the animal propensities (which we might call the impulses) are more in equilibrium and such persons "experience strong impulses both to good and
evil, and their actual conduct is greatly influenced by circumstances.
. . . If uneducated, and exposed to want and vicious society they
may lapse into crime . . ." and occasionally the opposite is true.
For these men, the fear of punishment is a desirable influence. In
this the phrenologist makes a departure from the judgment of
Owen, based on the same assumptions. The third class are those
in which the propensities overbear the moral and intellectual faculties and they "are incapable of resisting the temptations to crime
presented by ordinary society." The phrenologist came half way
to the ground now taken by the radical criminologist, for Combe
calls this third class "moral patients" and suggests not punishment,
but restraint. Other phrenologists, with a loftier conception of their
mission, believed that even a grown man could develop the counteracting propensity and be converted from a life of crime. In New
England, Combe's audience crowded around him after his lectures
and asked him to reconcile phrenology and the doctrine of total
corruption. He replied that that was the business of those who believed in that doctrine. The liberals, in these conversations, told him
that phrenology was highly considered among them because it

proved they were right in abandoning original sin. But as Combe left no place for repentance, conviction of sin, and regeneration even in his third class, he was obliged to say that "men must revise their interpretation of the scripture, and bring them into harmony with nature and truth."

In some ways, then, the phrenological cult had a profound effect on the development of American character. First it favored the cult of the individual. Or it would be equally accurate to say that phrenology drew from the American atmosphere certain tendencies to individualism and adapted itself to the American character. The two things, phrenology and the political and physical circumstances of American life, interacted. Phrenology and mesmerism both made man more interesting to himself, as psychology and psychoanalysis did half a century later. Mesmerism suggested unknown powers, and phrenology either justified action or taught the doctrine of self-development and self-control. This was dangerous doctrine in a country which lacked a strong disciplinary government, and was engaged in breaking down the tremendous discipline of morality imposed by a religion in which sin and punishment were essential features. Toward this break-down, again, phrenology contributed enormously, not only in its proper activity, but by suggesting new forms of thought to philosophers and publicists, and by substituting an indulgent habit of mind for the severer justice and the tyrannical temperament of the old type of divine. Had phrenology come to America before Methodism began its fermentation, it would have been persecuted as a heresy and possibly rejected entirely. Actually, when it came, it could count on the support of many sects, the Universalists and the Unitarians particularly and, by giving to them a supposedly scientific foundation, it sharpened the ax which liberalism was laying at the root of the old Christianity of Calvin with its disciplines and responsibilities, its punishments and its dubious rewards.

† Into a few luxurious houses "elevators or hoistways" were introduced and, at second-hand shops, as much as $20 each were given for
colonial chairs and $40 for Grandfather's clocks. Gobelin carpets, pic-
tures by Church, and statues by Powers, were possessed only by the few
and it was considered proper to skirt the edge of a room in order to save
the carpet. † The confectioners of New York imported pears from
France; the population of the city was about 600,000, and half that
number of immigrants passed through it annually. Brick for domestic
building was disappearing. † Railroads stopped to let passengers lunch on
ham, fried oysters, pumpkin pie, and spirits; the gauge was changed at
the state lines of New York, Pennsylvania, and Ohio, and the city of
Erie tore up rails of identical gauges in order to force trains to stop
there. † The Croton aqueduct was a great sight in New York and the
Astor house, opposite Barnum's, printed its own menu daily. The Five
Points was the rendezvous of the vicious and the impoverished. † Barbers'
chairs were built for ease and lassitude and city graft was enormous.
† The Editor's Table in *Harper's New Monthly Magazine* for November, 1853, contained the following: "The most serious importance of this
modern 'woman's rights' doctrine is derived from its direct bearing upon
the marriage institution. The blindest must see that such a change as is
proposed in the relation and life of the sexes cannot leave either marriage
or the family in their present state. It must vitally, and in time wholly
sever that oneness which has ever been at the foundation of the marriage
idea, from the primitive declaration of Genesis to the latest decision of
the common law. . . . That which makes no change in the personal
relations, the personal rights, the personal duties, is not the holy marriage union, but the unholy alliance of concubinage."
† After 1855 kerosene supplanted lard and other animal oils as an illu-
minant. † Women wore skeleton skirts made of strips of iron of the quality of watch springs and men wore false chests. † The Hungarian patriot,
Kossuth, was received by the government and started the vogue for soft
felt hats. Talma Capes were also worn.

# XX.

## The Business of Prophecy.

**P**HRENOLOGY doubtless had a helpful effect on the moral tone. At its best, it helped to analyze and to mold character. But the prophets were much more attracted to the creative processes of mesmerism, handling it as another weapon against orthodoxy. The earliest of them, Andrew Jackson Davis, began his career as the trance medium of that Professor Grimes who had discovered the science of Etherology by combining the principles of Mesmer and of Spurzheim. To Davis, the world owes its present respect for mediums. In Europe, the hypnotist had always been considered the significant figure; Davis was the first medium to claim divine inspiration.

He was born in Blooming Grove, Orange County, New York, in 1826. He was a delicate child, given to somnambulism, hallucinations and, possibly, to epileptic fits. His parents were desperately poor, and it is not remarkable that one of the first voices he heard from the Beyond commanded him to "eat plenty of bread and molasses." A little later he heard a voice saying, "A little leaven leaveneth the whole lump," and, as he was then without satisfactory occupation, he took to peddling yeast through the country. He attended revivals, but failed to "take it." In 1844, after he had acted as clairvoyant for two practitioners of animal magnetism, he had his revelation. Galen and Swedenborg appeared to him, in a cemetery, and revealed to him the secrets of healing. Davis forthwith proceeded to New York and went into business as a medical clairvoyant. His ministry was tremendously successful and his explanation of his methods was satisfactory to the public:

"By looking through space directly into Nature's laboratory, or else into medical establishments, I easily acquired the common (and even the Greek and Latin) names of various medicines and also of many parts of the human structure," he says. By looking through space, he diagnosed ills and, on one occasion, prescribed the fat of thirty-two weasels as an element in a cure. He became so popular that there was talk of making him physician-in-ordinary to the Senate of the United States. But his healing presently became less important than his revelation of a new order of the universe. He was swept away on the current of spiritualism—the first manifestations of which occurred soon after his own revelation—and, going into self-induced trances, he dictated book after book, on every subject, until he was justified in going into the publishing business to issue his own works. Scientists, philosophers, and ministers of the gospel stood around the young man as he lay with closed eyes dictating to stenographers. Albert Brisbane, fresh from communication with the finest minds of Europe, gave him respectful hearing during these trances. Out of them came *The Principles of Nature, Her Divine Revelations and a Voice to Mankind*, in which the editor of the *Westminster Review* discovered affinities with Kant, Hegel, and Goethe. The book was published in 1847 in the size of a family album with eight hundred pages. It ran into thirty-four editions and was eagerly read until after the Civil War. The opening paragraph explains why Davis called words "deceptive aprons of obscurity":

"In the beginning the Univercælum was one boundless, undefinable, and unimaginative ocean of Liquid Fire! The most vigorous and ambitious imagination is not capable of forming an adequate conception of the height and depth and length and breadth thereof. There was one vast expanse of liquid substance. It was without bounds—inconceivable—and with qualities and essences incomprehensible. This was the original condition of Matter. It was without forms, for it was but one Form. It had no motions, but it was an eternity of Motion. It was without parts, for it was a Whole. Particles did not exist, but the Whole was one Particle. There were no suns, but it was one Eternal Sun. It had no beginning and it was without end. It had no length, for it was a Vortex of one Eternity. It had no circles, for it was one Infinite Circle. It had no disconnected power, but it was the very essence of Power. Its inconceivable magnitude and constitution were such as not to develop forces, but Omnipotent Power!"

In other works Davis declared that free will did not exist, and therefore there was no sin—this being his deduction from phre-

nology and liberal theology—and predicted the coming of a socialist
state. It is said that Sir Arthur Conan Doyle still holds him in great
respect.

§

Among Davis's disciples was a young poet, Thomas Lake
Harris, who might have remained for ever in obscurity if he had
not drastically touched the life of a brilliant English family. Harris
was born in England. Like Davis, he was a visionary child. Like
him, he broke away from established religion. He first became a
Universalist, then a disciple of Davis. Eventually he quarreled with
his master. Davis had found his spiritual affinity and, with the consent of her husband, an Indiana divorce had been arranged, so that
the affinities might be joined in marriage. The disciple had other
ideals, as we shall see. He left New York and, "under divine
guidance," founded a socialist community at Mountain Cove, Virginia. This having failed, Harris went to England to preach his
gospel. In Marylebone Street and at Steinway Hall he attracted
handfuls of listeners. One of them was Lawrence Oliphant.

Oliphant was "the pet of society," a "child of fortune," who
had returned to England after a brilliant career in the diplomatic
service. His father had been Chief Justice at Ceylon. The son was
an amateur of big game shooting and exploring. He had traveled
in Russia, and up the Nile, and in Asia. He was so exceptional a
journalist that Delane, of the *Times*, offered him four guineas a
column, twice the usual rate, to keep him from a rival journal. His
life was gay and his mind untroubled except for an occasional weariness and a touch of wonder about the significance of human endeavor. When he came to America with Lord Elgin he enjoyed
champagne, ices, strawberries, and bright eyes. His first contact with
cranks startled him. On this occasion, he was staying at the home of
a Senator who was a Methodist and a teetotaler, whose wife was a
spiritualist medium, and whose daughter was married to an atheist,
and wore bloomers. Oliphant was merely amused; he had no
tendency toward cults. After service as First Secretary of Legation
in Tokio, where he narrowly escaped assassination, he returned to
England to be triumphantly elected to the House of Commons.

Before he took his seat, he met Thomas Lake Harris and fell

instantly under his sway. The first compulsion Harris put upon him was complete silence in the House for two years. Oliphant obeyed, and the political career which all of England expected to rival that of Pitt and Fox was at an end. Harris returned to America and founded a community at Brocton. In 1867, Oliphant followed and was set to work cleaning stables, "gloomy silent labor for days and days," he writes, during which he was not permitted to address a word to any living being. He cleaned stables until nine at night and then drew water for two hours. His mother came to live at the colony but she and her son were forbidden to meet except as strangers. Oliphant made over his entire estate to Harris who said, "Those who come here must have no country, no relations or friends, no pursuits but such as are given them of God." When Oliphant returned to Europe, Harris told him that he would be summoned back by a sign. The sign was to be a bullet entering the room in which Oliphant sat. (Later, when Oliphant was a correspondent in Paris during the Commune, the sign came, and he straightway left his work to return to Harris.)

In England, Oliphant met Alice L'Estrange. They fell in love and, although Oliphant explained his devotion to the mysterious American leader, the girl was willing to marry him. For a time Harris refused consent, and Oliphant wrote, calling Harris by the title given to him at the colony, "Father's pressure is an awful pressure, but it is a blessed one." Eventually, Harris permitted the marriage to take place, apparently in preparation for a more bitter test of his disciple. As soon as they came to America, Alice Oliphant was sent to Santa Rosa, where Harris had established a subsidiary community, and her husband was kept in New York and in Canada. The separation was long and, for Alice Oliphant, it was desperately hard. Having been set at work she could not do, she escaped from the colony and lived miserably as a teacher in a tiny settlement in California.

The lovers were united over the body of Oliphant's mother. Whether he specifically claimed it or not, Harris had given Oliphant the impression that he could conquer death. When he failed to save Oliphant's mother, the disciple turned on the master, "the scales fell from his eyes," he sued to recover his property, left America and, living in out-of-the-way places, wrote books on mysticism. It is recorded that General Gordon came to call on him and the two agreed that they were the craziest fellows alive. When his wife died, Oliphant married Rosamond, daughter of Robert Dale Owen, because he needed her as a medium to communicate with the dead woman.

What was the power which Harris exerted? In a novel which Oliphant wrote, he created a character, Mr. Massolam, obviously a picture of Harris. He tells us that the leader's voice was pitched in two keys; a near voice which was kindly and vivacious, a far-off voice, solemn and impressive; the two mingling in a ventriloquistic and slightly unpleasant effect. His gray-black hair fell in massive waves over his ears. His brows were bushy and overhanging. His eyes were two revolving lights in dark caverns. His face had a Semitic cast, emphasized by mustache and beard. The figure, in short, is that of an ordinary crank. Nor does the poetry of Harris give us any clew to his influence. In 1856, he wrote *A Lyric of the Morning Land*, dedicated (in Gothic lettering) to the Pure in Heart. The first part of the poem is entitled "History" and begins

> "This poem is a Love-child of the skies;
> 'Twas bred in Heaven with breath like bridal blooms."

The whole is a chaos out of which emerges the announcement of a further poem by the same author, *Marriage, a Lyric of the Golden Age*, which was to be a "page of angel history." Of the first poem, the author gives an account in an appendix:

"On the first of January, 1854, at the hour of noon, the archetypal ideas were internally inwrought by spiritual agency into the inmost mind of the Medium, he at that time having passed into a spiritual or interior condition. From that time till the fourth of August, fed by continual influxes of celestial life, these archetypal ideas internally unfolded . . . until at length . . . they . . . uttered themselves in speech, and were transcribed as spoken by the Medium, he, by spiritual agencies, being temporarily elevated to the spiritual degree of the mind . . . and the external forms being rendered quiet by a process which is analogous to physical death. . . . In his external waking condition he had not the remotest knowledge or conception of any part of the poem."

This is the trance of Andrew Jackson Davis again. In his leading ideas, however, Harris passed beyond Davis. The picture of Oliphant may remind modern readers of contemporary mystic colonies at Fontainebleau and elsewhere. The doctrine anticipates parts of Christian Science and of Yoga. A fundamental exercise was called "inner breathing" or "inner respiration." Both Harris and Oliphant claimed to be able to dispense with the ordinary forms of breathing and, by some mystic channel, to absorb "the atmosphere of Heaven not only into the spiritual, but also into the natural lungs." This is close to the inhalation of Prana which we shall find in Yoga. Harris gave it an extreme significance, for he says that internal respiration "leads to counterpartal marriage . . . man in his true or unfallen state being twain-one or dual in nature."

How it "leads" is not clear. Students of mysticism have established Harris' debt to Swedenborg in his emphasis on a non-physical breathing. Boehme is possibly the source of his idea of the bisexuality of the natural man. On this point, Harris is much clearer: "God manifested in the Flesh is not Male merely nor Female merely, but the two in one . . . in whose spiritual and physical likeness we seek to be reborn." Counterpartal marriage was, of course, a spiritual union, the ordinary union of the sexes being considered "a terrible thing," a hindrance to spiritual regeneration. Harris expected children to be born of these spiritual unions and declared with satisfaction that "propagation of the species (by ordinary unions) and physical death" were decreasing "among my people." He promised that, eventually, "physical transubstantiation" would take the place of death.

§

In many of these theories, Harris seems to be the immediate predecessor of Mary Baker Eddy. In Christian Science, bisexuality is often implied, and propagation without physical union is on record. But the actual forerunner of the new cult is a prophet who seemed indifferent to Harris' ideas, and who concentrated on one thing alone, healing. His name is Phineas Parkhurst Quimby.

There are dozens of pamphlets in existence affirming and denying the debt of Mrs. Eddy to Quimby. Except to the Christian Scientist, the question must be slightly academic, for Mrs. Eddy's

Andrew Jackson Davis

teachings are not only like Quimby's, they are like a great many others; but their peculiar quality—which has erected her doctrine into a Church—is entirely her own. If Quimby had no influence on Christian Science, he had a great deal on New Thought; and New Thought and Christian Science are of the same blood.

In 1838, Quimby heard a lecture by Charles Poyen, the most brilliant of the mesmerists in America. The idea of inducing hypnotic trances enchanted him, and he began to experiment with a certain Lucius Burkman as his subject. In the manuscripts which Quimby left (and which Mrs. Eddy is accused of having transcribed and elaborated into *Science and Health*) he says that Burkman could look into the bodies of patients and disclose their maladies. What is more startling, "He can go from point to point without passing through intermediate space. He passes from Belfast to Washington or from the earth to the moon . . . swifter than light, by a single act of volition." One would fancy such a power worth controlling, but magnetism did not come instinctively to Quimby. It was common property when he began his practice, and he learned a great deal about it from a book called *The Philosophy of Electrical Psychology*. Quimby's method of magnetic cure was to pass a current of magnetism from his body through the body of the patient, positive and negative contact being established when Quimby held his left hand on the abdomen of the patient and with the other hand rubbed the top of the head. This method was effective for diseases located in the torso. For the lower limbs, the rubbing was transferred to the legs, but the left hand sacredly maintained contact. The heat produced by these manipulations was considered proof of the electro-magnetic power of the healer.

Possibly Quimby was dissatisfied with this mummery because he knew that the power within him was of a finer grain. He felt, as he performed his cures, that he was giving something much more important than electrical fluid or animal heat to his patients. He knew that, if anything coursed through their bodies, it was the power of his mind. After a few years, he began to rely on this mental power without any physical interposition. In Portland, in 1859, he addressed a circular to the sick in which he says:

"My practice is unlike all medical practice. . . . I give no medicines and make no outward applications, but simply sit by the patient, tell him what he thinks is his disease, and my explanation is the cure. . . . If I succeed in correcting his errors, I change the fluids of his system, and establish the truth or health. The truth is the cure. This mode of treatment applies to all cases." (It may be noted that one of his first patients was Mrs. Julius Dresser who, with her husband, became a leader of New Thought.)

Truth is of course right belief and is not only the cure but is health itself; wrong belief, or error, is sickness. Although Quimby called his system a science and tried very hard to discover its laws—looking for a parallel to the miracles of Christ's healing and considering Christ the founder of his system—he never formulated it in such a way as to make himself the head of a school. He was persuading his patients that they were not ill, that there was no such thing as illness in the world, since God, who was All-Good, could not deliberately create evil and, being at the same time all-powerful, could not allow any other force to bring evil into the world. At first, he exercised the patient's mind by making him transfer his pains from where they were (erroneously) supposed to be to some other part of the body. Thus a rheumatic pain in the knee could be moved to the base of the thumb and its reality discredited; a few rubs, or passes, over the new location of the supposed pain made it disappear. Quimby insisted particularly on his patients being receptive to the thought of the All-Powerful God, being consciously in contact with the infinite of health and happiness which came from God, and letting the divine force flow through them. This required a surrender of the Will, much as a cure by psychoanalysis now requires it. The patient was instructed to banish his fears and to gain the pure benefit of floating fearlessly on the healing waters.

At this single point, the connection between mind healing and spiritualism becomes clear. For it is not an easy thing to persuade even a willing sufferer, even a pathological victim of imaginary ills, that disease and evil do not exist. There is an obstinate human habit of clinging to, exaggerating, exploiting, and taking pride in ills, real or fancied, which was known in the time of Molière and probably in the time of Aristophanes. Moreover, the recognized deficiency of certain orthodox Christian sects is that they fail adequately to account for evil, just as it is the supremely attractive quality of evangelical Christianity that it redeems men from evil and promises, in the future, redemption from the greatest indignity of all, the evil of death. Quimby held fast to the Christian miracle; but something new, something more easily demonstrable, was required, and spiritualism supplied it. For the essence of all spiritualism was, and is, that there is no death. By the time Quimby left manipulations and mesmerism behind and soared unencumbered into the high realm of the soul, spiritualism had passed far beyond communications and rappings: it had successfully materialized the spirits of those erroneously called dead. Death, the greatest of all evils, was at last shown to be an illusion. The spirit lived on and only belief on the part of the earthly spirit was needed to see, to hear, perhaps to touch, the spirit which had passed beyond. If this could be believed, and a cloud of witnesses gave testimony to its truth, how could one fail to believe that sickness, so much feebler than death, was also an illusion and could be thought out of existence?

We can judge from the nature of the reported cures that vapid, idle, and hysterical women were among Quimby's best patients and precisely these were most susceptible to the current of supernaturalism then flowing so freely through the American air. Without the annihilation of death which spiritualism had accomplished, Quimby and the other mind healers might have succeeded; but the way would have been harder. Once death was denied it was a simple thing to affirm health, and it is on the general basis of spiritualism that Quimby founded the early religion of mental healing and the early religion of commercial optimism.

† The best-known phrenologists, Fowler and Wells, also published *The Water Cure Journal and Herald of Reforms*. † A Boston paper noted that "the New York auctioneers treat the crowd to champagne and oysters" and that the Japanese "are delighted with us Yankees." † There were supposed to be 200,000 believers in spirit-rapping, and Fanny Fern and Mrs. E. D. E. N. Southworth were the most popular women writers. † Forrest refused $50,000 for fifty performances in California, and Christy and Woods combined their minstrel shows. The favorite operas included *Norma, Lucia, Ernani*, and *Don Giovanni*. † Men used Boyles Celebrated Hyperion Fluid for their hair and mustaches. † New Orleans was famous for its food. † The precocity of children was encouraged and moralists protested against a morbid taste for light reading in the country at large, although Goethe's *Correspondence With a Child* was influential among girls. † By 1853 the insecurity of life in New York had become proverbial, and a newspaper complained that "with few exceptions our police are the worst in the world." † A "ragged school" with soup kitchen was opened for children too poor to go to the public schools. † The rooms of the Astor House were an "Elysium of princely drawing rooms and boudoirs, in which velvet, lace, satin, gilding, rich carpets, and mirrors contribute to form a scene of indescribable luxury." † Women traveled alone and Americans addressed no conversation to strangers in public conveyances. † The citizens of Boston gave a splendid ball to the Prince de Joinville. † There were 111,000 Germans in Ohio, 51,000 Irish and 25,000 English; in New York one out of every five persons was foreign born. † A device by which cattle water themselves was patented.

† The United States consumed more silk than any other country on the globe. † At an auction the pews in the Brooklyn church of Henry Ward Beecher were rented for as much as $175. † A life-preserving jacket was perfected and, in one year, camphene and burning fluid caused fifty-nine deaths. † Bryant heard Negroes sing a singularly wild and plaintive air which he thought musicians would do well to reduce to notation. It was *Johnny, Come Down de Hollow*. He also heard, *John, John Crow*. † A traveler in the United States says, "Americans are always in a hurrry." † After marriage young people preferred to go to a hotel to live.

# XXI.

## The Good News from Rochester.

IF messages from beyond the grave had not existed in 1848, it
would have been necessary to invent them. The mental chaos
of the time required a catalytic agent, a power which would
give all ideas coherence and order. Liberal theology had quarreled
with the ancient specifications of life after death, and had failed to
provide new ones. Liberal science—animal magnetism, cures by
visions—having rejected the support of official science, lacked background. Social experiments were trying to diminish the significance
of death. Trances produced masterpieces—but where did the trances
come from? The age needed a revelation. It was left to two little
girls in a tiny village called Hydesville, in Wayne County, New
York, to supply what was needed.

In the family of John D. Fox and his wife Margaret there were
two daughters, Maggie and Katie, born of the second union of this
pair, which had rejoiced in three children, not destined to an equal
fame, in the first years of their marriage.* The first way in which
the Fox sisters made themselves a nuisance was innocent enough.
They used to tie strings to the stems of apples and, after they had
gone to bed, bounce them on the floor in the dark to frighten a
little niece who slept with them. These and other noises disturbed
Mrs. Fox who said that "sometimes it seemed as if the furniture
was moved; but on examination we found everything in order. The
children had become so alarmed that I thought best to have them
sleep in the room with us. . . . On the night of the first disturb-
ance, we all got up and lighted a candle and searched the house, the
noises continuing during the time, and being heard near the same
place."

Mrs. Fox's deposition is Exhibit A in the early story of spiritualism. It has since been duplicated a thousand times in other words,
but another excerpt may be given to show just what it was that took

* Students of heredity will be interested to know that, after the parents were
separated, the father took to drink.

in the whole country. For some reason, which no one understood at the time, the children used to call on Mr. Splitfoot to make noises. "Katie exclaimed: 'Mr. Splitfoot, do as I do'; clapping her hands. The sound instantly followed her with the same number of raps; when she stopped, the sound ceased for a short time. Then Margaret said in sport: 'Now, do just as I do; count one, two, three, four,' striking one hand against the other at the same time, and the raps came as before. . . . I then thought I could put a test that no one in the place could answer. I asked the noises to rap my children's ages, successively. Instantly, each one of my children's ages was given correctly pausing between them sufficiently long to individualize them until the seventh, at which a longer pause was made, then three more emphatic raps were given, corresponding to the age of the little one that died, which was my youngest child. I then asked: 'Is this a human being that answers my questions so correctly?' There was no rap. I asked: 'Is it a spirit? If so make two raps,' which were instantly given as soon as the request was made. I then said: 'If it is an injured spirit, make two raps,' which were instantly made, causing the house to tremble. I asked: 'Were you injured in this house?' The answer was given as before. 'Is the person living that injured you?' Answer by raps in the same manner. I ascertained by the same method that it was a man, aged thirty-one years; that he had been murdered in this house, and his remains were buried in the cellar; that his family consisted of a wife and five children, two sons and three daughters, all living at the time of his death, but that his wife had since died.

"Then the supposed spirit was asked if it would continue to 'rap' if the neighbors were called in to listen. The answer was affirmative."

All this sounds to us like a weak version of the exploits of Tom Sawyer, but actually these noises, and the blood-curdling melodrama offered in explanation, were the beginnings of the Rochester Rappings. The mother of the little children—the oldest was nine—encouraged them and, by skillful questions, the rappings were made to demand a public exhibition for which the largest hall in Rochester was hired. Margaret and Catherine Fox appeared on the platform in long trailing gowns, the dresses of grown women in those days, expressly made for them by their oldest sister Mrs. Ann Leah Fox

Fish. This eldest sister was eventually to be accused of being the evil genius of the younger ones. She claimed that, before Maggie and Katie were born, she had received messages promising great things for them and, when the young children became the medium for the first communications with the other world, Mrs. Fish formed the rather grand project of founding a new religion. According to the young women, however, they refused to carry their work so far. She did, however, promote the Fox sisters quite in the modern manner, coaching them, protecting their finances and, to a large extent, arranging their séances and publicity. There was of course no possible probable shadow of doubt of the genuineness of the manifestations. No one questioned the obvious conclusion that the rappings proved the persistence of the individual soul after death. The result was the spiritualistic movement in America, which alternately supported and drew support from European mediums until it became a world-wide religion. On that religion no one who has not entirely mastered all the documents can pass judgment, but the career of the Fox sisters is in itself a verdict on their part in it. The Fox sisters became the rage in literary circles and they, and a hundred other rappers, flourished throughout the decade. Although communication with the dead was the essence of their business, they managed to combine healing with it by transmitting to sufferers cures from great doctors of the past or aiding them by suggesting the names of living physicians.

§

It is not necessary to mark the progress of spiritualism in its early days. From one circumstance we may gather that it followed the usual course of superstitions, hysterias, and mass movements; namely, that it enlisted the support of a sufficient number of superior people to give it authority over the multitude. When spiritualism was only six years old, 15,000 signatures, most of them the names of educated and informed people, were appended to a petition to Congress asking for a federal investigation of the claims of the new movement, the intention being to wrest from the government its official approval. Whether Senator Shields of Illinois, who laid the petition before Congress, was in earnest is problematical. He himself brought in the name of Cagliostro, with his beds that guaranteed painless child-birth and, according to a contemporary report, the other senators were not more serious.

"A pleasant debate followed. Mr. Petit proposed to refer the petition of the Spiritualists to three thousand clergymen. Mr. Weller proposed to refer it to the Committee on Foreign Relations, as it might be necessary to inquire whether or not when Americans leave this world they lose their citizenship. Mr. Mason proposed that it should be left to the Committee on Military Affairs. General Shields himself said he had thought of proposing to refer the petition to the Committee on Post Offices and Post Roads, because there may be a possibility of establishing a spiritual telegraph between the material and spiritual worlds. The petition was finally, by a decisive vote, laid upon the table. The table did not, as we learn, tip in indignation at this summary disposal of Spiritualism in the Senate, by which we infer that the 'spirits,' if there were any in the Senate at the time, endorsed its action and considered the same all right."

"Mr. Sludge, the medium," was meanwhile having a great success in Europe. The New Orleans *Picayune* of November 14, 1857, has the following intelligence:

"Mr. Douglas Hume, the great American medium, is the lion of the season at Baden. Nobody else is talked about, nobody else is so stared at, nobody else is so courted. Whenever he goes to the gaming table and stakes money on a color, there is an avalanche of napoleons on that color; for the crowd thinks he can read the future course of chance, and vaticinate the color which is certain to win. He has received a fortune in presents from the Russian and German nobles, who have showered on him rings, breast-pins, watch-chains, rubies, diamonds, opals; the Princess Bubera gave him three pearl shirt-buttons, worth $600, for an evening's exhibition at her house; the Prince of Prussia offered him five thousand florins for a single evening's display of his powers—he refused it."

Amelia Bloomer went to a soirée at the home of Horace Greeley when a notable gathering discussed spiritualism, but Mrs. Bloomer does not express any opinion on the discussions which she reports:

THE SISTERS FOX, THE ORIGINAL SPIRIT RAPPERS.

"It was in the early days of spiritualism, when the Rochester rappings had excited much wonder throughout the country. Horace Greeley was known to have taken a good deal of interest in the subject; to have given time to its investigation and to have entertained its first propagandists, the Fox sisters, for days at his house. During the evening of our visit that subject came up and Mr. Greeley warmly espoused the side of the spiritualists. He said many things in confirmation of his belief in the new doctrine of spirit visitation. Standing midway of the two parlors and pointing to a table that stood against the wall and the front windows, he said: 'I have seen that table leave its place where it now stands and go back to its place without anyone touching it or being near it.' "

Greeley himself was the type of believer who has not lost all sense of criticism. The first séance he attended rather disappointed him, but he and his wife had recently lost their child "Pickie," to whom they were passionately attached, and Mrs. Greeley went to see the Fox sisters several times at their hotel and finally invited them to spend a week or two at the Greeley house in 19th Street. The sisters gave them "sittings," and Greeley got some significant responses, "evincing knowledge of occurrences of which no one, not an inmate of our family in former years could well have been cognizant," along with much that seemed trivial and "unlike what might naturally be expected from the land of souls." In his recollections, Greeley makes a further record and an interesting comment:

"Not long after this, I had called on Mademoiselle Jenny Lind, then a newcomer among us, and was conversing about the current marvel with the late N. P. Willis, while Mademoiselle Lind was devoting herself more especially to some other callers. Our conversation caught Mademoiselle Lind's ear, and arrested her attention; so, after making some inquiries, she asked if she could witness the so-called 'Manifestations.'

"I answered that she could do so by coming to my house in the heart of the city, as Katie Fox was then staying with us. She assented, and a time was fixed for her call; at which time she appeared, with a considerable retinue of total strangers. All were soon seated around a table, and the 'rappings' were soon audible and abundant. 'Take your hands from under the table!' Mademoiselle Jenny called across to me in the tone and manner of an indifferently bold archduchess. 'What?' I asked, not distinctly comprehending her. 'Take your hands from under the table!' she imperiously repeated; and I now understood that she suspected me of causing, by some legerdemain, the puzzling concussions. I instantly clasped my hands over my head, and there kept them until the sitting closed, as it did very soon. I need hardly add that this made not the smallest difference with the 'rappings'; but I was thoroughly and finally cured of any desire to exhibit or commend them to strangers. . . . But, while the sterile 'sittings' contributed quite as much as the other sort to convince me that the 'rappings' were not all imposture and fraud, they served decidedly to disincline me to devote my time to what is called 'investigation.' To sit for two dreary, mortal hours in a darkened room, in a mixed company, waiting for someone's disembodied grandfather or aunt to tip a table or rap on a door, is dull music at best; but so to sit in vain is disgusting. . . . I find my 'spiritual' friends nowise less bigoted, less intolerant, than the devotees at other shrines. They do not allow me to see through my own eyes, but insist that I shall see through theirs. If my conclusion from certain data differs from theirs, they will not allow my stupidity to account for our difference, but insist on attributing it to hypocrisy, or some other form of rascality. I cannot reconcile this harsh judgment with their professions of liberality, their talk of philosophy. But, if I speak at all, I must report what I see and hear."

Both the Fox girls being very pretty and very young, each soon found a patron. Greeley undertook the education of Katie and Dr. Elisha Kent Kane, the ill-starred Arctic explorer, reformed the character of Maggie and eventually married her. Among the other disciples or friends of the Fox sisters, were Bancroft, James Fenimore Cooper, Bryant, N. P. Willis, John Bigelow, Dr. Griswold, the enemy of Poe, Bayard Taylor, Theodore Parker, and Harriet Beecher Stowe. In 1857, an entire column of the *Practical Christian* listed sixty-seven books and magazines devoted to spiritualism. From the list, one gathers that Andrew Jackson Davis was not slow in linking himself with the new movement. At least a dozen of these works are from his pen, many of them including his favorite word "harmonial" in the title, as *The Penetralia; being harmonial answers to important questions. The Lily Wreath of Spiritual Communication,* through Mrs. J. S. Adams and others, and the *Bouquet of Spiritual Flowers,* received through the same mediumship, were to be had at 85 cents. For the pictorially inclined, there was Mr. Wolcott's amusing picture representing the attack of the allies on the Sebastopol of Spiritualism. Hudson Tuttle contributed *Sins in the Spiritual World.* Mrs. Adams' husband wrote a *Rivulet from the Ocean of Truth,* being an interesting narrative of the *Advancement of a Spirit from Darkness in to Light.* For the odd price of 38 cents, one could buy Alfred Cridge's *Epitome of Spiritual Intercourse.* The editor of the *Practical Christian,* Adin Ballou, wrote an exposition of *Views Respecting the Principal Facts, Causes and Peculiarities Involved in Spirit Manifestations.* Again for 38 cents, one could buy a work by the great infidel Thomas Paine, not usually listed under his name, *The Philosophy of Creation* credited to him "through the hand of Horace G. Wood, medium." The phrenomagnetist, La Roy Sunderland, contributed some sympathetic works on nutrition, and healing without medicine, and *The Book of Health,* and *The Birth of the Universe* are advertised as being "by and through R. P. Ambler." A skeptical work by E. W. Capron (who captivated Providence with animal magnetism) is also advertised. And there are books on the dynamics of magnetism, on Pneumatology, and on the celestial telegraph. An inharmonious note occurs in the title, *Spirit's Work Real but not Miraculous,* by Allan Putnam who, thirty years later, wrote a curious book in which he tried to explain the witchcraft of New England in the terms of modern spiritualism. He defines a witch as a "medium or a human being whose body becomes at times the tool of some finite disembodied intelligent being, or whose mind senses knowledge in spirit land." A few sentences from his argument are worth preserving as a curiosity of logic, the explanation of a delusion in the terms of the unproved:

"The chief non-intelligent instrumentality employed in producing miraculous, spiritualistic, necromantic, and other kindred marvels, is now generally called psychological force—force resident in and put forth from and by the soul. . . .

"The usurping capabilities of this force were strikingly set forth by the illustrious Agassiz in his carefully written account of his own sensations and condition while in a mesmeric trance induced upon him by Rev. Chauncy Hare Townshend. The great naturalist—the strong man both mentally and physically—says that he lost all power to use his own limbs—all power to even will to move them, and that his body was forced against his own strongest possible opposition to pace the room in obedience to the mesmerizer's will. Since such force overcame the strongest possible resistance of the gigantic Agassiz, it is surely credible that less robust ones, in any and every age, may have been subdued and actuated by it.

"Those who were accused of bewitching others were fountains from which invisible intelligences sometimes drew forth properties which aided them in gaining and keeping control of those whom they entranced or otherwise used. Also from such there probably sometimes went forth unwilled emanations that were naturally attracted to other sensitives, who perceived their source, and pronounced it diabolical, because the influx thence was annoying. Impersonal natural forces to some extent, and at times, probably designated the victims who were immolated on witchcraft's altar."

§

In the very year that this was published the great spiritualist hoax was exposed. The Fox sisters confessed that everything they had done, without exception, had been humbug! On the 24th of September, 1888, the New York *Herald* published an article under the startling headlines:

GOD HAS NOT ORDERED IT

A Celebrated Medium Says the Spirits
Never Return.

CAPTAIN KANE'S WIDOW

One of the Fox Sisters Promises
an Interesting Exposure of
Fraud

A fraud with the peculiar name of Madame Diss De Barr had recently been exposed, and the reporter who went to interview Mrs. Kane, ready to expose another, was not prepared for the sensation which she gave him. He found in a little house on West 44th Street, "a small magnetic woman of middle age," who was negligently dressed and not in the calmest mood. She told him the fantastic story of her life and intimated that she wished to balance her account, "which the world of humbug-loving mortals held against her, by making a clean breast of all her former miracles and wonders." The reporter was impressed by the fact that, when in London, Mrs. Kane had been entertained by some of the best-to-do of the great and comprehensive middle class. He therefore listened attentively while Mrs. Kane poured out her story, in the intervals of which she would break into sobs or go to the piano and "pour forth fitful floods of wild, incoherent melody, which coincided strangely with that reminiscent weirdness which, despite its cynical reality, still characterized the scene."

Mrs. Kane was prepared to deliver one lecture in which she would expose the humbuggery she had practiced. In the midst of her conversation she paused for a moment and the reporter heard a rapping on the floor beneath his feet and, as he walked around the room, the rappings followed him, under tables, across the threshold and, when Mrs. Kane sat on the piano stool, the legs of the instrument reverberated and the taps "resounded throughout its hollow structure."

"Spirits, is he easily fooled?" asked Mrs. Kane. Three raps came in reply. "I can always get an affirmative answer to that question," Mrs. Kane remarked cynically, and proceeded to explain to her caller that a slight dislocation of the bones in the foot enabled her to make these sounds with an imperceptible movement. "Splitfoot" and the long dresses of 1847 were at last explained and Mrs. Kane asserted that Ann Leah Fox Fish, by this time the wife of Daniel Underhill, respectable president of an insurance company, had known of the deception all the time and had forced the exploitation of it on her younger sisters. Mrs. Underhill, who was still highly thought of in spiritualistic circles, made no statement, but her husband reluctantly suggested that both Maggie and her sister Katie would do well to keep sober occasionally and particularly to avoid the ingratitude of attacking the eldest sister, since the Underhills had twice furnished apartments for them. Mr. Underhill admitted that there were frauds in spiritualism—Madame Diss De Barr, who had performed materializations, was one of them—but he deplored the fact that one of the founders of spiritualism should turn against the faith. The *Herald* story naturally caused a sensation, but most good believers attributed it to drink and to the long tragedy of Mrs. Kane's widowhood. In the next month, Katie Fox, now Mrs. Jencken, arrived from England on the *Persian Monarch*. She also had had difficulties in New York, especially with the Gerry society which had accused her of habitual drunkenness and had taken away her children, but now she declared herself done forever with drink and thoroughly in sympathy with her sister's attack on spiritualism. "Alleged immoralities," figured in the headlines, and Mrs. Jencken declared spiritualism one of the greatest curses the world had ever known. She too asserted that Leah, who was twenty-three years older than herself, had encouraged and managed the rappings from the very beginning. She made it clear that the furor they created, and the excitement, had caused herself and her sister to lend themselves to the fraud. On the 21st of August, Margaret Fox Kane, in spite of many threats sent to her by spiritualists, appeared at the Academy of Music. The New York *World* for the following day gave a brief account of the proceedings:

"A plain wooden stool or table, resting upon four short legs, and having the properties of a sounding board, was placed in front of her. Removing her shoe, she placed her right foot upon this table. The entire house became breathlessly still, and was rewarded by a number of little short, sharp raps—those mysterious sounds which have for more than forty years frightened and bewildered hundreds of thousands of people in this country and Europe. A committee, consisting of three physicians taken from the audience, then ascended to the stage, having made an examination of her foot during the progress of the 'rappings,' unhesitatingly agreed that the sounds were made by the action of the first joint of her large toe.

"Only the most hopelessly, prejudiced and bigoted fanatics of Spiritualism could withstand the irresistible force of this commonplace explanation and exhibition of how 'spirit rappings' are produced. The demonstration was perfect and complete, and if 'spirit rappings' find any credence in this community hereafter, it would seem a wise precaution on the part of the authorities to begin the enlargement of the State's insane asylums without any delay."

The Fox sisters, it is said, later recanted their confession, but the student of mass-manias and intellectual fads is impressed by one thing which the recantation does not touch, namely, that the exposure of a fraud is one of the least successful ways of combating it. It may work in isolated instances, it may help to detach those who are wavering but, apparently, the faithful are as readily nourished by exposure as they are by divine manifestations. The Fox sisters were confessed drunkards and, if they did not stick to their own "betrayal" of spiritualism, they showed at least that they were not precisely trustworthy. Yet if their career has had any deterrent effect on the progress of spiritualism, the Society for Psychical Research does not know of it. It is not within the scope of this book to analyze the proceedings of that society, nor to question in any way the validity of spiritualistic phenomena. The interaction of spiritualism with other manifestations of the radical spirit, which is our theme, is already sufficiently complicated.

§

Of this interaction, we catch glimpses through a flawed crystal, the temperament of Orestes Augustus Brownson, who was a spirit naturally radical, but was driven by despair of reform movements, and by the motions of his intellect, to end his life in the Catholic church; not serenely, but in violent controversy with Catholics and Protestants alike. Brownson's career and ideas offer us a sort of conspectus of the times and his one notable work of fiction, *The Spirit Rapper*, is as illuminating as any of the facts. He was at one time a member of the Presbyterian church and later preached to a Universalist congregation in Albany after which, at Utica, he fell under the influence of Fannie Wright.

This persecuted reformer, who suffered the concentration of all hostile abuse, since she was at once abolitionist, suffragist, anti-capitalist, infidel, and free lover, had already failed with the Nashoba plantation. The interrelation of radical movements was so

close in those days that it is worth while retreating a little chrono-
logically to take in the whole of Fannie Wright's career. She was
an Owenite not only by personal affiliation, but in theory and, as she
and Mrs. Trollope walked the deck of the steamer which brought
them to America, she told the snobbish Englishwoman that she proposed to prove the equality of all men by giving equal education to
blacks and whites. Like most reformers, she was unwilling to carry
one reform through. "Integral" reform was one of the watchwords
of the day and the stern, sturdy, Scotchwoman, who was then a
little over thirty years old, proposed to abolish the slavery of marriage as well as the slavery of serfdom. So, in her invitations to
Nashoba, she followed one of the Rappite principles and anticipated
one of the laws of John Humphrey Noyes, by making it clear that
married persons entering her community *ipso facto* relinquished
any special claim upon each other. A husband was to enjoy no precedence over any other member of the community in seeking the
favors of his wife. She lagged behind the dogmatism of Noyes,
however, because she did admit the propriety of lasting unions so
long as they were based on the affections and were entirely voluntary. She was one of the earliest defenders of unmarried mothers,
protesting against the prolonged and unwilling chastity and un-
fruitfulness of women who had to wait for an appropriate marriage.
She said that if a woman became a mother, under the influence of
"kind feelings," she hoped the time would come when no one would
care to inquire whether she was a wife. Miscegenation was another
doctrine to the practice of which Nashoba gave countenance. The
religion of manual labor was also one of the cults. However, by
paying $200 a year, gentlemen unused to work in field and factory
might be relieved from manual work and left free to enjoy the
other exceptional privileges of this community. After Nashoba
failed and the negroes had been settled in Hayti, Fannie Wright
began the propaganda of her ideas by publicity. With tireless energy,
she waged war against Owen's three great curses, marriage, property, and religion and, in connection with his son, Robert Dale
Owen, published a weekly, *The Free Enquirer*, at New York, and
lectured throughout the country. In Cincinnati, she caused a sensation with her speech on the *Nature of True Knowledge* and, in
Philadelphia, she came upon the platform of the pretty Arch Street

Engraved by A.C. Dick from a Daguerreotype Miniature by A. Morand.

O. A. Brownson.

Theatre with a bodyguard of Quaker ladies in their sober costumes and, in the course of a startling and eloquent lecture which was much applauded, she produced "an emotion" by announcing that according to Jefferson, the father of our country was not a Christian.

It was in 1829 that Brownson heard Miss Wright at Utica and was so impressed that he stayed after the lecture and had a long conversation with her. He then attended her series of four lectures at Auburn, and it was agreed between them that he should become a corresponding editor of her paper. In the issue of December 7, 1829, Miss Wright announced that "Mr. Orestes Augustus Brownson has held out to her the hand of fellowship and become attached to *The Free Enquirer*," a publication as infamous in its day as *The Masses* was in 1917.

The direction which the *Enquirer* was taking was made clear when Fannie Wright and Owen helped to organize the Workingmen's Party. This was at a time of unrest in American labor and the two methods of agitation which have continued to this day developed then their fixed character. Some of the hundreds of labor journals favored legislation procured by political action; others worked for solidarity in trade unionism. Strict party lines were being broken in minor elections by the success of labor candidates and, even if the labor party in any one place was insignificant in numbers, it could still make its influence felt if the major parties were so equally divided that a few votes could turn an election. On one side, we see Tammany Hall fighting or dickering with labor parties and, on the other, we note a growing body of social legislation intended to soothe the outraged conscience of laborers and liberals. The Workingmen's Party was founded in Philadelphia, in 1827, and became of some importance about the time Brownson joined Fannie Wright. At this time it sponsored a meeting of mechanics and laborers to protest against the foul conditions in which sempstresses were compelled to work in that city. "Into this Party," says Brownson, "I entered with enthusiasm." He might have added that he also left it with enthusiasm for, at the end of nine months, he swung to the support of a Jackson candidate and, after the election, gave up the Party entirely. The truth was, as he himself puts it, "I never was and never could be a Party man, or work in the traces of a Party." He denies that he ever gave up the cause of the workingman. It may be noted that, even twenty years later, Fannie Wrightism was still being used in Congress as a synonym for socialism and mob rule, and the Cincinnati *Mirror and Ladies' Parterre* always considered it funny to remark that Fannie Wright, "the high priestess of infidelity and all-things-in-common, had committed amongst other things, marriage." *

Brownson afterward withdrew himself more and more from radical movements, although they had a fascination for him which he could not resist. He would flutter among them, get his wings singed, and retire with some bitter commentary. But he was right in saying that he never gave up the causes for which the movements stood. Nothing could be more vehement than his denunciation of the factory system when, in 1839, the *Boston Times* caused a sensation by a series of articles on the morals of women workers in the Lowell mills:

"The great mass wear out their health, spirits, and morals, without becoming one whit better off than when they commenced labor. The bills of mortality in these factory villages are not striking, we admit, for the poor girls when they can toil no longer go home to die. The average life, working life we mean, of the girls that come to Lowell, for instance, from Maine, New Hampshire, and Vermont, we have been assured is only about three years. What becomes of them then? Few of them ever marry; fewer still ever return to their native places with reputations unimpaired. 'She has worked in a factory' is almost enough to damn to infamy the most worthy and virtuous girl. . . . The man who employs them, and for whom they are toiling as so many slaves, is one of our city nabobs, reveling in luxury; or he is a member of our legislature, enacting laws to put money in his own pocket; or he is a member of Congress contending for a high tariff to tax the poor for the benefit of the rich; or, in these times, he is shedding crocodile tears over the deplorable condition of the poor laborer while he docks his wages 25 per cent.; building miniature log-cabins, shouting Harrison and 'hard cider.' And this man too would fain pass for a Christian and a republican. He shouts for liberty, stickles for equality, and is horrified at a southern planter who keeps slaves."

* She married Phiquepal d'Arusmont, a disciple of Pestalozzi.

On the question of slavery, Brownson was, for once, a moderate. Although he disliked slavery, he would do nothing to put an end to it in those cities and territories where it legally existed but contented himself with opposing its extension elsewhere. The abolitionists, he considered hypocritical, self-seeking demagogues, destructive in mind and contemptible in character. Yet when a mob composed of Southern gentlemen and respectable Boston merchants prevented the anti-slavery society from holding a meeting, Brownson's sense of Justice was outraged and he denounced the city in *The Reformer*, of which he was then editor. In other things he was not so liberal. The recognition of Louis Kossuth provoked him to say that "the government has really let loose one of the most dangerous characters now living. The president knew it is a profanation to apply the term patriot. . . ." And although he was a great friend of Ripley's and, in fact, is said to have converted Mrs. Ripley to Roman Catholicism, he accepted no Brook Farm ideas of equality, saying:

"They carry their zeal for reversing so far as to seek to reverse the natural relation of the sexes, to dishonor woman by making her the head, and sending her to the legislature, the cabinet, or into the field to command our armies, and compelling man to remain at home, and nurse the children, wash the dishes, make the beds, and sweep the house. Already are the women assuming the male attire, and beginning to appear in our streets and assemblies dressed out in full *Bloomer* costume; and little remains for the men to do but to don the petticoat and draw the veil over their faces."

He was a genuine anti-feminist, protesting to the end against the idolatry of women, with its assumption that the Christian virtues are peculiarly feminine, "that the human character of our Lord was woman-like" and that, by the extension of suffrage and the privilege of holding office to women, "our whole system would almost instantly be elevated in its moral tone, our manners would be refined and purified, our legislative assemblies and courts of justice would be incorruptible. . . ." He was reactionary too in politics, detesting "European red-Republicans, socialists, Carbonari, free masons," and their parallels in America. And as he threw himself violently into an aggressive Catholicism, he developed a severe morality and, reviewing *The Scarlet Letter*, he called it a product of perverted genius and said, "The story is told with great naturalness, ease, grace, and delicacy, but it is a story which should not have been told." His one work of fiction had a definite moral purpose: to establish the connection of spiritual manifestations, "with modern philanthropy, visionary reforms, . . . and revolutionism." This connection, he claims with sufficient reason, is asserted by spiritualists themselves. Brownson said of the *Spirit-Rapper* that, while it was not biographical, it had a trace of biography in it. Its central character is carried through almost all the fads of the time, abandoning each one as Brownson himself abandoned them. There was phrenology:

"I paid some attention to Gall and Spurzheim's new science of phrenology. . . . I have since abandoned phrenology. . . . I was arrested for a moment by Boston transcendentalism, but I could not make much of it. Its chiefs told me that I was not spiritual enough . . . at that time I had not paid much attention to Mesmerism. . . . [He pays attention to it and abandons it for the communist theories of St. Simon which in turn are displaced by table turning and then by world reform.] Close by me lived the Fox family. There were three sisters; one was married, and the other two were simple, honest-minded young girls, one 15, the other 13. As I passed by their house I saw them in the yard. I greeted them, and offered them some flowers which I held in my hand. The youngest took them, thanked me with a smile and I pursued my walk. These were the since world-renowned Misses Fox. . . . They are in good faith, as they some time since evinced by their wish to become members of the Catholic Church. . . .

"Even now the first stage is hardly passed and the movement I commenced by a present of flowers to these simple girls has extended over the whole Union, invaded Great Britain, penetrated France in all directions, carried captive all Scandinavia and a large part of Germany, and is finding its way into the Italian Peninsula.

"The Public never suspected me of having had any hand in producing the Rappo-Mania; and the Fox girls, even to this day, suspect no connection between the flowers I gave them and the mysterious knockings which they heard; and nobody had supposed An-

drew Jackson Davis, the most distinguished of the American mediums, of having any relations with me. He does not suspect it
himself, yet he has more than once been magnetized by me. . . ."

The hero requires a certain Priscilla to accompany him on his
mission to young Italy. She was his moral inspiration and, although
she was married, she hardly pretended to conceal the fact that she
loved him and loved him madly. "But love or lust was not precisely
my ruling passion, and I would as soon have taken another with
me as Priscilla, could she have served my purpose as well. Even in
my worst days I was as much repelled as attracted by a woman who
could betray her husband's honor, and I always found a woman,
mastered by her passion, and ready to give up all for love, as it
is called, a troublesome rather than an agreeable companion."

The end of the book deals with an unsuccessful attempt to use
the Pope in the cause of Young Italy but "our magic failed us; a
more powerful magician . . . intervened." And the hero, himself
a mighty magician, admits that the world will laugh at him for
"starting back with fear of death and dread of hell."

It is not a very lucid book, but even its vagueness and obscurity
make it an excellent reflexion of the chaos of the time. Brownson is
typical of the intellectual debacle in the age of prophecy. He was
willing to accept any heresy if it promised salvation; but he was too
gifted to cherish his own illusions and too volatile to remain long
in one camp. He flitted from one to another. He joined, fought,
and deserted. In the end, he had to discover a discipline for his disordered spirit, and found it in the oldest Christian Church. Had he
waited a few years he might have been seduced into the newest. It
was just around the corner.

# XXII.

## Northbound Horses.

IN the gay flush of a new century the life of the spirit ought to have been a priceless thing for Americans. Lecturing in 1901 at the austere and venerable University of Edinburgh, William James gave his approval to America's "only decidedly original contribution to the systematic philosophy of life" and declared New Thought adequate "to the mental needs of a large fraction of mankind." Early in the new century, schools rose in America teaching how to cure baldness by holding the thought of life while rubbing the scalp. Instruction on how to go into the silence was purchasable at twenty-five cents from the same company which promoted an invention to "burn air"—"it will become a bigger money maker than Bell Telephone." In Washington, there was a school for attracting opulence and the Psychic Research Company gave courses in Zoism, personal magnetism, clairvoyance, and crystal-gazing, palmistry, phrenology, and astrology. Elsewhere, one could learn "Just how to wake the solar-plexus." William Walker Atkinson, who was known as the Yogi Ramacharaka, announced that he never got tired of the theme "I can and I will." Ralph Waldo Trine wrote some more books on the great advantage of being in tune with the infinite. Professor S. A. Weltmer made public his discovery of "the long-lost secret of regenerating the human body" by magnetic healing. Nicotine was eliminated from New Thought Cigars and sin and evil were banished from life. In the years of McKinley and Roosevelt, the Love-thought was triumphant. Conventions were held, churches founded, magazines published, songs written in honor of chewing food with the right mental attitude. The "Boston Craze" as New Thought had been called in its early day made its way to Chicago, where it became practical, and to the Pacific Coast, where it lost itself in the rapturous theosophy of Point Loma. It was the era of Success, of Prosperity, of the Will to Health, of Self-Development. Its offspring were Physical Culture and Addison Sims; the *Book of Etiquette* and Elbert Hubbard's *Scrap-book* for a University Education; wall mottoes counseling relaxation and the religion of "Don't Worry." People were forbidden to complain of the weather and were told "God is Well and so are you"; or at least they would be if they only held the health thought and said, "I am well," often enough. Ella Wheeler Wilcox was the sweet singer of the new religion; Dresser, its serious historian; Orison Swett Marden, its practical prophet; Trine, its reincarnation of Emerson; Elbert Hubbard, its bad boy; Elizabeth Towne, its gentle moderator; Atkinson, its leader to mysticism. It loved Jesus and Buddha, Tolstoi, and Nietzsche, liberalism and socialism and anarchism, Unitarianism and Ethical Culture and the wisdom of the East, free love and monogamy, wealth and ascetic virtue. It was scientific and poetic and adored Nature and exalted man. It was pacifist and admired successful brutality. It was precious and went in for simplicity. It was soft.

These are the qualities of New Thought as it ran to seed. Its first convention was held in 1899. By the beginning of the Great War, the systematic philosophy which James saw in it was buried under the multitudinous form-letters of charlatan mind-healers, the magazines of uplift and good-will, the arty folders and limp-leather books on Love and Health and Success. This seems a quick degeneration; but actually the process had begun half a century earlier. The sources of New Thought are in Emerson, in Mesmer, in Quimby, in Noyes, in Owen, and in Fourier. When time had weakened the powerful impulses of these men, their followers coined base metal and gilded it with the new words of Science or Sociology. Emerson, particularly, was the favorite philosopher of the sect, although it seems to have read him in extract only. The sage was forgotten who had lived through a score of movements and had written:

"How frivolous is your war against circumstances! . . . The impulse is good, and the theory; the practice less beautiful. The reformers affirm the inward life, but they do not trust it, but use outward and vulgar means. . . ."

Similarly, when they happened to return to Nature, they made an idol of Thoreau, without thinking deeply of his motives when he went to (and returned from) Walden Pond. They did not recall that he had said of the radicals of his time: "My objection to Channing and all that fraternity is, that they need and deserve sympathy themselves rather than are able to render it to others. They want faith, and mistake their private ail for an infected atmosphere. . . ." There was enough in the New England Transcendentalists to encourage the leaders of New Thought, and Emerson's style made him peculiarly adaptable to their needs. It is only surprising how little development they gave to what they took and how consistently each change was for the worse. "Trust your emotion," wrote Emerson and, out of this, New Thought developed sermons on Keeping Fit, Getting On, and Selling Things. He spoke with awe of the mystic Law of the Universe and one new prophet wrote:

"A New York business man recently told me that he never allows himself to go to his office in the morning until he has put his mind into perfect harmony with the world."

[And James, with all gravity, quotes another:]

" 'I know,' writes Mr. Trine, 'an officer on our police force who has told me that many times when off duty, and on his way home in the evening, there comes to him such a vivid and vital realization of his oneness with this Infinite Power, and this spirit of Infinite Peace so takes hold of and so fills him, that it seems as if his feet could hardly keep to the pavement, so buoyant and so exhilarated does he become by reason of this inflowing tide.' "

Where Emerson was mystical and vague, New Thought became simply unintelligible. He wrote: "Ineffable is the union of man and God in every act of the soul. The simplest person who in his integrity worships God, becomes God; yet forever and ever the influx of this better and universal self is new and unsearchable." And they:

"As the windows of the morning are unbarred, open wide the windows of the soul that the sunshine, the inspiration, the love-light may pour in as your Creator bids you a cheery good-morning. He sends His greeting through the twittering birds, the breath of the flowers, the murmuring night wind, the voices of the children, the sparkling waves, the mountain grandeur, and the deep sea roar. He bids you—

" 'Be still, and know that I am God.' . . . The Divine *letting go* relaxes you to receive the inflow of power. . . ."

"In the preceding lessons I have endeavored to show that Man is one with an all-comprehensive Being, which flows from center to circumference and from circumference back to center by its own intrinsic law or mode of motion. This law is not imposed upon it from the outside, for there is no outside, since Being is all there is. Being, or any part of being, moves as it does because it is what it is, and for no other reason. The reason is in itself, and nowhere else."

Or, to explain geometric diagrams of the Spirit, they wrote, "The blank space in the center of the radiant figure but poorly represents the wonderful reservoirs of Being from which all things proceed," adding blandly, "and yet that blankness may well symbolize the unexpressed." There was an effort, too, to get the emotional value out of religious phrases without accepting their obligations, and out of psychoanalysis without accepting its meaning, as in the profound statement that "the outer Consciousness is on its way to an at-one-ment with the inner."

One idea the New Thoughters rejected; they did not as a rule establish communities. They met and lived together in pretty villages, but the overmastering economic impulse was lacking and, for all their worship of simplicity, they preferred comfort and an income. Emerson had pithily said of the communities of his time that they attempted to make every member rich on the property which would naturally leave every member poor: the prophets of New Thought held poverty to be not quite the will of God. The practice of New Thought was in fact extremely accurate: only its doctrine haphazard and unfortunate. In this it precisely reversed the condition of the communities and movements of a century earlier when theory was the strong point and practice, disaster. Yet New Thought accepted patiently the theory which lay behind early American communism, the pet idea of the 1840's, Association. Of this Emerson had written with a fine individualistic scorn:

"Friendship and association are very fine things, and a grand phalanx of the best of the human race, banded for some catholic object. Yes, excellent, but remember that no society can ever be so large as one man. He, in his friendship, in his natural and momentary associations, doubles or multiplies himself, but in the hour in which he mortgages himself to two or ten or twenty, he dwarfs himself below the stature of one.

"But the men of less faith could not thus believe, and to such, concert appears the sole specific of strength. I have failed, and you have failed, but perhaps together we shall not fail. Our housekeeping is not satisfactory to us, but perhaps a phalanx, a community, might be. Many of us have differed in opinion, and we could find no man who could make the truth plain, but possibly a college or an ecclesiastical council might. I have not been able either to persuade my brother, or to prevail on myself, to disuse the traffic or the potation of brandy, but perhaps a pledge of total abstinence might effectually restrain us. The candidate my party votes for is not to be trusted with a dollar, but he will be honest in the Senate, for we can bring public opinion to bear on him. Thus concert was the specific in all cases. But concert is neither better nor worse, neither more nor less potent than individual force. All the men in the world cannot make a statue walk and speak, cannot make a drop of blood, or a blade of grass, any more than one man can. But let there be one man, let there be truth in two men, in ten men, then is concert for the first time possible, because the force which moves the world is a new quality, and can never be furnished by adding whatever quantities of a different kind. What is the use of the concert of the false and the disunited? There can be no concert in two where there is no concert in one. When the individual is not individual, but is dual; when his thoughts look one way and his actions another; when his faith is traversed by his habits, when his will, enlightened by reason, is warped by his sense; when with one hand he rows, and with the other backs water, what concert can be?"

The disciples of New Thought lived in an age of rapid communication. There was no necessity for Association to demand the bodily presence of many believers in a communal life. The telephone and telegraph, the railroad and presently the motor car made Association simple. Besides this, New Thought was enchanted by another idea which it borrowed from Science. There were waves in the air, waves of sound and of light. Inanimate objects were found to give off emanations. Things radiated. There was the promise that even the human voice would spring from one center to another. These things were facts and not merely symbols; but it did not seem possible that the Omnipotent Good, which had created them, should deny their counterparts and parallels to the mind of man. French scientists had restored the reputation of Mesmer. There *was* such a thing as hypnotism and the mind, or something, of one man affected the soul, or whatever it was, of another. So New Thought made itself into an Association of people whose spirits radiated appropriate sentiments in all directions and unheard, unseen, even unknown, affected the lives of others. Merely to subscribe to a magazine was to expose oneself to the irradiations of good will from 20,000 other subscribers and, to gain success in life, one had only to join an invisible circle by repeating a magic formula:

"I hereby join the success circle of the Psychic Club of America, with the right to withdraw whenever I see fit. While I am a member, I pledge myself to join my brethren in sending out thoughts of love, encouragement, help, and success, to myself, my brothers and sisters of the success circle; and all mankind. I will do my best to refrain from all thoughts of fear, discouragement, failure, and hate, and I will do my best to add to the loving and helpful thought wave being sent out by the circle. May peace, harmony, and success attend our efforts."

The triumph of New Thought is in its transformation of "evolution" into "progress." For a generation, the Darwinian hypothesis had made dark the anxious days of thoughtful men; life was brutal, calculating, and unjust, and nature red with tooth and claw. Yet this was the same nature which the transcendentalists had worshiped. The new science had to be reconciled to the All-Truth. The process by which New Thought effected this "at-one-ment" is a little obscure. There was a strain of mysticism in it; of the conviction, unfortified by experience that, however ill may be the plight of an individual, a nation, or an era, "the total frame of things absolutely must be good." There was a touch of German philosophy: this bit of evil and that bit of good together form a Good higher than Good. In the late 1890's, there was added a tiny element of estheticism. Just as the portrait of an ugly woman paring her nails might be a beautiful picture, so squalor and misery might be composed into a spectacle that would give pleasure to the highest senses. But as far as Nietzsche went in his glorification of the beauties of hardness and brutality New Thought did not venture. It was too irredeemably pledged to the Good.

In this faith in divine Goodness it gained support from the liberal movements within the Protestant churches; and made the most of this support because, unlike Christian Science, it did not establish an exclusive church itself. Avoiding rigidity, avoiding even precision, in all things, it preferred vague organizations. Its adepts could pray in any church which had abandoned the religion of pessimism and of sin. The old theology had insisted that God was powerful and that his Goodness consisted in being just. The new theology was based on the more disputable assumption that God is good within the terms of the human conception of Goodness. But as human goodness finds no place for the murder of pious men, for rape and thievery and loss, for cancer and lingering death, there was left a blank in the new theology. At the right of the page was the rubric of eternal goodness; at the left, the record of man's mortal unhappiness. The old theology balanced its accounts by adding the unutterable and incalculable sinfulness of man since the fall of Adam. The new theology having erased that item, was bound to look on the other side of the sheet for its equivalent.

Here Christian Science came in to suggest that unhappiness was accidental, wayward, and unplanned—in essence that unhappiness does not exist. And New Thought also more cautiously ventures upon the same ground. Unhappiness is only a symptom of man's imperfect development; it is destined to vanish in the course of evolution. For evolution is always upward, since the soul of man is at its present apex, and the oversoul and the higher man are promised. Better and better, day by day is not an incantation, but a literal description of the actual workings of this great law of progressive evolution. One passes beyond the trust that somehow good will be the final goal of ill; what is ill will perish and all that remains must be good.

There was still an obligation: to hasten this benevolent process by which evil will disappear. Fortunately, when cosmic duty says "thou must," New Thought answers "I can and I will." The mystic and the practical adept are assured of one thing: that, through the higher self, "we are partakers of the life of God . . . in essence the life of God and the life of man are identically the same." Until we become aware of our natural oneness with the divine power, we wander helplessly through the world suffering evil and doing no good. But:

"The great central fact in human life is the coming into a conscious vital realization of our oneness with this Infinite Life, and the opening of ourselves fully to this divine inflow. In just the degree that we come into a conscious realization of our oneness with the Infinite Life, and open ourselves to this divine inflow, do we actualize in ourselves the qualities and powers of the Infinite Life, do we make ourselves channels through which the Infinite Intelligence and Power can work." *

As we drink in this infinite power for Good, we arrive instantly at a state, not of drunkenness with the exaltation of knowing ourselves infinite, but of extremely desirable practical satisfactions:

"In just the degree in which you realize your oneness with the Infinite Spirit, you will exchange dis-ease for ease, inharmony for harmony, suffering and pain for abounding health and strength. To recognize our own divinity, and our intimate relation to the Universal, is to attach the belts of our machinery to the power house of the Universe. One need remain in hell no longer than one chooses to; we can rise to any heaven we ourselves choose; and when we choose so to rise, all the higher powers of the Universe combine to help us heavenward."

It is worth noting that "all the higher powers of the universe" work in our favor, for this gives us a clew to the astonishing success

* The droning repetitions of the revivalists reappear, with other phrases, in New Thought. The second time a word is used, it requires half the attention of the first time. By the tenth repetition, the word is hypnotic, magical. It lulls the brain to sleep—or what is called, in New Thought, receptivity. Emerson did not know the trick. He said simply, "If a man is at heart just, then in so far is he God." New Thought omits the qualification and repeats its assertions endlessly, for to assert and to repeat are essentials in the method. The foregoing and following quotations are selected by James from Ralph Waldo Trine as giving the "central point of view" of New Thought.

of New Thought. For centuries the effect, if not the intention, of
science had been to destroy the illusion that man is the center of
the universe. The great astronomers had literally done this by
proving the earth a satellite to the sun. The evolutionists had completed the work by indicating how coolly indifferent nature is to
our ideals and our well-being. The armies of inexorable law did not
protect man so much as confine him and 1900 years after God had
sent his only begotten son to save mankind, humanity found itself
where the psalmist had left it, a withered blade of grass, a dust
cloud in the wind. New Thought miraculously restored man, and
raised him to the stature of a God. It made him think that the indis-
cernible laws of the universe coincided with the laws of his own
existence. It gave him dignity and an unparalleled power. He had
only to think himself God in order to be God. For the weak-minded
even thought was dispensable. They had only to say.

The proof of power was in the destruction of everything evil.
New Thought, according to a trivial magazine bearing the name,
was "sweeping away antiquated dogma, crass materialism, bigotry,
superstition, unfaith, intolerance, persecution, suppression, fear,
hate, intellectual tyranny, and despotism, prejudice, narrowness,
poverty, disease, yea, perhaps even death," and bringing in its place,
among other things, freedom, courage, advancement, development
of latent powers, success, health, and life. The method of attaining
power was resolutely to banish pessimism and fear, to think no more
of sin, to be confident that all was, or shortly would be, for the
best. From the moment one became receptive to these happy invasions, not only the higher powers would coöperate, but every
thought sent out by every other happy person would inundate one's
being.

New Thought has had its miracles, no less than Christian Science.
They were for the most part miracles of right thinking, but they
were effective. Before they had heard of Freud, the practitioners
of the mind cure were suggesting that sometimes a lame leg, or a
blind eye, was due to some warping of the nervous system, some
obstruction to the strong will and the healthy mind. For the most
part, New Thought left actual physical cures to Christian Science
and to its gentle counterpart, the Emmanuel movement. To itself

it took other ills: awkwardness, and lack of confidence, fear, and thwarted ambitions, and frustrated lives. It called for a certain courage. It did not pamper its patients nor encourage them to dwell on their symptoms. If it failed to say "bear the pain," at least it did not say "enjoy the pain." It imposed no discipline on the mind and it made no fetich of facing reality. It did not deny the existence of what it disliked; it only denied its significance. The mind cure, in New Thought, is generally applied to the things of the mind. The method has its source in the direct spiritual healing of Quimby, for New Thought, holding that pain is in our consciousness, advises us to divert our attention, to shift it from what is painful to what is pleasing. According to an unfavorable critic, there is in New Thought even the idea that suffering is the result of struggle and, in fact, New Thought is always urging men to relax, to let beneficent spirits conquer us. Thus America's peculiar contribution to philosophy takes on the dim hues of an oriental nirvana.

Of necessity, New Thought is liberal in its social doctrines. While established Christianity taught that all men might partake of the grace of Jesus Christ if they were converted, if they lived the Christian life, it also noted the existence of the wicked and the unregenerate. In the vision of New Thought the latter were only individualized portions of the infinite spirit which had not yet become aware of their identity with God. In other words, all men are brothers and, potentially at least, all are equally good and noble and pure, since they share equally in the divine nature. The religions of altruism and communism found supporters in the ranks of New Thought and, just as it drew its doctrines from Transcendentalism, it drew its sociology from the altruistic spiritualism of the last century. For its comparatively feeble denial of the reality of death, it had roots in spiritualism. Its doctrine that all things are progressing to perfection and that, merely by thinking, we become part of the inviolable harmony of the universe, approached the mystic perfectionism of Finney and of Noyes. Thus we read that "the time is coming when man cannot suffer" and "the perfection of our individuality is at hand." A healing affirmation in the *Complete Christian Divine Scientific Philosophy* asserts, "I am one with health, wealth, and love . . . there is one mind in God (good)

and that mind is my mind now. I am one with the gifts of God.
. . . I am perfect in love, truth, and life eternal. . . ." *

§

So, in spite of its vagaries, New Thought is a culmination of
the radicalism which marked American thought from the very beginning to the very end of the nineteenth century. For that reason,
New Thought may be made a point of departure for a résumé of
the development of Calvinism in the period.

If we look back from New Thought to Jonathan Edwards, we
are conscious that somewhere there is a break in continuity. Between
the Puritan's pervading sense of sin and the attainable all-good of
latter-day cults, there seems to be no connection. The break of course
occurred when revivalists, in their greediness for saved souls, threw
off the letter of Calvinism and felt free to develop the idea of a
sinless and sanctified humanity. Finney and Mahan and the comparatively orthodox Perfectionists threw bridges of logic across this
chasm but, by making a sinless life possible on earth, they changed
the direction of man's search for salvation and aided their enemies,
the liberals in various Christian sects, and the infidels. They succumbed, in short, to the combined influence of French philosophers
and Anglo-Saxon engineers and allowed the transposition of the
golden age from the past to the future. They did not intend to do
this; for them the fall of man was real enough. But they permitted their sense of Christ's attainment to carry them to a restoration of Eden on earth at the very time when social philosophers,
scientists, and engineers, were indicating the possibilities of unlim-
ited progress for man.

Yet in another way the cults of New Thought march in a direct
line from the religion of Edwards: the glorification of the Will.
Here too we find a transposition; it was the will of God that Edwards so patiently adored; it is the will of man to which a thousand
advertisements now address themselves. Yet, in spite of his theology, Edwards did exalt the human will as well as the divine. He
called it stubborn and perverse and irremediably bent toward evil
but, as he magnified the power of God's Will, he could not help

* The succeeding affirmation does as much for astrology.

magnifying also the power of our own. It would belittle God for us to have puny powers and the very strength of our sinful will proved the superiority of our adversary. The moment the opposition of God's will was withdrawn—in the general breakdown of Calvinism—the human will sprang up like a dampened fire when it has eaten its way into the air. In the era of revivalism the will had been put to enormous exercises of self-restraint and at the same time was allowed unnatural gratifications. As it conquered time and annihilated space in creating a new physical universe, so it was to triumph over fear and desire and establish man in the higher spiritual order of omnipotent nature. The alternation of despair and hope in the camp-meeting, abasing and then exaggerating the will, helped in this process. It did away with the necessity of knowing one's normal powers and substituted for discipline a flow of external grace. Edwards had placed the raging beast of superhuman will in the cage of predestination. The later revivalists, after having prodded and pampered the beast, suddenly broke down the bars, letting the will run wild at the very moment when Force, regardless of its discipline or its objective, was beginning to be worshiped.

The simplest way to conceive the relation between the type of religion roughly known as mental healing and the Calvinism of the eighteenth century, is to think of the religion of universal good as a reaction against the religion of merciless anxiety. "Our young people," says Emerson, "are diseased with the theological problems of original sin, origin of evil, predestination, and the like." To cure this disease was one of the great functions of New Thought. It succeeded; but the malady had left ineradicable marks on the body of the victim. Calvinist theology was shattered, but Calvinist morality remained almost untouched. It was a morality always suitable to industrial democracy. It required men to be sober and women to be chaste. It exalted industry and condemned pride and envy. It offered no intermediary absolution for sins and its moral bookkeeping was complex and accurate. In a sense, it was a mercantile morality: the wages of speculation were bankruptcy. The only dignity it gave to man was in his responsibility.

The attacks on Calvinism have been noted. Owen with his "counteracting circumstance" and the phrenologists with their "faculties," were as effectively hostile as the infidels who denied the story of Adam's fall, and the Universalists who taught that all men are saved. The whole American experiment was opposed to the Calvinist theology. We see this marked in the extraordinary change of relationship between parents and children. The eternally damned infant might well be apprenticed to a tanner, or a printer, and brutally kept at work sixteen hours a day. Until he was saved by an act of grace, he was the devil's property, not God's. But the child, in America, escaped from perdition. Like America itself, its children were precocious and, from the 1820's on, it is universally remarked that American children are encouraged and pampered. Foreigners, finding them independent and fearless, counted this a charm. And the charm worked on the preachers for, slowly, the grim chord of damnation was resolved by successive modulations. In spite of the protests of doctrinaires who disliked poetry in ladies' parlors "about the angelic sweetness of infancy," it became established that infants are not necessarily damned; later that, if they died before baptism, they are certainly not damned; and, finally, that all that died in infancy are elect. The bitter fundamentalist does not admit infant election even to-day, but fear of infant damnation has dropped entirely from the American consciousness. In criminology, the same attack was made on Calvinistic principles. President Humphrey of Amherst noted that the opinion seemed to be gaining ground in some respectable and influential quarters that punishments are rarely if ever necessary in family government and, as the Calvinist father came to imitate less and less the Calvinist God, the democratic state became more corrective and less vindictive in its dealings with offenders.

Yet none of these things deeply affected the morality of daily life. Universalist, Unitarian, Transcendentalist, and disciple of New Thought, still agreed that sobriety and virtue, chastity and self-improvement were the foundations of a good life. Even phrenology preached self-culture and self-development to such a degree that its pamphlets read like parodies of twentieth-century advertisements. The old responsibility for sin was taught with a new emphasis. Man is responsible for his failures, for his poverty, for his ill-health, for his unhappiness. The moral accounting system drawn up by Franklin could have been endorsed by Jonathan Edwards, by Noyes, by Alcott, by Frances Willard, and by Elbert Hubbard. To perfect oneself morally is the goal of them all. The Puritan ethics suggested restraint on one's natural impulses because the impulses themselves were evil. Liberal morality practiced restraint for the exaltation of self and for the general good of humanity. Even the cult of love had a strong moralistic basis. The God who is all-love, no less than the God who is all-just, desires our natural instincts to be checked, so that those who are evil may become good and those who are good may become perfect.

§

But if the fundamental morality remained unchanged, New Thought pronounced the old law with shifted accents. It offered to every man, as his birthright, complete realization of himself. In one of Marden's books he taught: "That everybody ought to be happier than the happiest of us are now; that our lives were intended to be infinitely richer and more abundant than at present; that we should have plenty of everything which is good for us; that the lack of anything which is really necessary and desirable does not fit the constitution of any right-living human being, and that we shorten our lives very materially through our own false thinking, our bad living, and our old-age convictions, and that to be happy and attain the highest efficiency, one must harmonize with the best, the highest thing in him."

The whole idea of boundaries was offensive to New Thought. The finite must merge into the infinite at all costs and no man must be allowed to cut himself off from his fellows. Sharp lines, definitions, classifications, were all to be erased, so that the mind of man might again be in harmony with the unbounded universe. So each teacher promised everything. There was no discipline in this religion and the possibilities for every individual were without end. "There is a power inside of you which if you could discover and use it would make of you everything you ever dreamed or imagined you could become." Thus in a scientific age miracles were restored to mankind.

It was inevitable that the optimistic religion of New Thought should go into business. It was essentially a religion of success. The successful man had brushed away limitations, had denied contradictions and realized himself fully. Marden, Trine, and Hubbard in their various ways were successful enough, but for the most part the business side of New Thought is rather sad reading and one turns from its surface optimism in magazines of success and advertisements of Personality to wonder whether the defeat of Jonathan Edwards was as desirable as it seemed. A cut above the success cult is Horace Fletcher who opposed to the "fear-thought" his idea of menticulture, saying that "it had been proven that none are so ill-favored as to be exempt from regeneration by the influence of optimistic thinking" and suggesting that beauty, too, is the reward of happy thoughts. But, in general, the business men of New Thought advised stock-brokers to become at one with God so that they might put over big deals, and refined the old bluff of the Yankee into "we are what we assert ourselves to be," or "claim that you are what you desire to be." New Thought turned assumption into aggressiveness and sired the go-getter. When it went into business for itself it was incoherent and often fraudulent. It became a mail order religion with loud complaints against the "peculiar laws" by which the post office department prevented prophets from selling sacred handkerchiefs guaranteed to cure cancer and barrenness. In unsubtle ways it managed to connect regeneration with the restoration of sexual vitality. At the same time, its professions were always lofty and it gave rise to the current sanctimonious chatter about service. From it also came the highly organized business of self-improvement. The moderate claims of President Eliot that the careful reading of fifty volumes of great literature will lay a foundation for being considered a well-read man, are laughed to scorn by the higher advertising which promises *savoir faire* in French and in etiquette, in memory and public speaking, in a fragrant breath and a knowledge of philosophy, and offers to develop a great personality in addition to all learning and all graces. The degradation of the idea of the will in all this is as marked as the expansion of the idea of self-reliance. Between them has been created a new and distinct type of American and there are moments when one thinks that it is the dominant type.

§

This was not the intention of New Thought. As late as 1916, the scheduled purposes of the New Thought Alliance were "to teach the infinitude of the Supreme One, Divinity of Man and his Infinite possibilities through the creative power of constructive thinking and obedience to the voice of the Indwelling Presence which is our source of Inspiration, Power, Health, and Prosperity." And, the following year, some effort was made to bring the "creative power of constructive thinking" to bear on this sentence itself. As a result certain affirmations were made. New Thought, after accepting the universe, allowed itself to be precise:

"We affirm the freedom of each soul as to choice and as to belief, and would not, by the adoption of any declaration of principles, limit such freedom. The essence of the New Thought is Truth, and each individual must be loyal to the Truth he sees. The windows of his soul must be kept open at each moment for the higher light, and his mind must be always hospitable to each new inspiration.

"We affirm the Good. This is supreme, universal, and everlasting. Man is made in the image of the Good, and evil and pain are but the tests and correctives that appear when his thought does not reflect the full glory of this image.

"We affirm health, which is man's divine inheritance. Man's body is his holy temple. Every function of it, every cell of it, is intelligent, and is shaped, ruled, repaired, and controlled by mind. He whose body is full of light is full of health. Spiritual healing has existed among all races in all times. It has now become a part of the higher science and art of living the life more abundant.

"We affirm the divine supply. He who serves God and man in the full understanding of the law of compensation shall not lack. Within us are unused resources of energy and power. He who lives with his whole being, and thus expresses fullness, shall reap fullness in return. He who gives himself, he who knows, and acts in his highest knowledge, he who trusts in the divine return, has learned the law of success.

"We affirm the teaching of Christ that the Kingdom of Heaven is within us, that we are one with the Father, that we should judge not, that we should love one another, that we should heal the sick, that we should return good for evil, that we should minister to others, and that we should be perfect even as our Father in Heaven is perfect. These are not only ideals, but practical, every-day working principles.

"We affirm these things, not as a profession, but practice, not in one day of the week, but in every hour and minute of every day, sleeping and waking, not in the ministry of the few, but in the service that included the democracy of all, not in words alone, but in the innermost thoughts of the heart expressed in living the life. 'By their fruits ye shall know them.'

"We affirm Heaven here and now, the life everlasting that becomes conscious immortality, the communion of mind with mind throughout the universe of thought, the nothingness of all error and negation, including death, the variety of unity that produces the individual expressions of the One-Life, and the quickened realization of the indwelling God in each soul that is making a new heaven and a new earth."

Of the mind-cure literature of his own time, James said, regretfully, that some of it is "so moonstruck with optimism and so vaguely expressed that an academically trained intellect finds it almost impossible to read it at all." One wonders what he would have made of the affirmations just quoted. He might assume that to affirm the freedom of belief means to protect or stand for that freedom as a principle. To affirm the divine supply would be to announce a belief in that supply. But what, precisely, is the meaning of affirming the Good? Does it mean appreciation of the Good, or preference for it, or only belief in the existence of the Good? Or that the Good alone exists and evil only "appears"? And, if these questions suggest the exact nature of the meaning of "affirm," what is the meaning of affirming heaven here and now? Even a mind not academically trained becomes confused, wondering, if heaven is affirmed and established, what is the "nothingness of all error and negation," and how death is included and precisely in what? What is the "higher science," and what "the life more abundant," and in what way is a body full of light?

One wonders whether the vagueness of all these terms was not intentional. New Thought seemed to shrink from precision. Nothing in it was tough-minded. Its beliefs were all timid and timidly held. It lacked the power of dogmatic religions because it would not accept oppositions in nature and hostilities between men. It wavered between a mystic God and a scientific principle and, in practice, it exalted the aggressive American spirit on one day and taught ways of escape on another. It is not remarkable that, in the end, many of its leaders left New Thought behind and found a way of escape more sure than any of their own. For the only element in New Thought which is not a culmination of older native forces is its strain of Oriental mysticism. So far as it was strong at all, mysticism gave it strength.

# XXIII.

## The Path to Nothing.

THEY were all seekers for salvation, from the ecstatic Puritan to the vague yearners after New Thought. For some, salvation meant social equality; for others, an aristocracy in heaven. Some were fleeing from ills of the body and finding redemption in bran and water. Others, whose minds were sick, accepted any short way to the arms of the redeemer. For some, salvation was a means of escape from their own sins. Others, who had overcome Sin in themselves, sought the path to universal righteousness. The Christian felt his soul bruised by his separation from God; the abolitionist, by the bar between other men and himself. Even the dreary temperance worker looked forward to the perfection of mankind and the coming of God's kingdom. The differences between them are many. From what were they escaping? And to what? And by what means? The abomination from which New Thought offered an escape was, like everything else in that cult, synthetic. Physical ills, moral defects, political injustice, external pressures, and lesions of the soul, were all to be cured by this single method: the method of thinking. By this method was prosecuted the search for the One. As intentionally as Thales or Anaximenes, New Thought brushed away the diversity of the forms of life to seek the one underlying principle. They found it in that moral law which Emerson had announced to them as a suitable object of worship. There was something restful in the thought of Oneness: it was in itself salvation from the plaguing diversity of daily life, from lust and lethargy and greed, and even from success. In New Thought, the Law was given names more benign, Good or All-Good, Divine, Almighty Presence, Nature, Kindly Light, the Over-Soul. But it was hardly necessary to make this God kind. For worship had ceased to be adoration: one merely contemplated the magnificence of the Law. The high priest had arrived at some rapture in this contemplation. The lesser orders—it was a religion without laity—swooned on a perfumed sea of vague ideas.

But, again and again, there came into the mind of the believer a suspicion that this was not all. The crass world obtruded itself. One held fast to the thought of loyalty, yet servants deserted on the eve of a dinner party. One was aggressive and assertive and thought of nothing but prosperity, yet banks failed and factories burned. The world refused to be defeated. It would not be manipulated by thought into acceptable shape. It had been reduced to one, but from that one particles split off, apparently unaware of their identity with the infinite and the eternal. Somehow disease struck down the brightest and the best. Failure overtook the most confident and the most happily gifted. Perhaps there was some way of passing beyond the mystic One. Perhaps, by an effort, the believer could find nothing.

At the second general convention of disciples of New Thought (New York, 1900) there appeared the Swami Abhedananda, a prophetic presence, since New Thought was destined to be enormously influenced by Oriental mysticism. Always receptive, and always looking for some new thing, the leaders of New Thought were enchanted with Yoga. The 195 rules on which it is based were more than a thousand years old, but the great works on Yoga had only begun to make their way into English in the 1890's and a Swami, or even a Guru, was impressive. And there was something peculiarly sympathetic in the methods and devices of Yoga, especially if one did not consider too closely what the golden object could be. The Yogin knew how to breathe, and how to chew his food, and how to sit, and how to go, enormously, into the silence. There is for example the sutra on posture quoted by Professor Leuba, which mentions "the lotus-posture and the hero-posture and the decent-posture and the mystic diagram, and the staff-posture and the posture with the rest and the bedstead, the seated curlew and the seated elephant and the seated camel, the even arrangement, the stable-and-easy and others of the same kind." The sutra is explained by Max Mueller in a quotation from the Bhagavad-Gita: " 'A devotee should constantly devote his Self to abstraction, remaining in a secret place . . . fixing his seat firmly in a clean place, not too high nor too low, and covered over with a sheet of cloth, a deerskin, and blades of Kusa grass—and there seated on that seat, fixing his mind exclusively on one point, with the workings of the mind and senses restrained, he should practice devotion for purity of Self. Holding his body, head, and neck even and unmoved, remaining steady, looking at the tip of his own nose, and not looking about in all directions, with a tranquil self, devoid of fear, and adhering to the rules of Brahmakarins, he should restrain his mind and concentrate it on me (the Deity), as his final goal. Thus constantly devoting his Self to abstraction, a devotee whose mind is restrained, attains that tranquillity which culminates in final emancipation and assimilation with me.' Elsewhere the devotee is directed to exclude from his mind 'external objects,' concentrate the visual power between the brows, and making the upward and downward life-breaths even, confining their movements 'within the nose.' In another place, he is directed to repeat the single syllable 'om,' a mystical formula for Brahma."

§

To Americans who had been developing systems of eating and not eating, it was enchanting to find that the esoteric wisdom of the East was so desperately concerned with the human body. Here was a new field and they drove their mechanical plows into it without stopping to wonder what the crop would be. Philosophers of New Thought developed strange oriental names. William Walker Atkinson, Yogi Ramacharaka, published at least eighteen works on the Hindo-Yogi Science of Breathing, on the Science of Psychic Healing, on Auto-suggestion, on Hatha Yoga, and Moral Culture and Gnani Yogi and Raja Yoga and Thought Force in Business. Hatha Yoga, the philosophy of physical well-being, we learn is "first Nature; and last Nature." From which it is adduced that it is not necessary to wear rubber soles to prevent Nature ("mother earth") from drawing out the magnetism she has given the human body. The book also explains Prana, or Pranic energy, precisely in the terms of a medieval philosopher explaining that fire is hot because in fire there is a principle of heat which is called phlogiston. "Man obtains Prana as well as nourishment from his food—Prana as well as a cleansing effect from the water he drinks—Prana properly distributed as well as mere muscular development in physical exercises—Prana as well as heat from the rays of the sun—Prana as well as oxygen from the air he breathes—and so on."

"What is Prana?" he asks in our behalf, and explains—if it is an explanation:

"Occultists in all ages and lands have taught, usually secretly to a few followers, that there was to be found in the air, in water, in the food, in the sunlight, everywhere, a substance or principle from which all activity, energy, power, and vitality was derived. . . . We have preferred to designate this vital principle by the name by which it is known among the Hindu teachers and students—gurus and chelas—and have used for this purpose the Sanscrit word 'Prana,' meaning 'Absolute Energy.'

"Occult authorities teach that the principle which the Hindus term 'Prana' is the universal principle of energy or force, and that all energy or force is derived from the principle, or rather, is a particular form or manifestation of that principle." Of course Prana is a great deal more. It is the active principle of life and must not be confounded with the Ego since "Prana is merely a form of energy used by the Ego in its material manifestation. When the Ego leaves the body, the Prana, being no longer under its control, responds only to the orders of the individual atoms. . . . With the Ego in control, cohesion exists and the atoms are held together by the Will of the Ego.

"Prana is the name by which we designate a universal principle, which principle is the essence of all motion, force, or energy, whether manifested in gravitation, electricity, the revolution of the planets, and all forms of life, from the highest to the lowest. . . .

"This great principle is in all forms of matter, and yet it is not matter. It is in the air, but it is not the air nor one of its chemical constituents. It is in the food we eat, and yet it is not the same as the nourishing substance in the food. It is in the water we drink, and yet it is not one or more of the chemical substances which combining make water. It is in the sunlight, but yet it is not the heat or the light rays. It is the 'energy' in all these things—the things acting merely as a carrier.

"And man is able to extract it from the air, food, water, sunlight, and turn it to good account in his own organism.

"Prana is in the atmospheric air, but it is also everywhere, and it penetrates where the air cannot reach. The oxygen in the air plays an important part in sustaining animal life, and the carbon plays a similar part with plant life, but Prana has its own distinct part to play in the manifestation of life, aside from the physiological functions."

Prana is in the air and it is apparently to absorb Prana that the Yoga system has developed ways of breathing. Once the proper posture has been found, several kinds of breath-control are possible. Professor Leuba is a little impatient with them: "It is external in case there is no flow of breath after expiration; it is internal in case there is no flow of breath after inspiration; it is the third or suppressed in case there is no flow of either kind.* The puerile subtleties into which sutras and commentaries enter in this connection cannot interest us. We need note merely that the fourth and perfect control of the breath involves the total suppression of the passage of air to and from the lungs. Since death would speedily supervene should this be realized, we must suppose that the Yogin, in consequence of the bodily and mental attitude he assumes, is deceived into the belief that breathing is totally suspended. That he suffers many similar illusions and hallucinations there cannot be any doubt. But why this unnatural behavior? Because in restraint of breath, 'the central organ' becomes fit for fixed attention and complete mastery of the organs is attained; i.e., the sense organs are 'restricted,' their activity ceases, and that, as we know, is a step towards complete disinterestedness and passionlessness." But the American Yogin assures us that the Prana is important for, while the oxygen in the air feeds the blood, Prana feeds the nerves.

It was a happy day when the American orientalizers discovered that there was a sutra on eating. Oddly, the mystic teaching coincided with that of the good millionaire, Horace Fletcher. But the Yoga doctrine of mastication could hardly be expressed in the comparatively specific terms of an American, even of a New Thought American. It was important to know, first, that "the Yogin has conquered appetite, and allows hunger to manifest through him." This being so, and Prana manifesting itself in food as well as in the air, thorough mastication, which Mr. Fletcher advised because it

* The internal respiration of Thomas Lake Harris comes to mind.

made digestion perfect, is incorporated in the Yogi system because it permits the fuller absorption of food-Prana. "The act of mastication liberates this Prana, by separating the particles of the food into minute bits, thus exposing as many atoms of Prana to the tongue, mouth, and teeth as possible. Each atom of food contains numerous electrons of food-Prana, or food energy, which electrons are liberated by the breaking-up process of mastication, and the chemical action of certain subtle chemical constituents of saliva, the presence of which have not been suspected by modern scientists, and which are not discernible by the tests of modern chemistry, *although future investigators will scientifically prove their existence.* Once liberated from the food, this food-Prana flies to the nerves of the tongue, mouth, and teeth, passing through the flesh and bone readily, and is rapidly conveyed to numerous storage-houses of the nervous system, from whence it is conveyed to all parts of the body, where it is used to furnish energy and 'vitality' to the cells." (The italics are mine.)

This masticated food melts away in the mouth and "to describe this sensation is almost impossible"; it may be compared to a "kiss from the loved one," in its radiation of magnetism. It is of course to be understood "that the mental attitude aids materially in the process of absorbing Prana. This is true not only of the Prana absorbed from the air, but also of the food-Prana. Hold the thought that you are absorbing all the Prana contained in a mouthful of food, combining that thought with that of 'Nourishment,' and you will be able to do much more than you can without so doing."

§

The methods by which the oriental mystic obtains concentration are not appropriate subjects for criticism here. The whole language of Vedanta, or Yoga, is clear only to the adept. For a layman to criticize it without profound study is an impertinence. What the layman is justified in criticizing is the adaptation of this philosophy in America and one's first impulse is to say that this mysticism translated into a health cult is a peculiarly exasperating form of buncombe. Such a characterization, however, fails to explain and a somewhat closer analysis becomes necessary. The first thing that comes out is the special emphasis upon bodily health which the

American vulgarizers of Yoga gave it. For them, Yoga was only another mystic proof of God's intentions regarding the viscera. That this has almost nothing to do with the purposes of the Yogin's exercises is apparently considered unimportant in the American adaptation. The mania for health which brought into being on one side the cult of sport, fostered every variety of cure, from diet to Christian Science, on the other. To the true pagan, the true mystic, and the normal healthy individual alike, this preoccupation with health is as disquieting as hypochondria. To them, health either comes naturally or is not of supreme importance. The American cult-follower, for a variety of reasons, made a religion of being well and was most happy when he could add well-being to a mystic conception of the universe.

It happens that both the philosophy and the goal of Yoga are opposed to the underlying affirmations of American life, as they are opposed (in part) to the essence of Christianity. To the Yogin, "life is evil and death is merely the beginning of another painful existence . . . the goal is escape from the round of rebirths." The Christian perfects himself, and his reward is endless life in which his personal soul persists. The object of the Hindu mystic seeking perfection is different. In his philosophy, the pain he suffers is a penalty for evil done by himself in a previous incarnation and, if he lives one life without sin, he "considers that victory over his imperfections entitles him to an honorable dismissal from conscious existence." The object of his concentration, of his asceticism, and of his complete realization of self, is to be annihilated forever. The principle of Hatha Yoga (from which Americans drew methods of breathing and eating) is described by a French Orientalist as an effort to slow down the pace of life, to burn with the smallest flame, to make the nervous system almost insensible and to create in oneself a calm so profound that meditation is no longer troubled and ecstasy supervenes. This relaxation of the hold on life corresponds somewhat to the surrender of the ego in psychoanalysis and in religious conversion. Particularly, the sutras call for relaxation of the intellect. It is through the mind that we become conscious of the world and, when we know the world, we are possessed by ambitions, torn by desires and, beginning to worship our will, become personalities. According to Yoga, it is desirable that the self should be isolated, and become unconscious of any object, wholly passionless and without purposes, so that personality gradually fades and the self becomes pure. This is the way of deliverance. In the highest state the adept "ceases to become conscious of any object."

Yet—a point which endeared Yoga to the children of the Transcendentalists—at this very moment the believer becomes possessed of all truth. It is not the result of an active and disciplined intelligence. It is "the flash of insight which does not pass . . . through the serial order of the usual process of experience." Possessing all truth, the Yogin knows the essence of things and sees them as they are. The critical faculty is rejected and knowledge with it, just as they were rejected by uneducated revivalists, by mesmerists, by Mrs. Eddy. This is the familiar rapture of the saint. According to St. Teresa, feeling as well as thinking must abdicate in the truly mystical communion. "The soul," she says, "is fully awake as regards God, but wholly asleep as regards things of this world and in respect of herself. During the short time the union lasts, she is as it were deprived of every feeling, and even if she would, she could not think of any single thing. Thus she needs to employ no artifice in order to arrest the use of her understanding: it remains so stricken with inactivity that she neither knows what she loves, nor in what manner she loves, nor what she wills. In short, she is utterly dead to the things of the world and lives solely in God. . . ." And again: "If our understanding comprehends, it is in a mode which remains unknown to it, and it can understand nothing of what it comprehends. For my own part, I do not believe that it does comprehend, because, as I said, it does not understand itself to do so." The activities of the mind are repudiated and, in their place, comes either a direct revelation from the outside or an impulse from the unconscious. The two are not as far apart as is often imagined. Suppress the activities of the mind, say the sutras, contemplate the wheel of the navel, and you will learn intuitively the arrangement of the body. Concentrate on the well of the throat, and hunger and thirst will cease.

Professor Leuba's criticism of Yoga notes the points of similarity and difference between oriental and Christian mysticism; but Yoga, as brought to America, was intended less for mystics than for nervous and idle women. One may turn to a less intelligent critic to see what compromise could be affected between the self-annihilating doctrine of the East and the aggressive common philosophy of America.

The rules of Yoga are inexorable: Stamp out ambition, stamp out desire of life, stamp out desire of comfort. But in America:

"The lesson to be learned from these rules is that we should rise above the incidents of personality, and strive to realize our individuality. That we should desire to realize the I AM consciousness, which is above the annoyances of personality. That we should learn that these things cannot hurt the Real Self—that they will be washed from the sands of time, bv the waters of eternity."

Yoga is another way of transcending, but it is a way unknown to Americans. The typical response to desire in an aggressive western country is to strive for satisfaction; the way of Orientalism is to seek the cessation of desire. One is the life of effort, the other the life of renunciation. The western mode is individualistic. The individual holds himself apart, sharply defined from others, making his own way. The mystic way is to deny distinctions, to say, I am thee and thou art me. The western is the way of research; the eastern, that of contemplation. The danger of the western attitude of mind is that it may glorify effort for its own sake (records, championships, firsts) and aggression for its cwn sake, and believe that personality is greater as it expands and becomes influential through possessions. But these are the excesses of its nature. The philosophy of the East, as the East has reason to know, is opposed utterly to taking and grasping. Chesterton has contrasted the Buddha with closed eyes, his mind turned inward, rapt in an objectless contemplation, with the eyes of the Christian martyr, bright and burning, turned outward upon the world. Even the ascetic cannot turn his eyes away and, for the common man in the West, nothing serious exists except the material universe. To the West, the mind is the instrument by which the world is conquered; in eastern mysticism, it is the instrument by which the world undermines and enslaves the individual.

What then could be the appeal to Americans of Yoga, and theosophy, and Bahaism, and the other forms of oriental mysticism? If we could assume that these ways of salvation were thoroughly understood and honestly practiced by western people, the answer would not be far to seek. We would say that, possessing the world, men had lost their souls and were trying to find their way back to God. Or that satiety had set in, after all our grasping and possessing, and that we wished to rid ourselves of our encumbrances. Or that our nervous systems had broken down under the flogging demands of daily life. Mysticism would then be our escape from the implications of our own materialistic philosophy. Without question, in isolated cases, this is precisely the function which the philosophy of the East has fulfilled.

But it is almost impossible to believe that the wholly undisciplined followers of New Thought could understand or seriously practice the discipline of Yoga. A decade after its vogue had begun, a half dozen other ways of escape were taking its place. Yoga was a fad and not a philosophy. It served actually to soothe exasperated nerves and to throw an aura of mystery over certain types of infidelism. For the most part, those who practiced it had not the faintest intention of giving up the world. Yoga was for them a mystic way of renouncing whatever was irritating and preserving whatever was pleasing. It was an elaborate game of pretense by which noisy people went into silence and distracted people imagined that they were concentrating. The glamor of renunciation suffused the picture which they had of themselves. Actually nothing was renounced and whatever was desired was lifted to a transcendental plane where it could be enjoyed a hundred-fold. No doubt the delusion was as effective as the actuality might have been. One fancies oneself becoming ageless and deathless, and full of perfection, sinking into eternal nothingness. And if, in fact, one was only resting a little and sinking into a perfumed bath the result was about the same. For Yoga had given a reason beyond reason. It had, in a strange way, transfigured the commonplaces of life. One was lifted successively to higher and higher planes of being, not knowing exactly what they were, but vaguely satisfied because they were higher. The little irritations of the world fell away. One was alone with the mysterious spirit and, breathing in a refined way, one returned to conquer the world.

# XXIV.

## Christian Science.

CHRISTIAN SCIENCE is the culmination not only of the religion of mental healing and of spiritualism in America, but of the whole process by which the ancient disciplines of society have been destroyed. It is perhaps possible by acrobatic feats of logic to reconcile formal Calvinism with the letter of Christian Science, but I do not know of any attempt to do this and no master of dialectics can persuade the average intelligent being that the two religions are not poles apart. Essentially, the religion of Edwards assumed the reality of death and of hell, or paradise, hereafter. It was a religion of fear and hope, not a religion of comfort. It found, in a way which seemed inhumanly cruel, a place for sin and evil and disease and, in spite of its harsh determinism, it left some room for moral effort. The religion founded by Mary Baker Eddy specifically ranked death as a synonym of Error and, while it accepted the Christian promise of redemption, it never believed in the reality of death itself. Possessing true belief, the Christian Scientist needs to suffer no anxiety; he has assurance in a religion of love which surpasses justice. There is no need to discover the use or function of evil and disease because Christian Science denies their existence and, in common with New Thought, substitutes the intensity of belief for the discipline of moral effort.

The sensitiveness to criticism of Christian Science is easily understood. Against Mrs. Eddy are brought modern equivalents of all the accusations which founders of religions have been compelled to meet. One of the sources of strength of Christian Science, its existence in modern times with the power of publicity to spread its doctrines, turns out to be a weakness. For publicity is, as Emerson called it, pitiless, when applied to trivial things, to slips in grammar, to business dealings, to a few inconsistencies, or to the common symptoms of religious hysteria. There is no glamor of distinction about Mrs. Eddy. In a time over-anxious to "humanize" its prophets, she remains all-too-human and, by her own insistence, she has made it virtually impossible to separate her private life from the doctrines of her church. That is the fatality of claiming divine inspiration. If you utter your doctrine exclusively with the tongues of angels and claim authority chiefly because of your source, you must be prepared to let the doctrine drop into oblivion the moment the authenticity of your voice is successfully challenged. So long as Mrs. Eddy lived, at least, Christian Science had to stand or fall as she stood or fell.

She not only stood; she withstood the most withering ridicule, the most bitter attacks on her intelligence and probity, the most thunderous declamations from established pulpits, the most logical discussions of her whole edifice. Against the claim of divine inspiration, which at times amounted to an imputation of equality between herself and Jesus Christ, was offered the testimony of witnesses who had seen the Quimby manuscripts. When she repudiated Quimby they printed her pathetic little poem:

Lines on The Death of Dr. P. P. Quimby Who Healed with the Truth That Christ Taught, in Contradistinction to All Isms.

Did sackcloth clothe the sun, and day grow night,—
    All matter mourn the hour with dewy eyes,—
When Truth, receding from our mortal sight,
    Has paid to error her last sacrifice?

Can we forget the power that gave us life?
    Shall we forget the wisdom of its way?
Then ask me not, amid this mortal strife,—
    This keenest pang of animated clay,—

To mourn him less. To mourn him more, were just,
    If to his memory 'twere a tribute given,
For every solemn, sacred, earnest trust
    Delivered to us ere he rose to heaven;

Heaven but the happiness of that calm soul,
    Growing in stature to the throne of God
Rest should reward him who hath made us whole,
    Seeking, though tremblers, where his footsteps trod.
                     —MARY M. PATTERSON.

*Lynn, January 22nd,* 1866.

When they accused her of being a charlatan, her disciples pointed to the record of the law courts and to the fact that their leader used little enough of the money she earned. And to the more serious charges against her, they might well claim that these were common form whenever a new religion began. Mark Twain, in 1907, devoted a book to a vicious attack on Christian Science on the very first page of which he wrote, "It is the first time since the dawn-days of creation that a Voice has gone crashing through space with such placid and complacent confidence and command." This is not a literally accurate statement. Confidence and command have characterized a hundred prophets and a hundred charlatans in every age. They prove nothing of falsehood or truth. Origin in fact seldom does but, even if Mark Twain's statement were true to the letter, it would only mean to the believer that no one before Mrs. Eddy had had such absolute command of the truth.

Christian Science is a modern religion in the sense that it is connected with no shrine and has no sacred relics. It is a religion that accords with railroads and large editions of books and cheap postage. It is not incongruous that a rather fanatic group of Christian Scientists should have offered to broadcast, not only the doctrine, but the actual cures by radio. For the miracles of Christian Science, as compared with those of primitive Christianity, are performed by large-scale production. One almost expects interchangeable cures. And in keeping with this, the most vicious attack on Mrs. Eddy has had to do not with her religion, but with her financial success. Thus in America, which is supposed by foreigners to make a religion of Business, it was considered an impropriety to make a business out of religion. It was held against Mrs. Eddy that, in seven years, according to her own account, she had four thousand pupils each of whom paid $300—a total of $1,200,000, which ought to have assured her respect in financial circles. The price of three weeks' tuition at the Massachusetts Metaphysical College was not lowered when the course was reduced to seven lessons and Mrs. Eddy is quoted as having said, "This amount greatly troubled me. I shrank from asking it, but was finally led by a strange providence to accept this fee. God has since shown me in multitudinous ways the wisdom of this decision." She was accused of chicanery in regard to the mortgage covering the land on which the First Church stands and of ingratitude for not reimbursing those who lent her money to publish *Science and Health,* even after that book had sold a quarter of a million copies. On one occasion, the work of healing was suspended and it became obligatory for all good Scientists to buy a new edition of *Science and Health,* which is reported to have contained only one minor change in a single sentence. There was a traffic in spoons at $5 for gold plate and $3 for silver, both equally effective, as a token of grace, because there was a representation of Mrs. Eddy's home in the bowl and of her alert and earnest face on the handle. In December, 1878, Mrs. Eddy's husband was indicted for conspiracy to murder Daniel A. Spofford, who had been accused by a disciple of Mrs. Eddy of causing pain and illness by the exercise of "malicious animal magnetism." It is always said that Mrs. Eddy managed to get rid of those healers who, by publishing explanations of *Science and Health,* threatened to cut into the revenues of the mother church, and of those who became so adept and influential as to threaten the position of the Mother herself. So runs the first group of charges and it is easy to see how much more they are based on interpretation of facts than on facts themselves. Even if they were all true, they would not belittle the truth of Christian Science any more than the love affairs of Goethe detract from the poetry of *Faust.*

§

The second line of attack on Christian Science is that it is silly. Here Mark Twain, as was to be expected, found himself at home. He calls Mrs. Eddy the most erratic and contradictory and untrustworthy witness that has occupied the stand since the days of Ananias. He mentions the story of a fatally injured horse restored to health by the application of Christian Science and exclaims, "I can stand a good deal, but I recognize that the ice is getting thin here. That horse had as many as fifty claims; how could he demonstrate over them? Could he do the All-Good, Good-Gracious, Liver, Bones, Truth, All down but nine, Set them up in the Other Alley? Could he intone the Scientific Statement of Being? Now, could he? Wouldn't it give him a relapse? Let us draw the line at horses. Horses and furniture."

He tells the story of "little Gordon who 'came into the world without the assistance of surgery or anesthetics.' He was a 'demonstration.' A painless one; therefore, his coming evoked 'joy and thankfulness to God and the Discoverer of Christian Science.' This is a noticeable feature of this literature—the so frequent linking together of the two Bibles. When little Gordon was two years old, 'he was playing horse on the bed, where I had left my 'little book.' I noticed him stop in his play, take the book carefully in his little hands, kiss it softly, then look about for the highest place of safety his arms could reach and put it there.' This pious act filled the mother 'with such a train of thought as I had never experienced before. I thought of the sweet mother of long ago who kept things in her heart,' etc. It is a bold comparison; however, unconscious profanations are about as common in the mouths of the lay membership of the new Church as are frank and open ones in the mouths of its consecrated chiefs."

He examines the four fundamentals of Christian Science:

"1. God is all.
"2. God is good.
"3. God, Spirit being all, nothing is matter.
"4. Life, God, omnipotent Good deny death, Evil, sin, disease. Disease, Sin, Evil, Death deny Good, Omnipotent God, Life."

And he almost shrieks with delight over Mrs. Eddy's statement that these "will be found to agree in statement and proof even if read backwards." Other critics mark the meaningless jumble of words which Mrs. Eddy used with such zeal and swing and assurance that they have a persuasive effect regardless of the meaning. Thus a Catholic critic notes that:

"Issachar, Jacob's son, is defined as corporeal belief; Jacob himself as a corporeal mortal embracing duplicity, repentance, sensualism, and yet—mirabile dictu—representing at the same time Inspiration and the Revelation of Science (Christian Science of course); Jerusalem becomes mortal belief and knowledge, obtained from the five corporeal senses; Jesus is the highest human corporeal concept of the divine idea; Joseph is, like Jacob, a corporeal mortal, but with a higher sense of Truth, rebuking mortal belief or error; Judah is, like Issachar, only more so a corporeal material belief progressing and disappearing, while at the same time it is the spiritual understanding of God and man appearing."

Critics also point to the fact that Mrs. Eddy swung herself out of the normal orbit of consequence and proof by the simple process of defining her own terms. Thus she says:

"I named it Christian, because it is compassionate, helpful, and spiritual. God I called immortal Mind. That which sins, suffers, and dies I named mortal mind. The physical senses, or sensuous nature, I called error and shadow. Soul I denominated Substance, because soul alone is truly substantial. God I characterized as individual entity, but His corporeality I denied. The Real I claimed as eternal; and its antipodes, or the temporal, I described as unreal. Spirit I called the reality; and matter, the unreality."

One is reminded of some of the mad passages in *Alice in Wonderland,* but Mrs. Eddy herself recognized the difficulty and blamed it on the "inadequacy of material terms," a strange echo of Jonathan Edwards' complaint that words contradict themselves, and a strange forerunner of modernistic theories of literary expression. Mrs. Eddy reported that she had been a rather precocious pupil, making natural philosophy, logic, and moral science her favorite studies, and learning something of Hebrew, Greek, and Latin, but "after my discovery of Christian Science most of the knowledge I gleaned from school books vanished like a dream. Learning was so illumined that grammar was eclipsed. Etymology was divine history, voicing the idea of God in man's origin and signification. Syntax was spiritual order and unity. Prosody the song of angels. . . ."

This was no doubt convenient and parallels exactly the experience of teachers of Mesmerism who advised their pupils earnestly to forget all they knew of ordinary physics and chemistry. Hugo Münsterberg, wholly unsympathetic as he is, does not find *Science and Health* silly. He says that the system is by no means unskillfully constructed and implies that if Mrs. Eddy had had more aptitude in expression it might have been much more effective.

Beyond these external objections, there are two more serious charges. The first is that Christian Science is not in any way original. Münsterberg says that "one who is familiar with the history of philosophy will find in it not one original thought." The obligation to Quimby is insisted upon although Mrs. Eddy, confronted by articles in praise of Quimby "purporting" to be hers, said that she might have written them while she was under the influence of "mesmeric treatment" by the Portland doctor. It is also known that, when Quimby died, Mrs. Eddy wanted H. W. Dresser, a leader of New Thought, to take his place and would not then make any claims for herself. A more illuminating light on the sources of Christian Science is found in the religion of the Shakers whose great prophetess, Ann Lee, was considered as the female principle of God and identified as the woman of the Apocalypse. She was called Mother Ann and claimed the gift of healing, and the Shakers called their first establishment the Mother Church. In all of these points Milmine, an historian of Christian Science, has found sufficient parallels to justify his assertion that the Shaker colony near Mrs. Eddy's childhood home strongly influenced the character of her own religion. These criticisms take us by marked stages closer to the heart of Christian Science. The next one is that Christian Science is blasphemous. (It may be said in advance that it is only blasphemous if it is not true.) Mrs. Eddy frequently wrote her name in the same line with that of the Virgin Mary and the Saviour, confusing Mark Twain by the arrangement since he could not tell whether she meant to place herself above one or both of them. In *Christ and Christmas*, by Mrs. Eddy, there was a picture of Christ holding the hand of a woman in whose other hand was a scroll marked Christian Science. Women disciples of the new church upon several occasions claimed to have been blessed with virgin births * and the height of blasphemy, to the orthodox, is in the Christian Science version of the Lord's Prayer, especially in the invocation:

"1. Our Father-Mother God, all harmonious.
 2. Admirable One.
 3. Thy kingdom is within us; Thou art ever present.
 4. Enable us to know—as in heaven, so on earth—God is supreme.
 5. Give us grace for to-day; feed the famished affections.
 6. And infinite Love is reflected in love.
 7. And Love leadeth us not into temptation, but delivereth us from sin, disease and death.
 8. For God is now and forever all Life, Truth and Love."

* "In June, 1890, Mrs. Woodbury gave birth to a son, whom she proclaimed, Mr. Woodbury not dissenting, to have been conceived by mental generation, in accordance with the doctrine of Christian Science."—Frank Podmore, in *Mesmerism and Christian Science*.

This brings us to the heart of Christian Science where we may leave objections behind and examine only the intentions of the new cult and its relations with the other unorthodox movements of the time. The connection with spiritualism is obvious; it is precisely the same as the connection between spiritualism and Quimby, and it hardly needs the corroborating evidence of Mrs. Eddy's brief term as a spiritualistic clairvoyant before she founded Christian Science. She indicated her relation to the characteristic thought of her day when she announced her purpose "to relieve the suffering of humanity, by a sanitary system that should include all moral and religious reform," and her inclination to faddishness when she protested against giving babies their daily bath and said that "bathing and rubbing to alter secretions or remove unhealthy exhalation from the cuticle receive useful rebuke from Christian healing." That nature is always good, always healthy, always informed by a moral order, which man must discover and conform to, is as implicit in Christian Science as in transcendentalism and New Thought. And Christian Science is essentially a religion of perfection, without the theology of Noyes, and with a strong tendency to identify moral and physical perfection with the ineffable purity and power of God.

The methods of Christian Science are so subject to ridicule that they have obscured the essence of its teaching. To call pain an error, to deny the existence of evil, to proclaim that disease and deformity can be willed, thought, or wished away, significant as these things are in Christian Science, were not its philosophical essence. Ascetics and pagans have both attempted in their several ways to rid their lives of these same factors of unhappiness, just as there have been Puritans who attempted to kill all elements of joy and who rejoiced in the mortifications and indignities of common existence. Absent treatment and mental healing are the proofs which a pragmatic age demanded of the truth of Christian Science. It worked, it brought religion as an active force into daily life as a way of guaranteeing health and happiness. It infused warmth into the inert body of science and it gave scientific, even if pseudo-scientific, corroboration to the imperiled mysteries of Christianity. There were thousands who fell away from orthodox creeds because these failed adequately to reconcile the common facts of misery and failure, of disease and death, with the protecting benevolence of an almighty

God. And when these thousands turned their minds, still habituated to the Christian mythology, to science, they found it incapable of satisfying their ultimate demands. It is quite possible that no combination of words in the thousands of names of sects has ever been more canny and more finely calculated in psychological appeal than the name of Christian Science. In the person of the healer, Christian Science retained all that was powerful in the doctrines which stem from mesmerism. In the cold, rigid solemnity of the church, it kept the advantage of ritual. Through Mrs. Eddy it afforded the longed-for human touch and, at the same time, a fore-taste of divinity.

§

To what end? The closer one comes to the core of Christian Science the more one is impressed by a sense of its strangeness, the more one is compelled to retreat before it, in order to examine the essence of other religions, and find an adequate basis of comparison. Christian Science is confusing because, with all its novelty, it accepts the Christian idea of a redeemer. "No person," says Mrs. Eddy, "can compass or fulfill the individual mission of Jesus of Nazareth." His mission in all Christian theology is that of a Saviour, or Redeemer. But what can his mission be to a world in which sin is only error? The idea of redemption is found in many religions outside of Christianity. Persephone and Adonis are redeemers no less than Jesus and, in all theologies, the God who dies and lives again shares this function. Pagan and Christian alike have felt the bitter reality of evil, the misery of earthly existence and the terror of death. In one way or another, they have looked for an atonement of sin which brought these evils into the world. Or if they were less conscious of sin, they have hoped for some intercession and some mediation between them and their Gods. But the moment misery and evil are denied, the moment their acute and burdensome reality is declared an illusion, the function of the intercessor and the redeemer is logically at an end. One feels that Christ remains in the theology of Christian Science for another purpose. It is his thaumaturgy that makes him precious. As in the religion of business Christ has been called the first rotarian, and in the religion of altruism, the first socialist, so, in Christian Science, he is the first, the greatest, the supreme worker of miracles. Lazarus was raised from the dead—it is a familiar interpretation—so that there might be hope for all men; but only Lazarus, so that no man would presume. But in Christian Science there is no body, and no body of this death.

And there at last is the pivot and center of Christian Science. The organized religions and even the independent ways in which men face the plight of existence may be roughly divided into two classes. There are the religions which we too broadly call pagan and pantheistic, which exalt fertility and take joy in life, averting their eyes from a cold and rather insignificant existence after death. In some of these, the stress on the present is so marked that they become purely materialistic, exclaim that nothing exists but the world we see and touch and experience, and that death is the end. Other religions are essentially life-fearing. They seek death as the enviable culmination of a miserable existence. In them death is the return to the eternal Good. It is harps and halos, or an endless day without passions, disease, or gratifications. Buddha, "seeking relief from the tedious impermanence of personal experience," and the gluttonous Epicurean, seeking endless gratifications through his experience, stand at opposite poles. And it is the mark of Christianity, in some of its forms, that it approves or permits a degree of earthly happiness while it robs death of its ultimate terrors. The joy of St. Francis impresses us as more genuine than the pleasures of an epicurean emperor. But the debased Christianity of modern times is, in dogma, a death-seeking religion.

Not so Christian Science, which denies the reality of the body and is compelled to deny the reality of the body's death. Here we arrive at a peculiar paradox. For, while Christian Science denies the reality of death, it also opposes itself to a great part of the reality of life. To a rhapsodist like Nietzsche, the very brutality and pain of life is part of its essence, adding dignity and magnificence. The tragic sense of life, and the feeling of life as a great tragedy, have been held precious by pagan and Protestant and Catholic. To deny these elements is, in a serious sense, to diminish and belittle human destiny.

The negation in Christian Science goes deeper still. It is one of the many religions which is, in essence, opposed to life, to fertility and procreation, to the basic functions of sex. Logically, a religion which banishes death might well be either a cult of sensual indulgence or a cult of holy motherhood. Christian Science is neither. Sometimes explicitly, and sometimes in vague tendencies, it stands against the manifestation of sex. It does not stand alone. In German mysticism, and Yoga, in some cults of Perfectionism and the Shakers, we find versions of the same doctrine. The Rappites believed that Adam, before the creation of Eve, combined in himself both sexual elements. The Shakers, refraining like the Rappites from sexual intercourse, held that Ann Lee was the female principle of God, and prayed to "our Father and Mother who art in Heaven." Of Ramakrashna, Jules Bois writes, "He adored the feminine principle in Divinity. The divine mother was for him the supreme God nameless and without form, in personal tenderness and inexhaustible love." And the perfectionists, as we have noted, ran through every variety of dogma denouncing sexual intercourse and restraining procreation. In Christian Science we find this hostility to the sexual impulse erected into a divine principle. It is perhaps accounted for by Mrs. Eddy's two unhappy marriages and by the recurrences after her son was born of the fits of hysteria with which she was afflicted as a child. But beyond the personal reasons, or possibly fortifying them, there was the common cult which insisted upon denying all differences between the sexes. To a certain type of mind, the idea of difference and of opposition is displeasing. There must be only harmony and oneness. Not procreative intercourse of male and female, nor the equilibrium between positive and negative, nor the duality of right and wrong and good and evil, but the destruction of these oppositions in the creation of the One. Mrs. Eddy applied this principle to sex. She did not forbid, but she discouraged marriage. She said that "Jesus was the offspring of Mary's subconscious communion with God" and like Thomas Lake Harris made it clear that she expected virgin births to become quickly more common and eventually to be the rule. From some of the observations and discoveries of Professor Agassiz, Mrs. Eddy derived extraordinary proof of the truth of Christian Science:

"The propagation of their species without the male element, by butterfly, bee, and moth, is a discovery corroborative of the Science of Mind, because it shows that the origin and continuance of these insects rest on Principle, apart from material conditions. An egg never was the origin of a man, and no seed ever produced a plant. . . . The belief that life can be in matter, or soul in body, and that man springs from dust or from an egg, is the brief record of mortal error. . . . The plant grows not because of seed or soil."

In this we have the pure originality of Christian Science— a conception of humanity almost without appetites, rejecting natural birth and absolved of natural death. Stated in these terms Christian Science is neither absurd nor unique. It answers a deep desire in some human souls. Whether that desire itself is desirable, and whether those souls are sick or well, is another question.*

* While this book was being prepared for the press, a series of astonishing advertisements appeared in the New York *World*. In the first of these Mrs. Augusta E. Stetson, most famous of Mrs. Eddy's disciples and head of the chief dissenting sect of Christian Scientists, specifically declared that she herself is immortal and that Mrs. Eddy will presently manifest herself again on earth. This announcement, and others which followed, precipitated a controversy between orthodox and dissenting Christian Scientists. The leaders of the First Church repudiated Mrs. Stetson's conception of immortality. The head of the Publication Committee for the state of New York, Edgar Grant Gyger, said, in the New York *Times* of August 2, 1927, that "Christian Scientists at the present time accept the inevitability of death." Two days later a prophet, Carl Gluck, of Oakland, California, announced that Mrs. Eddy had already been born again, was, in fact, now twelve years old, living as a little girl, unaware of her future mission, "in the western part of the United States." Mr. Gluck's statement was based on an interpretation of the poem, *Christ and Christmas*. Mrs. Stetson, in a later announcement, said, "I, Augusta E. Stetson, C.S.D., by the spiritual authority which has been vested in me by my Teacher and Leader, Mary Baker Eddy, do now, once again, proclaim to the Christian Science field, and to universal mankind, that Mary Baker Eddy lives, and that she will reappear, for she is the ever-present Christ, the Son-Daughter of God, who is eternal Life and Love."

She also quotes many passages from Mrs. Eddy's writings, especially from volumes less known than *Science and Health*, to prove her statement that Mrs. Eddy denied the actuality of death. The thought of death, one gathers, is due to a false conception of creation. The "Adam-Eve" creation is false. The true creation is that of Adam created in the image of God, without the separation of the sexes. The true creation is spiritual: "I have never held," writes Mrs. Stetson, "that 'flesh and blood' will 'return to earth,' or, indeed, that Mary Baker Eddy ever lived in matter, flesh, and blood. I have always taught, as she taught me, that man is now, always has been, and forever will be, spiritual and immortal. . . ."

The fact that, to a great number of disciples, Mrs. Eddy seemed to teach literal immortality and to deny the corporeal existence of sexual man, is the chief issue of the controversy. A minor point is the complete identification of Mrs. Eddy with Christ— minor because it seems, so far, to be the idea of Mrs. Stetson alone. Some support is given to the idea, however, by interpretations of the pictures in *Christ and Christmas*, for one of which, at least, Mrs. Eddy herself posed. These interpretations also reveal the precise moment of the rebirth of Mrs. Eddy, according to Gluck, and are otherwise too involved for lay interpretation. The poem was withdrawn shortly after its original publication because the pictures in it were beginning to be used as talismans and to effect cures. Mrs. Eddy recorded the fact that a child, merely by looking at one of the illustrations, had been healed. Three of the illustrations which, according to Mrs. Eddy, were compared to Botticelli and perfect in art, were used as designs for stained glass windows in the Mother's Room of the original Mother Church in Boston, a room now closed to the public.

Long after Mrs. Stetson's announcement, the Christian Science Parent Church (the Church of the Transforming Covenant) with addresses in Washington and London, published in the *World* an appeal to "its beloved brethren of the outdated counterfeit Boston organization to return to Mrs. Eddy's system of organization in time to avert further catastrophe." The details of the catastrophe are interesting:

"According to statistics published by Mary Baker Eddy in 1896, Christian Science under legitimate organization had proved so effective within the circle of her five thousand students, nearly all of whom were middle aged, that only fourteen deaths occurred in a period of nearly thirty years." Yet, of the four hundred and sixty-two persons holding the degrees of C.S.B. and C.S.D. [i.e., graduates of the Metaphysical College and presumable practitioners of Christian Science] sixty per cent. have died since the decease of Mrs. Eddy in 1910. This "appalling mortality" is ascribed to "illegitimate Christian Science"; briefly, the increase in the death rate of Christian Scientists, leaders and followers alike, is due to the fact that, since Mrs. Eddy passed away, Scientists have accepted false doctrine. Further:

"Mrs. Eddy taught that the mind of an individual affects his body for good and ill. She also taught that the individual mind is influenced by the convictions of the majority in any circle within which he is bound. Death is caused by a majority of human beliefs that man must die, and a change in general belief will cause a change in human experience."

The advertisement ends with the statement that "Legitimate Christian Science, under scientific government, maintains health and happiness and unfolds immortality."

The numerical strength of the particular dissentients who inserted this announcement is not given. One gathers from it further evidence that Christian Scientists, outside the parent church, tend to believe that Mrs. Eddy taught immortality in the strictest and most literal terms. And also that the belief in the circle of emanations, the possibility of harm being done by projecting evil thoughts, which comes down from Mesmer to New Thought, is no stranger to Christian Science. The distinction between New Thought and Christian Science in this respect is that the latter, possessing a Church, stresses belief in immortality; the former, without a discipline, stresses the will.

In the later stages of the controversy started by Mrs. Stetson, it was claimed that Mrs. Eddy asserted her power over the forces of nature, had a special group of disciples to attend to the weather (particularly to avert snowstorms) and *had restored life to a favorite disciple after he had been dead for some time*. As all these revelations lack official authority, they cannot be used as the basis for criticism of Christian Science; but so far as they are in keeping with the essential principles of Christian Science they serve legitimately as signposts to the inevitable, though possibly unconscious, intentions of Mrs. Eddy's teaching.

# XXV.

## The Kingdom of God in Chicago.

IN what proportions the souls of Matthias, Moody, Quimby, and John Humphrey Noyes entered into the composition of John Alexander Dowie is too delicate a question for me to solve. He was an impostor, an extraordinary organizer, and an exceptional evangelist. In 1899, he declared himself a messenger of God's covenant. In 1901, he added to that the affirmation that he was the reincarnation of Elijah. In 1904, he consecrated himself first apostle announcing that, in 1906, he would consecrate the other members of the Apostolic college. A somewhat terrified church, fearing that he would announce himself as Christ incarnate, deposed him before this last step could be taken. The divine healing which he practiced then came to an end and, in 1907, he died. The rapid audacity of his aggrandizement, as shown by these dates, is characteristic. For, to the business of being Christ's messenger on earth, Dowie brought an unparalleled energy, a maniacal haste, and the business methods of a Get-Rich-Quick-Wallingford. Since the time of Brigham Young, there had been no phenomenon like the growth of the Christian Catholic Apostolic Church in Zion. A cynical foreigner, observing the phenomenon, would say that, at last, the business methods of the United States had created the perfect American religion. John Alexander Dowie was, however, born in Edinburgh, Scotland, and did not land in the United States until he was forty-one years old (in 1888). He had already labored for many years in Australia and New Zealand on his "worldwide work for God and for humanity." His pretensions to divine inspiration equal those of Mrs. Eddy. The foulness of his language makes the speech of a Billy Sunday prim in comparison. His business acumen brought him the respect of Chicago bankers. The community and the Church he founded summed up and burlesqued the American sects and the communities of a century. But he was in no sense a product of the American revival system nor was he directly affected by the breakdown in religious authority which followed those revivals. His disciples, however, were. They flocked to him from all the collapsing cults. For thirteen years he made himself, by violence and chicanery, and by a degree of self-hypnotism almost without parallel, the outstanding prophet of the country, as preposterous a figure as Carry Nation, who hated him for the publicity he got.

Dowie first went into business in Adelaide, Australia, but returned to Edinburgh for four years' study at the University and after that, in South Australia, was ordained as minister in the Congregational Church. He discovered his ability to heal the sick by the laying on of hands and, in 1882, went to Melbourne where he accomplished in a small way what he afterwards did on a large scale in Chicago. He established a Church, built a tabernacle, and founded the International Divine Healing Association under whose auspices he did mission work in the Antipodes and later on the Pacific coast. In 1893, he came to Chicago and, with characteristic appreciation of the opportunities of the site, built a tabernacle just outside the grounds of the World's Fair.

He had already published a little book called *American First Fruits* in which the results of his early labors were set down. A union of pastors on the Pacific coast having condemned his doctrine of healing, he issued a violent reply, reinforced by a sufficient number of public testimonials from women who not only were cured, but were made to love Christ better, and from doctors and business men who were cured and were not therefore "inclined to scoff at religion." In Chicago, the cures and the conquests came more rapidly and Dowie soon felt himself hampered by the International Association he had founded. He was going into business with a press, and a bank, and a college, and a hospice of healing. For a focus and center he needed a Church. As Matthias was commanded to find, Dowie received word from God to found and, in 1896, the Christian Catholic Church, to which the name Apostolic was later added, was founded in Chicago with Dowie as General Overseer. The Church, which was to prepare for the kingdom of God and held fast to the conventional idea of the present coming of Christ, had a three-fold gospel: salvation, healing, and holy living. Dowie was of such a pugnacious temperament that he spent most of his time in attacking the enemies of a holy life, from oysters to walking delegates. His art of healing, while he magnified it and undoubtedly lied about it, was generally used as a sort of advertisement for the Church. As for salvation it was conventionally sought.

The comparative specific gravity of these three principles in the theology of Dowie may be judged from a single tragic incident. A daughter, to whom he was devoted, lit a spirit lamp in order to heat some curling irons and her loose nightgown caught the flame. She was so horribly burned that she died, after twelve hours of mortal agony, without the attendance of a doctor, since doctors were forbidden in the holy living of the Church. Heartbroken, Dowie said over his daughter's grave, "She was a good girl, but she disobeyed me. I forbade the use of alcohol in any form, she violated my command, and she has been punished for it." The prohibition of alcohol to which he alluded was that of the ordinary opponent of liquor but, in his explanation, Dowie was specifically putting a holy life, that is, a life led in accordance with his commandments, above even his own power to heal.

The Church was, of course, primitive and restorationist. In 1902, Dowie organized the Theocratic Party as a political unit, including all the citizens of his city, and, in the platform, summed up the moral basis of the Church in the declaration "that the Holy Scriptures which contain the ten commandments, and the inspired Gospel of Jesus, the Christ the son of God, constitute the principles of all righteous government for the individual, for the nation, and for the whole world." To Dowie, the Bible was not only literally true but universally binding. It was the source of every law governing every human activity. Thus, within sight of the abattoirs of Chicago, he preached a violent crusade against the eating of pork. He denied that the vision of St. Peter taught us to sweep away the distinction between animals clean and unclean; for him, the story of the Gadarene swine was the last recorded statement of our obligation. He proved that swine were possessed of the devil by the fact that "our Lord Jesus Christ . . . never healed a case of cancer," adding that cancer was not known in Palestine at that time and "is unknown now in countries where swine's flesh is not eaten." He insisted that the pig eats rattlesnakes, "Yea, more, as I have said, it swallows the whole thing from snout to tail" and that, in eating pork, "you eat cholera, and trichinosis, and tuberculosis, and scrofula, and cancer, and all kinds of foul diseases."

The idea that cancer is the devil was entirely in keeping with Dowie's theory of disease. He did not, like Christian Science, refuse to recognize it; to him disease was real, present, and dangerous. It was evil, the devil, or the devil's child. There was but one way to cure disease—by prayer, which casts out the devil and purifies us of sin, after which it is impossible for disease to have hold upon us. The only condition is that one must have faith; and it was not in Dowie's temperament to tolerate a divided allegiance, so that there were neither drugs nor doctors in the City of Zion. For a year the physicians of Chicago had been persecuting Dowie under a municipal ordinance regulating hospitals. Dowie faced over a hundred charges and, by carrying a test case to a higher court, had the ordinance declared invalid. When he founded his own city he took his revenge by banishing all physicians entirely. In the tabernacle he asked a thousand women, "If you knew you were going to die in your next confinement would you want a doctor?" and the *Zion Banner* reports that the answer was "no." It would have availed them little if they had answered "yes," for Zion City was ruled with an iron hand and lay under the terror of an intricate spy system. In *A Voice from Zion*, one of the many official publications, we find an attack on the miracles at Lourdes and doctors are dealt with under the heading of "You Dirty Boy":

" 'The saved and healed shall walk in God's way of Holiness, praise His name.' (Amen)

" 'And an highway shall be there, and a way, and it shall be called the way of holiness; the unclean shall not pass over it.'

"You stink-pots! You'll not get there. (Laughter)

"You whiskey-pots, what business have you on God's Highway of Holiness?

"It is no place for you.

"You who are full of digitalis, nux vomica, arsenic, strychnine, cocaine, Mother Siegal's Soothing Syrup, Carter's Little Liver Pills, Pink Pills for Pale People, and Pale Pills for Pink People. (Laughter.) It is no place for you.

"What are you going to do on that road, ye who are full of deadly drugs, disease and uncleanness? Get rid of your dirt and muck, of sin and of disease, and of the dirty, filthy drugs, and of the effect of the unclean hands of these unclean devils who get foolish legislators to pass laws which give them power over humanity from the cradle to the grave. We repudiate these illegal enactments.

" 'But it shall be for those—' when they are cleansed; thank God, they can be made clean.

"We want this 'dirty boy' to be clean. The Lord scrub him to-day. (Laughter) Thank God, He can make the filthiest clean. May the dirty doctors repent and be made clean. The Lord scrub them to-day. Let all the people say Amen.

"Audience:—'Amen!' (This came as a 'sound of many waters' from the thousands present.)

"Dr. Dowie:—That is right.

"A voice:—Hallelujah, Dowie!

"Dr. Dowie:—I am on the road. (Laughter and applause.)"

§

It would be almost impossible to catalogue all of the things which Dowie hated and forbade. In the first issue of the *Zion Banner*, "a weekly-semi-secular paper devoted to the extension of the kingdom of God and the elevation of man," there is a badly drawn cartoon showing "Zion unfurling her banner for the conquest of the world for God." The motley host in opposition includes figures or banners representing war, drama, society, lust, Romanism, the mob rule of the Masons (with a phallic symbol on their banner), the unclean press, boss rule, trades unions, hog raisers, doctors, tobacco dealers (the package of chewing tobacco is marked "bread of hell"), druggists (represented as sorcerers), and rum sellers. But this is not all. In the advertisements for Zion City we read that there were no harlots' dens, or gambling hells, or opium joints, or secret lodges, or theaters, or oyster bars, and, in a 330-page book by the Reverend John Alex. Dowie, Elijah the Restorer, he attacks Protected Adultery and Impurity in the Home, the Devilish Spirit of the Daily Newspaper Press, the Polluted Advertisements of the Modern Religious Press, Church Apostasy, and Contempt for God's Messenger, Unscriptural Baptism (he believed in triune immersion), Craftiness in Devouring the Patrimony of Widows and Orphans, and the Blighting Influence on the Young of Bad Books and Pic-

tures. There was no dancing in Zion City and billboards warned
visitors that "swearing, smoking and bad language of any sort are
not allowed." He anticipated, in short, the complete program of
the puritan of 1927 and erected his dislikes into a system of religion.

The success of this religion is startling. The stout little figure
of Dowie with its bright bald dome fringed by black hair and set
off by the conventional patriarchal beard of white was, to the believers, a messiah. Through him they were in communication with
God and, more important to them, with Christ, the healer; but the
price paid for this immediacy of relationship was high. Mrs. Eddy
gave her disciples unalloyed happiness, but all that Dowie offered in
normal life was negative, and it was a triumph of intelligence for
him to transform his negations into a positive crusade. He made each
member of the Church a hater of the things denied. He gave his
community the sense of living in a beleaguered city out of which, at
great peril, they made sorties against the besiegers. Their purity and
their God were always in danger and Dowie played on this endlessly. He reprinted all the vicious attacks made upon him and so
became more precious in the eyes of his followers and more justified in the tyrannical powers he assumed. He was in everything an
absolute dictator and justified himself by the fury of his enemies.
When he declared himself the messenger prophesied in Malachi
he said, "I have the right to stand here and say in Zion you have
to do what I tell you! Oh! the whole church? Yes! the whole
church—Presbyterian, Congregational, Baptist, Episcopal. It is the
most daring thing I ever said. The time has come; I tell the church
universal everywhere, you have to do what I tell you, do you hear?
You have to do what I tell you, because I am the Messenger of
God's covenant."

Again two years later, when he took the next step in identification, his first words were another command: "You have to do what
I tell you, because what I tell you is in accordance with that word,
and because I am the Messenger of the Covenant, Elijah the Restorer."

He created the Zion Restoration Host, numbering as many as
10,000 in all parts of the world, and used it as a sort of flying wedge
under the following extraordinary oath:

"I vow in the name of God, my Father, and of Jesus Christ, His Son and my Saviour and of the Holy Ghost, who proceeds from the Father and the Son, that I will be a faithful member of Zion Restoration Host, organized at Shiloh Tabernacle in the city of Zion on Lord's Day, September 21, 1902, and I declare that I recognize John Alexander Dowie, General Overseer of the C.C.C. in Zion, of which I am a member, in his three-fold office, as the Messenger of the Covenant, the Prophet foretold by Moses, and Elijah the Restorer.

"I promise to the fullest extent of my powers, to obey all rightful orders issued by him directly or by his properly appointed officers, and to proceed to any part of the world, wherever he shall direct, as a member of Zion Restoration Host, and that all family ties and obligations, and all relations to all human governments shall be held subordinate of this vow, this declaration and this promise. This I make in the presence of God and of the visible and invisible witnesses."

Command over the lives of the ordinary members of the church was not so definite, but he drew from them a tithe of their earnings. He dictated the way of their lives and virtually compelled them to work in the factories he built at the comparatively liberal wage he chose to pay. In time of stringency, he ordered them to deposit money in the bank of which he was the head, saying: "I have a list of all persons in Zion who have made no deposit since I sent out my first command, and I tell you we have no use for them. If they don't show down to-morrow they will be expelled from Zion. I am not afraid of the financial condition of Zion. I do not know what fear is. The member of Zion who fears to put his money into our hands for safe keeping is a coward and we have no use for him here. He must get out. We can't have him here for he is opposing the Lord by refusing to entrust his wealth in Zion."

And, in the same year, he ordered Dowieites from all parts of the world to sell what they had and to bring their fortunes to Zion City. Like many other founders of communities he had a yearning for Mexico, a country favorable to his health, and one of his last enterprises was the Zion Paradise Plantation there. To it he compelled the individuals and the industries of Zion City to contribute money they could not spare. As one reads the advertising literature of the community, one finds Dowie's name at the head of every enterprise. He bought nearly 7,000 acres of land and, dedicating it to God, held the property in his own hands, leasing it for a term of 1,100 years at high prices. He was in charge of the Zion City general stores, and president of the educational institutions, and director of the lace industries, and president of the building and manufacturing association which took in all the activities of Zion City. Even the sugar and confectionery business bore his name at the head, and he managed the bank and the publishing house as certainly as he bossed the Theocratic Party he founded. He permitted no question of his divine inspiration. If his healing proved anything, it proved his right to command the lives and fortunes of every man who accepted his leadership: "If my ministry is from heaven, you must believe what I say and you must do what I want. God has sent a man and he has written his mission over twenty-three years. What more do you want? I tell you, it is an awful thing to have a message from God. . . . It is an awful thing to stand between the living and the dead, but it has been laid upon me. You have to do what I tell you, because what I tell you is in accordance with that Word, and because I am the Messenger of God's Covenant."

Even when he was approaching disaster, he compelled every voter in Zion City to cast his ballot for Roosevelt in 1904.

Dowie's high moment was at the creation of Zion City. With a great flourish, he compared himself to Carnegie, Frick, and Rockefeller and announced the purchase of the site on Lake Michigan, 42 miles from Chicago. One year from the day the land was consecrated, the gates were opened and, within ten months, Zion City was incorporated under the laws of the state. Dowie had built himself a great tower from which he intended to take the largest photograph ever made and to look down upon his people. Actually, the first important edifice in the City was the lace factory, the story of which illustrates almost all of Dowie's characteristics. The hysterical style of his own publication gives a rather incomplete account:

"Five years before, the 'Little White Dove,' *Leaves of Healing,* had gone forth across the ocean with its Message of Salvation, Healing, and Holy Living.

"It had gone into the hands of a family of brothers in far-away Nottingham, England.

"The truth of the Everlasting Gospel which that little Messenger of God brought to them found an answering echo in their hearts.

"They believed that Zion was of God.

"They were skilled and successful manufacturers of lace. They understood perfectly every detail of the business.

"As the years went by, God prepared them for the wonderful purposes which He had in view for them, and when Zion City was announced His Spirit put in their hearts the desire to come to America and to engage in the manufacture of lace in Zion for God.

"One of the brothers came to Zion in Chicago and preliminary arrangements were made.

"The General Overseer purchased the Lace Factory near Nottingham, England, for Zion, and preparations were pushed rapidly to completion for bringing the factory to America. . . .

"The annual imports of lace to this country amount to eighteen millions of dollars, and the enemy recognized that with that great market for its product, Zion Lace Industries would quickly become one of the greatest manufacturing institutions in the country.

"Every attempt was made to throw suspicion upon the motives of the General Overseer, to belittle Zion Lace Industries and to create a lack of confidence on the part of Zion's people. . . .

"But in spite of it all Zion prevailed. . . .

"Then began a terrific struggle on the part of organized labor in the United States to prevent the bringing in of these Lace Experts.

"Again Zion triumphed over all her enemies. The experts and the machinery were brought in, as the world now well knows.

"On the eighth day of October, 1900, a little party of Zion's people went to Zion City, where they consecrated the site of the first building to be erected by Zion in the Coming City. . . .

"This building is now complete, and its three large floors are filled with happy workers, living together in harmony and peace and purity as one large family."

The actual facts hardly rise to that level. It is even doubtful whether *Leaves of Healing* was the instrument of this business conversion, for the manufacturer alluded to, an Englishman named Stephenson, had been performing some cures by laying on of hands before he heard of Dowie. They entered into correspondence and Dowie saw a golden opportunity, for there was a high tariff against Nottingham lace and none was manufactured in this country. Stephenson was invited to America, and married Dowie's sister. Together they invested nearly a half a million dollars for the purpose of importing machinery and skilled operatives from England. It was Dowie's custom to import or summon adherents, sometimes making no provision for housing them or giving them employment. The disaffected manager of the lace factory declared that the building erected could have housed 22 machines but contained only 18, and that the machinery had often to be stopped because the financial managers of Zion City did not pay the bills for yarn which had been ordered. The factory was overcapitalized and, according to the manager, Dowie avoided all investigation by a wily trick. He had promised the stockholders that, if the dividends were not paid after one year, he would issue a financial report. This left him free of all interference if dividends were paid, and they were—out of the original capital.

§

It is unlikely that good Dowieites would have called for any investigation. Their minds, none too bright to begin with, were alternately lulled by endless ceremonials or distracted by the vituperative outbursts of their prophet. There were three fixed prayer meetings daily in nearly every home and Bible readings in the Tabernacle at odd hours. The Sunday services lasted four hours, with endless processions of children, youths, adults, and old men and women (many of them dressed in the mortar boards and gowns which Dowie affected), and recitations of the apostles' creed and the ten commandments, and singing by the choir, and scriptural reading, and Church notices, and involved prayers, and, the great event of the day, Dowie's attack on some institution or person he disliked. Rarely, he made a positive statement as shocking as his negations:

"I stand for the Restoration. As Elijah the Restorer I desire to bring back again the strength of the primitive man; and I be-

John Alexander Dowie

lieve from my spirit that if the yellow, the brown, the black, and the white man could, in the Christ our Lord, and in purity, mingle together in one great family we would probably get the type of man Adam was, and which we lost at Babel when language was confounded and man was scattered. . . . I trust that there shall be no difference, but that we shall have marriages in Zion between all the families of the one great race upon the earth. . . . I defend miscegenation."

In 1903, perhaps feeling the uncertainty of his fortunes, Dowie declared a foreign war to distract his people. With tremendous advance publicity, he descended upon Madison Square Garden in New York. Before an enormous crowd he came, flanked by his Overseers, advanced to the pulpit, and raised his delicate little hands as a signal for the choir to lead in singing *The Hallelujah Chorus* from— naturally—*The Messiah*. After the usual ceremonies, he announced that the doors would be closed and began reading the scriptures. Suddenly several hundred people moved to the doors and, as the infuriated preacher ordered a hymn to be sung, two or three thousand left the Garden. The whole of the sermon thereafter was a peculiar mingling of biblical exegesis and personal commands. With his rich Scot accent, Dowie went on, "Eyes have they, yet they see not. Ears have they, yet they hear not. I shall ask the gentlemen of the press to behave and not to talk . . . but they took hold of the Lord Jesus and they hurried him to the brink of the precipice and I have passed through the midst of my enemies and came to New York. . . ."

The New York press compared him with William Jennings Bryan and credited him with the combined genius of Morgan, General Booth, Croker, and Barnum. The *Sun* was cynical about his efforts to reclaim the modern Sodom and sink of iniquity and mentioned the fact that reporters' passes were issued for one day only so that, if anything unfavorable were written, the offending newspaper could be barred thereafter. In the program of the revival there was an advertisement for the Zion City Bank of which the last line was taken from the 19th chapter of Luke: "Wherefore then cast not thou thy money into the bank?"

The New York visitation, as Dowie called it, was a failure and, in the next year, the prophet departed on a European trip.* Later, troubles having broken out at Zion City, Dowie went to Mexico, leaving Wilbur Glenn Voliva, a devoted disciple, to look after his interests. Voliva either could not, or would not, check the hostility of the other Overseers and, in an outburst of anger, Dowie was deposed. What friends he might have held were turned against him by a vicious attack he made on his wife and, on the second of April, 1906, the Overseers wired Dowie "protesting against your extravagances, hypocrisy, misrepresentations, exaggerations, misuse of investment, tyranny, and injustice. You are hereby suspended from office and membership for polygamous teaching and other grave charges. See letter. You must answer these satisfactorily to officers and people. Quietly retire. Further interference will precipitate complete exposure, rebellion, legal proceedings. Your statement of stupendously magnificent financial outlook is extremely foolish in view of thousands suffering through your shameful mismanagement. Zion and creditors will be protected at all costs."

The charge of immorality came as a great shock to the followers of Dowie, for his personal life was generally considered irreproachable. An impartial investigator discovered that, as old age was setting in, Dowie had become indiscreet. It was rumored that he proposed to divorce his wife and to marry again and the name of a Swiss woman was frequently mentioned. Dowie had begun to study and sympathize with the Mormon doctrines and there was talk even of unnatural vices. In his private library were discovered copies of the *Decameron* and *Heptameron,* unexpurgated *Arabian Nights,* and an appropriately illustrated *Gil Blas,* "for which he had paid $600 of money received for religious purposes." After Voliva and the Overseers had abolished autocracy in Zion

* There is at least one record in contemporary letters of his European influence. Making his way through the streets of Dublin on the 16th of June, 1904, Mr. Leopold Bloom picked up a circular which set his active mind at work:

"Elijah is coming. Washed in the blood of the lamb. Come on, you winefizzling, ginsizzling, boozeguzzling existences! Come on, you dog-gone, bullnecked, beetlebrowed, hogjowled, peanutbrained, weaseleyed fourflushers, false alarms, and excess baggage! Come on, you triple extract of infamy! Alexander J. Christ Dowie, that's yanked to glory most half this planet from Frisco Beach to Vladivostok. The Deity ain't no nickel dime bumshow. I put it to you that he's on the square and a corking fine business proposition. He's the grandest thing yet and don't you forget it. Shout salvation in King Jesus! . . ." (James Joyce: *Ulysses.*)

City, they discovered that Dowie's finances were a trifle shaky. He had once declared against all borrowing and again that he was authorized to borrow $7,000,000 in order to hasten the kingdom of God but, when depression set in and he could no longer live as he liked, "as luxuriously as the Pope," he borrowed and did not trouble to remark that the land he offered as security was either mortgaged or sold. The new Elijah died in 1907 and, at the funeral services at Zion City, 300 of the 6,000 people present were still devoted to him; the rest had gone over to the new management. Twenty years later Voliva sold a portion of Zion City for the reported sum of $9,000,000. The Messiah had paid dividends, after all.

# XXVI.

## The Complex of Radicalism.

THE cults and the radical movements of the nineteenth century almost all came to a single end—failure—and, for the most part, the failure lacked dignity. There is a little pathos in the remorseless dimming of high hopes, but the impulses of the cults and the ambitions of the radicals, the hopes themselves, degenerated also. If tragedy is wanted, it lies in the steady decay of radical idealism and in the intellectual muddiness of the religious cults as compared with the high, clear sources from which they flowed.

The reasons for this decay—which has brought us into the hands of the modern type of reformer—are complex enough. The underlying motive of the radical cults was salvation—in modern jargon they were escape mechanisms—and the underlying motive of nineteenth-century America was the desire for mastery. Through cults, escape was offered: from the terror of sex, by refraining from intercourse or by a special sanctification of intercourse—the means differ, but the motive is the same; from working for a living, by communism or coöperation; from ill-health, by Christian Science; from awkwardness, by the cult of Personality; from moral responsibility, by Phrenology; from the drabness of life, by imagining a Utopia; from loneliness, by accepting the friendship of Christ; from fear, by accepting his intercession; from death, by Spiritualism, Christian Science, and Christianity. In the end radicalism and revivalism mingle and flow back, in part, to orthodoxy.

For most of these evils, the common sense of humanity and the particular circumstances of pioneering America offered other consolations. Progress in science, progress in politics, progress in mechanics, gave the American means to dominate his world. He escaped inconvenience and misery by "doing without" for a time, in order to conquer his universe. He could be healthy by living a healthy life. His loneliness decreased as good roads, canals, steam engines, and the telephone and telegraph, came to make communication easy.

There lay before him always the idea that he could slip out of the wage system, not by becoming a communist, but by becoming a millionaire. Moral questions convulsed him rarely and he compacted with the preacher to assure himself a ticket to Heaven. He was generally Protestant, lacking ritual to give him easy communication with Christ and lacking absolution to give him an easy conscience; but the very violence of the revivalists indicates how casual the average man was until he was awakened to his sins. The revivalist, like the radical, was intense about salvation. Both were burdened by a sense of alienation from the world, or from God. Neither could bear the unmitigated evil of life. The average man lacked sensibility. He did not believe life was utterly evil, and the evil he saw—in his private circumstances—he proceeded to destroy. For him, this process constituted sanity, and reason, and progress.

The one significant thing to be said in favor of the American radical is that, crackbrained or perverse as he was, he did not submit entirely to the dominant purpose. He was opposed to the system of "make-money." The conquest of the wilderness seemed secondary to him; the conquest of the spiritual world, primary. The circumstances of his own life were unlovely; but he cared intensely for beauty. He was beset by poverty; but he did not think riches a good in itself. He wanted a freer society, an easier life for men and women. In a society peculiarly preoccupied with things, he held to ideas. He cared for accomplishment more than for possessions. Likewise the revivalists, as has been noted, spoke in the harsh loneliness of the backwoods, of spiritual things, of communion and love. Ineffective as they were, they reminded people that the current mode was not the only one. They suggested the possibility of another way of life. For the sake of variety in the American scene, for the sake of not being utterly given over to material progress, even at its best, there was need of a gospel contrary to the orthodox doctrine preached by the spade, the rifle, and the steam-engine.

It might have been preached by philosophers and saints but, for the most part, it fell into the hands of sour fanatics, crackbrained enthusiasts, monomaniacs, epileptics, and mountebanks. They were either defeated men and women, or uneasy souls, so baffled by the conflicting stresses of life that they had to flee from the struggle. The world was so abhorrent to them, or so difficult, that no ordinary way of salvation would do. The world was so hostile to them, individually, that, in the end, most of them came to believe that they had to make man over in their own image—and declared themselves either God or his near neighbor.

To the psychologist, this indicates inevitably the presence of the inferiority complex. The common habits and the common experience of mankind are both repudiated by the maker of Utopias because, in his mind, these habits and experiences are the very sources of evil. Has man found it simpler to use coin than to barter: the radical suggests the abolition of money. Has he found it agreeable to eat filet mignon: the radical goes vegetarian. Has he persisted in breaking his adversaries in order to be rich: the radical goes in for communal living and poverty. Is he concupiscent: the radical forbids carnal intercourse. Common things must have glamor to redeem them: work and child-bearing must be sanctified. Gay things must also be transformed, so that play becomes purposeful, and one cannot lift one's voice in melody without being caught in a community sing-song.

There is an enormous exhilaration in the feeling of being against the current. The radical (in the phases, especially, of uplifter and prohibitory reformer) translates this into the aggrandizement of personality which comes from imposing one's own will on others. Underneath, lies the desire to prove one's own superiority; and under that, according to the analyst, lies the consciousness of inferiority. The classic mode of life—to know one's capacities and exercise them to the utmost; to know one's limitations and to overcome them by discipline; or, if that is impossible, to remain within them—encourages few neurotics and fewer radicals. The romantic mode—which considers singularity a proof of superior qualities— is the matrix of radicalism.

The inferiority complex is, at the moment of writing, the more popular; but it seems to me that, if we accept the psychoanalyst's terms, the older Œdipus complex is equally useful as a scalpel. The hatred for authority is obviously a "transference" from the individual's hatred of his father, the first source of authority. The desire to destroy society is equally a dramatization of the desire to overthrow parental authority. And, still to use these terms a little out of their original intention, the radical of the nineteenth century displayed a truly astounding "mother-fixation," often enough in the literal meaning of a fixation on the mother that bore him, and, almost universally, a fixation on Mother Earth.

It is not necessary to import Freud in order to explain these phenomena. In the cold age of reason, Dr. Johnson expressed the sense of the time when he said that one blade of grass was very much like another blade of grass; he preferred society to Nature. After him came the deluge: worship of romantic scenery, of ruined castles on promontories, of mountains, of wild ravines, of primroses by the river's brim, which were somehow ineffably more meaningful than primroses ever thought of being before. Rusticity, the peasantry ("a bold nation's pride" even to Goldsmith, gently romantic under the Mogul's baleful eye), and, finally the Land, became possessed of all virtue. The state of Nature, Natural Law, the Natural Man, the Noble Savage were discovered and idolized until, in the Transcendental movement, Nature was endowed with a Moral Law and, in the communist movement, Land became the beginning and the end of all good things. American communities were all land-hungry, says Noyes, ruefully observing the careers of his predecessors. They wanted to go back to Nature, to live as Nature intended man to live; they did so, and Nature saw to it that they perished.

The great dream of the land-hungry communist lies also in the psychoanalytic order. He wanted to creep back into the arms of his Mother Earth, to escape from complexity and the light of day into the darkness of primeval simplicity. All this is precisely parallel to the dream of being unborn, still in the mother's womb. Nature would understand, comfort. Nature would restore health. Nature would banish or sanctify lust. In Nature, all things would be beautified and good. The intellectually honest radical openly proclaimed his intention to depart from civilization, to cure civilization, in his return to the simple life. Somewhere, in the dim beginning of time, life had taken the wrong turning; the radical proposed to return to the crossroads and take the right one. But where was the mistake made? Perhaps it was when private property was established, or marriage, or murder, or priesthood. Or was it when man began to walk upright, or learned the distinction between Good and Evil, or ate of the Tree of Knowledge and came to know Death? It was lost in obscurity, this baleful turning point in human history; search broke down the illusion of human happiness in Hellas or in the Garden of Eden; the beginning of the evil retreated farther into the mist; anthropology was rude even to the Noble Savage with his rigid formalism, his cruelty, his weaknesses, his tabus. But the wrongness of humanity remained fixed in the radical's brain. To him, as to the orthodox Calvinist, there could be no explanation of human misery without the assumption of a primal sin, an Error of cosmic dimensions.

If one could only go back!

§

His intention was to make a better world. He declared himself the friend of the future. He accused conservatives and reactionaries of loving the past too much. But, before he could begin, he had to retreat for his jump into the unknown. If there had never been a Golden Age or an Eden, then the present muddle could justify itself—and the present was hateful to him. He had to assume the Perfection of man in the past in order to look forward to its second coming. Theology had left a deep mark on his soul, even if he rejected God and Christ together. Impressed with the sound of the name, radical, he spoke always of Trees to the roots of which he would apply his ax—it was the Tree of Knowledge. The root would be spared, because it clung to the earth; but the tree, and the blossom, and the fruit, were civilization and must be destroyed. Vegetation is good; cultivation, evil.

In the last quarter century, the radical has yielded ground. Mechanics and technology have instructed him. As an economic and political radical, he wants a transfer of power to himself or to his class. The ancient radical ideals are soft and ridiculous in the eyes of the modern communist, just as the old banners of democracy are trampled under the feet of Fascism. The destruction of the framework of Russian life was only an incident in the transfer of power from the upper classes to the proletariat. The destruction of Italian liberty was an incident in the transfer of power from the mass to the bourgeoisie. The next generation will learn whether the radical temper has fundamentally changed.

All one can be sure of at the moment is that the cults of the preceding hundred years have left an adequate progeny. Greatest

of all at present is the cult of diet. Throughout the past century, it
has been noted, almost all fanatics held some special belief about
food. In America, the attitude toward food is never based on taste;
it is ethical, not esthetic. Franklin stopped eating meat in order to
save money and to have a clearer mind; others could not bear the
thought of the slaughter of fellow-creatures; others felt themselves
out of the divine harmony if they ate anything but cereals and nuts.
But that change in the character of radical endeavor which is so
marked in social experiments and in revivalism, is noted too in diet.
For a century of high ideals ends in diet for health, in diet for a
slender figure, for beauty, and for financial success.

     After diet, run the commercial cults of personality and success
and, less popular but significant enough, the cults of esthetic or
interpretative dancing, of eurhythmics, of spinal elongation, of new
breathings. The House of David is a religious cult quite in the old
manner. The theosophists, the followers of Gourdjeff, repeat the
circle of mysticism. Eugenics is a cult with old roots. Free love is
another, with roots still older. Without prejudice to their intrinsic
value, Pacifism and Prohibition may both be included under the
head of cults. Each escapes from the classification to become something more significant, but each has some of the characteristics of a
mass-mania. The belief in psychoanalysis marks the intellectual
cultish mind of to-day. The worship of science may, in the future,
be considered another cult. Under fresh forms, the old habit of believing persists.

     In America, a number of forms of radicalism exist side by side.
There is still the political radical, diminished in ambition since the
Progressive Party vanished. There is the economic radical, socialist
or communist. There are the social radical, the uplifter, and the
puritan reformer. The first is the true inheritor of the Revolution-
ary patriot, through the Abolitionist and the muck-raker. The second is in a state of uncertainty, wavering between his inherent tendency to destroy and the obligation imposed upon him by Moscow—
to capture and command. The third is the triumphant type.

     In spite of superficial diversities of method these three types
have much in common. A dry world, a world of sanitary tenements,
a world of sexless friendliness, a world without bawdy plays, a
world in which capital and labor are friends—all these are the con-

cerns of a single temperament: the idealist. In the service of an Ideal there can be no compromise. As Carry Nation put it, one meddles. The radical-reformer-Prohibitionist is convinced of his God-given authority to interfere with the lives of other men, in order to improve them. Eighty years ago, he withdrew from society, founded his own community, and preached Abstention. To-day, he passes laws and cries, I forbid. He believes still in the depravity of man as he is. He has still the ideal of Man before the Fall.

To the average sensual, balanced man such concern with Perfection, Ideals, Purity is extravagant. He calls it mania. Contemporary psychology suggests that the radical is neurotic, ill-adjusted to life, and so explains his tendency to flee and his equally marked tendency to destroy. This uproar about a smutty book, or a suggestive play, suggests intolerable suppressions, impotence, and envy. The radical and the saint have an answer. They say that man lives not in a single system of ideas, desires, and ideals, but in a complex one. The average man satisfies his lower instincts and considers his life well spent; the superior man must satisfy his higher ones. Sometimes an accident, sometimes a revelation from Heaven, sometimes a conversion, sets free this higher system and, from that moment, the lower is dust, an evil memory, an impediment to the higher, a corruption. In order to burn with the greatest intensity, it is necessary to cast out the slag. That is why the saint is in rags, and the radical in ugly clothes. That is why one mortifies himself with a hair shirt and another rejects all pleasures of the flesh.

In the soul of the saint there is no regret; he has not renounced anything worthy, only dedicated himself to the single good. But when the radical is not a saint, the Old Adam persists. He cannot bear the idea that other men, in whom the higher and lower natures are in equilibrium, can care as much as he does for sanctity and beauty, and still enjoy the carnalities of life. The very fact of their enjoyment becomes proof in his mind that they do not care intensely enough—they are compromising the Ideal. To the revivalists of the great era, the infidel was not a danger. The men they hated were the ones who took their religion calmly, "the cold professors of Christianity." They denounced these men as worse than atheists. They denied that living the moral life of a Christian and believing in Christ were of the least avail before the judgment seat. If one had Christ, one had to be all Christ, a flame of testimony. The moment of acceptance must be a terrible agony; the possession thereafter, a terrible exaltation. All other things must be cast away. And the Prohibitionist, using the drunkard as an awful example, so fears the moderate drinker that he denies his existence. For the moderate drinker, the temperate balanced man, also hates drunkenness, but he fails to make a religion of it, and he refuses to give up his drink. He lives simultaneously in both systems, sometimes allowing one the upper hand, sometimes the other. Love and lust exist side by side; he rejoices in both, sometimes forgetting love to give rein to lust, sometimes checking lust to give play to love. The radical rejects this dualism utterly; love must drive out lust and, if it does not, it is not true love. In his own experience, the two emotions have conflicted and he will not tolerate the idea that, in others, they may supplement each other in perfect harmony.

The balanced man is rare. The average man's equilibrium is often disturbed, but he readjusts himself. The radical, fanatic about himself and his discoveries, refuses to make this adjustment. As the world neglects him, or punishes, he creates another world, full of hostile phantoms. He snatches at whatever is opposed to the established order. "What have people's clothes to do with their religion?" asks the geologist in *South Wind*, and proceeds to discuss a common phenomenon of radicalism: "Can't a fellow be a Messiah without sporting a pink shirt or fancy dressing-gown or blue pyjamas or something? . . . I defy you to name me a single-barreled crank. If a man is a religious lunatic, or a vegetarian, he is sure to be touched in some other department as well; he will be an anti-vivisectionist, a nut-fooder, costume-maniac, stamp-collector, or a spiritualist into the bargain. Haven't you ever noticed that? And isn't he dirty? What is the connection between piety and dirt . . . ?"

§

The accomplishments of radicalism are hard to value. Mrs. Bloomer was entirely right in protesting against the clothes of her era; yet it was not the protest that brought into being the beautiful clothes of our day. They are the result of women's slavery in fac-

tories and women's activity as courtesans in Paris and women's freedom in cycling, motoring, and sports. The Reform Dress merely
substituted what was hideous for what was absurd. The reformers
shouted for Abolition and created the moral atmosphere in which a
non-Abolitionist Executive could emancipate the slaves; but they
did nothing serious to solve the negro problem. The great change in
the status of women, quite apart from the ballot, is largely due to
their agitation, and that agitation is also largely responsible for the
high moral tone, the evangelizing fervor, the political astuteness
and chicanery of the Prohibition movement. Against the wage and
property system, the radical made insignificant headway; against
orthodox science, hardly any; against the American preoccupation
with material success, very little; against irreligion, very little. In
almost every case, the adversaries left the high ground of early
controversy and descended into mud and swamp. It may go against
the grain to say, There shall be no ownership—but the tone of nobility is in it; and that tone is not in the clamorous demand that I
shall own, and you shall not. There is dignity in speculating about
the attributes of God; none in quarreling over the text of the Bible.
Even the phrenologist, speaking of Character, was superior to the
commercial New Thoughter speaking of Personality.

As the radicals failed, the level on which radicalism operated
declined. Its preoccupations grew gradually ignoble. Mr. Mum-
ford's "Golden Day"—the time from Hawthorne to Whitman—
was streaked with murk; but it created radicals with intelligence and
fire, with more of vision and less of envy. In our day, the stature
of both adversaries is diminished. The Sacco-Vanzetti trial brought
forth no great reactionary and no great radical; for the issues involved, the protagonists were on both sides puny and insignificant.

§

What is left? To avoid complexes and neuroses, to compromise
and to adjust ourselves, to cultivate our gardens, to be mechanics
(if not mechanisms) in an age of machinery—these are the suggestions from Freud, and Spengler, and a host of others. The brave
young men are turning to science; the worried ones, to Rome; the
thoughtful ones, to a form of classicism. Are these, also, salvation
hunters? Is there no way but the way of normalcy to live with some

scope and some satisfaction? The history of radicalism suggests only that to live sanely one must avoid cults; but, as one is about to plunge headlong into sanity, one is recalled by a few casual sentences of Marcel Proust:

"The magnificent and lamentable family of the neurotics is the salt of the earth. Everything great that we know we owe to neurotics. It is they, and none else, who have founded our religions and composed our masterpieces. The world will never know all it owes to them, and more especially all they have suffered in giving what we possess."

And yet—

# SOURCES

Impeccable in taste and judgment throughout her *Trumpets of Jubilee*, Constance Mayfield Rourke is again perfect in her attitude toward bibliography. "To end a book," she says, "with a display of the machinery by which it has been assembled is to stress the toil which has gone into its making, not the pleasure." It is perfectly obvious that in a book of this kind, the principal sources are the works of each of the persons studied, and after their works (or when no printed records exist) the principal biographical studies. I have consulted pamphlets, magazine articles, old newspapers; nearly every book of travel or of social criticism which covers the United States of the nineteenth century has something bearing on the movements I took for my subject. The subject-index of any good library will provide the reader with sources in profusion.

There are, however, a few books to which I owe something more than facts. As a layman in respect to both history and psychology, I needed more than anything else an authority to which to refer the strange phenomena I found. I discovered, for instance, that when Bronson Alcott took a negro girl into his school all of New England seemed to rise against him; was that an accident or was it a commonplace at that time? I found extraordinary states of bliss in certain stages of conversion; were they aberrations or entirely normal? In the second case my book of reference has been William James' *The Varieties of Religious Experience*; on the historical side, the standard of reference was Charles and Mary Beard's *Rise of American Civilization*. By both of these works I have been able to check my own tendency to think everything new to me was exceptional; I have quoted them, borrowed from them, even borrowed their quotations; and only wish I could have done more to incorporate their qualities into my own work.

Some special sources have been exceptionally useful. Professor Benjamin B. Warfield's essay on *Noyes and his Bible Communists* (in volume 78 of *Bibliotheca Sacra*) is really a study of the whole revival movement in relation to cults; A. M. Bellwald's *Christian Science and the Catholic Faith*; Gaius Glenn Atkins' *Modern Religious Cults and Movements*; and Podmore's various books on allied subjects, not only cover the field, but establish interrelations of peculiar importance. The facts and the documents in the story of the early camp-meeting are all in Catherine C. Cleveland's work, from which I have borrowed much of the first-hand testimony.

The work of research has been comparatively easy because of the marked tendency of most of my subjects to write autobiographies; and easier still because they were such unusual people that strangers were moved to print in their behalf or against them. The first half of the past century, moreover, was the period of Europe's second discovery of America: Chevalier and George Combe and Mrs. Trollope and dozens of others noted the things which a foreigner found strange. Many of the notes in fine type, supplying the domestic background, are due to these foreign observers; most of the rest come from dailies and weeklies of the time.

# Index.

*(Italics indicate footnotes)*

THE
JOHN DAY

COMPANY
INC.